the social character of its production, the connection between social organization from the institutional and ideological point of view, and the rules governing verbal behavior. I am fully aware that this is not an original statement. My only reason for reiteration is to briefly outline a scientific shortcoming: the contours of a professional inertia in which regard for tradition outweighs respect for reality. This shortcoming, however is not due to mere accident, but is caused by theoretical, empirical, and normative factors.

1. Language is often used as purely stimulative material, like sound or visual patterns (for example, in the study of human memory, discriminatory, or associative ability). Consequently, its social and symbolic aspect is and can be left aside; no one cares very much that the individual using or responding to a linguistic or sound stimulus knows that his awareness of it determines his associational and mnemonic behavior.

2. The classic distinction between *language*—a stable system of relationships among lexical units—and *speech*—an ensemble of uses of this system by the members of a community of speakers—permitted a set of linguistic phenomena to be severed from their so-called extralinguistic foundation. As a result, a sort of polarization arose between the genotypic linguistic phenomena, which can be grasped by taking individual psychology as a starting point, and phenotypic phenomena, which are left to the domain of sociology, anthropology, and perhaps social psychology. But obviously only the former are considered basic, while the latter remain secondary. Under these circumstances, conceptual and experimental efforts are focused on eliminating all interference from the social component in order to attain something like a presocial state: thus the interest in the language of children and individuals with psychopathic symptoms.

3. The opposition between individual and collective elements is reflected in the contrast between biological and social aspects. The ultimate aim is to succeed in establishing a link between neurophysiological makeup and linguistic organization, thereby supplying a biological explanation of the process of linguistic creation. Lenneberg (3), with the help of an impressive array of facts, has recently attempted to prove the biological foundation of language. His main contentions are that: (a) there are anatomic and physiological correlates of language, particularly with respect to oropharyngeal morphology and cerebral dominance, as well as special coordination between motor and speech centers; (b) development of linguistic ability in children follows a uniform and

systematic pattern; (c) linguistic ability can be neither inhibited nor suppressed, nor can it be acquired by nonhumans, who probably do not have the same cerebral and motor organization; and (d) the existence of universal elements of language implies the presence of a corresponding biological foundation.

In the face of this accumulation of facts, why should one look for an alternative explanation in terms of social factors and undertake research to validate it? Perhaps this is the right approach to the problem. In any case, this is the approach generally accepted. Still, some conflicting pieces of evidence might be cited. First of all, the brain and human neurophysiology in general are cultural products that attempt to communicate and think with the help of words. In addition, language is not limited to organic correlates; it has social and technical ones as well. There is no a priori reason for giving precedence to one at the expense of the other or for claiming that one is more fundamental than the other. There is less justification than ever for this sort of precedence now that we know how important a role the social factor must have played in the evolution of the species. Finally, linguistic universals are for the moment postulated rather than proven. Even if it can be shown that they exist, it does not follow that they have a biological correlate.

We are familiar with many other universals: technological features, prohibition of incest, and hierarchic elements of the social order. Nevertheless, we interpret and explain these universals on the basis of the study of social structures and relationship with the environment. Surely all these universals, and others as well, presuppose the existence of a genetic program, but actual knowledge of this program would not account completely for their nature. Last but not least, we must take into account the fruitfulness of this orientation, of which it could justly be written that "in spite of the vast accumulation of knowledge, scholars are still unable to propose a biological *theory* of language. Advances in knowledge have only shown ever wider areas of ignorance" (4). Clearly, in spite of everything, the die is not yet cast, and we may justly deplore the fact that all efforts have so resolutely been expended in the single direction of individual psychology and psychophysiology, without simultaneously trying to see whether research in another direction might not throw some light on processes about which so little is known.

4. Scientific choices often are determined by value judgments. It seems as though there were something more creditable about

THE PSYCHOSOCIOLOGY
OF LANGUAGE

THE
PSYCHOSOCIOLOGY
OF LANGUAGE

edited by

SERGE MOSCOVICI

Ecole des Hautes Etudes, Paris

MARKHAM PUBLISHING COMPANY / Chicago

MARKHAM PSYCHOLOGY SERIES
Howard Leventhal, Advisory Editor

Duke and Frankel, *Inside Psychotherapy*
Moyer, *The Physiology of Hostility*
Moscovici, ed., *The Psychosociology of Language*
Sahakian, ed., *Psychology of Learning: Systems, Models and Theories*

PREFACE

There is no existing field that might be called the social psychology of language: linguists are not interested in the psychosociological aspect of language and psychosociologists are not concerned with the linguistic aspect of social behavior. Under these circumstances, the readings presented in this book do not survey an established field as readings usually do, but rather delineate what should or could be included in this field. The readings must be viewed and evaluated from this perspective.

Why, one might ask, is there any need for a social psychology of language and what, until now, has prevented its development? There are numerous reasons, both positive and negative, but listing them would fill a small book. I will therefore limit this list to reasons I have presented elsewhere in greater detail (1) (see reference section at end of Preface), and which one will also find in Ragnar Rommetveit's book (2).

Basically, two questions require an answer: wherein lies the importance of social psychology for the study of language, and why has no one drawn on social psychology in these sorts of studies? I will make clear at once that I do not know the answer to these questions, so that I can only venture some educated guesses.

In present studies language is ordinarily defined as a communication system that brings together an emitter, a receiver, and material communication channels. The function of language is described as information codification—the relationship between words and things—and the communication or transmission of these words from one person to another or from one group to another. In other words, language is a social and cultural system inextricably tied to different cultural and social systems.

If these definitions and descriptions are taken literally, it is natural to assume that a serious analysis of the meaning and use of syntactic rules and the semantic dimensions of language cannot be undertaken without proper attention to interaction phenomena (the individual and collective goals that presumably molded language and in whose organization it is involved in turn). One might even go farther and point out that language is a social product in the most direct sense. Systems of classification for objects, resources, and skills were produced in response to pedagogic and administrative requirements. Rhetoric was developed with all its fine points to serve the political and diplomatic needs of representatives of government. The isolation of grammar and philology as objects of study and, consequently, the formulation of their rules, have both ideological and historical explanations that many Renaissance scholars have brought to light. It is undeniable that the circumstances under which the various languages in our societies were created left their mark on them, just as was the case in primitive societies. For lack of a communication theory, we cannot reconstruct the mechanisms by which languages were produced, and no serious efforts have yet been made in that direction. Only knowledge of these mechanisms would give us a better understanding of the syntactic and semantic transformations and proliferations that are now noted and described. Finally, language as communication is often said to hold society together. However it would be just as correct to assert the inverse. Those cohesive forces, conflicts, negotiations, festivities, and rituals that characterize a given society—that is, the need to speak or to be silent, or to use a single manner of speaking for all occasions or distinctive manners for each of them—are factors that generate linguistic or metalinguistic rules and cause their combination and diffusion.

Each institutional, social hierarchical, or technological modification has a bearing on related linguistic systems. This association is so intimate and so natural that it is taken for granted. I would go so far as to say that this cavalier attitude even makes one forget that language is a special form of behavior—symbolic behavior. This means that language symbolizes something for somebody. Language is thereby embedded in the vast field of collective psychology—social conceptions, myths, and ideologies—from which one may at times wish to isolate it. But it would be wiser to link language and collective psychology more closely to emphasize that a sentence or a word are forms of thought and action that is, forms of human thought and action in a human setting.

Social psychology is the proper framework for making explicit and rigorously analyzing the communication function of language, studying the connection between linguistic phenomena and memory or the perception of a child or sick persons than the connections between linguistic phenomena and leadership, problem solving, or persuasion in interpersonal relations or in a group. And yet, would one not imagine that this latter setting was more natural and corresponded more to linguistic reality?

Noam Chomsky recently stressed linguistic creativity. This creativity is undeniably instigated and structured by collective exchanges. Obviously memory and perception have their share in determining information content, length of messages, and part of their architechtonic virtualities. Each of these factors presumes a range of variation and supplies the elements to be combined. The rules for this combination, however, are laid down by the society that uses and invents them, and by the emitters and receivers who are induced to formulate them. Language is not only stored in the brain but is also stored in society. The scrupulous respect for social values conditioned the choice of experimental methods—they were always "individualistic"—and of the topics of investigation, which all centered on the classic *"psychologie des facultés."*

Psycholinguistics itself did not produce many innovations; it is simply a junction of individual psychology and certain sectors of linguistics. "Psycholinguistics," as G. A. Miller puts it (5), "does not deal with social practices determined arbitrarily either by caprice or intelligent design, but with practices that grew organically out of the biological nature of man and the linguistic capacities of human infants. To that extent, at least, it is possible to define an area of empirical facts well within the reach of our scientific method." Thus, linguistic analysis, far from opening up new perspectives and establishing new links between its own reality and those realities that are usually of greatest interest to psychologists, has trapped itself in a Procrustean bed of traditional techniques and problems. From this point of view, the fields of study of both psychic and linguistic phenomena are narrowed simultaneously. "Attempts to construct a model of language without any relation either to the speaker or to the hearer," Jakobson writes (and I would add, their reduction to neuro-physiological mechanisms—S.M.), "and thus to hypostatize a code detached from actual communication, threaten to make a scholastic fiction of language." (6)

5. Honesty obliges us to confess that psychosociologists have a complete lack of interest in linguistic phenomena. It is difficult

to determine why. I imagine that their excessive preoccupation with social engineering problems made them lose contact with questions raised by other sciences, such as linguistics, anthropology, or economics. Thus, with respect to groups and communications, much attention has been paid to the productivity and effect of group communication, but the genesis, the general mechanism of groups and communication, has been neglected. Another factor may be the lack of interest in symbolic behavior or in intellectual processes. The lexical and syntactic indices of interaction are usually assimilated to any kind of indices, and their particularities are overlooked. All that is verbal in social contact seems to be of secondary interest and does not arouse any special curiosity. This explains why, on the whole, neither psychologists nor linguists were tempted to collaborate with them, and why they saw no scholarly value in such a collaboration.

This expresses, in a nutshell, the reasons justifying the existence of a psychosociology of language and explains why it has not yet been constituted. However, no matter what clever arguments can be marshalled, arguments alone will never lay the foundation of a scientific undertaking. Even if everyone admitted their validity, they could not take the place of theoretical and empirical studies. In science, as elsewhere, the proof of the pudding is in the eating. It is therefore perfectly useless to stop at such prolegomena and to convince ourselves or others that it would be important to do something, without actually doing it. Paradoxically, a careful bibliographical investigation demonstrates that although there is no established and acknowledged subfield of social psychology devoted to verbal behavior, there are numerous experimental and even theoretical studies (I counted more than three hundred) which are pertinent in one way or another. In many cases, the experimental techniques are very sophisticated and ingenious; the results are interesting and often the conceptual apparatus often does not compare unfavorably with the one used in other psychosociological subfields: social perception, conflict, problem solving, and the like. Starting with these studies, as well as certain theoretical interpretations I have presented elsewhere (1), I grouped these readings to highlight the problems that seem most fruitful at present, and to which it would be worthwhile to devote systematic studies.

The first topic concerns the analysis of the relations between verbal and nonverbal communication. This is a pivotal theme in a way, because it concerns the transformation of relations to an object, within the context of relations, to a subject; that is, changing signals into a system of symbols. Numerous experiments show how color categorization takes place, how the number of categories used varies with different colors, familiarity with them, and so forth. However, the number of categories used, that is, the code employed to deal with a given body of information, depends in the last analysis not so much on the physical qualities of the stimulus but the conditions under which this information is transmitted; on the exchanges linking the different persons involved. The articles by J. P. Van de Geer, Lantz and Stefflre, and Krauss et al. focus on the problem of how codification of an object takes place when the person doing the coding is simultaneously acting as an emitter toward a well-defined receiver. Ekman's and Argyle's articles deal with verbal and nonverbal aspects of communication. This distinction between verbal and nonverbal communication is undoubtedly valid; we certainly use several groups of expressive gestures, grunts, and glances to convey desires, opinions, or social status.

The empirical results are impressive and the theoretical approach to this subject is very interesting. An enormous amount of conceptual work remains to be done. First, one must find a way of distinguishing "symbolic" nonverbal behavior that merely serves as a substitute for words from nonverbal behavior that has no direct verbal equivalent. When, instead of saying "here," I point to the spot with my finger, this behavior basically serves the same purpose as verbal behavior. Second, some movements of the body, head, or eyes are purely descriptive of course; like red or green traffic lights they convey some information—that something is forbidden, desired, or rejected—although no verbal substitute exists. Now the ordinary spoken language has a binary structure, and words have an arbitrary connection with the things they designate. The language emanating from body, face, and eyes is based more closely on analogical structures, reproducing rhythms or constellations of external events and, as in the case with music, its coding and decoding are probably not linear. Thus, a theoretical analysis of the nature of this language is indispensable for further findings.

The second topic, communication as a process of linguistic production, takes us to the heart of psychosociological concerns. Speech planning is the first point examined because here lexical and nonlexical elements combine. The speaker's hesitation when he elaborates and emits a message is a very significant example. Researchers have rightly given special attention to this hesitation phenomenon, and the examples found in this book (Goldman-Eisler, Boomer, Tannenbaum et al.) are indicative of the work done along this line. Beyond that, on the basis of the knowledge one has of the relations between emitters and receivers, their motivation, and their distance with respect to the object under consideration, it is possible to predict the message characteristics—grammatical features, redundancy, degree of formalism—that correspond to the given situation. Sections III and IV contain a whole series of demonstrations and promising experiments whose success would permit us to understand and even explain how communication systems are linked to syntactic or lexical systems.

Our third topic is social interactions, which we have chosen since language is a clue to social interactions, whether political or personal, whether work or play-oriented. Space limitations have prevented my including all the articles I would have liked. But the articles in section VI are sufficiently typical to put across the point that, from the very beginning of research in group dynamics, psychologists have studied the linguistic manifestations of leadership, participation, group activity, and so on. Unfortunately, they discarded this approach all too soon. Nevertheless, enough experiments were carried out to attest to the fruitfulness of this approach to the problem of exchanges and of the organization of meaningful social units. Linguistic knowledge has expanded considerably since that time, and methods for analyzing linquistic material have become more sophisticated. A renewed interest in group dynamics, notably with respect to verbal behavior, would yield much information that was not available when the pioneers in the field first studied it.

The fourth topic we will consider is codes as the instrument of communication, which deserve a particularly detailed analysis. They play a principal role in the organization of individual and collective experiences, in the selection of lexical and syntactic speech elements, and in the modeling of social conceptions and behavior. The most significant research on this topic, evolving from the work done by Bernstein and Brown (see section V) brought out the importance of codes conceived on the basis of relations between social classes. But unquestionably those codes revolving around male-female, parent-child relations, or different ethnic groups within a country deserve equally careful study. The multiplication of such studies in many directions would form a foundation for our knowledge of how language is based in the concrete social context, and how much bearing it has on the institutional structure of society. After all, the real speakers, the real creators of language patterns, are groups: classes, nations, professions, and so forth. By observing these groups, rather than by concentrating on children or the mentally ill, we will learn why and how sentences are produced and selected, and evaluated as grammatical or ungrammatical, for these groups are the ones that lay down the norms. Linguistic memory is a collective phenomenon; associative processes are collective phenomena. In this respect, differences between classes, professional groups, cultural groups (for instance, rural and urban cultures) by far exceed quantitatively and qualitatively those differences that arise on the individual level. The introduction of experimental methods adapted to groups might possibly facilitate the study of these differences and clear away many preconceptions.

The fifth topic is the semantic realm which has, from the psychosociological point of view, remained a virgin territory. The study of meaning in the processes involving changes of attitude, social influence, conflict, or psycho-logic has never been undertaken systematically. Nothing has been done about the fields of meaning groups have set up and are setting up in relation to objects, individuals, and the like, except indirectly in research about impression formation. Ragnar Rommetveit's article in some way serves as a concrete work plan. The articles by Ervin, Handel et al., Osgood, and Walker propose theoretical and methodological approaches of great interest. Readers might do well to supplement these articles by looking into works on ethnoscience by anthropologists, in order to obtain an overall view of this question.

Sixth, I would like to draw attention to the work on persuasion. But I believe I should have mentioned the degree to which the linguistic, rhetorical dimension of communication has been overlooked. Exclusive preoccupation with effects, with channels or "deep" processes, has obscured the simple fact that communicating by means of words is not tantamount to communicating with sounds, money, or services. There is no concern, in this subfield, with sorting out the imprint left by the persuader's intention or desire to change the other's conduct or attitude. Little attention is paid to the style peculiar to the various media, or to messages likely to induce trust, attract others, induce fear, and so on. The experimental studies touch on such facts as the credibility accorded to the source of emission, the influence of the amount of threat contained in a message, the personality traits (self-esteem, persuadability) of the receiver, the effects of primacy or recency, etc.

Ideally, not only the *contents* but also the *structure* of the messages destined to express credibility, threat (in short, all speeches adapted to the expression of intention, social status, feeling, and so on) should be included in a thorough investigation of communication processes. As one can see from the last section of these readings, a promising start has been made along these lines.

The list of themes just mentioned is far from exhaustive. In a way it only highlights the problems that should most directly and easily accessible to psychosociologists: here techniques, concepts, and a research tradition are already at hand. But nobody has ever claimed that the royal road in science is also the path strewn with most difficulties. Difficulties will arise in any case, once the network of results, regularities, and phenomena become more tightly woven and more contradictory. The presence of difficulties must be viewed as a welcome state of affairs, because it will confirm that the study of language has gained a place in social psychology.

This preface might create the impression that the articles collected here are only of interest to the highly trained and specialized professional. Nothing could be further from the truth. Any student, any person interested in communication and education, will find information applicable to his own experiences. Ideally, the eight sections of the book were intended for two courses. The first four sections were to constitute the material for a course mainly oriented toward the linguistic aspects of social relations and intercourse. They do not require any advanced knowledge of psychology, social psychology, or linguistics in order to understand the meaning, results, and sequence of the experiments. The four final sections primarily focus on the social aspect of language. In terms of the concepts involved and the methods used, the articles they contain are intended especially for more advanced students or students with more clearly defined scientific interests. At least this has been my experience with French and American students, which I am taking the liberty of passing on. In the last analysis, books belong to the public. The author or editor harbors the illusion that his preface gives him control over the use of the book, and that it will eliminate ambiguities, and excuse errors or weaknesses that have been allowed to slip in. Prefaces are just as much acts of self-deception, ritual, or incantation as the dedications to the wives and children who have patiently waited for the husband and father to complete his work, to the secretaries responsible for the typing of the manuscript, to the friends who read it, and so on. But what choice did they have? What else could they have done?

Readers should thus feel entirely free in the face of this preface, which in the last analysis can only serve to explain according to what criteria and for what purpose this book of readings was put together; they should feel equally free with respect to the persons I consulted and burdened with technical tasks and who, in turn, did no more than their duty.

Serge Moscovici
June 1971

REFERENCES

1. Moscovici, S. 1967. Communication processes and the properties of language. In L. Burkowitz (ed.), *Advances in experimental social psychology*, Vol. 3. New York: Academic Press. Pp. 226–70.
2. Rommetveit, R. 1968. *Words, meanings and messages.* New York: Academic Press, and Oslo: Oslo University Press.
3. Lenneberg, E. H. 1967. *Biological foundations of language.* New York: Wiley.
4. Marshall, J. C. 1970. The biology of communication in man and animals. In J. Lyons (ed.), *New horizons in linguistics.* New London: Penguin Books. P. 241.
5. Miller, G. A. 1964. The psycholinguists. *Encounter* 23: 35.
6. Jakobson, R. 1961. Linguistics and communication theory. In *12. The structure of language and its mathematical aspects.* New York: American Mathematical Society. Pp. 245–52.

CONTENTS

Preface   v

Part One   **CODABILITY AND NONVERBAL COMMUNICATION**   1

1   Codability in Perception   3
John P. Van de Geer

2   Language and Cognition Revisited   11
DeLee Lantz and Volney Stefflre

3   "Inner Speech" and "External Speech": Characteristics and Communication Effectiveness of Socially and Nonsocially Encoded Messages   29
Robert M. Krauss, P. S. Vivekananthan, and Sidney Weinheimer

4   Body Position, Facial Expression, and Verbal Behavior During Interviews   40
Paul Ekman

5   The Communication of Inferior and Superior Attitudes by Verbal and Nonverbal Signals   54
Michael Argyle, Veronica Salter, Hilary Nicholson, Marilyn Williams, and Philip Burgess

Part Two   **INTERACTION AND PLANNING OF VERBAL BEHAVIOR**   67

6   A Comparative Study of Two Hesitation Phenomena   69
Frieda Goldman-Eisler

7   Hesitation and Grammatical Encoding   80
     Donald S. Boomer

8   Word Predictability in the Environments
     of Hesitations   93
     *Percy H. Tannenbaum, Frederick Williams,
     and Carolyn S. Hillier*

Part Three   THE IMPACT OF SOCIAL
              RELATIONS ON LINGUISTIC
              ATTRIBUTES   **105**

9   The Operant Conditioning of Conversation   107
     Gilbert Levin and David Shapiro

10   Power, Influence, and Pattern of
     Communication   120
     Kurt W. Back

11   The Effects of "Understanding" from the
     Audience on Language Behavior   135
     Kate Loewenthal

12   Speaking of Space   143
     David McNeill

13   Differences in Egocentricity Between
     Spoken and Written Expression Under
     Stress and Non-Stress Conditions   158
     Nancy J. Sunshine and Milton K. Horowitz

Part Four   STRUCTURING OF MESSAGES AS A
             FUNCTION OF DISTANCE TO THE
             REFERENTIAL OR TOPICAL
             MATERIAL   **167**

14   Changes in Reference Phrases as a
     Function of Frequency of Usage in Social
     Interaction: A Preliminary Study   169
     Robert M. Krauss and Sidney Weinheimer

15   Characteristics of the Three-Person
     Conversation   174
     Julius Laffal

16   Interviewer Specificity and Topical Focus in

Relation to Interviewee Productivity   181
Benjamin Pope and Aron W. Siegman

Part Five   **SOCIAL CLASS, HIERARCHY, AND
LINGUISTIC HABITS**   **189**

17   Perceptual and Verbal Discriminations of
"Elaborated" and "Restricted" Code Users   191
W. P. Robinson and C. D. Creed

18   Social Class and Modes of Communication   206
Leonard Schatzman and Anselm Strauss

19   Social Class, Language, and Socialization   222
Basil B. Bernstein

20   Address in American English   243
Roger Brown and Marguerite Ford

21   Forms of Address and Social Relations in
a Business Organization   263
*Dan I. Slobin, Stephen H. Miller, and
Lyman W. Porter*

Part Six   **LANGUAGE AS AN INDEX IN SMALL
GROUP INTERACTIONS**   **273**

22   Channels of Communication in Small
Groups   275
*Robert F. Bales, Fred L. Strodtbeck,
Theodore M. Mills, and Mary E.
Roseborough*

23   The Distribution of Participation in Small
Groups: An Exponential Approximation   288
Frederick F. Stephan and Elliot G. Mishler

24   The Effect of Talkativeness on Ability to
Influence Group Solutions of Problems   308
Henry W. Riecken

25   Some Factors in the Selection of Leaders
by Members of Small Groups   322
*John P. Kirscht, Thomas M. Lodahl, and
Mason Haire*

26   Problem Solving by Small Groups Using

Various Communication Nets   328
George A. Heise and George A. Miller

27   Communication and the Process of Work   345
Tatiana Slama-Cazacu

Part Seven   **MEANING IN THE PSYCHOLOGICAL STUDY OF LANGUAGE**   **355**

28   Linguistic and Nonlinguistic Components of Communication: Notes on the Intersection of Psycholinguistic and Social Psychological Theory   357
Ragnar Rommetveit

29   Language and TAT Content in Bilinguals   369
Susan M. Ervin

30   Reasoning and Spatial Representations   384
Stephen Handel, Clinton B. DeSoto, and Marvin London

31   Motivation and Language Behavior: A Content Analysis of Suicide Notes   396
Charles E. Osgood and Evelyn G. Walker

Part Eight   **LINGUISTIC DIMENSIONS OF PERSUASION**   **415**

32   The Effect of Variations in Nonfluency on Audience Ratings of Source Credibility   417
Gerald R. Miller and Murray A. Hewgill

33   Language Variables Affecting the Persuasiveness of Simple Communications   431
David E. Kanouse and Robert P. Abelson

34   Attitudinal Effects of Selected Types of Concluding Metaphors in Persuasive Speeches   442
John Waite Bowers and Michael M. Osborn

35   Frustration and Language Intensity   454
Carl W. Carmichael and Gary Lynn Cronkhite

Part One

CODABILITY
AND NONVERBAL
COMMUNICATION

1

CODABILITY IN PERCEPTION

John P. Van de Geer

1. INTRODUCTION

This paper describes two experiments[1] modeled after a study by Brown and Lenneberg (1). In Brown's and Lenneberg's paper the emphasis is on linguistic coding; an hypothesis inspired, to some extent, by Whorf's theory that language is a determinant of perception. For example, if there is no word for 'orange' in some cultural community, people in that community will perceive the color orange differently from those who do have the word. Particularly, those who do not have the word will see orange as a shade of red or yellow and therefore more easily confuse orange with red (or yellow) than if the word were available.

Such a theory implies that (a) the linguistic response shapes perception and (b) it is meaningless to talk about the perceptual datum as a given, that is only afterwards embedded in some categorial system. In fact, it has become more and more difficult to say what is given in perception. One always can define the stimulus in physical terms, of course, but such a description does not cover experiential data. Studies of reaction times, for instance, show that even the simplest reaction time is co-determined by response systems and is, therefore, not simple. Thus, the "information" implied by a stimulus cannot be defined in terms of that stimulus alone, but only in terms of the set of alternative stimuli, and the nature of this

This article, written while the author was a Fellow at the Center for Advanced Study in the Behavioral Sciences, Stanford, is published here for the first time.

set is a characteristic of the responding organism rather than of the physical world.

The following experiments demonstrate the presence of such a "coding system," in somewhat the same manner as earlier physics molecular processes were made observable in the macroscopic world. Certain laws relating to volume and specific heat of gasses were then found to obey particular quantitative relations. These relations strongly suggested that gasses could be thought of as consisting of small moving particles with specific mass and velocity. This is true, even though these particles could not be measured or made observable directly. Similarly, our experiments are meant to show that there is such a thing as codability, but we cannot offer a detailed explanation; we cannot identify the specific code system or show how it acts as intermediary between stimulus and response.

2.   EXPERIMENTS

2.1   General Description

In the two experiments we felt that a coding process should reveal itself in one domain of responses, and then should be shown to be present in a different domain. The two domains chosen are naming responses and recognition responses. Naming responses are partly dependent upon the available linguistic identifiers. If these identifiers are related to the essential coding process, we should be able to trace their influence, which is not directly verbal, on the recognition process.

The two experiments are very similar, differing only in choice of stimulus material: colors in the first experiment, and facial expressions in the second. The general procedure was to collect, for each stimulus, measures related to the naming process, and to discover whether they are correlated with measures related to the recognition process. Colors and facial expressions have one common characteristic: they have a tremendous amount of discriminable varieties but only a limited repertory of available common verbal responses. The number of color words might run into several thousands, of which only a very limited selection (about ten to twenty) is commonly used, although the number of noticeable differences in the entire color space can be estimated at many millions. Similarly, there are many words that can be used to identify facial expressions, but this number is also far less than the number of discriminable stimuli. In other words, a limited number of verbal identifying responses should serve to cover the entire stimulus space, so that each identifier has to encompass a certain range of stimuli. Stimuli within the range would become easily confused, while stimuli in different ranges should be more easily kept apart. This, then, is not a characteristic of the stimuli themselves, but is dependent upon the identification system in the organism.

2.3. Material and Procedure

For the color experiment (C) 120 different colors were used, chosen to evenly cover the color space. For the facial expression experiment (F) 60 photographs of expressions of one actress were used. The photographs were carefully chosen for similarity in all irrelevant details such as contrast, position of the face, size, and so on. A selection of 24 colors[2] was used in the naming part of the experiment. These colors were shown, one at a time, to each of 21 Ss who were asked to describe the color verbally. In experiment F, 30 photographs were used in the naming part of the experiment. These photographs were shown, one at a time, to each of 30 Ss. A list of 20 adjectives describing emotional states was read to the S first, to give the S some idea of words that might be used. The S was asked to describe each expression with three such words (this was done to prevent the subject from digressing into long stories about the expression).

In the recognition part of the experiment, one stimulus was shown briefly, and then the S had to identify this stimulus on a panel on which many exemplars were mounted. In experiment C the color was shown for 5 seconds, and after an interval of 10 seconds, had to be identified on a panel with 120 colors. In experiment F the stimulus was shown for 20 seconds, and immediately thereafter had to be identified on a panel with 60 photographs. The Ss in the recognition part were different from those in the naming part. Twenty-four Ss took part in the recognition part of experiment C, and 30 in experiment F. All Ss were undergraduates in the psychology department.

2.3. Measures

For the naming part of the experiment the following measures were calculated for each stimulus:

R = latency time (time elapsed between presentation of the stimulus and first response), averaged over Ss (with prior standardization for each S in experiment F); $K =$ number of different categories used by all Ss; $F =$ frequency of the most common category. In experiment C the categories are just color words as given by the Ss. In experiment F the responses were first condensed to a set of 110 different categories, the main purpose of which was to combine synonyms (like "astonished," "amazed," "surprised"). The categorization was done by independent judges who were given the complete collection of responses written separately on cards. In experiment C, therefore, F is the same as the number of Ss using the most common word, whereas in experiment F the frequency of the most common category will be higher than the number of Ss using it. The measures for the recognition part are the following:

$T =$ latency time (time elapsed from beginning to search until response is given);

$N =$ number of different stimuli on the panel identified with the stimulus;

$G =$ number of correct identifications.

In experiment F observations for latency time and number of correct responses were standardized per S prior to the averaging over Ss. In should be realized that K and F are dependent because of method of computation. The same applies to N and G (if G is large, N must be relatively small).

3.   RESULTS

The results are given as correlation matrices for the two experiments, between the six measures (Tables 1 and 2). Scores F and G were taken with negative signs (since they measure the coding process in different directions as compared to the other four measures). These tables show that there are substantial correlations between variables from different domains.

It was difficult to find an overall measure for the relation between naming responses as one set, and recognition measures as the other set. Previously, we took a canonical correlation as this overall measure and indicated the coefficients for linear composites of variables within each set so that there was maximum correlation between the two composites. The canonical correlation, however,

Table 1. Correlations Between Measures in Color Experiment

(Diagonal elements are given that assign rank one to upper left and lower right 3 × 3 matrix.)

R	K	F	T	N	G
(.788)	.837	.713	.557	.440	.628
	(.889)	.757	.698	.491	.726
		(.645)	.393	.276	.439
			(.695)	.683	.772
				(.671)	.759
					(.858)

Table 2. Correlations Between Measures in Facial Expressions Experiment

(Diagonal elements are given that assign rank one to upper left and lower right 3 × 3 matrix.)

R	K	F	T	N	G
(.375)	.524	.434	.172	.208	.127
	(.733)	.607	.443	.549	.428
		(.503)	.516	.632	.493
			(.603)	.707	.618
				(.829)	.725
					(.634)

might partly result from components common only to perhaps one measure in the first set and one in the second, whereas our theory claims that we should have a measure common to all variables within one set; this measure should then appear to be related to a component common to all variables in the other set.

To solve this problem, the following procedure was adopted. Let us call the naming variables X, and the recognition variables Y. Then the three variables X should measure the same thing, apart from specific components. Therefore the matrix of correlations, after subtraction of specific contributions in the diagonal cells, should have rank one. Since this matrix is a 3 × 3 matrix, diagonal values can be computed that give the resulting matrix rank one. This matrix then can be explained by a single "factor." Similarly, we can compute a single factor for the other set of three variables.

The theory is that the single factor in one set gives the common component of the variables in it, and this component should be related to the common component in the other set. Let us call the factor in the first set k, and that in the second set, so that we have $R_{xx} = kk'$ and $R_{yy} = mm'$ (where R_{xx} is the matrix of correlations between the x's and R_{yy} that between the y's both with diagonal elements corrected to achieve rank one). Then in the "ideal" case we should have for the matrix of correlations across sets R_{xy}: $R_{xy} = km'$. Or, if the common component in one set just correlates with that of the other set: $R_{xy} = \phi.km'$, with ϕ a proportionality factor that can be identified with the correlation across sets. Actually, R_{xy} will not satisfy this ideal arrangement, but we can calculate a value for ϕ in such a way that the discrepancy between R_{xy} and $\phi.km'$ is small; in particular, we can take the value for ϕ for which the summed squares of differences between R_{xy} and $\phi.km'$ is minimum. This value has been calculated for both data matrices. For the data in Table 1 we find $\phi = .694$, and for the data in Table 2 that $\phi = .675$. A good test for significance is not available, but if we look upon ϕ as a measure of correlation, it is highly significant. The corresponding vectors k and m are given in Table 3.

This shows that K (number of categories used) has the highest loading in the naming variables set for both experiments. N (number of stimuli identified) is the main contributor in the second set.

A more classical analysis might have been to find the contribution of the first principal component. This is given in Table 3. The analysis shows one common factor that explains 68 percent of the variance in experiment C and .58 percent of that in experiment F. A second factor distinguishes between the two parts of the experiment.

Table 3. Loadings in Common Factor for First Three and Second Three Variables in Color Experiment (column C) and Facial Expressions Experiment (column F)

	C	F	C* I	C* II	F† I	F† II
R	.888	.612	.849	.345	.476	.787
K	.943	.856	.919	.254	.771	.376
F	.803	.709	.719	.588	.816	.183
T	.834	.777	.732	−.551	.873	−.278
N	.926	.910	.834	−.331	.786	−.333
G	.816	.796	.878	−.360	.775	−.399
eigen value			4.084	1.036	3.468	1.140

*First two principal components in color experiment.
†First two principal components in facial expressions experiment.

4. DISCUSSION

The calculated measure of the relationship between the variables from two distinct domains shows that there is a common component underlying the responses. We should recognize, however, that because the relative discriminability of the stimuli in the recognition panel was uncontrolled, a certain weakness was inherent in the experimental design. If, for instance, a great number of nearly identical stimuli are on the panel, measure N for a stimulus belonging to this set will be artificially high (and G artificially low). On the other hand, the possible presence of such a source of contamination can hardly increase the relationship between the two sets.

Since K and F have the highest loadings in the common factors, we may interpret the results of an interobserver agreement. K and F are in fact measures for agreement between subjects. The result then could be phrased as: Stimuli for which a high interobserver agreement in verbal naming exists, are better recognized than stimuli for which a low interobserver agreement exists.

This can be explained in terms of the underlying linguistic identification response. A different interpretation however, cannot be excluded: Some stimuli are more salient or "pregnant" in their perceptual characteristics, and such stimuli are more easily recognized make an impression of being more like primary colors, whereas the "difficult" colors are more like pastels. A similar impression is obtained from the facial expressions, where the "easy" stimuli express a clear-cut and avowed emotion whereas the "difficult" ones seem to express more or less intangible nuances. One must then ask what is first: the linguistic label or the Gestalt-like characteristics of the stimuli? Such a question cannot be answered from our data.

Spontaneous remarks of Ss during recognition search seem to support the idea that the linguistic code is important. Ss may say "Now where is that quizzical one?" in the facial expression experiment or "I am looking for terra cotta, where is it?" and the observer sometimes can see that such a search strategy leads into error (since the S selects real terra cotta instead of the correct color).

In summary: codability is a factor in the cognitive process of identification and recognition. But we do not know what is first: do stimuli have particular characteristics that make it easy for a linguistic label to become associated to them, or is the linguistic label located at an arbitrary range of the stimulus space that, when present, makes the stimulus salient?

NOTES

[1]The first experiment was reported earlier only as an internal report (4). The second experiment was published earlier in (2).

9 R 5/4	9 G 2/2	10.0 R 7.5/2
3 GY 4.5/2	3.5 Y 5/6	1 Y 8/4
5.0 G 5/3	2.5 G 4/10	4 GY 7.5/2
2.5 PB 2/2	5.0 B 6.5/2	25 GY 2/2
2.5 R 6/2	5.0 PB 2.5/3	8.5 R 5/14
neutral 5/10	5 R 3/16	10 YR 7.5/7
7.5 Y 6/4	10 GY 8/2	6.5 Y 8/5
8 R 2/6	2.5 PB 3.5/14	6 Y 9/7

REFERENCES

(1) Brown, R. W., and Lenneberg, E. H. A study in language and cognition. *Journal of Abnormal and Social Psychology* 49 (1954): 454–62.
(2) Frijda, N. H., and Van de Geer, J. P. Codability and recognition: An experiment with facial expressions. *Acta Psychologia* 18 (1961): 360–68.
(3) Lenneberg, E. H., and Roberts, J. M. The language of experience. *International Journal of American Linguistics* (1956) Memoir 13.
(4) Van de Geer, J. P. Studies in codability: I. Identification and recognition of colors. Research Report 001-60, Psychology Institute, University of Leiden, The Netherlands.

2

LANGUAGE AND COGNITION REVISITED

DeLee Lantz
Volney Stefflre

The general problem with which this study is concerned is the relation between language and nonlinguistic behavior. One position which may be taken is that all languages deal with the same "reality" and that thought and behavior are independent of the language used by the person. Language is simply used to express what is arrived at independently. Another position is that language shapes the way we experience and conceptualize the world and that our cognitive operations are dependent on the language in which we describe things.

Studies of relationships between language and thought, or language and nonlinguistic behavior, have mainly been of two types: the first type attempts to measure the ease with which the same experiences can be described in different languages—or the ease with which different stimulations can be described in the same language—and relates these measures of codability to the accuracy of retention of the stimuli.

Lenneberg (1953) has developed a methodology for research of this type. His method employs the color continuum, but this is

Reprinted from *Journal of Abnormal and Social Psychology* 69, No. 5 (1964): 472–81. Copyright 1964 by the American Psychological Association, and reproduced by permission. Figures have been renumbered and footnotes deleted.

just one example of the type of stimuli that might be used. The words used to describe the color continuum are the designated aspect of the language to be studied. The variable of color terminology which Lenneberg chose to use was codability, which may be defined as the efficiency with which a color can be transmitted in a given language. There are various ways this can be measured. The nonlinguistic behavior to be related to codability was memory, as measured by accuracy of recognition.

A study by Brown and Lenneberg (1954) applied this method. They asked the question, does the differential way we code different areas of the color solid influence other behavior toward color (such as recognition). Codability was the language variable chosen for study. The *measure* of codability used was *intersubject agreement* on naming color chips. The higher the intersubject agreement on a name, the higher the codability for that name, as defined operationally. The cognitive variable they studied was ability to pick from an array of colors one or more colors previously shown to the subject. These two variables were found to be positively correlated. Positive relationships between these same variables, using both colors and photographs of faces, were also found by Van de Geer (1960) and Van de Geer and Frijda (1960). Glanzer and Clark (1962, 1963) successfully predicted accuracy of reproduction of black and white figures and binary numbers from the brevity of verbal descriptions of these stimuli given by the subjects. This brevity measure was also used by Brown and Lenneberg in developing their original index. These studies seemed to be evidence that ease in naming a stimulus may influence ease in remembering that stimulus.

However, Lenneberg (1961) noted that the conclusions of the Brown and Lenneberg (1954) study could not be generalized beyond the specific stimulus array they used. He compared recognition scores found by Burnham and Clark (1955) using a different array of colors, with naming behavior for that same array from a previous study of his own. This time he found not a positive correlation, but a negative correlation between his measure of codability and recognition. These differing results were explained on the basis of the differences in the color arrays with respect to salient anchoring points. However explained, the fact remained that this measure of codability could not predict recognition for color arrays constructed in very different ways.

The second type of study of the relationship between language and other forms of behavior attempts to predict nonverbal measures of the similarity of pairs of stimuli from properties of the language spoken by subjects from different cultures. For example, the prediction might be made that objects having the same name or requiring the same verb stem will be put into the same category. Carroll and Casagrande (1958) asked Hopi- and English-speaking subjects to decide which two of three pictures "went together." The hypothesis was that differences in the lexicons would lead the two groups of subjects to make different judgments. Maclay (1958) and Carroll and Casagrande also investigated grammatical categories used in Navaho and compared the way Navahos and English-speaking Americans sorted objects. The results of these studies have been ambiguous.

The current consensus among those engaged in this type of research (Carroll, 1959; Furth, 1961; Greenberg, 1959; Lenneberg, 1962) appears to be that relations between language and nonlinguistic behavior are weak and equivocal. An alternative interpretation might be that we have not yet developed adequate techniques for prediction of other forms of behavior from language or verbal responses. We will describe below some alternative measures of codability and item-item similarity. These are members of a large family of possible techniques described in Stefflre (1963).

We will view memory as though it were a situation in which an individual communicates to himself through time using the brain as a channel. This communication process can be approximated by having individuals communicate with other people. Items accurately communicated interpersonally would then be predicted to be more accurately communicated intrapersonally as measured by the usual memory tests. And, pairs of items confused in interpersonal communication would tend to be confused in tests of memory.

Thus, for our measure of codability, people were presented with a stimulus array and asked to make up messages that would enable another person to pick out the stimulus it refers to—for example, "describe this item in such a way that another person will be able to pick it out." In this way we can measure the accuracy with which each item can be communicated by the messages composed by the subjects. This offers a direct measure of codability rather than the indirect measures such as agreement among people in selection of names (Brown & Lenneberg, 1954) or the mean number of words in the description (Glanzer & Clark, 1962). Stefflre used this direct measure of codability to predict recognition of pictures (1958) and recall of nonsense syllables (1963).

To attempt to predict confusions among color chips in the

recognition task several techniques are possible. A measure of the tendency of chips to be confused in the communications task can be compared with a measure of confusions in recognition, or a measure of subjects' tendency to describe pairs of stimuli in the same way can be used as a measure of item-item similarity (Stefflre, 1958). Here we asked the subject which color chip was the most "typical" of the description he had given for each chip.

This experiment attempts to unravel the conflicting relations found between codability and recognition in the studies of Brown and Lenneberg (1954) and Lenneberg (1961) by using a different measure of codability. We predicted that communication accuracy (as our measure of codability will be referred to) will correlate positively with recognition for both the original Brown-Lenneberg color array and the Farnsworth-Munsell color array, which, it will be recalled, yielded a negative correlation between recognition and the Brown and Lenneberg measure of codability, name agreement (Lenneberg, 1961). We also examined the Glanzer and Clark (1962) measure (brevity of descriptions) in relation to our stimulus materials. Finally, we wished to see if our measures of item-item similarity allowed us to predict the pattern of errors found in the recognition task.

METHOD

Subjects

College undergraduates were used. All subjects were native English speakers who had had no specialized training with color. They were screened for color blindness.

Stimulus Materials

Two sets of Munsell color arrays were used: a portion of the Farnsworth-Munsell 100 Hue Test and the Munsell colors used by Brown and Lenneberg (1954). The Farnsworth-Munsell array is a circular array of colors varying only in hue and having nearly constant saturation and brightness (Farnsworth, 1949). These colors are perceptually equidistant steps apart. The array consists of Munsell color papers mounted in black plastic caps.

The Brown-Lenneberg array varies on both hue and brightness, saturation being relatively constant. It is constructed so as to sample the outer shell of the color space evenly (highest saturation). They are not perceptually equidistant steps apart. These colors were mounted on cards.

Test Apparatus

The apparatus used for showing the Farnsworth-Munsell array was a modified version of the apparatus used by Burnham and Clark (1955). It consists of a wheel on which two sets of chips are mounted in concentric circles. There are 20 chips on the inner circle. We will refer to these as the "test colors," since they are the ones on which subjects were tested in the memory task. The outer circle consists of 43 colors—to be referred to as "comparison colors"— including duplicates of the 20 test colors. The wheel itself is enclosed in a case with a flat black finish. When the lid of the case is closed, a handle for rotating the wheel protrudes through the center. Near the edge of the cover is a set of four sliding panels that may be opened individually or together to present to the subject's view one to four of the test chips in the inner circle. Another aperture allows the subject to see the comparison colors in the outer circle one at a time.

No special apparatus was used to present the Brown-Lenneberg colors. The 24 test colors were mounted on individual 3×5 cards. Mounted on a large chart were 120 comparison colors, including duplicates of the 24 test colors. The chart was covered by a curtain which could be pulled back to reveal the chart to the subject. Throughout all the procedures, General Electric standard daylight fluorescent lights were used.

Procedures

Codability. It was first necessary to establish codability scores for each test color in the two stimulus arrays. Codability was measured in three ways: by *communication accuracy, naming agreement,* and *brevity of description.* Communication accuracy is the measure we described in the introduction which we feel will more adequately predict nonlinguistic behavior than previously used measures. Naming agreement is the measure used by Brown and Lenneberg (1954), and brevity of description is the measure used by both Brown and Lenneberg and Glanzer and Clark (1962, 1963).

Communication accuracy is a measure of how accurately a

color can be communicated. If one person names a color, and that name is given to another person, how accurately can he pick out that same color from an array? Communication accuracy required two groups of subjects: one group who named colors and another group who recieved the names and tried to find the colors the names originally referred to.

These two groups can be called, respectively, *encoders* and *decoders*. For the Farnsworth-Munsell array, the general procedure for encoding was to show each of 20 subjects (10 men and 10 women) the 20 test colors 1 at a time in the modified Burnham-Clark-Munsell apparatus. The following instructions were given:

> I'm going to show you some colors, one at a time, through this opening and I'd like you to name each color using the word or words you would use to name it to a friend so that he or she could pick it out. Do it as quickly as you can, but take time to be satisfied with your answer. Before we begin, I'll show you the colors you'll be naming. [This is to give the subjects a chance to see the range of colors he will be naming.] All right, we're ready to begin. Here's the first color. [The color was then shown through one of the openings.]

The next step in determining communication accuracy for the Farnsworth-Munsell colors was having another group of subjects decode the names given by the first group. Since there were 20 encoders and each named 20 colors, there was a total of 400 messages to be decoded. This was obviously too many messages to ask each subject to decode. Therefore, 4 messages (or names) from each encoder's total of 20 were read to each subject, making a total of 80 randomized messages for him to decode. In this way individual differences in the subjects' encoding and decoding ability would affect all colors equally. Twenty decoders were used. Every message from each encoder was decoded 4 times by different receivers. Therefore, each color had 80 decoded messages.

The decoding subjects were shown the 85 Farnsworth-Munsell colors with these instructions:

> I'm going to read some color names to you, one at a time. After I say a name, look at the colors in front of you and point to the color that seems to be the color that name refers to.

The experimenter began reading the names and wrote down the Farnsworth-Munsel number (written on the underside of the cap) of the color chosen.

By comparing the accuracy with which decoders could refer back to the color the encoder had originally described, a score of communication accuracy could be obtained for each color. Communication accuracy can be scored simply by determining the number of correctly decoded messages regarding each chip or by calculating the mean error score for each chip. This latter procedure entailed recording the difference between the code number of the chip each decoder selected when read a name and the code number of the chip to which the encoder originally gave the name, dropping the sign, and then summing the differences for all the messages referring to a chip and dividing by N. This averaging procedure was possible because Farnsworth-Munsell code numbers correspond to hue steps and the steps are perceptually equidistant. These two ways of computing communication accuracy were found to correlate .712 with one another. Since there was a wider range of scores and fewer ties with the mean error score it was used as the measure of communication accuracy for these chips.

The procedure for establishing communication accuracy for the Brown-Lenneberg colors was essentially the same. The 24 test colors were shown to the subject one at a time on 3×5 cards. The naming instructions were the same as for the Farnsworth-Munsell subjects and the same kind of decoding procedure was followed. Scores for communication accuracy for the Brown-Lenneberg colors were simply the number of correct selections made by decoders. Since the colors are not equidistant and they vary on two dimensions, a mean error score could not be computed.

The second measure of codability was naming agreement. The scores for naming agreement were derived from the data from the first group of subjects, the encoders. The Brown and Lenneberg computational formula was used. The naming agreement score for a particular color was determined by the amount of intersubject agreement on naming that color. While some colors are consistently given the same name by most speakers, others are given a variety of names. From the total of 20 responses given to a color, the number of *different responses* was subtracted from the number of times the most *common response* was given. A constant of 20 was added to keep the resulting scores positive.

The third measure of codability was brevity of descriptions.

The brevity score for each color chip was the mean number of words used to describe that chip.

Recognition.   To be related to these measures of our linguistic variable, codability, was a nonlinguistic memory task. For both sets of stimulus materials, three different recognition conditions were used. Condition I consisted of showing the subject one color at a time for 5 seconds followed by a 5-second interval, after which the subject was instructed to find the color just shown him. In Condition II, four colors were presented simultaneously for 5 seconds, and after a 5-second interval the subject was asked to find each of the four colors. Condition III presented four colors for 5 seconds followed by a 30-second interval after which the subject was asked to find the colors.

The subjects using the Farnsworth-Munsell array were told:

> You will be shown one [four] color[s] at a time through this opening [referring to the openings in the test wheel]. You will have 5 seconds to look at it, then it will be covered for 5 [30] seconds. After that time I'll give the wheel a turn and open this hole [referring to the opening above the comparison chips]. You take the wheel and find the color[s] you were just shown.

For the Brown-Lenneberg array, the recognition procedure consisted of holding one or four colors in front of the subject for 5 seconds. Also in front of the subjects was the randomized chart of 120 comparison colors which was covered by a draw-curtain while the test chips were being presented and during the interval following the presentation. After the interval, the curtain was drawn and the subject tried to find the colors he had just been shown.

Recognition scores were necessarily computed slightly differently for the two arrays, again because the Brown-Lenneberg colors were not amenable to a mean error score. The Farnsworth-Munsell recognition score was obtained by recording the difference between the code number of the comparison chip selected by the subject and the code number of the test chip presented. The total score for a chip was the sum of each of these individual scores divided by N. This yielded a mean error score for each chip which could be compared to the mean error score for communication accuracy for that chip.

The method used for obtaining recognition scores for the

Brown-Lenneberg colors was that originally devised by Brown and Lenneberg (1954). The number of correct identifications made by each subject was found and considered to be unity. Each individual correct response was given a fractional value of unity. The score for each color was the sum of all 20 subjects' fractional scores for that color.

The Farnsworth-Munsell colors were also scored this way to determine the comparability of the mean error scores and the scores weighted to take account of a subject's ability to correctly identify colors, that is, the Brown and Lenneberg formula. There was a rank-order correlation of .801 between the two ways of scoring the Farnsworth-Munsell results. The mean error score was used in preference to the fractional score because it is directly comparable to the scores for other measures of the same data, which the fractional score is not.

Measure of item-item similarity. In the introduction we referred to the giving of the same name to more than one color chip as a measure of similarity. We obtained this measure by asking the subjects for the most "typical" instance of each name they used. After the encoders had given names to the 20 test colors, they were shown the entire Farnsworth-Munsell array of 85 colors, or the chart of 120 Brown-Lenneberg colors. The subject was told:

> I'm going to read back to you, one at a time, the names you just gave me. When I say the name, look at the colors on the table and point to the "best" example, or the most "typical" example of that name. You may choose the one to which you originally gave the name, but there may be another color you think is an even better example of that name. If so, point to that one.

RESULTS

Codability and Recognition

Our hypothesis was that communication accuracy is a superior measure of codability and therefore would be a better predictor of memory than the other measures of codability which have been used. Communication accuracy should therefore correlate more highly with all recognition conditions on both the Farnsworth-Munsell and the Brown-Lenneberg color arrays. It was also our

Table 1.　Correlations Between Codability Measures and Recognition Conditions

Codability	Recognition condition		
	I	*II*	*III*
Farnsworth-Munsell array			
Communication ac-curacy	.32	.71***	.66**
Naming agreement	−.18	−.05	−.30
Brevity of description	−.29	.31	.23
Brown-Lenneberg array			
Communication ac-curacy	.51**	.86***	.78***
Naming agreement	−.02	.40*	.32
Brevity of description	.19	.42*	.33

*p ≤ .05.
**p ≤ .01.
***p ≤ .001.

expectation that communication accuracy would predict recognition for any color array, no matter how the array is constructed, whereas naming agreement probably would predict only for specific kinds of arrays, such as the Brown-Lenneberg array. The results of Spearman rank-order correlations among the variables are shown in Table 1 and intercorrelations among the codability measures are shown in Table 2. As predicted, communication accuracy was positively correlated with both sets of stimulus materials. (See Figures 1 and 2 for a graphic illustration of the strength of this relationship.) Moreover, communication accuracy was an even better predictor of Brown-Lenneberg recognition scores than the Brown-Lenneberg measure of naming agreement.

While naming agreement did correlate significantly with the second recognition condition for the Brown-Lenneberg colors, it was not correlated with recognition of the Farnsworth-Munsell

Table 2.　Intercorrelations Between Measures of Codability

Measure	Name agreement	Brevity of description
Farnsworth-Munsell array		
Communication accuracy	−.10	.13
Naming agreement		.09
Brown-Lenneberg array		
Communication accuracy	.43	.45*
Naming agreement		.54**

*p ≤ .05.
**p ≤ .01.

Figure 1. Relationship Between Codability and Combined Recognition Scores (all three conditions) for Brown-Lenneberg Colors

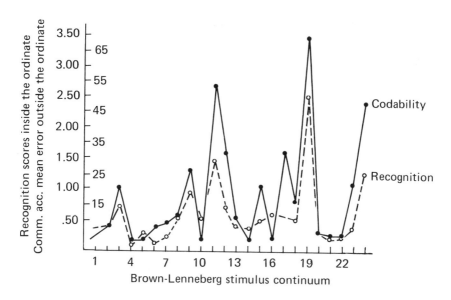

Figure 2. Relationship Between Codability and Combined Recognition Scores for Farnsworth-Munsell Colors

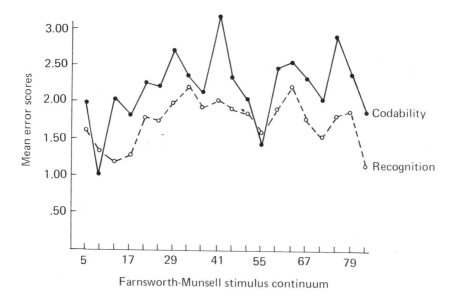

colors, as Lenneberg (1961) had reasoned. As one would expect, communication accuracy and naming agreement correlated −.10 *(ns)* with each other on the Farnsworth-Munsell data, and .43 (*p* < .05) on the Brown-Lenneberg data. We examined the correlation between naming agreement and Recognition Condition II on the Brown-Lenneberg array (the best of the naming agreement predictions) to see what would remain when communication accuracy was partialed out. The resulting partial correlation was .06. Thus, it is because naming agreement is related to communication accuracy for the Brown-Lenneberg array that it is able to predict, not because of anything unique to naming agreement.

We also examined the relationship between Glanzer and Clark's (1962, 1963) measure of brevity of description and recognition. None of the correlations between this measure and the recognition conditions was significant for the Farnsworth-Munsell color array, nor was brevity of description found to be significantly correlated with naming agreement or communication accuracy for these colors. For the Brown-Lenneberg array, the correlation between brevity of description and recognition reached significance on Condition II. The rather close parallel between the naming agreement and brevity of description correlations with recognition conditions for the Brown-Lenneberg colors suggests that these two codability measures are related for this array. The correlation between naming agreement and brevity of description was found to be .54 (*p* < .01). Since we know naming agreement and communication accuracy are related for this array, we would, then, also expect a relationship between brevity of description and communication accuracy. That correlation was .45 (*p* < .05). Again, a partial correlation was made between brevity of description and the Brown-Lenneberg Recognition Condition II with communication accuracy held constant. And, as with naming agreement, the correlation dropped to .07.

Thus, communication accuracy is a codability measure superior to naming agreement and brevity of description, both in strength of relationship and in ability to predict regardless of what kind of stimulus array is used. Where the latter two measures do predict, it is because, in those cases, they are related to communication accuracy.

In both stimulus arrays, the correlation between codability and recognition was greatest for the second recognition condition (four colors, 5-second interval). However, although Conditions II and III both differed significantly from Condition I in number of errors made, they did not differ significantly from one another (as determined by *t* tests), Brown and Lenneberg discussed their lack of correlation between codability and recognition in Condition I (which we also found) as possibly being due to the shortness of time between presentation of the test chip and recognition. Direct visual memory can be relied on for a 5-second interval, but when several colors must be remembered, or when there is a longer interval, the necessity of storing a name is increased.

Verbal Similarity Measures

There were two kinds of data on judgments of the "typical instance" of a color. First, there were *aggregate* typical judgments for each chip, where each of the 20 encoders found the most typical example for his name for that chip. For Chip Number 55 of the Farnsworth-Munsell array, for example, there are typical judgments for 9 names for that chip, because 9 different names were given by the 20 subjects. A single typical judgment was scored by taking the difference between the number of the chip to which the name was originally given and the chip that was judged to be the best example of that name. The 20 judgments were averaged, keeping the sign, and this average was the overall typical score for that chip. For Chip 67, the average of the typical judgments was +.925, meaning that, on the average, the color nearly one hue step beyond Number 67 was judged by the subjects to be a better example of the names elicited by 67 than 67 itself.

The relationship between the mean recognition errors and the judgments of the typical instance for that chip was examined (see Figure 3). Errors in recognition went in the same direction as the judgment of the typical 16 out of 20 times. A sign test for the sameness of direction was significant at the .01 level. But more than this, not only did recognition errors go in the direction of the typical instance, they were less extreme than the typical. That is, they assimilated toward it. There are only two exceptions to this—Chips 55 and 59, where the recognition errors were slightly more extreme than the typical.

Although the results were quite marked, one might argue that these were, after all, aggregated judgments and may or may not have anything to do with what goes on in the individual. Therefore a second means of examining the relations between recognition errors and judgments of the typical was used. A group of 15 subjects were asked individually to name the color chips, select the

**Figure 3.   Relationship of Combined Recognition Scores
to Judgments of the Typical**

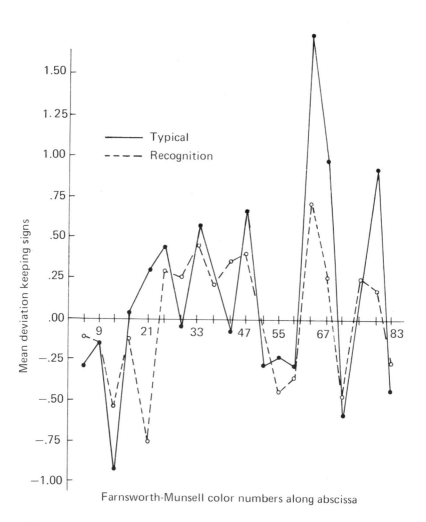

Farnsworth-Munsell color numbers along abscissa

typical chips for those names, and then were given the recognition
test as in Condition II. The chip each subject picked as his recognition response for each of the test chips could then be compared with
the chip he had picked as "typical" for the name he had given the
test chip. We then compared for each chip the number of people
making errors in the expected direction—that is, toward the chip

they had picked as typical—with the number making errors in the opposite direction. For 5 chips a majority went in the expected direction while for 15 chips the majority went in the other direction (away from the typical). A result like this would occur less than once in 20 times through chance, but it was, interestingly enough, in the wrong direction.

Considering this paradoxical result we decided that by asking the subject to select the chips typical of his description before he attempted the recognition task we were forcing him during recognition to reconsider the adequacy of his original descriptions. That is, we were warning our subjects against the phenomena we were attempting to demonstrate and altering the ways in which stimuli were encoded in the recognition task. To test this speculation 10 more subjects were run but the order of tasks reversed. First these subjects were given a recognition task, then they were asked to name the color chips, and finally they were asked to select the chips typical of each of the names. This alternation in procedure led 17 of the chips to exhibit more errors in the expected direction (toward the typical) and 3 chips to exhibit more in the opposite direction. This result was beyond the .002 level of significance, and in the expected direction.

It has been our experience that any modification in an experimental procedure that alters the way subjects describe the situation to themselves may alter the results of the experiment. The example above is simply one case in point.

DISCUSSION

The results are clear-cut evidence that communication accuracy is a superior predictor of memory for colors than naming agreement or brevity of description. It is superior in two senses: it correlates more highly with recognition results than do the other measures, and it predicts for at least two very different stimulus arrays, which naming agreement and brevity of description do not. It thereby brings together what were formerly disparate results.

It had previously been assumed that communality in verbal response reflected ease and accuracy in communication. The fact that naming agreement and communication accuracy were not highly positively correlated demonstrates that this assumption is not justified. These measures will not correlate when the appearance of numerous names simply indicates a proliferation of vocabulary for describing the item, or when there are a number of items in the stimulus array that are all named in the same way. Naming agreement will predict recognition only when it reflects communications differences.

The nature of the context in which a color—and presumably any other sensory stimulus—is found is very important in determining what kind of verbal measure will successfully predict nonverbal behavior in regard to it. For example, a color call "blue" by 100 per cent of the subjects (high naming agreement) will almost always be correctly decoded (high communication accuracy) if it is set in a context of reds, yellows, oranges, and greens. It will also be recognized quite easily. In this case, naming agreement and communication accuracy will correlate with one another and both will predict recognition. If that same color is in a context of 20 other shades of blue, there may still be high communality in naming it "blue," but ease of recognition would be sharply altered, as would communication acccuracy. Here the communication accuracy measure reflects the effects of context on ease of recognition, while naming agreement does not. If the nonverbal measures obtained on a given item can be radically altered by context—as recognition can—then the verbal measure from which we are trying to predict should also have this property, as communication accuracy does.

Communication accuracy also predicted far better than the brevity of description measure for the type of stimulus arrays used here. For a fair test of the relative generality of the two measures, communication accuracy should be obtained on the Glanzer and Clark stimulus materials to determine if it would still predict as well or better than brevity of description.

The communication accuracy technique described here will fail to work under certain conditions. If we used subjects who each had a different native language but shared a common *lingua franca* the intrapersonal coding for each individual might be in his native language while the interpersonal communication would be in the *lingua franca*. Here communication accuracy would not predict recognition. Also, if our stimuli were of a type such that each individual had his own personal language to describe it to himself, and used a different description for interpersonal communication, the relation between codability and recognition could be sharply attenuated. The private and the public descriptions may have very different properties in terms of their adequacy in communicating specific stimulus materials and in the pattern of errors they imply.

The key problem in predicting memory from the interpersonal measures is to insure that the description given by the encoding subjects are comparable to the descriptions given by the recognition subjects. The kind of incomparability described above is obvious. However, minor differences in the situation in which the verbal measures are obtained may also lead to differences in the way stimuli are described in the two situations. For example, the subjects in the recognition task in this study necessarily saw the entire array of comparison colors on their first trial. Having seen all the colors may have led them to describe the test chips to themselves differently than if they had not seen them. Therefore, we showed the subjects who named colors (the encoders) the entire array before they began their task. This procedure was followed in order to make the situation in which the verbal data were obtained as equivalent as possible to that in which the nonverbal data were obtained. It is difficult to tell what alterations in the situation may make a difference in how subjects describe even such simple stimuli as color chips. Therefore, everything possible should be done to assure comparability, for otherwise verbal measures will not predict nonverbal measures effectively. Fortunately, it is usually possible to test directly to see if the descriptions given in the encoding situation are in fact comparable to the descriptions generated covertly by the subjects in the nonverbal task.

The kind of formulation presented here of relations between language and behavior emphasizes the productivity of language— new descriptions may be formed spontaneously and function to encode stimuli effectively. For example, "light sky blue with a tinge of pink" may communicate (either to oneself or to another) quite well, while a more commonly agreed upon name such as "blue" may not be so effective. Any description of the relations between language and behavior or language and thought that does not take this into account and emphasizes only the role of dictionary words and/or grammatical categories will find it difficult to deal with the facts found in a particular experimental context.

Although the correlations found in this study between language and nonlinguistic behavior are striking, it might be argued that they do not necessarily demonstrate any causal relations. However, Lantz (1963) was able to manipulate the relationship experimentally. She taught subjects new names for previously poorly communicated chips and in this way increased the accuracy with which they were recognized. This type of experimental procedure allows inferences to be made about causal relations.

REFERENCES

Brown, R. W., and Lenneberg, E. H. A study in language and cognition. *J. abnorm. soc. Psychol.*, 1954, 49, 454–462.

Burnham, R. W., and Clark, J. R. A test of hue memory. *J. appl. Psychol.*, 1955, 39, 164–172.

Carroll, J. B. Language and thought studied across languages: A report of the "Southwest Project." Paper read at American Psychological Association, Cincinnati, September 1959.

Carroll, J. B., and Casagrande, J. B. The function of language classifications in behavior. In Eleanor E. Maccoby, T. M. Newcomb, and E. L. Hartley (eds.), *Readings in social psychology.* (3rd ed.) New York: Holt, 1958. Pp. 18–31.

Farnsworth, D. *The Farnsworth-Munsell 100 Hue Test for the examination of color discrimination: Manual.* Baltimore: Munsell Color Company, 1949.

Furth, H. The influence of language on the development of concept formation in deaf children. *J. abnorm. soc. Psychol.* 1961, 63, 386–389.

Glanzer, M., and Clark, W. H. Accuracy of perceptual recall: An analysis of organization. *J. verbal Learn. verbal Behav.*, 1962, 1, 225–242.

Glanzer, M., and Clark, W. H. The verbal loop hypothesis: Binary numbers. *J. verbal Learn. verbal Behavior.*, 1963, 2, 301–309.

Greenberg, J. H. Current trends in linguistics. *Science*, 1959, 130, 1165–1170.

Lantz, DeLee. Color naming and color recognition: A study in the psychology of language. Unpublished doctoral dissertation, Harvard University, 1963.

Lenneberg, E. H. Cognition in ethnolinguistics. *Language*, 1953, 29, 463–471.

Lenneberg, E. H. Color naming, color recognition, color discrimination: A reappraisal. *Percept. mot. Skills*, 1961, 12, 375–382.

Lenneberg, E. H. The relationship of language to the formation of concepts. *Synthese*, 1962, 14, 103–109.

Maclay, H. An experimental study of language and nonlinguistic behavior. *SW J. Anthropol.*, 1958, 14, 220–229.

Stefflre, V. An investigation of the role of language in E. Heidbreder's experiments on concept formation. Unpublished honors thesis, Reed College, 1958.

Stefflre, V. An outline for the study of some relations between language and nonlinguistic behavior. Paper read at Social Science Research Council Conference on Transcultural Studies of Cognitive Processes, Merida, Yucatan, June 1963.

Van de Geer, J. P. Studies in codability: I. Identification and recognition of colors. Report No. E001-60, 1960, State University of Leyden, Psychological Institute, The Netherlands.

Van de Geer, J. P., and Frijda, N. H. Studies in codability: II. Identification and recognition of facial expression. Report No. E002-60, 1960, State University of Leyden, Psychological Institute, The Netherlands.

3

"INNER SPEECH" AND "EXTERNAL SPEECH": CHARACTERISTICS AND COMMUNICATION EFFECTIVENESS OF SOCIALLY AND NONSOCIALLY ENCODED MESSAGES

Robert M. Krauss
P. S. Vivekananthan
Sidney Weinheimer

It frequently seems the case that the way a person encodes information for himself differs from the way he encodes it for some other person. One way of conceptualizing this difference is in the distinction between social or "external" speech and nonsocial or "inner" speech (see Vygotsky, 1962; Werner & Kaplan, 1963).

The difference between these two forms of verbal behavior is most clearly seen in the speech of young children. As Piaget

Reprinted from *Journal of Personality and Social Psychology* 9, No. 4 (1968): 295–300. Copyright 1968 by the American Psychological Association, and reproduced by permission. Footnotes have been renumbered.

(1926) has noted, the speech of young children is largely composed of verbalization which lacks a communicative function or is, to use Piaget's term, "egocentric." In more recent research, Glucksberg, Krauss, and Weisberg (1966) found that the messages uttered by four-year-old speakers in a dyadic communication task communicated inadequately to others, although the same messages could be employed effectively in communication with the speaker himself.

Two relevant studies of inner and external speech using adult subjects (Kaplan, 1952; Slepian, 1959) have been reported in the literature (see Werner & Kaplan, 1963). In both, the inner speech of normal subjects was found to contain fewer words and fewer "communal referents," compared to the external speech of the same subjects. However, both studies have serious defects. In the first place, in both, the inner speech condition always preceded the external speech condition, thereby confounding treatments and sequence effects. Second, in both, the external speech condition was presented immediately after the subject had received negative feedback, that is, he had been told that the information provided in his message was insufficient to enable a listener to select the correct referent. Maclay and Newman (1960) have found that such feedback increases the number of words used by speakers to encode referents, and Krauss and Weinheimer (1966) have shown that this effect is especially strong where there is no direct interaction between speaker and listener, as was the case in the Kaplan (1952) and Slepian (1959) studies. So the effect of the negative feedback, taken together with the sequence by treatment confounding, can explain the results of these two studies insofar as the number of words used is concerned. In addition, neither of these studies attempted to assess the communicative adequacy of inner or external speech by having listeners actually attempt to select a referent from among a set of referents on the basis of the two types of messages.

The present experiment attempts to examine differences in both the communication effectiveness and the lexical characteristics of inner and external speech. In addition, the data will enable some conclusions to be drawn concerning the relations between communication effectiveness and lexical characteristics. Following Werner and Kaplan's (1963) usage, messages which are socially encoded (i.e., encoded for others) will be defined as external speech and messages which are nonsocially encoded (i.e., encoded for oneself), as inner speech. The present measure of communication effectiveness is the same as that used by Lantz and Stefflre (1964), namely, the accuracy with which a message enables a listener to select an object from a set of objects.

METHOD

Overview of the Experiment

Fifty-two female subjects named each of 24 color chips. Half of the subjects were told that the names would later be used by the subjects themselves to identify the colors (nonsocial encoding condition); the remainder were told that the names would be used by some other person (social encoding condition). Approximately 2 weeks later all 52 subjects were called back, seated before the original 24-color stimulus array, and asked to match each of 72 names with the appropriate color. Twenty-four of these were names the subjects themselves had given in the first session (self-decoding condition), 24 were names given by another subject under social instructions (other-social decoding condition), and the remaining 24 had been given by another subject under nonsocial instructions (other-nonsocial decoding condition).

Subjects

Fifty-two female undergraduates, naive to the purposes of the experiment, served as subjects. All were randomly assigned to their treatment conditions. They were paid $1.50 for participating in the two sessions, which together ran about 35 minutes. In view of the low frequency of defective color vision among females (about .4 percent according to Judd, 1952), subjects were not screened for color blindness.

Stimulus Materials

Twenty-four $\frac{1}{2} \times \frac{7}{8}$-inch Munsell color chips comprised the stimulus array. The color array used here was originally employed by Brown and Lenneberg (1954), and the reader is referred to their paper for the Munsell renotation values of the 24 colors. Each chip was mounted on a white 3×5-inch card.

In the encoding sessions the chips were presented individually. The white card containing the color chip was placed in the center of a neutral gray field laid out on a table. Illumination was provided by two high-intensity lamps mounted 9 inches above and to either side of the stimulus display, $3\frac{1}{2}$ inches apart, providing an illumination level of 170 foot-candles. The subject, seated in front of the display, viewed it from above at an incident angle of about 75 degrees.

In the decoding sessions, the cards containing the 24 chips were displayed on a 25×20-inch sheet of white illustration board. They were systematically ordered on the hue dimension in four rows of six chips each. The illustration board was mounted upright, and the subject viewed it at eye level from a distance of about 3 feet.

Procedure

In the first phase of the experiment, the encoding session, subjects were run individually. They were first shown the 24-color array and asked to examine the colors for about 1 minute. This procedure was followed to acquaint the subjects with the range of differences among the stimuli.

They were then told that they were participating in the first part of a two-part experiment and that they would be shown several color chips and asked to name them. Subjects were told that in the second part of the experiment they themselves (for nonsocial encoders) or some other girl (for social encoders) would be asked to identify the colors from these names. In part, the instructions read:

> ... by the name of a color what I mean is any verbal label which will help [this other girl/you] to pick out that color in the second part of the experiment. That is, you don't have to restrict yourself to conventional color names if you don't want to.

The experimenter then exposed the 24 colors sequentially, using a different random order for each subject. The subject named each color aloud, and the experimenter transcribed each name verbatim.

In the second part of the experiment (the decoding sessions) all 52 subjects received a deck of 72 punch cards, each containing a single color name. Twenty-four of these names were the subject's own, 24 were those of a subject in the social encoding condition, and 24 were those of a subject in the nonsocial condition, randomly ordered. Random sampling without replacement was used, so that the names given by each subject were decoded by exactly two other subjects, one of whom had initially participated in the social encoding condition and the other in the nonsocial condition. Subjects were run in groups numbering from two to four and worked in separate booths. They were instructed to go through the deck of punch cards, read the name at the top of the card, search the 24-color array in front of them and locate the color referred to, and write the identifying number of the color on the punch card. Subjects were told to go through the cards in the order given and not to skip any or go back. The instructions stressed that they were to assign a number to every name and, if necessary, to guess when they were uncertain.

RESULTS

Communication Effectiveness

The communication effectiveness of socially and nonsocially encoded messages was assessed by determining the frequency with which the names given in the encoding sessions enabled subjects in the decoding sessions to identify the colors which had elicited them. It is clear from an examination of the Brown and Lenneberg (1954) series that hue-adjacent colors are not equidistant. Initally, it had been the intention to multidimensionally scale the decoding data and establish intercolor distances so that values representing the degree of inaccurate identification could be assigned. Unfortunately, the decoding confusion matrices were unsuitable for multidimensional scaling. Hence, subjects' responses were assigned a binary score, 1, when the identification was correct and 0 when it was incorrect, regardless of how discrepant from the originally designed color it was. It should be noted that analyses based upon more refined scoring schemes produced the same configuration of results.

The configuration of treatments forms a 2 (encoding conditions) × 3 (decoding conditions) × 24 (colors) factorial experiment. Encoding condition is a between-subjects variable, and decoding condition and color are within-subjects variables. A mixed analysis of variance was performed on the data for accuracy of identification, and the results of this analysis appear in Table 1. The means, summed across colors, are shown in Table 2. As these analyses indicate, there are clear differences in communication accuracy

Table 1. Analysis of Variance of Identification Data

Source	df	MS	F	Error term
Between Ss	51			
Encoding condition (A)	1	0.0974	<1	Error (b)
Error (b)	50	0.2500		
Within Ss	3692			
Decoding condition (B)	2	11.0758	93.94*	E_1
Color (C)	23	3.1693	14.33*	E_2
A × B	2	0.1505	1.28	E_1
A × C	23	0.0726	<1	E_2
B × C	46	0.5135	4.54*	E_3
A × B × C	46	0.0854	<	E_3
Error (w)	3550			
E_1 (B × Ss within groups)	100	0.1179		
E_2 (C × Ss within groups)	1150	0.2211		
E_3 (BC × Ss within groups)	2300	0.1130		
Total	3743			

*$p < .001$.

Table 2. Mean Proportion of Correct Identifications in the Six Decoding Conditions

Original encoding condition	Decoding of messages encoded by		
	Self	Other-social	Other-nonsocial
Social instructions	.615	.744	.577
Nonsocial instructions	.620	.744	.542

in the three decoding conditions ($F = 93.94$, $df = 2/100$, $p < .001$). Subjects were most accurate in identifying colors from their own encodings, they were next most accurate in identifying colors named by another person in the social encoding condition, and they were least accurate in identifying colors named by another person in the nonsocial encoding condition. As the Encoding × Decoding condition interaction indicates, a subject is equally good at identifying colors from his own (or others') names, irrespective of his original encoding condition. Indeed, the self-decoding means are identical for subjects who encoded under social and nonsocial instructions, and this is the only contrast in which one would expect to find differences.

As the significant main effect for Color ($F = 14.33$, $df = 23/1150$, $p < .001$) indicates, colors vary in the accuracy with which they can be identified on the basis of a name. However, it is clear from the significant Decoding condition × Color interaction that this is not true to the same degree across colors; the same colors are differentially identifiable in the three decoding conditions. Upon further analysis these differences seem attributable to the fact that the 24 colors differ as to the ease with which they can be named — a property which Brown and Lenneberg (1954) termed "codability." Correlations, computed across colors within each of the three encoding conditions between the Brown and Lenneberg codability score (see Brown & Lenneberg, 1954, Table 1) and the decoding accuracy score show marked differences. For the self and other-social conditions, the correlation coefficients are not significantly different from zero (r's $= .27, .31$, respectively). For the other-nonsocial condition, $r = .58$ ($p < .01$). That is, decoding accuracy was more strongly associated with a color's codability in the other-nonsocial decoding condition than in the two other decoding conditions. It may be the case that nonsocial encoders tend to give idiosyncratic names to colors for which socially accepted names are not readily available. Because these names are idiosyncratic, they are difficult for another person to use in the identification task, although they present no great problem for the encoder himself.

Lexical Features

Name length. The length of each name (in number of words) was calculated for the two encoding conditions. In cases where it was not clear whether a pair of words should be counted as two separate words, a single word or a hyphenated word the preferred usage as given by *Webster's New Collegiate Dictionary* (1949) was used as the criterion. For hyphenated words, hyphens were removed and the number of separate words counted. An analysis of variance performed on this measure indicated no significant difference in name length between the social and nonsocial encoding conditions ($F = 2.69$, $df = 1/50$, $p < .10$) contrary to the findings of Kaplan (1952) and Slepian (1959). This failure to confirm their results suggests that the confounding discussed above may indeed have been responsible for the greater length of external speech messages in Kaplan's and Slepian's experiments.

Type-token ratio. One commonly used measure of vocabulary diversity is the ratio of the number of different words a speaker uses (types) to the total number of words he uses (tokens). A type-token ratio (TTR) was computed for each subject in each of the two encoding conditions, and a t test was performed on the TTR transformed to its radian. A significant difference in the TTRs for the two conditions was obtained ($t = 4.07$, $df = 50$, $p < .01$). Subjects in the nonsocial encoding condition employed more diverse vocabularies (i.e., larger TTRs) than their counterparts in the social encoding condition.

Word-frequency analysis. One may also characterize a vocabulary in terms of the portion of rank-frequency distribution from which it tends to be sampled. Persons using relatively esoteric vocabularies would tend, on the average, to use a great many low-frequency (high-rank) words. The authors compiled a lexicon of all the words used by subjects in both encoding conditions, ordered in terms of frequency of occurrence. Each word was assigned a rank corresponding to the ordinal position of its frequency. Each subject was then given a score based on the mean rank of the vocabulary she employed in encoding the 24 colors. A t test performed on the difference between mean rank of the vocabularies of subjects in the two encoding conditions revealed a significantly greater use of high-rank (i.e., relatively unusual) words for subjects in the nonsocial encoding condition ($t = 2.06$, $df = 50$, $p < .05$).

Another way of assessing differences in the word frequencies of the color names given in the two encoding conditions is in terms of the frequency of unique words (i.e., words used by only one subject). Subjects in the nonsocial encoding condition tended to use nearly twice as many unique words as subjects in the social condition (5.2 versus 2.8 words, respectively), but this difference does not quite achieve the conventionally accepted level for statistical significance ($t = 1.63$, $df = 50/.10 > p > 05$).

Lexical features and decoding. The authors have indicated above some aspects of the lexical differences between socially and nonsocially encoded color names. Another area of interest concerns the relationship between the lexical features of color names and the extent to which they give rise to accurate identification. One may ask whether the use of unusual words tends to lead to accurate identification by *(a)* the subject who used them, and *(b)* other subjects. For socially encoded color names there is a significant negative correlation between mean rank and accurate identification in the self-decoding condition ($r = -.54$, $p < .05$), while for nonsocially encoded names the relationship is significant in a positive direction ($r = .42$, $p < .05$). In neither condition is mean rank related to decoding accuracy by others. The same pattern of relationships is found for the correlation of frequency of unique responses with accuracy. Apparently, then, the use of unusual words in the two encoding conditions reflects rather different processes.

DISCUSSION

It seems clear that subjects instructed to produce color names either for their own use or for the use of others produce quite different sorts of names. Under nonsocial encoding instructions, subjects employ vocabularies which are more diverse and contain more unusual and unique words. However, their color names contain approximately the same number of words as the names given by subjects encoding under social instructions. Further, these lexical differences seem to be related to the accuracy with which names can be matched to the colors which elicited them. Socially encoded names elicit more accurate identification than do nonsocial names. However, in the self-decoding condition, social encoders and nonsocial encoders were equally accurate. This result is somewhat surprising, for intuitively it seems that the language one uses to encode messages for oneself is, in some sense, a more efficient code than the language one uses to communicate with others. Two factors may have mitigated this effect in the present experiment. First, subjects were not under time pressure for encoding or for decoding. It may be the case that inner speech is more efficient (if, in fact, it is more efficient) because one has readier access to it; that is, it permits production of names with shorter latencies. The second factor relates to the domain of stimulus objects. English provides a rich variety of conventional names for colors (see Chapanis, 1965), and it may well be the case that females are especially conversant with these names. Under such circumstances it may not be too surprising that self-decoding for socially or nonsocially encoded names is equally accurate. But it is clearly not the case that all subjects map color names onto the color array in precisely the same way. A subject using her own socially encoded names to identify colors performed more accurately than did other subjects using the same names. Undoubtedly there is some degree of idiosyncrasy in the way individuals use certain conventional, but relatively rare, color names.[1] Perhaps with stimuli for which conventional names are less applicable (e.g., random shapes) or for which idiosyncratic associations might provide better mnemonics (e.g., faces), a difference in self-decoding would be found for socially and nonsocially encoded names.

The fact that accuracy in the self-decoding condition relates differently to the use of low-frequency words in the social and nonsocial encoding conditions (negatively in the former case and positively in the latter) suggests that rather different processes are represented in the two encoding conditions. One critical aspect of communication skill involves the speaker's ability to infer from a set of assumptions he makes about his listener the appropriateness of alternative ways of encoding a given informative content. As Brown (1965) put it, "Effective coding requires that the point of view of the auditor be realistically imagined [p. 132]." In the social encoding condition this would require that the subject assess the likelihood of another person being familiar with a given unusual color name or with objects whose color can be incorporated into a color name (as in "the color of the yolk of a hard-boiled egg"). The fact that a given social encoder finds it necessary to employ a great many unusual words might be taken to suggest a certain ineptness on his part, since good social names are by definition names which have a high degree of communality. And as these data indicate, this ineptness is reflected in the inability of such subjects to identify colors accurately on the basis of their own names. In contrast, the use of unusual words by a nonsocial encoder suggests the opposite, an ability to take advantage of his special knowledge of the characteristics of the message's recipient (i.e., himself) by using a special vocabulary. This enhances the subject's ability to identify colors, as is indicated by the positive correlation between frequency of unusual words and self-decoding. What is surprising in all of this, and weakens the foregoing argument considerably, is the fact that in neither case is a relationship found between frequency of unusual words and decoding accuracy of others. Since, for social encoders, the frequency of unusual words and accuracy of self-decoding are negatively related, and, at the same time, self-decoding and other decoding are positively related, the authors are led both by speculation and by the configuration of relationships to expect a negative relationship between frequency of unusual words and decoding accuracy by others. The data simply do not support such an expectation.

NOTE

[1]The authors observed this in an early pilot study in which a non-color-defective male subject applied the name "chartreuse" to a pinkish-red color chip and insisted that the name was appropriate. It is the authors' impression that females tend to use such relatively rare color terms as "fuchsia," "cerise," etc., both more frequently and more accurately than do men. However, the operative factor here would seem to be familiarity (with color, names, or both) rather than perceptual acuity, given subjects whose color vision is normal (Pickford, 1951).

REFERENCES

Brown, R. *Social psychology.* New York: Free Press of Glencoe, 1965.

Brown, R., and Lenneberg, E. H. A study in language and cognition. *Journal of Abnormal and Social Psychology,* 1954, 49, 454–462.

Chapanis, A. Color names for color space. *American Scientist,* 1965, 53, 327–346.

Glucksberg, S., Krauss, R. M., and Weisberg, R. Referential communication in nursery school children: Method and some preliminary findings. *Journal of Experimental Child Psychology,* 1966, 3, 333–342.

Judd, D. B. *Color in business, science and industry.* New York: Wiley, 1952.

Kaplan, E. An experimental study on inner speech as contrasted with external speech. Unpublished master's thesis, Clark University, 1952.

Krauss, R. M., and Weinheimer, S. Concurrent feedback, confirmation, and the encoding of referents in verbal communication. *Journal of Personality and Social Psychology,* 1966, 4, 343–346.

Lantz, D., and Stefflre, V. Language and cognition revisited. *Journal of Abnormal and Social Psychology,* 1964, 69, 472–481.

Maclay, H. S., and Newman, S. Two variables affecting the message in communication. In D. K. Wilner (ed.), *Decisions, values, and groups.* New York: Pergamon Press, 1960.

Piaget, J. *The language and thought of the child.* New York: Harcourt, Brace, 1926.

Pickford, R. W. *Individual differences in colour perception.* London: Routledge & Kegan Paul, 1951.

Slepian, H. A developmental study of inner vs. external speech in normals and schizophrenics. Unpublished doctoral dissertation, Clark University, 1959.

Vygotsky, L. S. *Thought and language.* New York: Wiley, 1962.

Webster's New Collegiate Dictionary. Springfield, Mass.: Merriam, 1949.

Werner, H., and Kaplan, B. *Symbol formation.* New York: Wiley, 1963.

4

BODY POSITION, FACIAL EXPRESSION, AND VERBAL BEHAVIOR DURING INTERVIEWS

Paul Ekman

There has been relatively little systematic investigation of the information which may be transmitted through spontaneous nonverbal behavior shown during interpersonal transactions. Research on body movement and facial expression has had to deal with a phenomenon which is continuously occurring, has no readily apparent unit of measurement or method of evaluation, and is both difficult and expensive to record. Despite the clinical conviction that nonverbal behavior provides important clues about an individual's emotional experience, such beliefs rest on little more than anecdotal evidence or speculation. In fact, research on interview behavior has increasingly focused on verbal rather than nonverbal interactions.

The major problem in exploration of the nonverbal aspects of interview behavior, may at least initially appear to be the acquisition of a permanent record. Actually, unless the body movements and facial expressions are obviously meaningful from simple

Reprinted from *Journal of Abnormal and Social Psychology* 68, No. 3 (1964): 295–301. Copyright 1964 by the American Psychological Association, and reproduced by permission. Footnote has been deleted.

inspection, the investigator is quickly overwhelmed with a mass of photographic stimuli, which are just as baffling and complex as were the original behaviors themselves. The central difficulty in research on spontaneous nonverbal behavior is the development of fruitful techniques for evaluating the information which may be contained in records of nonverbal behavior. Two approaches can be distinguished which, although related, usually have been separately pursued.

The first approach has measured variations in nonverbal behavior as a *response* to some other factor, such as interview structure of patient mood. Sainesbury (1955) and Dittmann (1962), for example, have reported a relationship between changes in nonverbal behavior and the content or structure of an interview. They did not study the related question, however, of what may be communicated to an observer by these changes in nonverbal behavior.

In the second research approach, nonverbal behavior is presented as a communicative *stimulus* and an observer's response to that stimulus is measured. Most of the experiments using this second approach have been performed with posed behavior which occurred during isolation rather than in the midst of an interpersonal interaction (for example, Schlosberg, 1954). Moreover, these studies have focused upon judge agreement rather than accuracy in understanding communication through nonverbal behavior. Attempts to measure the information transmitted through nonverbal behavior during an interview have been inconsistent in their methods and results (Giedt, 1955; Mahl, Danet, & Norton, 1959). These experiments have not allowed specification of the actual nonverbal cues which served as the basis for the judgments required. A further criticism of the research studying nonverbal behavior as a communicative stimulus, is that it has relied on the application of highly complex verbal concepts for evaluating the information transmitted by the nonverbal cues. A judgment task which requires ratings on emotional scales, diagnostic or psychodynamic formulations, may well miss much of the information which nonverbal behavior can communicate to an observer.

The present series of experiments combined features of both research approaches by measuring an observer's response to nonverbal behavior (Approach 2), in a task which required him to relate nonverbal behavior to another aspect of the interview situation (Approach 1). A relationship between what a person does with his body and what he is saying was assumed, and a matching procedure was borrowed from the early research on expressive behavior (Vernon, 1936; Wolff, 1943) to test the following hypothesis: Judges can detect a relationship between nonverbal and verbal behavior which was simultaneously emitted during an interview.

Four separate experiments with different groups of judges will be reported. In each of these experiments judges responded to verbal and nonverbal stimuli which had been gathered during the course of two interviews.

GENERAL METHOD

Interview Procedure

A standard rather than clinical interview was employed to increase the comparability of the two interviews and to insure the presence of different affective reactions. The interview structure was achieved by programing both the style and content of the interviewer's (the experimenter) behavior toward the interviewee (the subject). After an introductory affectively neutral period of 10 minutes, the experimenter attacked and criticized the subject's choice of occupation, competency, and motivation. Throughout this stress phase, the experimenter continually questioned and interrupted the subject, responding tangentially to his replies, and generally giving little opportunity for any defense. After 10 such minutes, the experimenter initiated the catharsis phase by apologizing for being hostile, explaining it had been necessary in order to study the subject's reaction to stress. The subject was praised for his resiliency and performance under stress, and humor was introduced. Throughout the following 10 minutes of catharsis, the experimenter was reassuring in manner and attempted to bring about a release of tension.

Interview Participants

Two such standardized interviews were recorded, with completely different participants in each of the interviews. All four interview participants were from the field of psychology. The two different experimenters were staff research psychologists at a veterans' hospital, having a position of some authority over the two different trainees who served as subjects. All of the participants were told that the experiment was concerned with interviewing, and that their behavior would be tape recorded and observed. The experimenters also knew that they would be photographed and nonverbal behavior would be studied.

Recording Method

Photographs showing a profile view of both the experimenter and the subject were taken through a one-way vision screen with a 35-millimeter still camera. The verbal behavior was tape recorded. The verbal and nonverbal records were synchronized by a switching device mounted on the camera which placed an audible signal over the tape recorded voices whenever a picture was taken. The frequency of photographic sampling, one frame every 30 seconds in Interview A and one frame every 15 seconds in Interview B, was dictated by limitations in the film capacity of the camera.

Selection of Verbal and Nonverbal Stimuli

The judgment task involved presenting short written speech samples from the interviews along with pairs of photographs. On each trial the judge was required to pick from a pair of pictures the one which best fitted or matched the verbal behavior.

The universe of verbal behavior which could be sampled for presentation in the judging task was delimited by the number of occasions during the interview in which a photograph had been taken. There were 26 such points during Interview A and 71 points during Interview B. Speech samples of from 30 to 60 seconds were chosen from this pool of verbal behavior if they appeared intelligible when lifted from the context of the total conversation. There was no inspection of the photographs during this selection procedure. An index card was prepared for each speech sample which stated whether the verbal interaction had been taken from the stress or catharsis phase of the interview; provided a one-sentence background synopsis; contained the speech sample of one or two statements by both the experimenter and the subject with the actual moment which had been photographed indicated by a circled word.

Pairs of photographs, correct and incorrect, were then selected to accompany each speech sample. The correct photographs were the ones which actually had been taken during the speech samples. Incorrect photographs were randomly selected from a photograph pool delimited by two factors: The mouth position, open or closed, had to be the same in both the incorrect and correct photographs, and if the experimenter (or the subject) were speaking when the correct photograph was taken, then the incorrect photograph had to be selected from photographs also taken while the experimenter (or the subject) was speaking.

Two types of incorrect photographs could be chosen for pairing with each correct one. The incorrect photograph could be taken from the same phase of the interview as the correct picture, or taken from the other phase. Since speech samples had been selected from both the stress and catharsis phases of the interview, there were four types of correct-incorrect photograph pairs which could be presented to the judges. With a verbal sample from the stress phase of the interview, the judges could be required to choose between two stress photographs or between a stress and a catharsis pair. Similarly, with a verbal sample from the catharsis phase of the interview, the judges could be presented with either two catharsis photographs or with a catharsis and a stress photograph.

Experiment I

The problem was to determine if any relationship between verbal and nonverbal behavior simultaneously emitted is communicated to an observer. Hypothesis: untrained judges can choose from a pair of photographs the one which was taken during a given speech sample.

Subjects. Eighteen college freshman, consisting of the entire introductory psychology class taught by the author, served as judges. There were 10 males, 8 females; the median age was 18.5.

Method. Fourteen speech samples and accompanying correct-incorrect photographs were selected from Interview B by the method described above. Eight of these speech samples were from the stress phase of the interview; six, from the catharsis phase. Four × five-inch enlargements were made of each photograph, showing a profile view of both the experimenter and the subject. The judgment task was individually administered in order to allow random variation of the order of presenting the 14 speech-photograph items. The judge was shown pairs of photographs, each of which came from the same interview phase on half the items, while on the remaining trials the incorrect-correct photograph pairs were drawn from different interview phases. A table of random numbers were used to determine whether for a particular judge the choice on a particular speech would be between photograph pairs from the same or different interview phases.

Prior to the task, the judge was given the following intstructions to read:

> This is a test of your skill in interpreting and understanding gestures and body movements. You will be shown some photographs which were taken every 15 seconds during a thirty minute interview. The interviewer, or Examiner, was a staff psychologist at a hospital, and the person interviewed, the Subject, was a student in training to become a psychologist. The Subject was told that he was participating in a research project on interviewing techniques, and that he would be observed through a one-way vision screen and tape recorded. The interview was pre-arranged for the Examiner to ask factual questions during the introductory first 10 minutes, and then to become hostile and challenging, questioning the Subject's academic training, the adequacy of his preparation to take his examinations coming up the following month, and to continually interrupt him. This Stressful period lasted about 10 minutes. In the Final phase of the interview the Examiner explained what he had been doing; that it had been part of the research to try and provoke the Subject, and generally attempted to reassure the Subject. In actuality, this interview plan did not work out perfectly. There was not as clearly defined a difference between the three phases of the interview as had been expected. There was some stress for the Subject throughout the interview. The final phase was not completely successful in producing some relief from the stress since the Subject knew that the experiment was still continuing, and perhaps was apprehensive about what might be coming next. Nevertheless, there were some important differences between the various phrases of the interview. The stress phase did have more overt expression of hostility and tension; and in the final phase the Subject did experience some relief, at least knowing that the worst was over. You will be given to read 14 excerpts from the tape-recorded conversation. The verbal excerpts each took less than a minute of interview time. One photograph was taken during each of the verbal excerpts, and the actual words spoken when the photograph was taken are circled in red. After you read each verbal excerpt you will be shown a pair of

photographs, and your job as a judge will be to pick which of the two pictures in the pair fits the best or matches the verbal excerpt. In all of the photographs, the Examiner appears on the left and the subject on the right. Your task, then, is to determine for each set of two photographs which one is most likely to have been taken during the verbal excerpt.

Results.   The number of correct or accurate choices for each judge was tabulated. This distribution of obtained accuracy scores was evaluated by comparison with a theoretical median representing the score which might be expected if only chance factors were operative. An assumption was made that if there had been no information in the situation, and the judges' choice had simply reflected chance factors, then there would have been an equal probability of either photograph being selected on each trial. The expected median was therefore equal to a correct choice on half of the trials. Significance tests were derived by applying Wilcoxon's matched-pair ranks test (Siegel, 1956, p. 75) to the difference between the obtained scores and the expected median.

It can be seen in Table 1 that the obtained median accuracy score was significantly better than might be expected by chance. Table 1 also shows that more than three-fourths of the judges scored above the expected median.

Experiment II

Problem.   The purpose of this experiment was to replicate the findings reported above with a different group of judges and to extend the generality of the results by utilizing verbal and nonverbal stimuli drawn from an additional interview. A second purpose was to determine if it was still possible to match verbal and nonverbal behavior with more restricted nonverbal cue information. In a pilot study (Ekman, 1961) an attempt was made to specify the nonverbal cues required for the judgment task by limiting the judges to seeing either head or body. The results indicated little difference in accuracy if the judge saw head or whole person cues, but accuracy was much lower with photographs showing only body position. Hypothesis: Judges can choose from a pair of photographs the one which was taken during a given speech sample when responding to pictures of the whole person. This discrimination between photograph pairs is also possible when the judges are limited to pictures showing only body position.

Table 1. Results of the Four Experiments

Trials	Experiment I N=18 Whole person	Experiment II N=16 Body	Experiment II N=16 Whole	Experiment III N=15 Body	Experiment III N=15 Whole	Experiment IV N=27 Body	Experiment IV N=29 Head
Interview A (6 trials)							
Obtained median		3.2	4.0*	2.5	3.6	2.6**	3.9**
Percent above *expected* median of 3		44	56	13	56	7	76
Interview B (14 trials)							
Obtained median	9.5***	7.5	8.2***	9.1***	8.1	8.1*	7.7
Percent above *expected* median of 7	78	50	69	75	56	67	55
Interviews A and B combined (20 trials)							
Obtained median		10.7*	12.7*	11.2***	11.8***	10.6	11.3*
Percent *expected* median of 10		62	75	67	60	52	73

*p < .05.
**p < .01.
***p < .001.

Subjects. Since the pilot study had suggested that working with body position photographs was a difficult task, an attempt was made to select as judges individuals who might be able to best understand this type of nonverbal behavior. Sixteen professional modern dancers served as judges; 14 were female, the median age was 25, the median education was 16 years.

Method. The same task was employed, but the procedure was modified for group presentation rather than individual administration. A booklet was prepared which contained an instruction sheet, similar to the one used in the first experiment, and 20 speech samples. Fourteen of these were the samples used in the first experiment, the other 6 speech samples were drawn from Interview A. Twelve of the 20 samples were from the stress phases of the interviews, the remaining 8 samples were drawn from the catharsis phases. Half of the correct-incorrect photograph pairs were composed of pictures taken during the same interview phase, the remaining 10 pairs of photographs consisted of pictures from different interview phases. The photographs were made into two sets of positive transparencies. The heads of both the experimenter and the subject were covered with opaque ink in one set of transparencies, so that only the body position could be seen.

Two projection screens and two 35-millimeter slide projectors were used to show the correct-incorrect photograph pairs simultaneously to the group of judges after they read each of the speech samples in the booklet. The judges first completed the 20 trials responding to photographs of body position, and then after a 10-minute intervening task, repeated the procedure with photographs showing the whole person. The appearance of the correct photograph on either the left or right projection screen differed under the body and whole person cue conditions and was balanced across the 20 trials.

Results. The technique of data analysis was the same as described in the first experiment. The results on Interview A trials and Interview B trials in this experiment and in Experiments III and IV will be interpreted together in the discussion section of this paper. The results in Table 1 show that accuracy on all 20 trials (Interviews A and B combined) replicated the findings of the first experiment. The judges were able to pick the photograph which matched a verbal sample when limited to seeing body position and also when shown the whole person. While it appears that the level of accuracy was greater when the whole person was seen, the difference between the two cue conditions was not tested since there had been no control for practice effects.

Experiment III

Problem.   In interpreting the results from Experiment II, it was not clear whether the judges' ability to match "body only" photographs with speech samples was due to any special characteristics which might be associated with dancers or if such accuracy might be found in a more unselected group of judges. The major purpose of this experiment was, then, to determine if a heterogeneous group of judges could match body position photographs with speech samples. A secondary purpose was to replicate the findings of the two earlier experiments. Hypothesis: A heterogeneous group of judges can choose from a pair of photographs, showing only the body position, the one which was taken during a given speech sample.

Subjects.   Fifteen undergraduate students in the author's introductory psychology evening class served as judges. Twelve were males; the median age was 22.5 with a range from 18 to 55.

Method.   Exactly the same procedure described in Experiment II was followed. Twenty speech samples were presented in booklet form. The judges first responded to body position photographs, and then to pictures showing the whole person.

Results.   The techniques of data analysis were identical to those reported earlier. Table 1 shows that for the results of all 20 trials, the hypothesis was confirmed and the earlier findings were replicated. No comparison was made between the accuracy achieved by the dancers in Experiment II and this group of evening psychology students, since the two groups of judges differed in age, education, and sex distribution as well as in their choice of vocation.

Experiment IV

Problem.   The design in Experiments II and III did not permit study of relative accuracy in matching nonverbal and verbal behavior as a function of the nonverbal cue information available. The purpose of this experiment was to test impressions from the pilot study referred to earlier by comparing accuracy between groups of judges who were limited to seeing either head or body position nonverbal cues. Hypothesis: Judges can choose from a pair of photographs the one which was taken during a given speech sample when responding to either head or body position cues. The judges shown head cues will achieve greater accuracy than the group of judges seeing body position cues.

Subjects. Female students in two freshman psychology classes served as judges. There were 27 judges in the group seeing body position photographs, 29 judges in the group responding to head photographs. The median age in both groups was 18.

Method. The general procedure described in Experiments II and III was followed except that two separate groups served as judges, each group responding to only one cue condition, either head or body.

Results. The technique of data analysis described earlier was again used to evaluate the results which are shown in Table 1. Considering the group which responded to head cues, the results on all 20 trials combined generally conform to the findings reported earlier for judgments of the whole person. The group responding to body position cues, however, did not achieve a significant level of accuracy in their scores on all 20 trials. Examination of the results on Interviews A and B separately revealed that while accurate judgments were achieved on Interview B, the judges were significantly (two-tailed test) below the chance level of expectation in their responses to body position photographs from Interview A. There was a tendency for body photographs from Interview A to be similarly misjudged in Experiment III, although it had not reached statistical significance.

Differences in accuracy under the two cue conditions were evaluated with a Mann-Whitney U test. The group responding to head cues achieved greater accuracy than the body position judges in their performance on all 20 trials ($p < .001$).

DISCUSSION

Accuracy in matching materials from the two different interviews was related to the type of cue information provided—head, body, or whole person cues. Although there was some inconsistency across the four experiments, by and large a significant level of accuracy was achieved on both Interviews A and B if either the whole person or the head were shown. There were marked differences in the accuracy obtained on Interviews A and B, however, when only the body positions were shown. The body cues in Interview B seem to have provided sufficient information for matching in two out of three experiments. Table 1 shows that such accuracy was never reached on body cue judgments of Interview A. This difference in accuracy was evaluated with the McNemar test for the significance of change (Siegel, 1956, p. 63) by comparing the scores on the two interviews for each cue condition in Experiments II, III, and IV. Judgments on Interview B trials were more accurate than Interview A trials only under the body cue condition (Experiment III, $p < .02$; Experiment IV, $p < .001$). The results of Experiment IV on differences between judgments made on the basis of head or body cues provide related information. Head judgments were superior to body position judgments for Interview A ($p < .001$), while a trend in the reverse direction was seen for judgments made of Interview B.

There are a number of hypotheses which might explain why in one of the interviews head but not body cues could be related to verbal behavior. These explanations involve differences in sending behavior, that is, the extent to which people may differ in the information which is conveyed to an observer through their nonverbal behavior. The experimenter and the subject in Interview A may have been head rather than body senders; or, they may have been sending information in their bodies which was unrelated or contradictory to the verbal behavior; or, the body cues while related to the verbal behavior may have either anticipated it or lagged behind it. The choice between these hypotheses will have to await further research.

A communication paradigm involves consideration not only of sending behavior but also of receiving behavior, that is, possible differences across observers in their skill or sensitivity in understanding nonverbal behavior. While these experiments were not designed to study this question, one aspect of receiving behavior can be analyzed by determining whether accuracy in judging one interview was related to accuracy in judging the other. Spearman rank-order correlations were calculated between accuracy in judging Interview A and Interview B for the various cue conditions in the last three experiments. Of the six possible correlation coefficients, only two were significant and these were both in a negative direction. Thus, it would seem that accuracy in matching verbal and nonverbal behavior from one interview was independent of such accuracy in working with materials from another interview. The more general question of whether sensitivity as a receiver is specific to the behavior of a particular sender, or group of senders, must also await further research.

The overall results on the four experiments suggest that some information related to the verbal behavior is conveyed by spontaneous nonverbal behavior during interviews. In attempting to specify just what may be communicated through body position and facial expression, both specific and general classes of information can be outlined. The most obvious example of specific nonverbal communication would be a gesture such as a smile or fist shake which has a direct verbal equivalent or translation. Even less symbolic nonverbal acts such as swaying of the body or tapping of the foot may have a specific communicative value by emphasizing or focusing attention on a particular part of a verbal message. Although not studied in these experiments, nonverbal acts, such as movement towards or away from another or direction of eye gaze, may not necessarily be related to the verbal message, but instead may communicate specific information in the language of the relationship (Ekman, 1962). In addition to these specific meanings, nonverbal behavior may also communicate more general or gross information about the sender. Examples would be information about activity level, anxiety, or the accumulation and discharge of tension.

In the present experiments, specific information must have been communicated by the nonverbal behavior. The judges were not simply responding to the gross differences between the behavior shown under stress and catharsis, since they had been able to discriminate between photograph pairs taken from the same emotional phase of the interview. This discrimination between two stress or two catharsis pictures was as accurate as the judgments made of pictures from different interview phases.

Although the majority of the results obtained were statistically significant, and the distribution of scores was skewed towards accuracy, the absolute level of correct choices was far from perfect. There were a number of factors which made this judgmental task extremely difficult. If the nonverbal behavior photographed had contradicted or was not directly related to the verbal behavior, accuracy would suffer. Similarly, if the nonverbal behavior anticipated or lagged behind the verbal behavior, the photograph could not have been matched with the short speech sample provided. Presenting the speech sample as a typescript without any vocal cues may have served to increase the ambiguity of the verbal behavior. Finally, the use of still photographs rather than motion pictures eliminated any cues from sequence or movement patterns which are customarily available to an observer.

In light of these limiting factors, it is particularly impressive that consistent evidence was found for at least a partial relationship between verbal and nonverbal behavior. These experiments indicate that body position and facial expression spontaneously shown during an interview are not random activity or noise, but have specific communicative value related to the verbal behavior. Furthermore, this relationship is not obscure or available to only the privileged few, but can be detected by untrained observers.

REFERENCES

Dittmann, A. T. The relationship between body movements and moods in interviews. *J. consult. Psychol.*, 1962, 26, 480.

Ekman, P. Body language during interviews. Paper read at Inter-American Congress of Psychology, Mexico City, December 1961.

Ekman, P. The communication of interview stress through body language. Paper read at Western Psychological Association, San Francisco, April 1962.

Giedt, F. H. Comparison of visual, content, and auditory cues in interviewing. *J. consult. Psychol.*, 1955, 19, 407–416.

Mahl, G., Danet, B., & Norton, Nea. Reflection of major personality characteristics in gestures and body movements. *Amer. Psychologist*, 1959, 14, 357. (Abstract)

Sainesbury, P. Gestural movement during psychiatric interview. *Psychosom. Med.*, 1955, 17, 458–469.

Schlosberg, H. Three dimensions of emotion. *Psychol. Rev.*, 1954, 61, 81–88.

Siegel, S. *Nonparametric statistics for the behavioral sciences.* New York: McGraw-Hill, 1956.

Vernon, P. E. The matching method applied to investigations of personality. *Psychol. Bull.*, 1936, 33, 149–177.

Wolfe, W. *The expression of personality.* New York: Harper, 1943.

5

THE COMMUNICATION OF INFERIOR AND SUPERIOR ATTITUDES BY VERBAL AND NONVERBAL SIGNALS

Michael Argyle
Veronica Salter
Hilary Nicholson
Marilyn Williams
Philip Burgess

INTRODUCTION

Michael Argyle has already stated the hypothesis that language evolved and is normally used for communicating information about events external to the speakers, while the nonverbal code is used, both by humans and by nonhuman primates to establish and maintain interpersonal relationships (Argyle, 1969). In an earlier experiment by Mehrabian and Wiener (1967) the relative effects of verbal and nonverbal signals for emotions were compared. Single words were tape-recorded, affective tone of the words themselves varying (such as, love versus terrible) and tone of voice varying from positive to negative affect. It was found that judgments of stimuli were based mainly on tone of voice.

The authors are indebted to the S.S.R.C. for financial support for this research, and to Florisse Alkema for statistical help.

The experiments to be reported were concerned with one major dimension of interpersonal attitudes—superior-inferior (compare Lorr and McNair, 1965). It has been found that such attitudes can be conveyed by head position, facial expression, posture, and tone of voice (see, for example, Mehrabian, 1968).

Hypothesis 1. Nonverbal cues for interpersonal attitudes have more impact than verbal signals.

Another line of research has suggested that conflicting verbal and nonverbial stimuli along the love-hate dimension are very disturbing and can induce schizophrenia in children (Bateson et al., 1956), though subsequent research has failed to provide much support for this hypothesis (Schuham, 1967). It is not known whether conflicts on other dimensions such as superior-inferior will have similar effects.

Hypothesis 2. Conflict between verbal and nonverbal cues for interpersonal attitudes is an emotionally disturbing experience.

It is normal, during interaction, for verbal and nonverbal cues to operate together. An interesting question is whether either set of cues can operate effectively alone, without support from the other.

Hypothesis 3. Either verbal or nonverbal cues can operate alone, without support from the other.

Hypothesis 4. There are individual differences in the relative weight given to verbal and nonverbal stimuli: females, introverts, neurotics, and those with low scores in deliquency scales should attach more weight to nonverbal cues.

The general method used was to prepare series of videotapes, with sound, of a speaker. Each film embodied some combination of verbal and nonverbal cues for interpersonal attitudes, the verbal and nonverbal being equated with respect to their impact on ratings by observers. Subjects were asked to imagine they were meeting the person appearing on the monitor, and asked to record their impressions on a number of 7-point scales. This was thus a semi-realistic situation, more controlled than a real encounter, but with almost as much data as a short encounter would provide. It was decided to manipulate whole groups of nonverbal cues together, rather than alter them one at a time. The nonverbal renderings were arrived at, after some trial and error, from the combined views of the authors of this article, and in the light of previous research.

METHOD

The experiment was carried out three times, once with a practical class, and later with less sophisticated Ss. The results were very similar and only the second version will be reported. A third version of the experiment will be referred to in the Discussion.

Subjects

There were 20 males and 20 females, all students at technical and secretarial colleges. There were 40 psychology students in the preliminary experiment.

Materials

The social stimuli consisted of 18 films shown on a videotape recorder. There were three different messages, delivered in three nonverbal manners, by two female performers.

The two independent variables were superior-inferior attitudes expressed in verbal content and in nonverbal manner. There were three verbal messages, as follows.

Superior
It is probably quite a good thing for you subjects to come along to help in these experiments because it gives you a small glimpse of what psychological research is about. In fact the whole process is far more complex than you would be able to appreciate without a considerable training in research methods, paralinguistics and kinesic analysis, and so on.

Equal
It may be fairly interesting for you to come along and see what some people in the university are up to. You may like to stay on afterwards so that we can discuss the whole experiment together—we may be able to ex-

change ideas on some of these matters. I like to think of the university as a sort of community of people, doing different things, but all equally interesting and important.

Inferior

These experiments must seem rather silly to you and I'm afraid they are not really concerned with anything very interesting and important. We'd be very glad if you could spare us a few minutes afterwards to tell us how we could improve the experiment. We feel that we are not making a very good job of it, and we feel rather guilty about wasting the time of busy people like yourselves.

The messages were typed out and shown to 12 Ss, half of each sex, who rated them on 7-point scales. The average ratings on *inferior-superior* and *submissive-dominant* were as follows:

Inferior   1.66
Equal   3.92
Superior 5.13
range 3.47

The nonverbal stimuli were as follows:

Superior. Unsmiling, head raised, loud dominating speech.
Neutral. Slight smile, head level, neutral-to-pleasant speech.
Inferior. Nervous deferential smile, head lowered, nervous eager-to-please speech.

The performers were two attractive females, aged 22, who both gave all 9 performances.

In order to obtain ratings of these nonverbal stimuli, independently of verbal content, three further films were made in which one of the speakers counted "one, two, three . . ." in the styles as described, in the same period of time (20 seconds) as the original messages. These films were rated by a separate set of 20 Ss, half of each sex. The average ratings were as follows:

Inferior   2.10
Equal   4.30
Superior 5.50
range 3.40

It can be seen that the range is very similar to the range for verbal messages alone.

Procedure

The 18 performances were filmed in random order, and put on a videotape. Subjects were assembled in groups of from 5 to 8 persons and given the following instructions:

> Thank you very much for coming along. This is rather an unusual experiment: we are going to show you some TV films and we would like you to imagine that you are actually meeting the people in person. There will be film of two people who will each speak to you several times.
> We would like to know what impression these people make on you each time they appear, and we would like you to fill in a set of these rating scales after each performance. Is that clear, and do you understand how to fill in the scales? There will be a pause and some coffee after the first 9 goes in order to let you have a rest. Now here is the first performer—try to imagine that this person is actually in the room speaking to you.

Subjects recorded their impressions of each performance on a series of 7-point semantic scales, as shown in Table 1. Ss were given a stapled set of 18 pages of the scales at the outset of the experiment. Finally Ss were given the following personality tests: Neuroticism and Extraversion (MPI), Psychopatic Deviate scale (MMPI), and Anomie scale (S role, 1956).

RESULTS

Analyses of variance were carried out for each of the 10 scales for each version of the experiment. We shall report here the results for the second version only, since it was carried out under more rigorous conditions and with nonpsychology students. The results of the first experiment were, however, very similar.

Effects of Verbal and Nonverbal Stimuli

The effects of the nonverbal variables are shown in the summaries of the analyses of variance (Tables 1 and 2).

Table 1.   Variance in Ratings Due to Verbal and Nonverbal Cues

Rating scales	Source of variance (F value)		Ratio Nonverbal/verbal (F value)
	Verbal	*Nonverbal*	
1. Hostile-friendly	7.08**	212.11***	
2. Stable-unstable	4.34*	14.74***	
3. Confusing-straightforward	4.73*	0.37**	
4. Inferior-superior	12.69***	154.90***	12.22
5. Unpleasant-pleasant	1.85^{ns}	198.80***	
6. Sincere-insincere	8.71***	98.17***	
7. Submissive-dominant	11.08***	145.28***	13.11
8. She liked me-she disliked me	1.29^{ns}	147.72***	
9. Great versus small emotional impact	1.00^{ns}	131.20***	
10. Pleasant-unpleasant emotional impact	1.12^{ns}	57.74***	

*$p < .05$
**$p < .01$
***$p < .001$
^{ns}Not significant

It is apparent that the verbal variable significantly affects 6 of the 10 scales, and the nonverbal variable affects all the scales. However, the effect of the nonverbal variable is considerably greater; the average ratio of total nonverbal/verbal variance was 21.7, and in the scales directly related to inferior-superior it was 12.7.

Another way of analysing the data is in terms of the actual ratings of the different performances. We can compare the scale shifts produced by verbal and nonverbal cues *alone* in the initial measurements, and their effect (with different but similar Ss) in combination.

It can be seen that nonverbal cues, when combined with verbal cues of almost identical strength, have 4.3 times as much impact as verbal cues. There is a "shrinkage" in the impact of both kinds of cue but this is far greater for the verbal cues—14 percent versus 62 percent.

Interaction Between the Effects of Verbal and Nonverbal Cues

There were interactions between these two variables for 8 of the 10 scales: 5 were significant at $p < .01$, 2 at $p < .01$, and 1 at $p <$

Table 2. Analyses of Variance for Inferior-Superior and Dominant-Submissive

Source	Inferior-superior					Dominant-submissive				
	S.S.	D.F.	M.S.	F.	P.	S.S.	D.F.	M.S.	F.	P.
Between Ss										
Sex of Ss (A)	4.05	1	4.05	2.03	ns	2.39	1	2.34	1.11	ns
Ss within groups	58.40	38	1.54			80.00	38	2.11		
Within Ss										
Nonverbal cues (B)	532.84	2	266.42	154.90	$p < .001$	502.66	2	251.33	145.28	$p < .001$
A × B	6.46	2	3.23	1.88	ns	1.95	2	0.97	<1.00	ns
B × Ss within groups	131.03	76	1.72			131.62	76	1.73		
Verbal cues (C)	30.77	2	18.38	12.68	$p < .001$	26.16	2	13.08	11.08	$p < .001$
A × C	1.26	2	0.63	<1.00	ns	3.28	2	1.64	1.39	ns
C × Ss within groups	109.97	76	1.45			89.79	76	1.18		
Stooge (D)	18.69	1	18.69	13.35	$p < .001$	18.37	1	18.37	13.71	$p < .001$
A × D	.01	1	.01	<1.00	ns	2.50	1	2.50	1.91	ns
D × Ss within groups	53.30	38	1.40			50.91	38	1.34		
B × C	24.30	4	6.09	4.17	$p < .01$	11.48	4	2.87	1.83	ns
A × B × C	5.13	4	1.28	<1.00	ns	3.39	4	.85	<1.00	ns
B × C × Ss within groups	221.85	152	1.40			239.23	152	1.57		
B × D	1.77	2	.88	<1.00	ns	0.10	2	.05	<1.00	ns
A × B × D	1.30	2	.65	<1.00	ns	3.13	2	1.56	1.19	ns
B × D × Ss within groups	102.60	76	1.35			99.43	76	1.31		
C × D	5.04	2	2.52	1.38	ns	17.34	2	8.67	8.06	$p < .01$
A × C × D	0.76	2	.38	<1.00	ns	3.59	2	1.79	1.25	ns
C × D × Ss within groups	139.20	76	1.83			108.39	76	1.43		
B × C × D	18.95	4	4.74	5.51	$p < .001$	18.81	4	4.70	4.05	$p < .01$
A × B × C × D	10.43	4	2.61	3.03	$p < .0025$	9.18	4	2.29	1.97	ns
B × C × D × Ss within groups	130.95	152	0.86			175.69	152	1.16		

Table 3. Scale Shifts Due to Verbal and Nonverbal Cues Alone and in Combination

	Alone	*Combined*	*Percent effect*
Verbal	3.47	0.49	14
Nonverbal	3.40	2.10	62
Nonverbal / verbal	0.98	4.3	—

.05. The main hypothesis was that there would be double-bind effects, that is, conflicting verbal and nonverbal cues would be perceived as *confusing, unstable, unpleasant,* as having an *emotional impact,* and an *unpleasant emotional impact.* The superior (NV) performance was judged as more *unpleasant* etc. with all verbal messages, and combined with superior (V) was judged as more unpleasant, etc., not less. However, the equal (NV) and inferior (NV) performances did produce a cross-over pattern, as would be expected on the double-bind hypothesis. This is shown for the scale *emotional impact pleasant-unpleasant* in Figure 1a.

A similar pattern is found for the scales *pleasant-unpleasant* ($p < .001$), *great* versus *small emotional impact* ($p < .05$), and *confusing-straightforward* ($p < .001$), as well as for several other scales for which a double-bind effect was not expected, but which belong to a general pattern of favorable-unfavorable. These results are created by a single combination of stimuli—equal (NV) with inferior (V), which is generally disliked and found disturbing, compared with equal-equal.

The interaction plots can also be examined to see whether verbal or nonverbal cues are effective alone, that is, when the other one is equal or opposed. Nonverbal cues can certainly act alone, as is shown by the plot for the scale inferior-superior (Figure 1b). With equal (V) the nonverbal cues have their greatest effect, both on scales such as inferior-superior, and on those like pleasant-unpleasant (Figure 1c). From the interaction plots in Figure 1 it appears that verbal cues have a multiplying effect when combined with inferior (NV) and superior (NV).

Sex of Subjects. Separate analyses of variance were computed for males and females for the ratings of *inferior-superior* and *dominant-submissive.* The ratio of combined nonverbal/verbal variances was 11.2 for males, 24.5 for females, mainly because the females were less responsive to verbal cues.

Figure 1. Interactions Between Verbal and Nonverbal Cues for Three Scales in Experiment 1

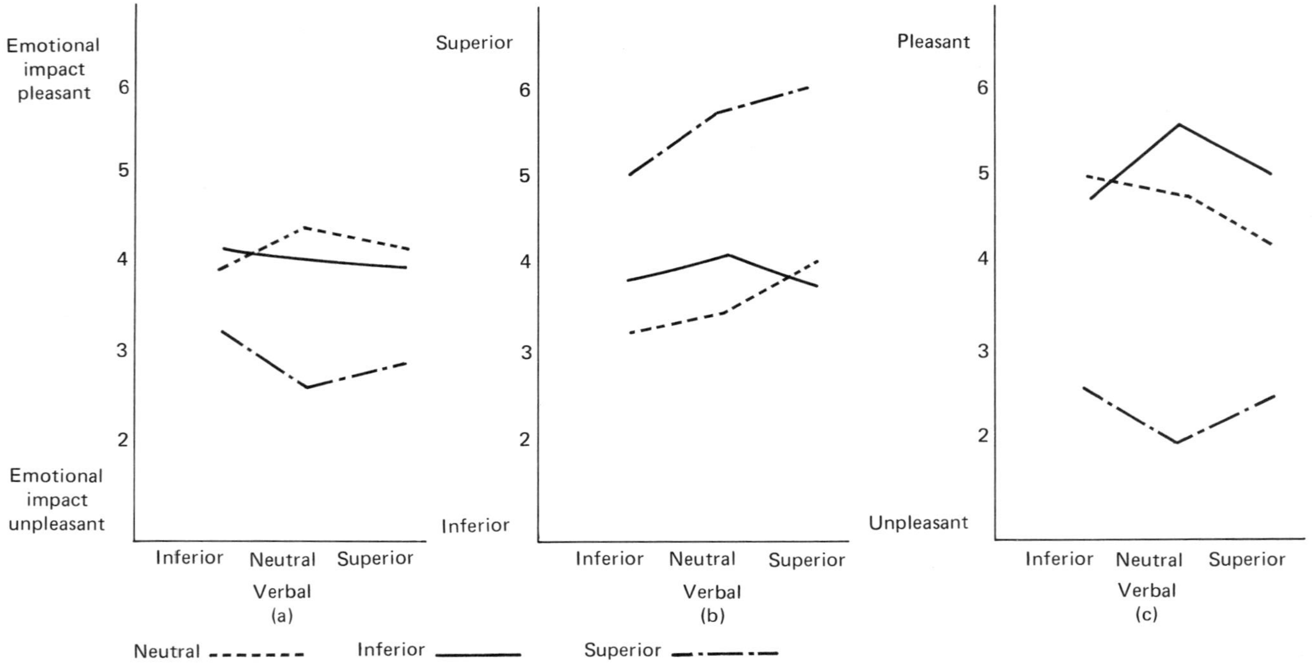

Correlations with Personality Measures

Correlations were computed for each rating scale between the personality measures and for: (1) the difference between ratings of the 3 verbal inferior and the 3 verbal superior performances ("verbal"); (2) the difference between ratings of the 3 nonverbal inferior and the 3 nonverbal superior performances. ("non-verbal"); (3) reactions to the conflicting cues, inferior (V) -superior (NV), etc.; and (4) the ratio of (1) and (2).

The total pattern of correlations was significant in relation to the number computed. *Verbal* variations in inferior-superior produced more effect on the inferior-superior scale for neurotics ($r = .40$, $p < .01$); there were no other correlations between personality measures and *inferior-superior* or *dominant-submissive*, though there were with other scales. The nonverbal/verbal ratio correlated for several of the other rating scales with the *Pd* scale. Of the inconsistent stimuli; inferior (V)-superior (NV) was judged more unpleasant by neurotics (.38, $p < .025$) but this was not the case with the other conflicting combination.

DISCUSSION

The first and main hypothesis was that nonverbal cues would have a greater effect than equated verbal cues. A ratio of 21.7:1 was found between the total variances, and 12.7:1 for variance on scales most directly related to inferior-superior. Nonverbal cues had 4.3 times the effect of verbal cues on shifts in ratings.

It was felt that this result might be spurious, since each message was repeated 6 times, and Ss clearly were not attending very much to verbal cues during the later presentations. On the other hand it could also be argued that *nonverbal* cues were repeated 6 times. To check this possibility, the experiment was repeated with one of the original performers with a different message in each film, and a 2 × 2 design, omitting the equal condition. This time the nonverbal/verbal variance ratio on relevant scales was 30.1:1.

Why should nonverbal cues be more effective than verbal cues in communicating interpersonal attitudes? First, perhaps there is an innate pattern of communication and recognition of the cues for these attitudes. This is clearly the case in animals, and

certain aspects of human emotional expression appears to be un-
learned and culturally universal (Vine, 1969).

Second, perhaps speech is normally used for other kinds of
messages—information about other people, solving problems and
the like—and not for handling the immediate social situation,
which nonhuman primates can do perfectly well without language.
Experiments are in hand to determine whether people find it more
difficult to talk about interpersonal relations than about less personal matters.

Third, it appears that we normally use two channels of communication, verbal and nonverbal, that function simultaneously.
Conscious attention is focused on the verbal, while the "silent"
nonverbal channel handles interpersonal matters, including feedback on what is being said. It is thus a disturbance of the normal
division of channels to put interpersonal material into the verbal
channel.

Fourth, one advantage of interpersonal matters being dealt
with nonverbally is that things can be kept vague and flexible—
people need not reveal clearly what they think about one another.

The second hypothesis was that conflicting verbal and nonverbal cues would create double-bind effects and be experienced
as unpleasant, insincere, and so forth. There was some suggestion of
this between inferior and equal (NV) and verbal cues, but the effect
was weak, and was not found for the superior-inferior combinations.
In a later experiment clear double-bind effects have been found
with inconsistent cues for hostile-friendly.

The third hypothesis was a query about whether verbal or nonverbal cues are effective alone. The written messages produced a
shift along *inferior-superior* scales of 3.47, but combined with *any*
nonverbal cues their effect was reduced to about 0.5 points . From
the verbal-nonverbal interactions it was found that verbal cues only
operate as multipliers—they can make an inferior nonverbal signal
more inferior, or a superior one more superior, but have no effect
on a neutral signal and are ineffective when in conflict.

The last hypothesis was concerned with individual differences.
As predicted it was found that female Ss were relatively more
affected by nonverbal cues. The stimulus person was a female, but
this might be expected to generate greater effects for *males*. The
only correlations with personality traits that can be interpreted
are that neurotics find inconsistent, "double-bind" cues more
unpleasant, and neuroticism correlates with responsiveness to
verbal cues for inferior-superior.

SUMMARY

Ratings were made by 120 subjects of 18 videotapes in which verbal and nonverbal cues for inferior, equal, and superior were varied and combined in a 3 × 3 design. The typed messages (verbal alone) were rated by further Ss, as were videotapes of a performer reading numbers (nonverbal alone); the two sets of cues alone had identical effects on ratings. In combination, both kinds of cues had a reduced effect, but it was found that nonverbal cues now had 4.3 times the effect of verbal cues on shifts of ratings, and accounted for 10.3 times as most variance; verbal cues were only able to act as multipliers of consistent nonverbal cues. There was little evidence of double-bind effects. Analysis of individual differences showed that females were relatively more responsive to nonverbal compared with verbal cues, and that more neurotic Ss found the combination of superior (nonverbal) with inferior (verbal) unpleasant, and responded more to verbal cues for inferior-superior.

REFERENCES

Argyle, M. 1969. *Social interaction*. London: Methuen. New York: Atherton Press. P. 196.

Bateson, G., et al. 1956. Towards a theory of schizophrenia. *Beh. Sci.* 1: 251–64.

Lorr, M., and McNair, D. M. 1965. Expansion of the interpersonal behavior circle. *J. pers. soc. Psychol.* 2: 813–30.

McDavid, J., and Schroder, H. M. 1957. The interpretating approval and disapproval by delinquent and non-delinquent adolescents. *J. Pers.* 25: 539–49.

Mehrabian, A. 1968. The inference of attitudes from the posture, orientation, and distance of a communication. *J. consult. Psychol.*, 32: 296–308.

Mehrabian, A., and Wiener, M. 1967. Decoding of inconsistent communication. *J. pers. soc. Psychol.* 6: 109–14.

Schuham, A. L. 1967. The double-bind hypothesis a decade later. *Psychol. Bull.* 68: 409–16.

Srole, L. 1956. Social integration and certain corrolaries. *Amer. sociol. Rev.* 21: 709–16.

Vine, I. 1969. Communication by facial-visual signals. *In* J. H. Crook (ed.), *Social behaviour in animals and men*. London and New York: Academic Press.

Part Two

INTERACTION AND PLANNING OF VERBAL BEHAVIOR

6

A COMPARATIVE STUDY OF TWO HESITATION PHENOMENA

Frieda Goldman-Eisler

INTRODUCTION

Previous work by the writer on hesitation pauses concentrated on the silences which interrupt speech utterance (Eisler, 1958a, b). A recent paper by Maclay and Osgood on "Hesitation phenomena in spontaneous English speech" (1959) deals with four types of hesitation phenomena; beside the silent pauses which they call *unfilled pauses* (UP) they also studied the occurrences of sounded hesitation devices, i.e., the /ɑ, ɛ, æ, r, ə, m/ sounds of hesitation which they call *filled pauses* (FP), as well as repeats and false starts. We shall here be interested only in the hesitation phenomena of unfilled and filled pauses.

Maclay and Osgood recorded these phenomena by taking counts of their frequency. Thus unfilled pauses are counted by occurrence irrespective of their duration, in the same way as the filled pauses. (The writer's own method of recording unfilled pauses consists, apart from recording their occurrence, in measuring their duration from visual speech recordings (Eisler, 1956, 1958a, b).)

Maclay and Osgood have also taken note of the position of filled and unfilled pauses in the sentence, and in relation to the grammatical function of words.

Reprinted from *Language and Speech* 4, Part I (Jan./March 1961): 18–26.

The following results relevant to the present paper emerged from their analysis:

(1) Both filled pauses and unfilled pauses are found to occur more frequently before lexical words than before function words. But unfilled pauses are relatively more likely to appear before lexical words.

(2) For those constructions that can be analysed statistically, filled pauses occur more frequently at phrase boundaries than within phrases. These are statistically significant tendencies, not cases of absolute complementary distribution in the linguistic sense.

(3) Filled pauses and unfilled pauses were a matter of individual differences; the relative "preference" for hesitation phenomena of different types seems to be an aspect of individual style of speaking.

It should be noted that conclusion (2) is a corollary of conclusion (1) as phrases commonly start with function words while most lexical words occur within phrases. With the greater uncertainty in the choice of lexical words it follows that unfilled pauses are better indicators of uncertainty of choice than filled pauses.

Maclay and Osgood suggest that the distinction between filled and unfilled pauses as indicated in (1) and (2) lies mainly in the duration of the non-speech interval. They write:

> Let us assume that the speaker is motivated to keep control of the conversational "ball" until he has achieved some sense of completion. He has learned that unfilled intervals of sufficient length are the points at which he has usually lost his control—someone else has leapt into the gap. Therefore, if he pauses long enough to receive the cue of his own silence, he will produce some kind of signal (ah, m, er) or perhaps a repetition of the immediately preceding unit, which says in effect: "I'm still in control—don't interrupt me". We would thus expect filled pauses and repeats to occur just before points of highest uncertainty, points where choices are most difficult and complicated. . . . This assumption that "ah" type pauses are reactions of the speaker to his own prolonged silences at points of difficult decision is consistent with our finding that these two pause-types are merely statistically, not absolutely, different in distribution. . . . The less probable the sequence, the more

prolonged the non-speech interval and hence the greater the tendency for an "ah" or a repetition.

Maclay and Osgood's suggestion concerning unfilled pauses and their relation to difficult decisions is in keeping with the writer's own experimental results as was pointed out by these authors (Maclay and Osgood, 1959), and further evidence derived from measurements of pause duration has since been produced by the writer (1961) to demonstrate that "the less probably a sequence the more prolonged the non-speech interval."

Maclay and Osgood's observations on the distinction between filled and unfilled pauses raising the question of the relative significance of the former has stimulated the present investigation. Its purpose has been to see to what extent the introduction of the criterion of time might help to illuminate further the relative functions of filled and unfilled pauses.

MATERIAL

The speech samples used for this investigation were taken from an experiment, reported elsewhere (Eisler, 1961), which was concerned with the relation of hesitation pauses to degree and level of selection and uncertainty. It consisted in showing subjects cartoon stories without captions (of the kind regularly published in the "New Yorker" magazine) asking them first to describe the content of the stories and then to formulate the meaning, point, or moral of the story. Experimental conditions were thus created for the study of pauses (a) in speech produced within a relatively concrete situation, i.e., a given sequence of events (through their description) and (b) in speech uttered in the process of abstracting and generalising from such events (through summarising their meaning).

The speech produced by the subjects was recorded, transcribed and visual records obtained of the sequences of sound and silence, the length of which were measured, as described in a previous paper (Eisler, 1956).

The results showed that (a) speech described observed events contains considerably less hesitation (as measured by duration of pauses) than speech produced in conveying the meaning of these events.

(b) Hesitancy (pause length per speech unit) which is independent of the length of utterances in descriptive speech, becomes a function of brevity of verbal expression when the meaning of the cartoon stories is summarised. Greater conciseness in summarising was associated with more hesitation.

(c) A transitional analysis executed on descriptive speech and summaries separately showed the summaries to carry words of significantly greater uncertainty than the descriptions. (Oral communication at 4th London Symposium on Information Theory, 1960, to be published.) The material of this experiment was used for the present study.

Measurements were taken of the durations of the filled as well as the unfilled pauses; this was done for descriptions and summaries separately.

RESULTS

1. Relative Length of Filled and Unfilled Pauses

Time measurements of the filled pauses which occurred in the speech of nine subjects, describing and summarising 7–9 cartoons each, showed that the duration of filled pauses ranged between 0.2 and 0.8 sec. each. The total length of time taken up by filled pauses in relation to the total non-speech pauses (filled plus unfilled pauses) covered a range from 0.0 to 18.5 percent of the total pause time with a single stray value of 57.1 percent where there was very little pausing of any kind and the verbal statement itself was very short. The mean percentage of the total pause time taken up by filled pauses was 5.7 percent (including the value of 57.1 percent in the total). This figure, however, covers a very wide spread (see Table 1) with nearly two-thirds of the filled pauses taking up less than 5 percent of the total pause time, and three-quarters less than 6 percent.

Table 1.
Percentage of Total Pause Time Taken up by Filled Pauses

	Descriptions		Summaries	
	Cartoons		Cartoons	
Subjects	*1*	*2*	*1*	*2*
Ha	5.88%	0.00%	0.00%	2.45%
Tr	0.62	2.56	0.88	2.35
Co	4.80	4.26	15.38	7.14
Sa	1.23	0.88	10.34	0.00
Gi	5.26	2.21	9.01	5.45
Ne	3.48	5.81	18.52	2.78
Am	4.63	1.06	1.47	4.21
Do	0.00	0.00	57.10	1.33

Table 2. Time Occupied by Filled Pauses (FP/w) and Unfilled Pauses (UP/w) in Descriptions and in Summaries, Expressed in Seconds per Word Produced: Mean Values Based on 7−9 Cartoon Experiments with Each Subject

Subjects	Descriptions		Summaries	
	FP/w	*UP/w*	*FP/w*	*UP/w*
Ha	0.00 sec.	0.53 sec.	0.01 sec.	1.69 sec.
Tr	0.02	0.56	0.04	1.88
Wi	0.01	0.30	0.02	1.00
Sa	0.01	0.33	0.01	1.62
Gi	0.02	0.27	0.01	0.46
Ne	0.01	0.38	0.04	0.72
An	0.09	0.40	0.50	0.74
Do	0.00	0.30	0.01	0.77
Th	0.01	0.22	0.01	0.61

Relating the length of filled pauses (EP) and unfilled pauses (UP) to the output of speech (number of words produced), in the descriptions FP time per word produced (FP/w) was 0.013 sec. against UP time per word (UP/w) of 0.365 sec. and in the summaries, 0.023 sec. against 1.054 sec.

2. Filled Pauses, Unfilled Pauses and Points of Uncertainty

The relation was studied of the frequency of filled pauses to the total time of unfilled pauses (FP/UPt) in descriptions and those summaries which were long enough to permit such correlation, for each of four subjects separately. (The correlations were based on nine and seven cartoons for each of two subjects.) The frequency and variability of filled pauses for the rest of the subjects were too low to justify correlation. Table 3 shows that for three out of the four subjects the frequency of the filled pauses is a function of the duration of the unfilled pauses. It has been shown (Eisler, 1961)

Table 3. Rank Correlations Between Filled Pause Frequencies (FP) and the Total Time Occupied by Unfilled Pauses (UPt)

Subjects	Descriptions (FP, UPt)	Summaries (FP, UPt)
Tr	0.928**	0.667*
Sa	0.867**	—
Gi	0.372	0.596
An	0.955**	—

**Significant at 1 percent level.
*Significant at 5 percent level.

Figure 1. The Rate of Growth of Unfilled Pause Time with Total Speaking Time, Measured by the Number of Words Produced, for 9 Different Subjects

(Each section shows the results for four verbal tasks: spontaneously describing pictures and abstracting their meaning at a first trial, and repeating both kinds of statement after practice (seventh trial).)

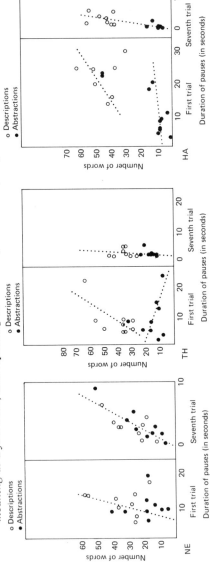

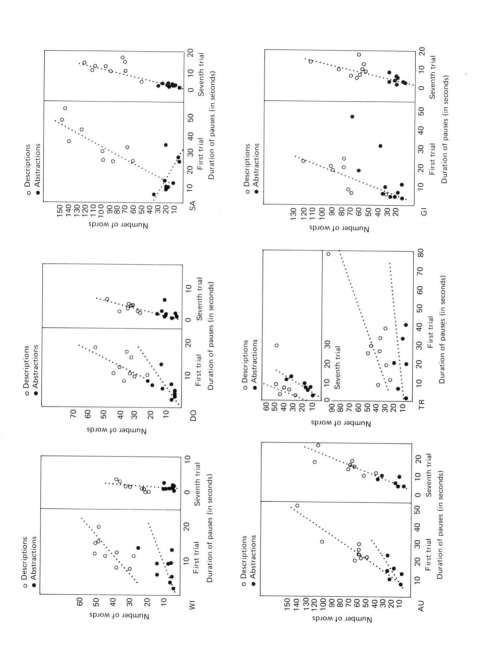

that the total length of unfilled pauses is a function of the total length of verbal productions. The longer we speak, the more words we produce and the more time we spend being silent. As linguistic and speech phenomena are functions of time, it is not surprising to find that the frequency of filled pauses increases with the increasing total length of unfilled pauses.

Figure 1 shows however that the rate of growth of unfilled pause time with total speaking time differs for different individuals, and in the same way we must expect that the rate of increase of filled pauses relative to unfilled pause time will be a discriminating factor in different individuals, and under different conditions.

Table 4 shows the ratio for nine subjects of the frequency of filled pauses to the duration of unfilled pauses (in seconds) for descriptions and summaries. It illustrates the considerable differences among individuals in the silence they can tolerate without breaking it with vocal activity. The exceptional ratio 1 : 114 for subject Do. must however be interpreted in the light of the fact that this subject was particularly curt in utterance and short in pausing.

Table 4.   Ratios of Filled Pause Occurrence to the Time Occupied by Unfilled Pauses (in seconds)

Subjects	Descriptions EF/UPt	Summaries FP/UPt
Ha	1 : 77	1 : 83
Tr	1 : 13	1 : 14
Co	1 : 19	1 : 13
Sa	1 : 7	1 : 16
Gi	1 : 4	1 : 6
Ne	1 : 7	1 : 4
Au	1 : 4	1 : 4
Do	1 : 114	1 : 19
Th	1 : 9	1 : 10

Table 5.   Mean FP/UPt Rates

Subjects	Descriptions	Summaries
Ha	0.013	0.012
Tr	0.079	0.074
Wi	0.052	0.079
Sa	0.138	0.062
Gi	0.249	0.175
Ne	0.140	0.250
An	0.264	0.273
Do	0.009	0.005

Table 6. Analysis of Variance: Filled Pause Rate (FP/UPt) for Descriptions and Summaries, Based on 6 Subjects and 128 Cartoons (5 cartoons for 4 subjects and 7 cartoons for 2 subjects)

Source	Sum of squares	df	Variance estimate
Descriptions and summaries	0.0172	1	0.0172
Between subjects	0.5226	5	0.1045
Interactions	0.5969	5	0.1195
Within subjects (error)	0.6041	116	0.0052
Between subjects/error	$F = 20.1$	$p < 0.001$	
Descriptions and summaries/error	$F = 3.3$	Not significant	
Interaction	$F = 22.9$	$p < 0.001$	

The infrequency of filled pauses under these circumstances falls in well with Maclay's and Osgood's suggestion that "ah" or "m" sounds are speakers' reactions to their own prolonged silences. The silences of subject Do. were rarely long enough to stimulate him into signalising vocally that he was still talking. For the rest, the consistency of individual ratios of filled pause frequency to unfilled pause duration is evident even from these average figures when we compare descriptions and summaries. An analysis of variance based on filled pause occurrence per second of unfilled pause time for six subjects shows the degree and significance of the consistency (Table 6).

A coefficient of reliability calculated from the variance ratio was 0.950. It is also evident from this analysis of variance that the different levels of speech production operating in descriptions and summaries which were reflected most significantly in the length of unfilled pauses (Eisler, 1961) showed no systematic effect on the rate of filled pause occurrence per second of unfilled pauses. However, individual differences accounted for only about half of the variance whilst the other significant half was due to interaction effects between subjects and cartoons.

CONCLUSIONS AND DISCUSSION

Three conclusions seem to be justified on the basis of the above results:

(a) That the ratio of filled pause occurrence to the time occupied by unfilled pauses can be classed as a speech habit characteristic of individuals.

(b) That in contrast to silent hesitation (unfilled pauses) which also have shown to contain a habitual factor (Eisler, 1961) deviations from habitual filled pause rate are not stimulated by cognitive factors such as degree of abstraction in speech production or difficulty of choice as measured by transition probability.

(c) That on the other hand, judging by the significant interaction between subjects and cartoons, factors connected with the content of the cartoons do seem to stimulate subjects to deviate from their habitual filled pause rate. This suggests an emotional factor.

The two hesitation phenomena of filled and unfilled pauses would thus appear to reflect different internal processes, cognitive activity being accompanied by an arrest of external activity (speech or non-linguistic vocal action) for periods proportionate to the difficulty of the cognitive task, while emotional attitudes would be reflected in vocal activity of instantaneous or explosive nature.

This interpretation was put to the test by correlating the mean filled pause rate (FP/UPt) for nine subjects with their mean hesitancy (unfilled pause length per word, P/w). The correlation Spearman's r, was -0.665, significant at the 0.05 level of probability for the summaries. There was no significant relation ($r = 0.100$) for the descriptions, but this might have been expected from the small range of individual differences in hesitancy (P/w) which was not only less in extent, but also less discriminating between individuals in the descriptions. The summaries which represent responses to a considerably more difficult cognitive task resulted not only in greater hesitancy generally, but also in wider differentiation between the specific hesitancy of individuals, as may be seen from Table 7. The negative correlation of these latter values (P/w) with the subject's mean filled pause rate (FP/UPr) shows that subjects whose hesitancy in formulating summaries was greater, were less inclined to break their silences with "ah" or "m" sounds, while subjects whose silent pauses were shorter, uttered more of such sounds. This would seem to contradict Maclay and Osgood's suggestion that filled pauses are responses to length of unfilled pauses, but it is a conclusion applicable under specific conditions, namely in a situation requiring high level cognitive activity. Under conditions requiring processes of abstraction and generalisation those who hesitated longer in silence, who also produced more concise statements and words which were less predictable, produced fewer filled pauses per second of unfilled pause time, while

Table 7. Pause Time per Word Produced in Descriptions and in Summaries

Subjects	Descriptions P/w	Summaries P/w
Th	0.22 sec.	0.61 sec.
Ha	0.53	1.69
Tr	0.56	1.88
Wi	0.30	1.00
Sa	0.33	1.62
Gi	0.27	0.46
Ne	0.38	0.72
Au	0.40	0.74
Do	0.30	0.77

the less hesitant subjects who produced the more long-winded summaries and more predictable words produced filled pauses at shorter intervals of silence.

Thus those who consistently achieved superior (more concise) stylistic and less probable linguistic formulations are consistently inclined towards delay of action and tolerance of silence, whilst the inferior stylistic achievement (long-winded statement) of greater predictability is linked to greater verbal as well as vocal activity.

REFERENCES

Goldman-Eisler, F. 1956. The determinants of the rate of speech output and their mutual relations. *J. Psychosom. Res.*, 1: 137.

Goldman-Eisler, F. 1958a. Speech production and the predictability of words in context. *Quart. J. exper. Psychol.*, 10: 96.

Goldman-Eisler, F. 1958b. The predictability of words in context and the length of pauses in speech. *Language and Speech*, 1: 226.

Goldman-Eisler, F. 1961. Hesitation and information in speech. In *Proceedings of the 4th London Symposium on Information Theory* (in the press).

Maclay, H. and Osgood, C. E. 1959. Hesitation phenomena in spontaneous English speech. *Word*, 15: 19.

7

HESITATION AND
GRAMMATICAL ENCODING

Donald S. Boomer

This study is concerned with two varieties of hesitations in spontaneous English speech: silent pause and "filled pause" (*uh* /e/,
ah /a/, *um* /em/, and similar variants). The data to be presented
concern the location of these hesitations in extended utterances,
but the basic theoretical issue involved is the nature of the grammatical encoding process in speech. The data and the theoretical
issue are inferentially related. The linking hypothesis is that
hesitations in spontaneous speech occur at points where decisions
and choices are being made. On this basis, the patterning of hesitations should provide clues as to the size and nature of the encoding units which are operative.

If the encoding units are single words then hesitations should
occur more frequently before those words which involve a difficult decision; i.e., a choice among many alternatives. If the encoding unit is a sequence of several words then the hesitations
should predominate at the beginnings of such sequences, rather
than occurring randomly wherever a difficult word choice occurs.
The present inquiry has sought to establish a critical confrontation
of these two alternatives.

Reprinted from *Language and Speech* 8, No. 3 (1965): 148–58. Footnotes have
been renumbered.

BACKGROUND OF THE PROBLEM

In general, previous investigations have considered hesitations to be a function of the statistical transition probabilities which obtain in the sequencing of words. Lounsbury (1954, p. 99), in an extended discussion of this issue, puts the case in the form of a hypothesis:

Hypothesis 1: Hesitation pauses correspond to the points of highest statistical uncertainty in the sequencing of units of any given order. (High statistical uncertainty = high transitional entropy.) The observations which lead us to formulate this hypothesis have been focussed on the sequencing of words. We are relatively hopeful for the substantiation of the hypothesis when the units are of this order.

Goldman-Eisler (1958) tested this hypothesis experimentally on a small language sample with positive results. A set of 12 spontaneously uttered sentences containing 60 unfilled pauses were transcribed and subjected to the Shannon guessing technique for estimating transitional probabilities between successive words. The words which had been preceded by a pause when originally uttered proved to be significantly harder to guess than were the words which had been spoken fluently. The sample sentences, however, were a markedly biased sample of spontaneous speech, since the experimental design dictated that only grammatical, well-constructed sentences be chosen. The difficulty Goldman-Eisler reports in finding such utterances in her corpus attests to their unrepresentativeness. The function of pauses in this restricted context cannot safely be generalized to ordinary spontaneous speech.

In a larger corpus of 50,000 words tape-recorded in a work conference, Maclay and Osgood (1959) studied the incidence of both filled and unfilled pauses relative to lexical words and function words. About 59 percent of all hesitations occurred before lexical words and 41 percent before function words, a finding which, although statistically significant, leaves sufficient unexplained variance to warrant further investigation.

The present study was based on the belief that a systematic account of hesitation phenomena may require a unit larger than the word. Previous empirical studies based on this idea have turned to formal grammar for the definition of the larger units. Maclay and Osgood (1959) used some of the grammatical test frames of Fries (1952), and Little (1963) used a structural classification system described by Francis (1958). Both investigations found that hesitations occur within many syntactic structures as well as at their boundaries. Some systematic variability was found in both investigations; that is to say, hesitations were significantly more probable at some syntactic positions than at others. Although both studies are enlightening, neither provides any systematic basis for defining speech encoding units in terms of formal structural linguistics.

In another hypothesis Lounsbury (1954, p. 100) also considered units larger than the word:

Hypothesis 2: Hesitation pauses and points of high statistical uncertainty correspond to the beginning of units of encoding.

This could serve as the basic hypothesis of the present study if the words "and points of high statistical uncertainty" were deleted. The reason for this qualification will be clarified later in the paper in the course of an argument against the assumption that pauses occur at points of low word-to-word transition probabilities.

In discussing Lounsbury's hypotheses Maclay and Osgood (1959, p. 23) say, "Hypothesis 2 has an element of circularity in that no independent method of defining encoding units has been developed." This is the point of departure of the present study. The *phonemic clause*, as defined by Trager and Smith (1951), has been adopted as a provisional encoding unit. This unit is defined phonologically and does not depend on the presence or absence of hesitations. The incidence of hesitations in phonemic clauses, then, may be examined, with the hypothesis that they occur predominantly at the beginnings of these units.

The phonemic clause is a phonologically marked macrosegment which, according to Trager and Smith, contains one and only one primary stress and ends in one of the terminal junctures /I, II, #/. In practice, the instances of terminal junctures are determined from the tape recording and marked on the transcript. The boundaries so marked determine successive phonemic clauses in the corpus.

PROCEDURE

Speech samples

Tape recordings of spontaneous speech of 16 male native American speakers of English had been made for an earlier study (Boomer and

Dittmann, 1964). These recordings were used in the present investigation. After a "warm-up" chat each subject had been asked to speak extemporaneously to an interviewer for about three minutes on any subject he chose; hobbies, sports, summer vacations, or the like. Every effort was made to provide a relaxed atmosphere in which the subjects could talk naturally.

Speech was recorded on an Ampex 350 tape recorder, and a simultaneous oscillograph record was made for the purpose of locating silences. An automatic timer registered signals at 30 sec. intervals on both the oscillograph record and the audio tape to facilitate subsequent matching of the records. Careful typewritten transcripts were prepared in conventional orthography. The location of each silence exceeding 200 msec. was determined from the oscillograph records and marked on the transcripts. This is just slightly below the 250 msec. cutting point proposed by Goldman-Eisler (1958) for distinguished hesitation pauses from nonpausal phonetic effects. All filled pauses were also located and underlined.

Linguistic Analysis

The phonemic clause boundaries were established without knowledge of the purpose of the study by a colleague[1] who had been taught suprasegmental analysis by Trager. His task was to listen to the recordings and to record terminal junctures on an otherwise unmarked transcript. Repeat reliability of 0.93 has been reported by Dittmann and Wynne (1961) for the location of terminal junctures.

Hesitations

The object of analysis was to establish the location of each hesitation form in the phonemic clause in which it occurred. Our experience accords with statements made by previous investigators (Maclay and Osgood, 1959; Little, 1963) that filled and unfilled pauses occur almost without exception at word boundaries.[2] The successive word boundaries in a given phonemic clause, then, can the regarded as an ordered series of opportunities for hesitation. The possible locations in a five-word clause are illustrated below:

$$_1 \text{and}_2 \text{the}_3 \text{weather}_4 \text{was}_5 \text{hot} \; \#$$

The position after *hot* is not considered as a part of the clause, since the utterance is closed by the terminal contour over *hot.* More generally, the presence or absence of a pause after the terminal contour is irrelevant to the determination of juncture and is thus not linguistically a part of the preceding clause. A pause in this position, then, must be assigned to the following clause. Whether or not it functions as a true hesitation is a separate issue.[3]

In general, there will be as many possible locations as words in the clause, each location being labelled with the ordinal number of the word it precedes. Occasional arbitrary exceptions were made in this study for multiple-element proper nouns such as *Bill Smith* and *San Francisco,* for combinatory groups like *thank you* and *what-you-may-call-it,* and for certain "tags" such as *you know* and *you see.* These were counted as single words, as were syntactically superfluous repetitions of words, as in *I took the . . . the train.* Filled pauses themselves and word-fragments were also excluded from the count.

The corpus contained a total of 1593 phonemic clauses of which 713 contained one or more hesitations. Hesitations totalled 1,127: 749 unfilled pauses and 378 filled pauses. Each hesitation in the transcript was tabulated by its location number within the clause. The location and tabulation were done independently by two people and cross checked to minimize error.

RESULTS

The hypothesis that hesitations tend to occur at the beginning of phonemic clauses was strongly supported with, however, an unpredicted reversal. As may be seen in Table 1,[4] the greatest fre-

Table 1.   Frequencies of Hesitations Located at Successive Word Boundaries in Phonemic Clauses Classified by Length

Number of	*Boundary locations*										
words in clause	*1*	*2*	*3*	*4*	*5*	*6*	*7*	*8*	*9*	*10*	*Totals*
2	18	28									46
3	16	68	29								113
4	34	81	39	27							181
5	28	80	37	22	21						188
6	21	65	22	26	16	17					167
7	14	67	25	20	13	19	8				166
8	9	38	18	11	11	14	13	7			121
9	7	19	13	15	4	6	6	4	13		87
10	4	15	4	8	5	7	5	3	4	3	58
Totals	151	461	187	129	70	63	32	14	17	3	1127

Table 2. Frequencies of Unfilled Pauses Located at Successive Word Boundaries in Phonemic Clauses Classified by Length

Number of words in clause	(J)	Boundary locations										Totals
		1	2	3	4	5	6	7	8	9	10	
2	(65)	6	22									28
3	(99)	5	46	18								69
4	(101)	16	49	29	21							115
5	(109)	10	50	29	15	17						121
6	(98)	9	47	16	18	11	12					113
7	(76)	5	45	19	14	11	13	7				114
8	(55)	4	27	14	9	9	12	8	4			87
9	(36)	2	14	10	12	3	3	4	4	7		59
10	(20)	1	10	3	4	5	6	5	3	3	3	43
Totals	(659)	58	310	138	93	56	46	24	11	10	3	749

quency of hesitations is not at the outset but at position 2, after the first word of the clause. This is true for all nine of the array distributions representing clause lengths from two to ten words. An interpretation of this result will be offered in the final discussion.

Tables 2 and 3 show the separate distributions of unfilled and filled pauses respectively. This breakdown was included to demonstrate that the distributions of both kinds of hesitation conform essentially to the total distribution. Of the 18 arrays in the two tables, 16 show the same pattern with the highest frequency at position 2. The two discrepant arrays, clause lengths 2 and 9 in Table 3, may represent sampling error resulting from the small number of entries.

In order further to clarify the data in Table 1, they are pre-

Table 3. Frequencies of Filled Pauses Located at Successive Word Boundaries in Phonemic Clauses Classified by Length

Number of words in clause	Boundary locations										Totals
	1	2	3	4	5	6	7	8	9	10	
2	12	6									18
3	11	22	11								44
4	18	32	10	6							66
5	18	30	8	7	4						67
6	12	18	6	8	5	5					54
7	9	22	6	6	2	6	1				52
8	5	11	4	2	2	2	5	3			34
9	5	5	3	3	1	3	2	0	6		28
10	3	5	1	4	0	1	0	0	1	0	15
Totals	93	151	49	36	14	17	8	3	7	0	378

sented graphically in Figure 1 against a hypothetical chance distribution. The dotted line represents the expected total distribution of hesitations in the entire set of phonemic clauses if their occurrence were governed by chance. The solid line represents the distributing of column totals from Table 1. Both sets of values are represented in percentage terms to facilitate comparison. As may be readily seen, only the frequency at position 2 exceeds chance. All other frequencies are at or below chance expectancy.

One other aspect of these data requires discussion at this point. In Table 2 the frequency of juncture pauses is separately tabulated in column (*J*). In column 1 are tabulated the unfilled pauses in position 1 which are not juncture pauses, that is to say, those pauses which were preceded by an initial *ah* or a word fragment which opened the clause but was not counted as a word. Had the juncture pauses been simply included in column 1 the totals would be greater than for position 2 in each array. The initial hypothesis that hesitations occur at the beginning of phonemic clauses would be even more strongly supported, but the interesting reversal between 1 and 2 would be obscured. We have therefore chosen to maintain the distinction between these types of pauses, but to present all of

Figure 1.   Comparison of Theoretical and Obtained Total Percentages of Hesitations Occurring at Successive Boundary Locations

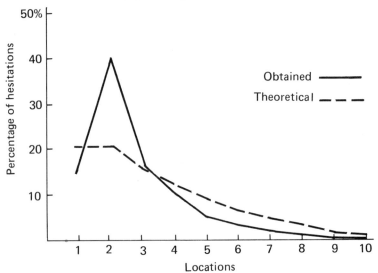

the data for full consideration. Some of the theoretical issues involved will be discussed in the concluding section of this report.

Additional Findings

Two minor issues regarding hesitations were examined in this body of data. Although peripheral to the central hypothesis of the study they are at least tangentially of interest.

These data permitted a test of a psycholinguistic interpretation of *ah* offered by Maclay and Osgood (1959, p. 41). These authors say:

> Let us assume that the speaker is motivated to keep control of the conversational "ball" until he has achieved some sense of completion. He has learned that unfilled intervals of sufficient length are the points at which he has usually lost this control—someone else has leapt into his gap. Therefore, if he pauses long enough to receive the cue of his own silence he will produce some kind of signal ([m, r], or perhaps a repetition of the immediately preceding unit) which says, in effect, "I'm still in control—don't interrupt me."

This hypothesis is subject to quantitative test although Osgood and Maclay were unable to make such a test because of the limitations of their data. The oscillographic recordings available in the present study permitted the measurement of unfilled pauses immediately preceding instances of *ah*. The results of this test do not support the Maclay-Osgood hypothesis. More than 72 percent of the *ahs* were preceded by no pause. An additional 11 percent were preceded by pauses which were shorter than the subject's mean pause length. Thus only 17 percent of the *ahs* in this study were preceded by longer than average pauses.

The other issue concerns a possible durational distinction between juncture pause and hesitation pause. This widely cited distinction was originally formulated by Lounsbury (1954, p. 98):

> Even if "junctures" sometimes consist of short pauses, the [hesitation] pauses under consideration here are not the same. For one thing, there is a difference in duration. Juncture pauses which we have seen in spectrographic analyses of speech were in the order of a hundredth of a second or less in length. The pauses referred to here, however, are appreciably longer.

In the present data about half the junctures were followed by a pause. According to Lounsbury these pauses should be much shorter than the hesitation pauses, that is, pauses which occur at locations other than following junctures. This does not seem to be the case. The juncture pauses as measured are, in fact, somewhat longer than the hesitation pauses. The overall means are 1,027 msec. and 747 msec. respectively, a difference which is significant, $p < 0.001$. Furthermore, 15 of the 16 subject mean comparisons are in the same direction.

DISCUSSION

This study has used the location of hesitations in spontaneous speech as evidence in support of the theory that speech encoding at the grammatical level operates with units larger than the word. When sustained speech is marked off in successive phonemic clauses, bounded by terminal junctures, it has been shown that hesitations are not randomly located throughout such clauses, but tend to occur near the beginnings. This tendency characterizes both types of hesitation studied, all clause lengths from two to ten words, and each of the 16 individual subjects.

If words were in fact the operative encoding units there would be no reason to expect such a finding. In fact, a strict word-transitional model should predict just the opposite. The argument is as follows: primary stress typically occurs toward the end of a phonemic clause; almost invariably the last or next to last word in the clause received the stress. And, as Berry (1953) has shown, primary stress is negatively related to word frequency; that is, the less frequent a word, the more likely it is to receive phrase stress when uttered in sustained speech. Thus the high-information lexical words tend to occur toward the end of phonemic clauses, and this is where a word-unit model should predict the most hesitations to occur. That, in fact, they do not argues strongly for the phonemic clause rather than the word as the molar encoding unit of speech.

Let us now consider the unexpected finding that the most frequent pause location is after the first word in the clause, rather than before it, as had been predicted. This fact may have some additional implications for the psycholinguistic process of speech encoding.

Carroll (1953) suggested a two-stage, hierarchical encoding process with larger units chosen first, followed by the selection of smaller components. The larger units may be thought of as involving grammatical decisions and the smaller units as involving lexical choices. The reality of these separate aspects of speech production is strongly supported by evidence from clinical research (Wepman and Jones, 1964) that in aphasia either function can be impaired, leaving the other relatively intact. A medicolinguistic distinction was drawn earlier by Jakobson (1956) between "contiguity" and "similarity" disorders.

In the neurologically intact speaker these processes are so smoothly co-ordinated that they seem to be a single process. The temporal ordering of these two encoding stages, if indeed there is an ordering, remains a subject of dispute. Skinner (1957) has speculated that lexical selection is the fundamental process and that such features as syntactic arrangement, inflection and qualification are added as intraverbal, "autoclitic" responses, that is, verbal responses to previously uttered verbalizations.

In a carefully reasoned review of Skinner's work, Chomsky (1959, p. 54) argues that the opposite is just as likely—". . . . that the 'key responses' are chosen only after the grammatical frame."

The present data suggest that Chomsky's view is the more correct one. The initial word in a phonemic clause sets certain constraints for the structure of what is to follow. The selection of a first word has in greater or lesser degree committed the speaker to a particular construction or at least a set of alternative constructions, and has also foreclosed the possibility of other constructions.[5]

According to this view, then, the hesitations in phonemic clauses are most likely to occur *after* at least a preliminary decision has been made concerning its structure and *before* the lexical choices have been finally made.

This interpretation rests on the preponderance of hesitations at position 2, which in turn rests on our rather arbitrary decision not to consider juncture pauses as true hesitations. There is some theoretical and empirical basis for our decision. Previous experimentation (Boomer and Dittmann, 1962) has shown that listeners do not distinguish between minimal-pair utterances contrasting a closed juncture and a juncture followed by a 500 msec. pause, whereas a hesitation pause of 200 msec. is discriminated. This empirical finding supports the generally accepted theoretical view that juncture pauses are facultative accompaniments of terminal junctures and essentially linguistic, while hesitation pauses are extra-linguistic.

To be sure, neither the evidence nor the theoretical distinction is compelling, but pending better information we will continue to regard these two pausal phenomena as functionally different.

In passing, it is suggested that the above-mentioned experiment may have some bearing on the generally-held opinion that juncture pauses are vanishingly short as compared to hesitations. This is perhaps true for closed junctures, and about half the junctures in this study were not followed by pauses exceeding 200 msec., our cut-off point. Half, however, were followed by juncture pauses which were significantly longer than hesitation pauses. Even at these lengths, however, the unaided ear fails to register them. It is likely that impressionistic judging procedures and even stopwatch pause timing miss many of these pauses.

Hesitations and Transition Probabilities

The prevailing view that hesitations reflect low transition probabilities at the point of their occurrence has been directly challenged by this study. The transitional-probability hypothesis contains the unexamined assumption that the speech encoding process does not involve any anticipatory planning beyond the next word. The speaker is, according to this view, not aware that he is at a loss for a word until he is on the point of uttering it, at which point he hesitates long enough to make the choice. This would seem to be an unnecessarily primitive assumption in view of the demonstrable capacities of the human brain for short-term storage, delay, and "feed-back" control of rapid, complex sequential motor activities.

Our data imply a rather more complex process in which planning ranges forward to encompass a structured "chunk" of syntax and meaning. As a given clause is being uttered the next one is taking shape and focus. At the terminal juncture the next clause may be ready, in which case it will be uttered fluently, as were more than half the phonemic clauses in this corpus.

If, however, the emerging clause has not yet been subjectively formulated, speech is suspended until the entire pattern is clarified. This suspension may be manifested as either a pause or a vocalized hesitation sound. Our data do not support any functional distinction between these hesitation signals.

This hypothetical description, of course, fails to account for all the data. Our distributions show that some hesitations occur at each successive position in some clauses, although with declining probability overall. It would be surprising if the case were otherwise. The psychological monitoring process are undoubtedly delicate, sensitive, and subject to modification at any point. Our data argue only that most decisions in most clauses occur at the first internal word boundary.

Notes

[1]Allen T. Dittmann, whose interest in psycholinguistics preceded and stimulated my own.

[2]In order to sidestep the prolonged linguistic dispute about this unit it should be emphasized that "word" is used here in its most traditional sense, as defined by a typist when she presses the space bar.

[3]The pause following terminal juncture is mentioned in the systems of Bloomfield (1933), Harris (1951), and Hill (1958). Despite terminological differences, there is general agreement that this pause is linguistically determined, an intermittently occurring free variant of the terminal juncture. Hesitation pauses, that is, pauses occurring at other than structural boundaries, when mentioned at all are attributed to non-linguistic or extra-linguistic factors.

[4]A few clauses, 30, to be exact, longer than 40 words were omitted from this tabulation because there were too few in any length category to permit statistical treatment. In order to exceed 6 or 7 words a clause must usually include one or more extended anacolutha, a fact which may account for the "humps" near the ends of the distributions for the 8 and 9 word clauses. The data tabulated here include 97 percent of the hesitations in the original corpus.

[5]Cf. Hockett, C. F. (1960).

REFERENCES

Berry, J. 1953. Some statistical aspects of conversational speech. In *Communication theory*, ed. W. Jackson (London).

Bloomfield, L. 1933. *Language* (New York).

Boomer, D. S. and Dittmann, A. T. 1964. Speech rate, filled pause, and body movement in interviews. *J. nerv. ment. Dis.*, 139: 324.

Carroll, J. B. 1953. *The study of language* (Cambridge, Mass.).

Chomsky, N. 1959. Review of "Verbal Behavior" by B. F. Skinner. *Language*, 35: 26.

Dittmann, A. T. and Wynne, L. C. 1961. Linguistic techniques and the analysis of emotionality in interviews. *J. abnorm. soc. Psychol.*, 63: 201.

Francis, W. N. 1958. *The structure of American English* (New York).

Fries, C. G. 1952. *The structure of English* (New York).

Goldman-Eisler, Frieda 1958. Speech production and the predictability of words in context. *Quart. J. exp. Psychol.*, 9–10: 96.

Harris, Z. S. 1951. *Methods in structural linguistics* (Chicago).

Hill, A. A. 1958. *Introduction to linguistic structures* (New York).

Hockett, C. F. 1960. Grammar for the hearer. *Proc. Symposia in Applied Mathematics, Vol. 12, New York*, 220 (Providence, R.I.).

Jakobson, R. and Halle, M. 1956. *Fundamentals of language* (The Hague).

Little, L. 1963. The syntax of vocalized pauses in spontaneous cultivated speech. Ph.D. Dissertation, George Peabody College for Teachers.

Lounsbury, F. G. 1954. Transitional probability, linguistic structure and systems of habit-family hierarchies. In *Psycholinguistics: A survey of theory and research problems*, ed. C. E. Osgood and T. A. Sebeok (Baltimore).

Maclay, H. and Osgood, C. E. 1959. Hesitation phenomena in spontaneous English speech. *Word*, 15: 19.

Skinner, B. F. 1957. *Verbal behavior* (New York).

Trager, G. L. and Smith, H. L. 1951. An outline of English structure (Norman, Okla.).

Wepman, J. M. and Jones, L. V. 1964. Five aphasias: A commentary on aphasia as a regressive linguistic phenomenon. In *Disorders of communication*, ed. D. M. Rioch and E. A. Weinstein (Baltimore).

8

WORD PREDICTABILITY IN THE ENVIRONMENTS OF HESITATIONS

Percy H. Tannenbaum
Frederick Williams
Carolyn S. Hillier

Various hesitation phenomena apparently occur in almost all speakers of all languages. Generally, they have been taken as interruptions in the "normal" flow of speech and, as such, have been used to index variations in the encoding state of speakers (e.g., Mahl, 1956, 1959; Feldstein and Jaffe, 1962; Stolz and Tannenbaum, 1963). Recently, attention has been focused on the role of hesitations as indices of different encoding decision points (Lounsbury, 1954; Goldman-Eisler, 1958a, 1958b, 1961a), and it was to this issue that the present investigation was directed. More specifically, the present research was concerned with assessing the predictability of words in hesitation versus fluent encoding contexts, across and between different types of hesitations.

The impetus for such research stems from a series of studies by Goldman-Eisler. Originally interested in language phenomena in psychiatric interviews, she found that speech interruptions involved both breathing and hesitation pauses, but while the former

Reprinted from *Journal of Verbal Learning and Verbal Behavior* 4 (1965: 134–40. Footnotes have been renumbered.

related more to the emotional state of the encoder, hesitation pauses were more cognitive in origin, apparently characterizing conditions of encoder uncertainty (Goldman-Eisler, 1955, 1956).

In subsequent tests of this "cognitive decision point" hypothesis, she found that the first lexical word subsequent to an unfilled pause was less predictable (Goldman-Eisler, 1958a) and took significantly longer to replace (Goldman-Eisler, 1958b) than lexical words uttered in fluent contexts. In addition, the word preceding unfilled pauses tended to be even more predictable than in other fluent contexts. Thus, it was reasoned that hesitation pauses had occurred at junctures representing transitions from relatively high to low redundancy, the original speaker having paused at that point in order to make a particular encoding decision. Further support for this interpretation came from another study (Goldman-Eisler, 1961a) in which the frequency of hesitation pauses was found to vary with the level of cognitive activity required of encoders. Such pauses were more frequent in "interpretations" rather than "descriptions" of subtle cartoons, and diminished with increasing repetition of the same encoding task.

A related descriptive study led to the conclusion that hesitations were non-random in their occurrence and that such phenomena "are clearly related to the dynamics of grammatical and lexical selection" (Maclay and Osgood, 1959, p. 40). An important aspect of this study was the use of a variety of hesitation phenomena; a classification of four different types (false starts, repeats, and filled and unfilled pauses), representing a reduction of Mahl's (1956) eight categories, was employed. In keeping with the Goldman-Eisler and Lounsbury (1954) theoretical positions, unfilled pauses tended to occur antecedent to likely encoding choice points, but so did filled pauses and, to a somewhat lesser extent, repeats. False starts, on the other hand, often involved blocking subsequent to a lexical unit and then retracing to correct it. Goldman-Eisler (1961b) pursued the suggestion that filled and unfilled pauses might characterize similar decision points by re-analyzing the data from her earlier "cartoon" study (Goldman-Eisler, 1961a) for the occurrence of filled pauses. Unlike the findings of unfilled pauses, there were no significant differences between the description and interpretation encoding conditions for filled pauses. This suggested that these two hesitation phenomena reflect different internal processes—unfilled pauses still relating more to the encoder's cognitive decisions, but filled pauses more to his emotional state.

The present research involved two separate but related studies investigating the cognitive decision point theory from a somewhat different methodological standpoint, and leading to the implication that different hesitation phenomena characterize different types of encoding decisions. Because of their somewhat different foci, the two studies are reported separately.

EXPERIMENT I

The first phase of the research was a direct test of the hypothesis that words immediately following hesitations are less predictable than those originally uttered in other, more fluent, sequences. As such, this study represented a replication of the earlier Goldman-Eisler (1958a) test of the same hypothesis. However, it involved some distinctive methodological modifications, including the selection of appropriate language samples as test materials, the inclusion of a wider variety of hesitation types, and the use of a different procedure to assess word predictability. These methodological variations were designed to provide for a more sensitive assessment of contextual predictability and, hence, of relating hesitation phenomena to encoder uncertainty.

Method

Language samples.   In order to allow for a closer correspondence between the original encoding behavior and the decoding behavior involving word replacement, the present study employed an entire single message, rather than a variety of independent sentences (cf. Goldman-Eisler, 1958a). Spoken messages are rarely encoded as independent sentences, and the constraints influencing word predictability can certainly exist beyond sentence boundaries.

The message used was encoded as part of another study dealing with the effects of cognitive feedback on oral encoding behavior (Stolz and Tannenbaum, 1963). Under the guise of an examination, students in a psychology of speech course replied to a set of three questions; the instructors' apparent evaluations being provided on a mechanical feedback meter. The first question was answered by all Ss under the neutral, or no feedback condition, and the remaining two questions were systematically varied between positive (favorable meter reading) and negative (unfavorable) feedback conditions. The message selected for this study was encoded by a male under neutral feedback.

Identification of hesitations. The recorded message was transcribed, and the location of the various hesitations was noted in the manner suggested by Maclay and Osgood (1959): *Unfilled pauses* were judged by trained coders as "silences of unusual length," rather than the Goldman-Eisler measure of including all silences over .25 sec duration. This admittedly more subjective index was used to assure that true hesitation silences were included without possible contamination from non-hesitation silences, such as those due to different speaker rates, "emphasis" pauses, etc. *Filled pauses* included all non-phonemic vocalizations—usually "ahs." *Repeats* included all repetitions judged to be semantically non-significant—from a phoneme to a series of words, although the most frequent case involved a single word. *False starts* involved all incomplete or "self-interrupted" utterances. The experimental message was of moderate length (273 words) and was marked by a relatively wide-spread hesitation distribution, including three false starts, eight repeats, sixteen filled pauses, two unfilled pauses, and four combinations.

Predictability measures. Another important distinction involved the manner in which the main dependent variable of word predictability or uncertainty was assessed. Goldman-Eisler used a variation of the Shannon (1951) method of estimating entropy in English, allowing for the influence of the antecedent or the subsequent, but not both contexts. Obviously, different semantic and syntactic constraints governing word predictability can operate in the complete context than in its components. Accordingly, cloze procedure (cf. Taylor, 1953, 1954; Osgood, 1959), which involves the systematic deletion of a sample of words from the entire passage, was employed here.

Procedure. Two versions of the transcribed message were prepared. One had a 10-space underlined blank in the place of words which had followed each of the 33 hesitations. The second version had an equal number of blanks in place of words selected on a purely random basis from the remaining corpus.

A total of 82 Ss was randomly assigned to each of two equally-sized ($N = 41$) groups, each group receiving one of the two message versions. The Ss were students enrolled in the same course which supplied the original encoder, but in a subsequent semester, thus also providing a closer correspondence between the encoder and response groups than in the Goldman-Eisler procedure.

In the manner characteristic of cloze procedure (cf. Taylor, 1953), all Ss were instructed to "try to replace the missing words so that the passage makes sense." The S s were urged to respond on all blanks, even if it involved guessing.

Results

The responses were first analyzed in terms of a set of measures related to the degree of agreement between the original encoder and the responding S s: the proportion of verbatim replacements *(V)* of the deleted word; a similar measure of agreement of the grammatical form class between the original and replaced words *(FC)*; and a *V/FC* index, reflecting the predictability of an actual word given that its grammatical classification has been correctly ascertained (*cf.* Fillenbaum and Jones, 1962).

For the present study, the prediction was that V, since it reflects a semantic choice, would be lower in the after-hesitation position than in fluent sequences of the message. It can be argued that the *FC* score is more related to the syntactic nature of the language than to deliberate semantic decisions and, thus, it should not necessarily discriminate between the two versions to the same degree as does V. Following the above reasoning, *V/FC* may be regarded as a more sensitive index of cognitive activity, since it adjusts for variations in the form class replacement.

The data for these three measures of encoder-respondent agreement are indicated in Table 1, and conform to the above predictions. The differences on V and *V/FC* are both in the predicted direction and statistically significant ($p < .02$, one-tailed Mann-Whitney U test, in each case). Although also in the predicted direction, the FC data do not show a significant difference.

Table 1 includes an additional relevant measure relating to degree of uncertainty among the actual responses, independent of the original deleted word. It is indexed by the relative entropy *(Rel. H)* of the response distribution, the measure assuming a range of zero to $+ 1.00$, corresponding to the range of minimum to maxi-

Table 1. Mean Word Replacement Measures in Fluent and After-Hesitation Contexts

Measure	*Fluent context*	*After hesitation*
V	.58	.37
FC	.79	.74
V/FC	.73	.50
Rel. H.	.28	.42

mum uncertainty.[1] Thus, for the present study, the prediction would be for a higher value of *Rel. H.* in the after-hesitation condition. Again, the data in Table 1 confirm this prediction, the difference being significant beyond the 0.5 level.

EXPERIMENT II

The second study involved a more detailed attempt to explore word predictability in the environment of hesitations. Instead of a mere dichotomy between "after-hesitation" and "other" word locations, predictability measures were obtained for all words in the sample; and these could then be related to the position of a given word relative to the nearest hesitation.

Such a more detailed approach obviously allows for a more sensitive test of the basic hypotheses derived from earlier work. Again the predictions are for the greatest uncertainty at the position immediately subsequent to a hesitation, while significantly less uncertainty should obtain in all the other positions in the hesitation-environment. Further, in keeping with the Goldman-Eisler (1958a) finding, we would expect the lowest uncertainty of all in the position immediately preceding the hesitation.

Method

For this experiment, two additional messages were selected from the same feedback study that produced the first message. The two passages, totaling 440 words and including 56 instances of hesitation, came from two separate encoders—a male and a female—both encoding under conditions of negative feedback (cf. Stolz and Tannenbaum, 1963).

By systematically rotating the selection of the first word to be deleted and then maintaining an every nth word deletion scheme, one can exhaust all the words in n versions of the passage. In the present case, Taylor's (1954) procedure was followed, and an every-*fifth*-word deletion pattern was used, five such versions for a passage. Thus, in any one version, there was a four-word context presented both antecedent to and subsequent to every response blank. To keep this pattern constant, the first four words and last four words in each passage were not included in the deletion scheme.

The same 82 Ss who served in the first experiment were involved in the present one. They were randomly assigned to one of five groups; each group being exposed to one of the five versions of each of the two experimental passages. The instructions to the *S*s were the same as those in the first study.

The original tape recordings of the two spoken messages were again scrutinized for the location and type of each hesitation, as in the first experiment. Thus, each of the deleted words could be identified as to its position in the environment of a given hesitation—i.e., by how many words it preceded or followed the hesitation. This was originally done for all words in the samples. However, because of the nature of the distribution of hesitations, it was decided to restrict the analysis to the immediate six-word environment—the three antecedent words (designated as a_3, a_2, a_1) and the three subsequent words (s_1, s_2, s_3)—of a given hesitation. Going beyond this limit would have involved too much confounding of both hesitations and words.

Results

In addition to the dependent variables employed in the first study, another measure, referring only to replacement of *lexical* words in the environment (V_{lex}), was included. This restriction to lexical items stems from Goldman-Eisler's (1958a) reasoning that it is specifically such words that are directly related to the cognitive activities involved.

Table 2 presents the word predictability means for the word positions both antecedent and subsequent to hesitations. Rather uniform results obtain across the various measures. The largest predictabilities are in the more peripheral positions (a_3, a_2, and s_2, s_3). The greatest uncertainty is in the s_1 position, as predicted. But surprisingly, the a_1 position exhibits an equal degree of uncertainty.

Table 2. Mean Word Replacement Measures in Antecedent and Subsequent Hesitation Contexts

Measure	*Word position*					
	a_3	a_2	a_1	s_1	s_2	s_3
V	.51	.53	.40	.39	.51	.53
V_{lex}	.46	.44	.29	.31	.42	.40
FC	.76	.78	.67	.66	.73	.77
V/FC	.67	.68	.60	.59	.70	.69
Rel. H.	.44	.43	.49	.48	.42	.41

These findings are underlined in comparisons between adjacent positions, with the number of words in each category used as the replicates in a Mann-Whitney U test. The differences between the a_2 and a_3 positions fall far short of statistical significance, as does the difference between the s_2 and s_3 positions. Comparison of the a_2 and a_1 locations yields a significant ($p < .05$) difference in all cases, as does the s_1 vs. s_2 comparison. The differences between the a_1 and s_1 positions are statistically negligible. These findings hold for each of the five indices employed, including the FC score.

While the results are in general agreement with the predictions, there is one clear and significant exception: *Both the a_1 and s_1 locations are the points of lowest predictability, with no difference between them.* The theoretical expectation was that the a_1 position would be the most redundant, at least more so than the s_1 position.

DISCUSSION

Clearly, a most intriguing aspect of this research is contained in this last finding of no difference in predictability between words immediately preceding and immediately following a hesitation. Why this unexpected finding, in contradiction to Goldman-Eisler's (1958a) conclusions?

One possible answer is that the different results merely reflect differences in what was being compared. Goldman-Eisler restricted her study to unfilled pauses, identifying these as silences beyond .25 sec. The present study not only used a much more stringent criterion for the inclusion of unfilled pauses, but also incorporated these within a larger undifferentiated category involving other hesitations. Thus, unfilled pauses as such were relatively obscured here; hence, the present study should perhaps not be expected to yield the same findings as Goldman-Eisler.

Such considerations may explain the lack of an a_1-s_1 difference, but it does not account for the fact that a_1 represents a position of significantly lower predictability than other (e.g., a_2 and a_3) locations. A plausible explanation for both findings may be that other hesitation types behave differently than do unfilled pauses. Consider the possibility that for one or another hesitation type, an a_1-s_1 difference does in fact exist but in a direction opposite to that for unfilled pauses. Under such circumstances, the final results, since they included all hesitations within a single category, could represent a cancelling-out among several significant but opposing response tendencies in the a_1 and s_1 positions.

Such a hypothesis can readily be tested by comparing the world predictability scores for the a_1 and s_1 positions separately for each hesitation type. Unfortunately, the data from this investigation allowed for only a limited analysis on this point. After elimination of the many instances of mixed hesitations in order to conduct the analysis only on pure cases of each hesitation type, enough cases remained to represent only repeats ($N = 13$) and filled pauses ($N = 20$). But even from such a restricted comparison, important clues emerged.

The data presented in Table 3 clearly indicate a differential pattern of word predictability between the two types of hesitations. The filled pause category exhibits the results originally predicted— greater uncertainty in the s_1, as opposed to the a_1, position. This is true on all but the FC measures where the reversal is relatively small. Examination of the repeat category, however, indicates precisely the opposite trend; the a_1 location being the one of higher uncertainty (again, the one reversal, in V/FC, is of minimal magnitude). When the a_1-s_1 difference scores are compared between the two hesitation categories by a Mann-Whitney U test, the difference between filled pauses and repeats is significant ($p < .05$) on all but the FC measure.

This evidence is admittedly quite sparse and tentative, but it does raise a legitimate theoretical question: what accounts for the differential distributions observed? One interpretation is that *different types of hesitations index different kind of encoding decision points*. The fact that Maclay and Osgood (1959) found various hesitation types to be somewhat differentially distributed with respect to syntactic environment lends credence to this viewpoint

Table 3. Mean Replacement Measures of Words Immediately Antecedent to and Subsequent to Repeats and Filled Pauses

Measure	Filled pause a_1	s_1	Repeat a_1	s_1
V	.42	.30	.37	.43
V_{lex}	.32	.23	.29	.39
FC	.72	.75	.58	.70
V/FC	.58	.40	.64	.62
Rel. H.	.40	.53	.51	.45

(although their data do not lead to the particular prediction for repeats and filled pauses). Similarly, while the Goldman-Eisler (1961b) distinction between the role of filled and unfilled pauses does not relate directly to the differential choice-point hypothesis, it does suggest that different hesitation phenomena may differ in the kind of psycholinguistic behavior they characterize.

The theoretical position offered here does not necessarily assume that each hesitation type indexes a distinctively different type of encoding-decision juncture. It may be suggested that two basic types of psycholinguistic phenomena underlie the occurrence of hesitations in encoding. One is a type of *groping* phenomenon, similar to that suggested by Goldman-Eisler. The speaker reaches a point where, for one reason or another, he cannot immediately elicit the "right" word, phrase, or sentence. Accordingly, his speech is interrupted as he gropes for the appropriate term. Under such circumstances, we would expect that the next encoding unit would be the more difficult to replace in cloze procedure—the encoder paused because he was uncertain, and this degree of uncertainty would be reflected in the cloze responses. Both filled and unfilled pauses may particularly characterize such encoding blocks.

An alternate type of hesitation-producing behavior stemming from *feedback* during encoding can also be postulated. The speaker, hearing himself say what he may not intend, interrupts his message production. Under such conditions he may backtrack to correct himself or may be momentarily stunned and repeat himself. This approach implies, then, that such feedback-induced hesitations will be characterized more by false starts or repeats. Moreover, it would predict that the highest uncertainty would be not in the subsequent, but in the preceding word that precipitated the hesitation.

This idea of a contrast in the function of different hesitation phenomena is obviously still speculative at this stage. The theoretical position is more a consequence of the investigation than the study was a test of the theory. The implications, however, are amenable to further exploration—both through more detailed descriptive analysis of the occurrence of hesitations, and through experimental tests of specific hypotheses suggested by the theory.

Note

[1]Relative entropy represents the ratio of the obtained entropy of the response distribution to the maximum entropy if all the events were equiprobable, i.e.,

$$\text{Rel. H.} = \frac{-\sum_{i=1}^{m} p(i) \log_2 p(i)}{\log_2 m}$$

where $p(i)$ is the probability of the occurrence of the ith event of m possible events (cf. Wilson, 1954; Taylor, 1954).

REFERENCES

Feldstein, S., and Jaffe, J. A note about speech disturbances and vocabulary diversity. *J. Communication*, 1962, 12: 166–170.

Fillenbaum, S., and Jones, L. V. An application of "cloze" technique to the study of aphasic speech. *J. abnorm. soc. Psychol.*, 1962, 65: 183–189.

Garner, W. R., and Carson, D. H. A multivariate solution of the redundancy of printed English. *Psychol. Rep.*, 1960, 6: 123–141.

Goldman-Eisler, F. Speech-breathing activity—a measure of tension and affect during interview. *British J. Psychol.*, 1955, 46: 53–63.

Goldman-Eisler, F. The determinants of the rate of speech output and their mutual relations. *J. psychosom. Res.*, 1956, 1: 137–143.

Goldman-Eisler, F. Speech production and the predictability of words in context. *Quart. J. exp. Psychol.*, 1958a, 10: 96–106.

Goldman-Eisler, F. The predictability of words in context and the length of pauses in speech. *Language and Speech*, 1958b, 1: 226–231.

Goldman-Eisler, F. Hesitation and information in speech. In C. Cherry (ed.), *Information theory—Fourth London symposium*. Washington: Butterworths, 1961a. Pp. 162–174.

Goldman-Eisler, F. A comparative study of two hesitation phenomena. *Language and Speech*, 1961b, 4: 18–26.

Lounsbury, F. G. Sequential psycholinguistics. In Osgood, C. E., and Sebeok, T. A. (eds.), Psycholinguistics: A survey of theory and research problems. *J. abnorm. soc. Psychol.*, 1954, 49, suppl.: 93–125.

Maclay, H., and Osgood, C. E. Hesitation phenomena in spontaneous English speech. *Word*, 1959, 15 (1): 19–44.

Mahl, G. F. Disturbances and silences in the patient's speech in psychotherapy. *J. abnorm. soc. Psychol.*, 1956, 53: 1–15.

Mahl, G. F. Exploring emotional states by content analysis. In I. De Sola Pool (ed.), *Trends in content analysis*. Urbana: University of Illinois Press, 1959. Pp. 89–130.

Osgood, C. E. The representational model and relevant research methods. In I. De Sola Pool (ed.), *Trends in content analysis*. Urbana: University of Illinois Press, 1959. Pp. 33–88.

Shannon, C. E. Prediction and entropy of printed English. *Bell System tech. J.*, 1951, 30: 50-64.

Stolz, W., and Tannenbaum, P. H. Effects of feedback on oral encoding behavior. *Language and Speech*, 1963, 6: 218-228.

Taylor, W. L. "Cloze procedure": A new tool for measuring readability. *Journ. quart.*, 1953, 30: 415-433.

Taylor, W. L. Application of "cloze" and entropy measures to the study of contextual constraint in samples of continuous prose. Unpublished doctoral dissertation, University of Illinois, 1954.

Wilson, K. The information theory approach. In Osgood, C. E., and Sebeok, T. A. (eds.), Psycholinguistics: A survey of theory and research problems. *J. abnorm. soc. Psychol.*, 1954, 49, suppl.: 35-49.

Part Three

THE IMPACT OF SOCIAL RELATIONS ON LINGUISTIC ATTRIBUTES

9

THE OPERANT CONDITIONING OF CONVERSATION

Gilbert Levin
David Shapiro

One describable feature of any conversation is the order in which the speakers converse. This order may be an important property of social behavior. These experiments were designed to test whether differentially reinforcing a group of speakers, when the contingency respects the order in which they have spoken, would tend to increase the frequency of speaking in that order.

EXPERIMENTAL PROCEDURE

Several Ss are asked to carry on a conversation in order to reach a series of unanimous decisions on which of several possible solutions to a problem is the correct solution. After each decision, the instructions require that the group stop the conversation and wait silently until it is informed whether or not its solution is correct. Each unanimous decision constitutes one "trial."

Speakers in a three-person group are designated A, B, and C.

Reprinted from *Journal of the Experimental Analysis of Behavior* 5, No. 3 (July 1962): 309–16. Copyright 1962 by the Society for the Experimental Analysis of Behavior, Inc. Footnotes have been renumbered.

The record of conversation may look like this:

  (a) Trial 1—ABCABCA
  (b) Hypothesis X
  (c) Silence
  (d) Intervention
  (e) Trial 2—CBACBA . . .

The first item (a) is a list of the sequence of all speakers during that trial. Next (b), there is an indication of the hypothesis the group chose unanimously which brought an immediate end to (a) and ushered in (c), leading then to (d). The experimenter's intervention consists of telling or signalling the group that its hypothesis is correct or incorrect. What the group is told is determined by some property of (a) which is the response the experiment is designed to bring under control. In no case is the whole of (a) taken into account. Immediately after (d), the group begins (e) and the whole process is repeated without interruption, with the number of trials ranging from 50 to 165. Length of an *S*'s speech or of a group's trial is not fixed, and experimental sessions last from 30 min. to more than 2 hrs.

RESULTS

Experiment I

In the first experiment, four college students were seated at random around a table on which there were two stimulus cards. Cards I and X of the standard Rorschach series were used. They were told that they were participating in an experiment in mental telephathy. It was their job to send messages telephatically to a "receiver" (who was a role player) in an adjoining room. They were asked to discuss and decide which of the two messages on the table to try to send to the receiver. They were encouraged to relax and to use their imaginations freely. As soon as they all agreed on a single message, they were asked to stop talking immediately and concentrate on that message as they waited for the receiver to come into the room. The receiver indicated which message had been received by pointing and saying "this."

Two of the four *S*s, designated A and B, were selected at random as experimental Ss. The behavior of the remaining Ss was completely disregarded. During each trial, a record was kept of the order in which A and B spoke.

A trial was reinforced; *i.e.*, the receiver claimed to have correctly received the message selected by the group, only if the last utterance of B followed the last utterance of A. Attention was paid to the last few speakers in the trial on the assumption that a group learns a social response more effectively when the delay between the response and its reinforcement is at a minimum. The following is a sample protocol:

Trial	Sequence	Intervention
1	ACBDCBDAC*BA*	not reinforced
2	CBACBC*AB*	reinforced
3	DBACB*A*C*B*D	reinforced
4	DCACD*BA*DC	not reinforced

The psychological hypothesis is sufficiently straightforward: The frequency of AB is expected to increase as a function of the number of reinforced trials. On the other hand, the statistical hypothesis leaves some room for choice. One possibility is to take a sample of the behavior from an early part of the experiment and another from a later part and test the difference between the two observed frequencies. A second possibility is to make some use of a theoretical frequency. Irrespective of the individual frequencies of A and B, they should appear in sequence equally often as AB or BA.

Neither of these approaches is ideal. The first approach is a rather stringent test. Because the experimental conditions have been in effect throughout the 50-trial experiment, a comparison of the early trials with the later ones is really a test of the difference between two levels of the experimental effect. A much longer experiment would minimize this factor. The addition of an initial "emitted behavior" or operant period in which no reinforcement is given would provide a base line for comparison with the achieved level of learning. Both of these solutions make for less economical use of experimental time than in this experiment.

The expected frequency approach is considerably more efficent for these data. It assumes a level of emitted behavior and allows all observations to be reckoned as a measure of the experimental effect. The disadvantage of such an approach is the degree

Table 1.   **Frequency of Two-Person Verbal Sequences in Experiment I**

		Sequence	
Trials		*AB*	*BA*
1–5		1	4
6–10		3	2
11–15		3	2
16–20		4	1
21–25		3	2
	Total	14	11
26–30		5	0
31–35		3	2
36–40		4	1
41–45		5	0
46–50		4	1
	Total	21	4
	Grand total	35	15

of uncertainty associated with the assumption, namely, that the pre-experimental level of AB=BA= 50 percent. The assumption is probably accurate for the sampling of a large number of groups, but any conclusion based on the performance of a particular group, or two or three groups, is open to question.

One way to test the assumption for a particular group is to compare that group's performance in a block of early trials with the expected frequencies, accepting the assumption as tenable if the null hypothesis (AB=BA) cannot be rejected. This procedure is not free from defects either; with a small sample size, the probability of accepting the null hypothesis is high if the true difference is not large. On the other hand, the fact that the experimental conditions are in effect during the first block of trials might have the opposite effect on the null hypothesis. Recognizing the difficulties of both the empirical and the theoretical approaches, the latter was arbitrarily chosen in the analysis. In recent studies, as yet unpublished, base-line measures were obtained by using random reinforcement procedures.

The results of Experiment I are given in Table 1. The pattern AB occurred in 35 trials out of a total of 50. This proportion ($\frac{7}{10}$) is significantly greater than the expected $\frac{1}{2}$ ($\chi^2 = 8.0$; $P < .01$). The results in the first set of 25 trials (14 out of 25) look different enough from the second set (21 out of 25) to cast serious doubt on the possibility that AB would have been the more frequent pattern in the absence of the experimental conditions.

Table 2. Frequency of Three-Person Verbal Sequences in Experiment II

	Sequence											
	Heterogeneous						Homogeneous					
Trials	ABC	ACB	BAC	BCA	CAB	CBA	ABA	ACA	BAB	BCB	CAC	CBC
1–25	5	2	4	1	3	3	0	1	1	2	3	0
26–50	7	1	4	3	1	2	1	1	1	1	1	2
51–75	7	1	4	2	2	2	0	0	1	1	1	4
76–100	8	2	3	1	0	2	0	0	1	3	4	1
101–125	7	0	7	2	3	2	1	0	0	1	2	1
Total	34	6	22	9	9	11	1	2	4	8	11	8
Grand total			91						34			

Experiment II

A second experiment was designed to permit a test of the hypothesis that a *three-person sequence* can be conditioned. Three Ss took part in this 125-trial experiment, and in each trial the last three speakers were recorded. Because no speaker can precede himself, each trial has 12 possible outcomes: ABC, ACB, BAC, BCA, CAB, CBA, ABA, ACA, BAB, BCB, CAC, or CBC. The last six of these (hereafter called homogeneous patterns) were expected to occur infrequently because of the nature of the instructions emphasizing *group* decision. And this was the case. In all, these patterns occurred 34 times out of a total of 125. (See Table 2.) For purposes of the analysis to follow, the trials with homogenous outcomes are omitted.

Two of the six heterogeneous patterns, ABC and BAC, are of special interest. The response ABC was chosen as the one to be reinforced. The expectation is that the frequency of ABC will increase as a function of reinforcement. But an increase in ABC is not a guarantee that this specific conversational pattern has been conditioned. Suppose that C alone learns to speak last in every trial. In this case, a critical test is that of the difference between the frequency of ABC and BAC. Because these are the only two three-person outcomes in which C can occur last, a preponderance of ABC over BAC would be evidence that the social response has been conditioned.[1]

Table 2 gives the results of Experiment II. The response ABC occurred a total of 34 times out of 91 heterogeneous trials. This ratio is significantly greater than the $\frac{1}{6}$ chance expectancy ($\chi^2 = 48.0$; $P < .001$). The difference between ABC and BAC is in the predicted direction, but it is not significant ($\chi^2 = 2.6$; $P < .10$).

The frequency of ABC when plotted against trial number lacks some of the properties of a typical acquisition curve. The correct response occurred first at the second trial, and then it did not occur again until the 22nd trial. At this point, it shows an upward spurt which is maintained but does not accelerate further during the remainder of the experiment. (See Table 2.) The Ss exhibited mounting impatience with the experiment, beginning somewhere between trial 50 and 100. This impatience grew to such proportions between the 100th and 125th trial that the experiment which had been planned for 150 trials had to be terminated after 125 trials in a total time of 2 hrs. and 45 min.

REVISED EXPERIMENTAL PROCEDURE

The work following Experiment II was devoted primarily to increasing the amount of information obtained per unit time, simplifying the instructions, and improving the conditions of observation. To accomplish these goals, a number of innovations were made in (a) the position of the experimenter, (b) the form of reinforcement, (c) the nature of the task, and (d) the method of recording data.

(1) In the first two experiments, the experimenter was in full view of the *S*s. This led to difficulties on two counts. First, it was a possible source of contamination. The *S*s may have been responding to unintended cues presented by the experimenter. Second, the continued presence of the experimenter made it possible for the group to communicate with him in spite of instructions to the contrary, thus disrupting the flow of conversation. For these reasons, and with the knowledge of the *S*s, the experimenter was removed to the other side of a one-way screen.

(2) Reinforcement delivered personally by a serious-looking stranger added interest to the task but was wasteful of experimental time. A tone defined as "correct" and a buzzer defined as "incorrect" replaced the human receiver, with the result of a saving in time greater than 50 percent.

(3) The task of the *S*s was altered in two respects. Instead of looking at several stimulus cards and deciding among them, the *S*s are seated around a table on which a bank of different-colored lights is arranged in a circle. The number of lights can be varied from one to six. Each *S* has before him a small control box with a number of buttons on it corresponding in number and color to the lights in the center of the table. A central light can be turned on only if all three *S*s press the appropriate button. The light remains on as long as all three buttons are held down.[2] The *S*s are asked to decide unanimously among the colors and to turn on the appropriate light the instant a decision is made and to keep it on while remaining silent until they are signalled right or wrong. This serves to bring a more clear-cut finish to each trial, to inhibit conversation while waiting for reinforcement, and to facilitate recording of hypotheses made by subjects.

Another change in the task was to instruct the *S*s that they were to play a guessing game rather than to attempt mental telepathy. They were told that the experimenter has a long list of color names in the next room comprised in the colors before them, and they were to guess the items in this list. The effect of this change seems to depend on the attitudes of the *S*s. It may reduce interest in the task, but it also prevents the extremely hostile disruptive reaction observed in one *S* in the second experiment who was avowedly anti-ESP. The guessing-game procedure may be more nearly free of complications for most *S*s.

(4) A persistent difficulty is obtaining an accurate record of the sequence of speakers. This is essential, not only as a means of measuring the experimental effect, but also for deciding, on the spot, whether or not a trial is to receive reinforcement. Incorrect reinforcements may entirely wash out the effect of the independent variable. Sound recordings of the experimental sessions were made, but they offered little help as a postmeeting accuracy check because of the difficulty of identifying voices, particularly in speeches of only one or two words.

In discussing observer reliability, some of the reactions of *S*s to the experimental procedure should be described. They have expressed a wide range of attitudes, ranging from a request from members of one group to "do it again for a hundred trials" to quite negative sentiments in another

Apart from these group differences, some of the important determiners of behavior seem to be (a) the percent reinforced trials, (b) the number of hypotheses the group is asked to choose from, and (c) the ratio of (a) to (b). In Experiment I, two stimulus cards (*i.e.*, two possible hypotheses) were presented to the group. This matched very well with the chance probability of the response. The AB sequence would occur about one-half the time by chance; and because the presence of two stimuli led to the same subjective probability estimate, the experiment made sense to the *S*s. At the beginning, they were correct in about one-half of the trials, and gradually the ratio changed in the direction they would expect if mental telephathy were taking place.

In Experiment II and in subsequent experiments, the sequential response sometimes had an expectancy different from 50 percent. When the sequential response is expected to occur in one out of six trials, the choice of one out of two hypotheses would tend to make the group feel that it was not doing well, even after the rate of the response had increased appreciably.

In both Experiments I and II, we were careful to create some sort of correspondence between these two sets of probabilities. In the second experiment, in which the correct sequence response was expected to occur by chance somewhat less often than in

$\frac{1}{6}$ of the trials, the group was given six hypotheses to choose from. This rather precise matching of the two sets of probabilities proved to be not entirely adequate. The rate of the correct response increased appreciably, and so did the rate of reinforcement. Nevertheless in postmeeting questionaries and interviews, the group felt that the experiment had been a failure.

In some groups, the procedure resulted in so much frustration that the Ss were unwilling to carry out the instructions. A number of solutions were attempted; but, finally, the sequence response itself had to be changed for one with a higher probability. The most successful combination proved to be three stimuli and a sequence response with probability .50. With these values, the groups were compliant, trials were short, and task satisfaction was relatively high.

The variety of these behaviors was reflected in differences in interobserver reliability scores gathered on several groups. Two observers, one experienced and one inexperienced, kept a record of an 80-trial experiment. In this experiment, the group was asked to choose from six hypotheses; the expected frequency of the sequence response was somewhat less than $\frac{1}{6}$; and the final three speakers were focussed upon. On 17 of these trials, one or both of the observers were unable to record complete data. Of the remaining 63 observed trials, the two observers were in complete agreement 18 times, or 29 percent of the time. This result is typical for the groups that worked under conditions of low rate of reinforcement.

When the experimental procedure was less frustrating, observation seemed easier and the data more reliable. In a 165-trial experiment (Experiment IV, discussed below), in which the group was asked to choose from three hypotheses and the expected frequency of the sequence response was $\frac{1}{2}$, and in which the last two speakers were focussed upon, two observers produced incomplete data in 43 trials. Of the remaining 122 trials, the observers were in complete agreement in 112 trials, or 92 percent complete agreement.

RESULTS

In both Experiments III and IV, the revised procedures discussed above were used, and reliable measures were found of the order of conversation. The Ss in each group were three boy scouts of fairly equal rank in their organization who knew one another before the experiment but were not close friends. The colored-light apparatus with three possible hypotheses was used; the instructions were those of the guessing game task. Reinforcement was in the form of a tone signifying "correct" and a buzzer signifying "incorrect."

The last two speakers in each trial were recorded, giving six possible outcomes: AB, BC, CA, BA, CB, and AC. Positive reinforcement was given after every occurrence of AB, BC, and CA (clockwise patterns). The remaining three outcomes (counterclockwise patterns) received negative reinforcement. By chance, the conversational pattern to be reinforced is expected to occur half the time.

We predicted that the reinforced clockwise patterns would occur more frequently than the counterclockwise patterns and that each clockwise pattern would occur more frequently than its counterclockwise mate (matched for individual rates of responding), *i.e.*, AB > BA, BC > CB, and CA > AC.

Tables 3 and 4 summarize the results for Experiments III and IV, respectively.

In Experiment III, both the general predictions (total clockwise > total counterclockwise) and specific predictions (AB >

Table 3.　Frequency of Two-Person Verbal Sequences per Block of 15 Trials in Experiment III

| | | | | *Verbal sequence* | | | |
| | | | | | | | One speaker |
Trials	AB	BC	CA	BA	CB	AC	only
1–15	3	3	3	1	2	2	1
16–30	1	2	2	3	3	2	2
31–45	3	3	3	1	2	3	0
46–60	2	5	2	0	4	2	0
61–75	3	3	3	1	2	3	0
76–90	6	5	1	1	1	1	0
91–105	2	8	2	0	3	0	0
106–120	3	3	2	1	6	0	0
121–135	0	5	1	3	1	2	3
136–150	2	4	2	2	1	0	4
151–165	0	6	0	4	2	0	3
Total	25	47	21	17	27	15	13
		Clockwise			Counterclockwise		
		patterns			patterns		
Grand total		93			59		13

Table 4. Frequency of Two-Person Verbal Sequences per Block of 15 Trials in Experiment IV

				Verbal sequence			
Trials	AB	BC	CA	BA	CB	AC	*One speaker only*
1–15	2	5	3	0	1	0	4
16–30	2	1	1	1	6	2	2
31–45	1	3	2	1	3	1	4
46–60	0	4	1	2	3	2	3
61–75	1	5	2	0	5	1	1
76–90	1	3	3	1	2	1	4
91–105	0	5	0	0	2	3	5
106–120	1	7	0	1	1	1	4
121–135	1	3	1	1	2	1	6
136–150	0	5	1	0	1	0	8
151–165	1	7	0	0	0	1	6
Total	10	48	14	7	26	13	47
		Clockwise patterns			Counterclockwise patterns		
Grand total		72			46		47

BA, BC > CB, and CA > AC) are in the expected direction, although the latter differences are significant only for the BC-CB comparison. Table 5 shows the chi square values.

The results of Experiment IV closely resemble those for Experiment III. The total clockwise versus counterclockwise and the three specific pattern differences are all in the expected direction,

Table 5. Chi Square Tests on Frequencies of Verbal-sequence Pairs

Sequence pair	*Clockwise*	*Counterclockwise*	χ^2	*Degrees of freedom*	*P*
		Experiment III			
AB BA	25	17	1.5	1	P < .15
BC CB	47	27	5.4	1	P < .01
CA AC	21	15	1.0	1	P < .20
Total	93	59	7.5	1	P < .005
		Experiment IV			
AB BA	10	7	0.5	1	P < .25
BC CB	48	26	6.5	1	P < .01
CA AC	14	13	0.03	1	P < .45
Total	72	46	5.8	1	P < .01

although two of the latter are very small. Again, the BC-CB comparison yields the only significant difference. (See Table 5).[3]

The results of Experiments III and IV confirm the hypothesis that preselected conversational sequences would occur more frequently than others. The results also indicate that not all of the three possible conversational patterns increased in frequency, but, rather only one of them. In Experiment III, this finding is highlighted in trial blocks 91–105 and 151–165; in Experiment IV, similarly, it is definite by trial block 91–105 and persists until the end of the trial run.

In effect, both groups appeared to learn a more specific social response, namely, of one person talking last, preceded by a specific other person, and not a general positional response (clockwise or counterclockwise). The next-to-last speaker functions as a discriminative stimulus for a given speaker whose final response brings reinforcement.

Reinforcing a category of two-person sequences may have served to "shape up" a specific conversation sequence. Scrutiny of the results in Tables 3 and 4 indicates the relative fixing of a specific clockwise sequence at about the fourth trial block (46–60). This same sequence is relatively higher than each of the remaining sequences, trial block by trial block, until the end of the runs.

An interesting exception is apparent in trial block 106–120 in Experiment III: CB occurred six times, whereas in the previous block, BC occurred eight times. The reinforcement of conversation between two persons, B and C, in one direction, B to C, seemed to generalize to its reverse sequence, C to B. By the same token, Speaker A learned to be quiet during this particular section of the conversation.

No specific hypothesis was made about increases over time in the frequency of given conversational patterns as a function of the number of reinforced trials. Such a change was observed for the single sequence (BC), as Tables 3 and 4 show. However, the acquisition of this response does not follow an incremental path, but rather seems to become stabilized at some point along the way.

DISCUSSION

We have shown in this paper how the operant conditioning of serial order of conversation may be carried out. In postgroup interviews with subjects, not one noticed a connection between conversational

sequence and getting the right answers, although several sus-
pected that the guessing game was rigged in some way. During the
experimental sessions themselves, Ss offered a great variety of complex and often inconsistent hypotheses to account for their increasing success in figuring out how the experimenter devised his list
of colors.

The results of the studies are all consistent with the hypothesis
that the order of speakers in a conversation can be brought under
experimental control by manipulating the variable of group reinforcement—success and failure—in a task in which the group has
to make a number of unanimous decisions about a number of
hypotheses. In each group, a conversational sequence became established at a given level after about 50 to 100 trials, or within a
half-hour of conversation.

Further studies are now proceeding on the acquisition and ex-
tinction of conversational patterns in three-person groups and on the
basic assumptions of the operant techniques used. The procedure
is also being adapted to study the course and stability of other
kinds of social responses under different conditions of group reinforcement.

NOTES

[1]So far, we have ignored the possible influences upon the results of each individual's overall rate of responding. In a three-person situation in which no person
may precede himself, the upper limit for any participant is slightly more than 50
percent of the total number of speeches. If C learned simply to talk a great deal,
to a degree approaching the limit, the frequency of outcomes which include C
would increase relative to those outcomes which do not. It would have a still
greater effect on those homogeneous outcomes which include C as both ultimate
and antepenultimate speaker (*i.e.*, CAC and CBC). However, this effect would
not alter the significance of a difference between ABC and BAC.

[2]The experimental apparatus was designed and constructed by Bernard
Tursky, Instrumentation Engineer.

[3]The seat positions and clock patterns were not in fact the same for Experiments III and IV; and the specific verbal sequence was clockwise in one instance,
and the reverse in the other. The learning was therefore not the same spatially
in both groups. Results were expressed in similar terms for simplicity.

10

POWER, INFLUENCE, AND PATTERN OF COMMUNICATION

Kurt W. Back

This article deals with the patterns of interaction and communication through which a person makes his intent to influence known to other people, and the different effects these patterns may have.

Before stating an abstract theoretical scheme on the function of communication in this context, let us first define a few terms, namely: power, influence, and authority. Only situations in which one person wishes to change another's behavior will be considered. The degree to which a person is able to do this will be called *power*. We can conceive of a person as a system with a describable input and output, and we can infer the internal state. The overt output we will call *action*; the inferred state of the internal system that determines which outputs will be used will be stipulated *attitude*. The kind of power that changes attitudes is defined as *influence*, and that which changes or produces action as *authority*. It is thus possible to have influence without authority and authority with little or no influence. However, authority combined with in-

From Leadership and Interpersonal Behavior edited by Luigi Petrullo and Bernard M. Bass. Copyright © 1961 by Holt, Rinehart and Winston, Inc. Adapted and reprinted by permission of Holt, Rinehart and Winston, Inc. The article was written as part of the program of the Organizational Research Group of the Institute for Research in Social Science, University of North Carolina, which was supported by the Office of Naval Research [Nonr-855(04)].

fluence will be more enduring as the predisposition of the person to later act spontaneously is changed, while direct authority is represented typically by compliance to one command.

In the following sections we will propose several hypotheses about conditions under which influence and authority are exerted. Before doing so we will present a general model from which specific relations can be derived. In turn, these relations can be interpreted as the proposed hypotheses.

THE MODEL

The model we use to visualize the different patterns of communication and interaction is taken from automata theory. In this theory simplified mechanisms are constructed with specified properties of input and output. The units—called fibers—correspond to logical operators by whose aid a theory can be constructed. These units are also physically similar to nerve fibers and thus simulate a nerve network. A psychological theory constructed in this way is at least locally compatible with a physiological substratum.

The fiber is a system with several inputs and one output; each input and output is represented by a line. The output reacts (the fiber fires) after a time delay during which a certain number of inputs are stimulated. The number of inputs necessary for firing is a characteristic of the fiber. In addition, some inputs can be inhibitory, cancelling out active stimulation. Thus a fiber which will fire when one input is stimulated needs two stimulations if one inhibitory input is stimulated.

Specific types and combinations of fibers can be constructed and are called organs. One of these, the majority organ, is important for application of the theory: it is a fiber that will fire if a majority of its inputs are stimulated. For instance, if there are three inputs, at least two of them must be stimulated before the organ will fire. Logically this corresponds to a disjunction of three conjunctions. For example, if we call the three input lines a, b, and c, then (a and b), or (a and c), or (b and c), or (a and b and c) must be active. It can be shown that this organ is self-sufficient to perform all logical operations. In other words, a message, analyzed into its logical components and used as input, will be represented by the output pattern.

We can now construct a system from these basic units representing the relations of inputs and outputs to interpersonal inter-actions. A system of this kind has to account for two effects: a direct effect on output and an indirect effect that changes the organism with respect to future reactions to output.

The system must have two levels of functioning, both of which work like majority organs. That is, inputs are distributed such that a certain critical proportion of live inputs is necessary for one unit to fire and a certain proportion of firing units is necessary for the whole system to fire.

(a) In the first system, a stimulation of any kind may leave an input live and thus less stimulation is needed the next time for the whole system to fire. The scaler may include a memory and thus may be more easily stimulated after earlier stimulations. We shall call this first set the *attitude system.*

(b) The second set fires when a specified majority of its input system has been stimulated. As its inputs are the outputs of the attitude set, this means that it will be active if a certain level of attitude is reached. We shall call this system the *motoric* (or action) *system.*

We have now constructed a model of a person that can account for the two effects we have mentioned. Inputs may change the attitude system without leading to overt output, but in so doing they change the probability of a later output. If the attitude system is in a favorable condition, then an additional stimulus may fire the motoric system and hence produce an output for the whole system, without changing attitudes appreciably.

INTERPRETATION OF THE SYSTEM

We restate the condition formally to conform with the model:

(1) Behavior at any time is a function of communication and of the state of a person at a previous time; this describes the effect of authority communication.

(2) The state of the person at any time is a function of the state of the person at a previous time and a communication at a previous time; this describes the effect of influence communication.

We can further interpret multiplexing (the uses of bundles of inputs) as repetition of the content of messages in different form. One bundle corresponds to a certain kind of information, but each fiber corresponds to a different way of putting the message across.

FOUR HYPOTHESES

The system leads to some derivations about the effect of particular kinds of inputs or communications. Let us assume that some of the fibers in one bundle are stimulated. This will change some of the organs in the attitude system toward a higher probability of firing. Increase in stimulation can proceed in two ways: an increasing number of fibers in the same bundle can be stimulated or some fibers in the other bundles can be stimulated.

In the first case, there will be an increase of readiness in all parts of the attitude system. This situation is therefore unlikely to increase the attitude above a critical level and to translate an impulse into overt action. Interpreted, this means that the same content transmitted in different forms will change attitudes but is unlikely to lead to corresponding actions.

In the second case, fewer of the units or elements of the attitude system are likely to be stimulated, but in some of the elements the increase will amount to several steps. Hence some of the units will have sufficient proportion of live inputs and will be active, and there is an appreciable likelihood of the attitude system reaching a critical level, firing, and stimulating the motoric system. With a great distribution of input bundles being stimulated weakly, it is possible that just enough impulses will come out of the attitude system to fire the motoric system. In this case we have an output, but the situation is clearly unstable and depends on the input being kept up. This means that many messages of different content will lead to action, especially when favorable attitudes are present, but the action is unlikely to be kept up.

Thus we have two hypotheses about the power of differing types of communication:

Hypothesis 1. Repetition of the same or similar content in different form will lead to change in attitude, but not necessarily to corresponding actions; that is, these messages will have influence.

Hypothesis 2. Single messages of differing content will lead to transition between attitude and action; this type of communication is appropriate to the exercise of authority, with only a fleeting change of attitude.

Going beyond the individual system, it is possible to make some inferences about the conditions under which different types of communication will be used and under which authority and influence will occur.

Let us consider the situation in which the attitudes of all participants are stable and also similar. Stability will occur when, in each unit, more fibers than the critical proportion are stimulated. Then the units will keep firing even if some lines are changed to inactive conditions. Messages that run counter to the prevailing attitude—that neutralize part of the input—will be insufficient to change the attitude. The output of each person, in this case, will reflect a fairly constant attitude and thus be constant itself. It will be repetitious in content. As the attitudes overlap, most of the communications will be conforming to the attitudes already existing and thus reinforce these attitudes. These are the conditions for producing influence.

The conditions describe the situation of individuals who agree strongly on many issues; whose interaction serves mainly to reinforce this common core in various ways until the attitudes are identical. This also implies that no individual has a different function and that the roles are interchangeable. This description tends to identify a team, in the sense of a group with "we-feeling" or "group spirit." As the theory does not include the motivation of members to enter a group but only the communication patterns, the usual definition of the group in terms of cohesiveness cannot be used. It has been shown, however, that groups defined in the two ways are closely related.

Because of high redundancy, the relation of output to input in these systems will be low. However, the possible long-run effects may compensate for this low efficiency in the short run, and result in the creation of common attitudes that will lead to easier triggering and hence greater efficiency on later occasions. The relationship of amount of communication to efficiency depends therefore on the kind of redundancy, whether content or form, and on the time span considered.

The opposite condition is one in which all the systems are different and unstable. They are likely to send out varied impulses resulting in behavior by other systems. This behavior will be varied as different attitudes are activated by different messages. As the messages will differ in content they will stimulate different bundles and perpetuate the differences in output of the different systems. These differences are not random variations as they are determined by the outputs of the other systems. In fact, we have here a model of functional interdependence.

The conditions of the systems describe a situation in which each member of an organization has a different role or function; hence his messages will be different, pertaining to a certain action the recipient has to carry out. All recipients will be ready to carry out these actions, but their general attitudes are not likely to be affected. The processes described are thus characteristic of a formal organizational setup, the condition for authority relation.

We can summarize the results of our conditions of the interactions of the systems in two additional hypotheses:

Hypothesis 3. Communication that is redundant in content but varied in form is
   a. Likely to occur in cohesive groups
   b. Likely to lead to a common framework of attitudes within a social system.

Hypothesis 4. Communication that consists of messages on different topics with little redundancy in content is
   a. Likely to occur in functionally interdependent formal organizations
   b. Likely to lead to effective action within a social system.

TYPES OF CONDITIONS

This set of hypotheses can be summarized by constructing four types of communication situations out of the combination of redundancy of form and content:

1. If both form and content are low in redundancy, we have the vivid kind of discussion, varied in content, that is characteristic of interpersonal, sociable situations.

2. If the content is high on information and the form is stereotyped or redundant, we have the organizational setup that performs work without changing opinions.

3. If content is redundant but the form is varied, the communication is of the kind we associate with primary, face-to-face groups that have influence on attitudes but frequently do not lead to any corresponding actions.

4. Finally, if both form and content are redundant, communication becomes a ritual. This ritualistic communication is mainly characteristic of the sacred type of social structure, uniting a great number of people in common beliefs and common actions.

THREE APPLICATIONS OF THE MODEL

A. A Field Experiment: Communication in Planned Social Change

The preceding four hypotheses provide a set of relationships between group structure, communication, and the effects of attitudes and action. Although they have been stated as four different principles, the significance of the whole set will be illustrated to clarify the implications of the system and the operational meanings of the terms. The following is an experiment on educational methods of promoting family planning in Puerto Rico; (Back, Hill, and Stycos, 1957a; Hill, Stycos, and Back, 1959). The same experiment was replicated in its essential features in Jamaica and let to substantially the same results (Stycos and Back, 1965).

As subjects of this study a representative sample of rural lower-class families was selected. The wives in the families were matched on attitude toward family planning, adequacy of family organization (adequate communication between husband and wife), and information about methods of family planning. On the basis of previous research, these three sets of variables were assumed to represent the internal set necessary for action on family planning. The subjects could be classified into those who were favorable on all three factors and those who were deficient on one of them. The content of the educational program was designed to produce favorable changes in one or more of the factors.

The educational program was transmitted by two methods: group meetings and distribution of pamphlets. The two methods correspond roughly to the two modes of communication described in the previous section. Meetings employed a variety of techniques that put the main points into different forms. The effort to have all group members participate resulted in much repetition and weighing of the same content from different points of view. This method thus can be seen as an application of the second mode. Pamphlets are of necessity much more direct and less repetitious. In this case especially, the text was kept to a low-literacy level that prevented elaboration of the points to be made and kept the language structure to the repetitiousness of primer level.

The effect of the two methods shows a sharp division in change of readiness for action, start of action, and consistent continuation of it. Some of the respondents had been using contraception, although not consistently or efficiently, while others had never used any.

Table 1. Influence of Type of Communication on Start, Consistency and Reinforcement of Use (Field experiment in contraception)

	Nonuser		User	
	Meetings	Pamphlets	Meetings	Pamphlets
Positive effect * in				
Reinterview	31%	55%	50%	29%
User in follow-up	67%	58%	79%	80%
Nonuser in follow-up	33%	42%	21%	20%
No positive effect in				
Reinterview	69%	45%	50%	71%
User in follow-up	38%	19%	89%	56%
Nonuser in follow-up	62%	81%	11%	44%
N	42	60	38	35

Positive effect means any use of contraception by nonusers and change to a better method or improvement in regularity by users. (From Table 127, Hill, Stycos and Back, 1959.)

Pamphlets were more likely than meetings to result in prompt action. Meetings tended to insure that action was consistently maintained and had a stronger effect on those women who had been using some birth-control method.

The repetitious messages in meetings stabilize a few parts of the attitude system. If sufficient parts are activated at all (and sometimes later events or perhaps even the stimulation of reinterview will do that) the resulting activation of the motoric system will result in a consistently maintained action.

These results are in accordance with the first two hypotheses. The conditions under which these two communication systems were employed corresponded almost of necessity to the group and functional organization: the meetings were conducted in groups and techniques were adapted to the creation of influential group atmospheres. On the other hand, the pamphlets were delivered, without any discussion, by a messenger who had a clearly defined, somewhat distant, function from the respondents.

Content Analysis

Redundancy and variety in form of the message can be measured by comparing the length and structure of the different sentences in the message. An analysis of parts of speech can give a rough measure of the quantity of information in a passage or a message. If we want to send a message that contains a maximum of information in a minimum of words (as in a cable with high word rates) the main words to be used will be nouns or adjectives. It is reasonable to use the ratio of nouns and adjectives to total words as a measure of information.

In line with the first two hypotheses, communications that have as their main intent and effect change of attitude will show great variation in form and a relatively low percentage of the "content words" (nouns and adjectives). The reverse will be true of communications that intend to initiate action. An analysis of this kind was made on two topics in which action or attitudes may be induced: politics and religion.

As an example of political power, two speeches by Franklin D. Roosevelt were analyzed (Zevin, 1946). Both were given in the same year, 1940; they were carried over national radio networks, and hence had the same potential audience. The context of the two speeches was different, however. The first was given at the beginning of the year at a Jackson Day dinner for party officials.

It was directed mainly at people with a favorable attitude quite in advance of any concrete action (election campaign). This speech was intended principally to reinforce attitudes. The second speech was given at a party rally at Madison Square Garden, one week before the Presidential election. This speech was directed at immediately obtaining votes, hence to initiate a specific action. The two speeches represent an attitude and an action appeal.

In the field of religion, sermons of two contemporary ministers with considerable popular appeal were compared: Billy Graham and Norman Vincent Peale. Both religious leaders exert their power in favor of a religious revival and both appeal to wide-range audiences that probably overlap considerably. Graham is a revivalist who urges an immediate "testimony" of revelation, while Peale exhorts his listeners to follow a general way of life ("positive thinking"). Graham represents an action-arousing and Peale an attitude-changing message. One of each minister's most effective sermons was used: Graham's "America's Decision," (given in 1953) and Peale's (Poling, 1944) "The Power Flows from the Cross."

In each of the four speeches the first fifty sentences were analyzed. As measures of variation of form, the variances of the sentence length, of the number of subordinate clauses, and of the proportions of nouns and of adjectives to total number of words in the sentences were used. Measures of information in the sentences were the mean proportion of nouns and adjectives. Table 2 shows the results of this analysis. With one exception the variances are larger in the attitude communications than in the corresponding action communications, most of them significantly so. On the other hand, although there is a consistent numerical difference in the predicted direction of the mean proportion of nouns and adjectives, only one of the four is statistically significant. As the differences in variances may be related to corresponding differences in means, especially between the two religious leaders, the relative dispersions (coefficients of variation) are also shown. In general, these coefficients preserve the differences shown in the variances; only one difference, that in the variability of number of subordinate clauses between Graham and Peale, seems to be due to the differences in means. On the other hand, the large reversal—in the variance of proportion of adjectives between the same two speeches —is also accounted for by the difference in the mean proportion, and the coefficients of variance differ in the predicted direction.

The type of content analysis of communications that has been proposed here shows itself as a first approximation to con-

Table 2.   Uniformity and Information in Attitude and Action Appeals

	Political (F. D. Roosevelt)			Religious		
	Attitude (Jackson Day)	Action (Madison Square Garden)	Significance of difference or of F ratio	Attitude (Peale)	Action (Graham)	Significance of difference or of F ratio
Variability in form						
Words per sentence						
Variance	558.08	182.81	<1%	206.00	69.70	<1%
Coefficient of variation	.8544	.5696		.6239	.5543	
Subordinate clauses per sentence						
Variance	1.91	1.05	<5%	2.97	.76	<1%
Coefficient of variation	1.50	1.13		1.32	1.5625	
Percent nouns in sentence						
Variance	118.00	36.78	<1%	88.52	76.19	ns
Coefficient of variation	.4862	.2527		.4613	.3856	
Percent adjective in sentence						
Variance	63.00	57.55	ns	30.08	110.46	[<1%]*
Coefficient of variation	.8277	.6465		.8145	.0852	
Measures of information						
Mean percent of nouns	22.42	23.98	ns	20.40	22.64	ns
Mean percent of adjectives	9.58	11.74	ns	6.74	12.32	<1%
N	50	50		50	50	

*Contrary to hypothesis

sistent measurement of information content and as a lead to data that confirm the theoretical model. The action communications have more nouns and adjectives, they have more uniform sentences that vary less in length and organization than the attitude communications. At the same time, the method is still quite crude and needs supplementation. In a different context, Yule (1944) has developed a method of vocabulary analysis, counting the occurrences of different words in an author's work. Yule defines a statistic K that measures the degree of occurrences of words. A large K designates certain words that are more likely to be used than others. Repetition of a word implies a degree of redundancy, that is, repetition of information. We can thus advance the hypothesis that the size of the K coefficient will be related to the attempts to influence attitudes through writing. The ranking of K coefficients in texts analyzed by Yule is as follows: the Gospel according to St. John has the largest coefficient; next comes Thomas à Kempis, a medieval monk and devotional writer; next John Bunyan, the author of *Pilgrim's Progress*; then Jean Charlier de Gerson, a medieval theologian; and finally Thomas B. Macaulay, the historian. This order seems to correspond to the rank order of the intent to influence attitudes.

The same type of analysis has been applied to an experiment relevant to hypotheses three and four. Applications of this analysis will be considered here. Groups of three students were each given the task of constructing a pamphlet. Three jobs were defined: research for data, selection of design, and coordination. The students were led to believe that they would be assigned to different jobs. The actual tasks were performed separately and, in fact, each student was a designer. It was clear that the work of the designer—evaluating the design of an excessively large number of Chamber of Commerce pamphlets—could not be completed in the time alloted, and it was also apparent that the coordinator had sufficient time left from his own task to help the designer. Communication was possible only by written messages. Two experimental conditions were introduced: In the *group* condition, teamwork was stressed, rewards were given to the group as a whole, and positions were considered to be interchangeable, presumably assigned by lot. In the *organization* condition, efficient organization for the work was stressed, rewards were given to individuals (though they were not competing with each other), and different functions were distributed by ability, presumably on the basis of tests.

The students were given four opportunities during the experimental session to write messages. For our two measures of information, percentage of nouns and adjectives, we have thus four possible comparisons each or a total of eight comparisons. Table 3 shows the eight pairs of mean percentages. In seven of the eight comparisons the organization condition produced a higher percentage of "content" words (significant at 5 percent level by sign test). In addition, a measure of variability of sentence length could be computed. As in this case, when we are comparing the communications of several individuals within each condition, we cannot assume that all the sentences produced in the organization condition will be more uniform than those in the group condition. We can infer, however, that each individual in the organization will produce sentences of uniform length in all his messages. Hence, the variances of the words in all the sentences of each student's messages were computed. The means of the variances in each condition (or rather the logarithm of the variances for a more normal distribution) are shown in the last column in Table 3. The organization

Table 3. Uniformity and Information under Group and Organization Conditions (Experimental data)

	Group	*Organization*	*Direction of difference (+ according to hypotheses, − contrary to hypotheses)*
Sentence length			
Mean 100 (log of variance)	129.44	107.77	+
N	36	35	
Message I			
Mean percent nouns	15.73	17.1	+
Mean percent adjectives	8.20	18.5	+
N	15	9	
Message II			
Mean percent nouns	12.39	14.47	+
Mean percent adjectives	5.97	7.29	+
N	33	34	
Message III			
Mean percent nouns	19.7	15.67	−
Mean percent adjectives	8.63	10.33	+
N	16	9	
Message IV			
Mean percent nouns	10.60	15.18	+
Mean percent adjectives	6.97	9.18	+
N	34	33	

condition shows a lower variability, that is, smaller variances (significant at 5 percent level, one-tailed *t*-test).

By taking actual examples of communication, and communication under special experimental conditions, the systems of analysis proposed here show promise of measuring the semantic content of communication and of being able to test mathematical models of social communication.

CONCLUSION

The principle of the distinction between the attitude and action systems within the model is not new. Allport (1936) summarizes under the name of "determining tendency" a number of concepts psychologists have been using. What the model does is to lead to an explicit statement of the relation between interpersonal relations and effect on attitude and action on one hand and with communication patterns on the other. This in turn can lead to a precise analysis of the communication itself and of its effects.

Starting with the common problem of several disciplines— how power is exerted—an attempt was made to approach this question through an analysis of the communication process. Using some recent developments in applied mathematics, automata theory, and communication theory a model was set up that could account for the effects of different kinds of communication. The main result of this analysis was the definition of two kinds of communication: repetition of a few main points by different means, and single transmission of many points in standard form. The former type was seen to be related to establishment of attitudes—that is to influence—and occurs in cohesive groups; the latter type was related to initiation of action, to authority, and occurs in functional organizations. The application of these hypotheses was then shown in several contexts; in field experiments, in content analysis, and in the theory of opinion leadership.

REFERENCES

Allport, G. W. 1937. *Personality.* New York: Holt, Rinehart and Winston.

Back, K. W., Hill, R., and Stycos, J. M. 1957a. The Puerto Rican field experiment in population control. *Human Relations 10*: 315–334.

Back, K. W., Hill, R., and Stycos, J. M. 1957b. Manner of original presentation and subsequent communication. *Psychological Report 3*: 149–154.

Poling, D. A. 1944. *A Treasure of Great Sermons.* New York: Greenberg.

Stycos, J. M., and Back, K. W. 1965. *The Control of Human Fertility in Jamaica.* Ithca, N.Y.: Cornell University Press.

Yule, G. U. 1944. *The Statistical Study of Literary Vocabulary.* Cambridge, England: Cambridge University.

Zevin, B. D. (ed.). 1946. *Nothing to Fear: The Selected Addresses of Franklin Delano Roosevelt.* Boston: Houghton.

11

THE EFFECTS OF "UNDERSTANDING" FROM THE AUDIENCE ON LANGUAGE BEHAVIOR

Kate Loewenthal

Language behavior may vary in different social situations (Ervin-Tripp & Slobin, 1966, review some recent work in sociolinguistics). The behavior of the addressee may also have effects: for example, a number of experiments show an increase in the rate of "verbal operants" with reinforcement (see review in Krasner, 1958). This experiment is concerned specifically with what happens to language behavior when the speaker is aware that his listener "understands" him. Maclay & Newman (1960) carried out an experiment which demonstrated that "misunderstanding" from the listener was associated with an increase in the length of spoken messages. In Maclay & Newman's experiment, subjects were required to describe one of an array of visual stimuli in such a way that a listener (who could not be seen) could identify the stimulus described. Sometimes subjects were told that the stimulus has been correctly identified (positive feedback), sometimes they were told that the stimulus had been incorrectly identified (negative feedback), and sometimes they were given no feedback. Messages became longer

Reprinted from *British Journal of Social and Clinical Psychology* 7 (1968): 247–52.

in the negative feedback condition, and were briefest in the positive feedback condition. One interpretation of these findings is that subjects feel that there is a need for lengthy explanation when the listener is likely to misunderstand.

Such an interpretation conforms well with Vygotsky's (1934) ideas about language. Vygotsky argued that the "inner" speech associated with thinking is an internalized form of the egocentric monologues observed by Piaget (1926) in young children. Inner speech, according to Vygotsky, is highly abbreviated, condensed, ungrammatical, and contains words with idiosyncratic meanings. Further, social speech may sometimes resemble inner speech: this happens in circumstances when the speaker feels "close" to his listener—when he feels that his listener is likely to "understand what he means." There is, then, the suggestion that "inner speech" and social speech lie on a continuum at whose extremes are two types of audiences. At one extreme is the "remote" audience, who is unlikely to understand with ease, for whom the speaker has to choose words carefully. At the other extreme is the "very close" audience—in fact, the speaker himself.

Werner & Kaplan (1963) also considered that in self-addressed speech the addressee is less distant than in social speech. It is not possible to test this idea directly, since silent "inner speech" cannot be observed. However, self-addressed speech can be observed by the simple technique of asking the subject to make a description of some object, for his own use. Using this technique, E. Kaplan (unpublished, cited by Werner & Kaplan) found that self-addressed descriptions of visual and olfactory stimuli were briefer, and contained more idiosyncratic terms than descriptions addressed to another person. The present writer (Loewenthal, unpublished) has observed similar differences between self-addressed and social speech: it was concluded from two experiments that, in social speech, the speaker has to define explicitly "what he means" by the terms he uses.

Hypothesis

The evidence reviewed above suggests that, with increased understanding from the audience, social speech will increase in resemblance to private speech. The available evidence suggests that abbreviation and the use of idiosyncratic (less "communal") terms are features of private speech. Therefore it was predicted that these features would increase in social speech with increased understanding from the audience.

METHOD

Outline of Method

Subjects sent a series of written messages describing different colored shapes (from an array in front of them) to another person, who was (ostensibly) to use the message to select the shape described from an array of the shapes. Subjects saw the shape selected, and recorded whether or not it was the one described. In fact, the receiver of the message was a confederate of the experimenter, and the proportion of "correct replies" which the subject received varied according to the experimental conditions: A: 20 percent correct replies (a 0 percent condition could not be used, since this would be likely to arouse the subject's suspicions); B: 50 percent correct replies; C: 100 percent correct replies. It would perhaps have been more desirable to have used a spoken means of communication. However, there was a fourth experimental condition (D) in which the subject wrote messages for his own use after the experiment. It was felt that asking subjects to speak aloud messages to themselves would have been less natural than asking them to write them down.

Subjects

Subjects were eight undergraduate psychology students (three men, five women).

Materials

The subject and the confederate each had an array of 24 2 × 2 in. cards, on each of which was a colored shape. The cards in each array were numbered from 1 to 24. There were six different shapes and four different colors (two shapes of blue and two shades of green). The shapes were taken from a children's stencil card, purporting to be of seashells and other marine flora and fauna; they were selected because it was anticipated that they would be fairly difficult to describe.

A type of predecessor-balanced Latin square design was used (based on Williams, 1949). There were four experimental conditions (A, B, C, D) and four "sets" each of 10 stimuli (randomly preselected from the array of 24) were described, one under each condition.

Each subject received each condition and each stimulus-set

once, and conditions and stimulus-sets were counterbalanced, so that each treatment and stimulus-set occurred the same number of times in each order of presentation, and in conjunction with each other. Each treatment was preceded the same number of times by each of the other treatments (and similiarly for the stimulus-sets).

Procedure

The subject and confederate were seated at opposite ends of a table divided by a screen, so that they could not see each other. Messages were posted through a rectangular hole covered by a hinged flap.

Every attempt was made to treat the confederate as though he were another subject. The experimenter asked him his name at the beginning of each session with a new subject, and gave him instructions as though he were a new subject. Instructions were given as follows: "This is a message-passing game. Both of you have in front of you a set of cards with different colored shapes on them. You both have exactly the same cards. However, each card is numbered, and the numbers are not necessarily the same in both sets. I want one of you to write messages describing certain of the shapes to the other person, who must try to pick out the shape described. I want you [to the subject] to write the messages, and you [to the confederate] to receive them. Here is some paper and a pen [giving a numbered pad of paper to the subject]. I am going to call out the number of a card, and I want you to write a description of the colored shape on the card, and post your message through. [To the confederate]: When you get the message, read it carefully, pick out the colored shape which you think he/she means, and post it through. Keep the messages you are sent. [To the subject]: When you get the card that he has picked out, I want you to score a point on here [giving a sheet of paper to the subject] if it is the right one. Put a cross if it's wrong. When you've done that, post the card back again. I want you both between you to try and get as many points as possible."

The subject and confederate were forbidden to speak to each other, and the subject was asked to use entirely verbal means of communication in the message—drawing was forbidden. The experimenter then called out one by one the numbers of the 40 stimuli to be described. Subjects were not informed of changes in experimental conditions, except that before condition D (the self-addressed messages), the following instructions were given: "Now

I want you [to the confederate] to have a short rest. I would like you [to the subject] to write some messages about the shapes, for your own use, so that you will be able to use the messages to pick out the shapes described from another array of the shapes after the experiment is over."

After condition D, the subject and confederate were asked to continue with the messages as before.

RESULTS

From the written messages, the following dependent variables were analyzed: (*a*) message length (mean no. morphemes per message); (*b*) percentage of "function-words" (prepositions, articles, etc. as opposed to "content-words"—nouns, verbs, adverbs, adjectives); (*c*) frequencies of content-words.

Variables (*a*) and (*b*) were assessed from the last two messages produced in each experimental condition: only towards the end of a condition would the full effects of the treatment be shown. (*c*) The analysis of frequencies of content words was carried out in an attempt to give a quantitative basis to the term "idiosyncratic"; it is argued that in private speech (and in conditions of understanding from the audience) the content-words used in descriptions of a given figure should have a smaller frequency of occurrence than words used in social speech, where the audience shows decreased understanding. Descriptions of one shape, which had been encountered in all conditions by each subject, were considered. From the total of 32 descriptions, a frequency score was obtained for each content-word, corresponding to the number of times it had appeared in the 32 descriptions. For each description, a mean frequency score (for the content-words in the description) was obtained. The frequency score gives a measure (an inverse one) of the "idiosyncrasy" of the content-words in a message.

Table 1 shows how the four experimental conditions affected the three dependent variables. Messages became shorter with increased understanding from the audience, and self-addressed messages were shortest.

The proportion of function-words declined with increased understanding, and was lowest in self-addressed messages.

The analysis of frequencies of content-words was disappointing; although self-addressed messages contained less frequent words, messages in the three communicative conditions did not

Table 1. Description Length, Percentage of Function-Words and Content-Work Frequency under Three Conditions of Understanding from the Audience, and in Self-Addressed Language

(Messages understood: A, 20 percent; B, 50 percent; C, 100 percent; D, self-addressed messages)

Condition	Description length (mean no. morphemes per message)	Function-words per message (percent)	Frequency of content-words
A	14.9	21.1	3.8
B	11.6	16.7	3.8
C	8.9	13.4	3.8
D	8.1	9.8	2.7
F (d.f. = 3, 12) conditions*	5.03	5.31	2.26
Significance	$P < 0.025$	$P < 0.025$	$P < 0.05$ (ns)

*Other sources of variance were stimulus-sets (4), subjects (8) and periods (4). Full analyses of variance are not shown, since these sources of variance seldom had significant effects.

differ with respect to frequencies of content words. An inspection of the subjects' messages suggested that the apparent similarity of frequency scores over conditions A, B and C may mask certain qualitative differences. In condition A the less frequent content-words seem to be "padding," added for greater clarity. (For example, one subject described one shape as a "three-pronged figure" in condition A, while in condition B it was described simply as "three prongs.") In conditions B and C "padding words" tend to be omitted; only "essential" words are included. It is possible that the "essential" words are of lower frequency in conditions of increased understanding. However, it is difficult to find a suitable *a priori* basis for assessing whether a word is "essential" or "padding."

DISCUSSION

The results provide some support for the hypothesis that, with increased understanding from the audience, social speech increases in resemblance to self-addressed (private) speech, particularly with respect to brevity. This seems, in part, to be due to a decline in the proportion of function-words with increased understanding from the audience. Function-words generally carry little lexical content, and they are usually relatively predictable from context. With an audience who is likely to understand, function-words can be "taken as read." In this context it is interesting to remark Brown & Bellugi's (1964) observation that young children's "imitation" of their mother's speech is often stripped of the function-words (and that function-words, in the mother's speech, were usually least stressed).

Vygotsky (1934, chap. 7) described the laconic, ùngrammatical, "meaning-loaded" nature of inner speech, and of social speech in situations of increased understanding from the audience, and the findings of the present experiment support his speculations.

The analysis of content-word frequencies, although inconclusive, suggests that further research might be valuable. It is possible that the "closeness" of the audience might be an important factor in word selection (a factor which has largely been ignored in recent accounts of the word-selection process, e.g. Wales & Marshall, 1966).

The experiment, then, provides some evidence that social speech increases in resemblance to private speech with increased understanding from the audience. In this context it should be stressed that "private speech" is unlikely to be a constant, invariable phenomenon. It is likely that it varies from person to person, and within a particular person from situation to situation. The simplest way of accounting for this variation is to suggest a sort of internalized "imaginary audience" (children have been observed talking to imaginary companions) analogous to the Freudian internalized "judge"—the superego. The imaginary audience may vary from person to person, and within a given person from time to time. This variation would be associated with differences in "cognitive style" (or linguistic style—the distinction is difficult to draw when considering thought expressed in language).

What remains to be determined is the mechanisms involved in the formation of the speaker's judgment of his audience (whether real or imaginary), and the processes involved in the influences of this perception of the audience on language behavior.

REFERENCES

Brown, R. & Bellugi, U. 1964. Three processes in the child's acquisition of syntax. In E. H. Lenneberg (ed.), *New directions in the study of language*. Cambridge, Mass.: M.I.T. Press.

Ervin-Tripp, S. & Slobin, D. 1966. Psycholinguistics. *Ann. Rev. Psychol.* 17: 435–474.

Krasner, L. 1958. Studies of the conditioning of verbal behavior. *Psychol. Bull.* 55: 148–170.

Maclay, H. & Newman, S. 1960. Variables affecting the message in communication. In D. Willner (ed.), *Decisions, values and groups.* Oxford: Pergamon Press.

Piaget, J. 1926. *The language and thought of the child.* New York: Harcourt, Brace.

Vygotsky, L. S. 1934. *Thought and language.* Cambridge, Mass.: M.I.T. Press. (English edition, 1962.)

Wales, R. & Marshall, J. C. 1966. The organization of linguistic performance. In J. Lyons & R. Wales (eds.), *Psycholinguistics papers.* Edinburgh: Edinburgh University Press.

Werner, H. & Kaplan, B. 1963. *Symbol formation.* New York: Wiley.

Williams, E. J. 1949. Experimental designs balanced for the residual effects of treatments. *Aus. J. Sci. Res.* A 5: 149–168.

12

SPEAKING OF SPACE

David McNeill

We read of "space speak" on every hand. Newspapers and magazines discuss it in their science columns, and popular fancy seems to have been captured by it. The belief is that the space effort has given us, in addition to the possibility of going to the moon, a new linguistic phenomenon. However, it is not easy to escape the confines of English, and in "space speak" there is nothing novel, nor even very much that is unique. The name itself is a misnomer. "Space speak" is not much spoken; and, linguistically, the most important thing that NASA engineers do is not peculiar to the space effort. On the other hand, there is a jargon of engineering that is fully used by space technologists. My task in this article is the analysis of such jargon.

The major part of space jargon is an overabundance of a linguistic form that is available to all speakers of English. There is,

Reprinted from Science 152 (May 13, 1966): 875–80. Copyright 1966 by the American Association for the Advancement of Science.

Preparation of this article was supported in part by a grant (No. NsG–253–62) from the National Aeronautics and Space Administration to the American Academy of Arts and Sciences, Committee on Space, and in part by a grant (No. 5–TI–1011–02) From the National Institutes of Health to Harvard University, Center for Cognitive Studies. Final preparation of the article was supported in part by a grant (No. 1P01 HD01368–01) from the National Institute of Child Health and Human Development to the Project on Language Development, University of Michigan, and in part by a contract (No. OE–5–14–036) between the U.S. Office of Education and the Center for Research on Language and Language Behavior, University of Michigan.

however, a much smaller part that is unique; these are the words, seemingly occult, that give rise to the impression of linguistic novelty. Some familiar examples are *pad, abort, umbilical*. Others, less well known, are *eyeballs in* and *eyeballs out* (describing conditions of extreme acceleration and deceleration respectively) and *milk stool* (describing an arrangement of three rocket engines on the lunar spacecraft). As these examples show, such terms in the jargon of space engineering are of two types. Most are metaphors (for example, *umbilical, milk stool*), where the conventional meaning of the word and its meaning in space jargon have something in common. A much smaller number are metonyms (for example, *eyeballs in*), where the conventional term refers to something that typically accompanies the referent of the space term. Metaphors depend on similarity of referent; metonyms depend on contiguity. Both types of term are the ingredients of most professional jargons. Psychologists, for example, talk of *thresholds*; anthropologists, of cultural *diffusion*; sailors, of *Jacob's ladders*.

Metaphors and metonyms are usually apt, but, by the same token, they are difficult to come by. The process of finding a good metaphor or metonym is not given automatically by the rules of English syntax. It demands a kind of creativity that is unregimented. Thus, whereas metaphors and metonyms are ordinarily "good," in the sense of capturing an intended meaning succinctly and vividly, they are also rare. If a technical jargon must provide large numbers of terms, reliance on metaphors and metonyms simply will not be sufficiently productive.

What is needed is a systematic procedure. One solution is to coin new words, as the medical sciences have done. Their procedure is systematic and useful if one knows a little Greek or Latin and the rules for combining roots in these languages. Had engineering experienced its great growth at a time when schooling in Greek and Latin was still part of the college curriculum, perhaps space jargon would have followed in the same path. (NASA's penchant for naming programs and vehicles after the Greek and Roman gods is, of course, a different matter altogether.) Words also can be created *de novo* within English, and there are some examples of this in space jargon (for instance, *rockoon*, a rocket launched from a balloon). Neologism, however, is no more systematic than the formation of metaphors, though it may demand less in the way of creative powers, and so it is not likely to have a larger yield of technical terms.

In official NASA dictionaries of space terms (*1*), metaphors and metonyms account for about one-eighth of the entries. In absolute terms, this is less than 100 words. Most of the remaining entries are combinations of words, put together into a particular grammatical construction, the so-called nominal compound. The solution for increasing the technical vocabulary, then, has been to resort to English syntax.

The advantages of this solution are considerable. The method is endlessly productive, since there are no limits on the constructions that may be generated by a grammatical device. It requires no exotic knowledge, since it draws only on the English lexicon and employs only rules that are general in English. Moreover, nominal compounds, however long, are always nouns and this means that they have all the maneuverability of single words. Some examples will make clear the type of construction a nominal compound is: *launch vehicle; escape propulsion system; battery discharger test set; separation and destruct system ordinance equipment (2)*. These terms reveal several features worth noting about engineers' nominal compounds. Most obvious is the flexibility in length. Two words are the minimum, but there is, in theory, no upper limit. The longest nominal compound I have seen occurred in the *Congressional Record* and contained 13 words—*liquid oxygen liquid hydrogen rocket powered single stage to orbit reversible boost system*. The statement that each compound is grammatically a noun can be verified by placing the compounds in the sentence frame, "The ——— is here." Actually, the grammatical class of the compound is the class of the final word, which is always a noun. Perhaps less obvious than the grammatical class of nominal compounds is the constraint on the order in which words can appear. *Vehicle launch* is not the same thing as *launch vehicle*; nor is *discharger set battery test* the same as *battery discharger test set*. I return below to the constraint on word order, but first I must support two points already made.

One is the statement that nominal compounds are part of general English grammar, a relationship that can be simply exemplified with some familiar compounds from ordinary English. We buy from *vending machines*, park in *driveways*, and worry about *girl friends*; and we even read in Dr. Seuss of "three seater zatzit nose patting extensions" *(3)*. It is not accidental that the obvious examples of nominal compounds in general English are short; the main difference between engineering jargon and general English is that long compounds are more frequent in engineering jargon. Otherwise, the two classes of compounds are the same—that is, order of words makes a difference, and the compounds are grammatically nouns.

The second point is basic to the theme of this article and so

warrants elaborate treatment. It is, actually, two related points:
(1) in spite of the fact that nominal compounds are general in
English, they are used by engineers in response to a special pressure for technical terminology; (2) because of this, nominal compounds are not peculiar to the space effort but appear equally often
in the jargon of other engineering fields.

There is no way to measure pressure on a field to form a
technical vocabulary. But it seems safe to assume that engineers
are under greater pressure to do this than social scientists, who in
turn experience greater pressure than literary critics or historians.
Therefore, we should expect that writings by these three groups will
show corresponding differences in the frequency with which nominal compounds are used, and such is the case. Samples were taken
from 18 technical reports published by NASA, from six papers by
psychologists, which appeared in the *Psychological Review* and
the *Psychological Bulletin* (both professional journals), and from
six articles from *The American Scholar*. The samples ranged in
size from 3000 to 6000 words in the NASA reports and were in nominal compounds. The corresponding average for the psychologists
was 8 percent, and for *The American Scholar*, 3 percent. The number
of metaphors and metonyms, on the other hand, did not differ among
the three samples, which perhaps indicates that this source is
used to its fullest even in *The American Scholar*. Thus, most of
the nominal compounds used by the engineers were probably used
in response to the need for technical terms.

The average for NASA—19 percent—is duplicated almost
exactly in the technical writing of other engineering fields. Twenty
percent of the words in a sample of reports issued by the Operations
Center of M.I.T. were in nominal compounds; most of the writers
were electrical engineers. Similarly, 17 percent of the words in
the departmental announcements of the M.I.T. departments of
mechanical engineering and physics were in nominal compounds.
In short, the nominal compound is used by diverse fields, apparently to meet the common need for technical terms in greater
numbers than metaphors, metonyms, or neologisms can supply.

LINGUISTIC ANALYSIS

The basic fact about nominal compounds is that they all derive
from underlying phrases, through the application of one or more
grammatical rules. It is in this sense that the nominal compound is

a grammatical device. *Launch vehicle,* for example, comes from the phrase *vehicle for launching.* The grammatical transformation has the effect of reversing word order and deleting the preposition and the bound morpheme *-ing.* Phrases with different structure are similarly transformed, but by different rules. *Simulation of flight,* which is a sequence of noun-preposition-noun (in contrast to noun-preposition-verb in the foregoing example) becomes the compound *flight simulation.* The rule is slightly different, but it has the same effect of reversing order and deleting the preposition. The various rules thus have similar effects; their differences consist in the type of underlying structure on which they operate.

The rules for transforming underlying phrases into compounds have been formulated in detail by the linguist R. B. Lees (4). I need not restate these rules here, nor take into account their complete forms. For present purposes it is sufficient to note that such rules exist and that they pair compounds with underlying phrases (5).

An underlying phrase can be regarded as the origin of the corresponding compound, and the process of forming nominal compounds in space jargon can be conceived of as taking place in two steps: production of the underlying phrase and transformation of the phrase into a compound by the appropriate rule. There are many rules, and so virtually any phrase can become a nominal compound. Also, as we shall see shortly, underlying phrases can be of any length, and so, therefore, can their compounds. In these two points lie the major advantages of the nominal compound as a means of increasing technical vocabulary. Given a knowledge of the rules, all that is required is a capacity to produce phrases in English.

The process is illustrated in Table 1. On the left are phrases; each row contains everything contained in the immediately preced-

Table 1. Nominal Compounds and Corresponding Phrases

Phrase	*Nominal compound*
the system	the system
the system that controls	the control system
the system that controls attitude	the attitude control system
the system that controls attitude of the ship	the ship attitude control system
the system that controls attitude of the ship by ejecting	the ejection ship attitude control system
the system that controls attitude of the ship by ejecting gas	the gas ejection ship attitude control system
the system that controls attitude of the ship by ejecting gas through nozzles	the nozzle gas ejection ship attitude control system

ing row plus one additional phrase or word. On the right are the corresponding compounds. We can see here how compounds grow in length, and we can also see something of the variety of phrase structures that can be transformed into nominal compounds.

Also, we can now see the basis of the constraint on the order of words in a compound. It is simply the order of words in the underlying phrase. Note that one can roughly reconstruct each phrase from the corresponding compound by reading the words of the compound in reverse order.

One way to demonstrate that compounds correspond to phrases is to show that they can be bracketed in the same way. Bracketing is grammatical parsing done with brackets; it is a notation showing where the constituents of the compound or phrase are. (In the present case, contrary to usual practice, the brackets have been drawn above and below the string of words.) For the compound of Table 1 we get,

The nozzle gas ejection ship attitude control system,

which corresponds exactly to

The system that controls attitude of the ship by ejecting gas through nozzles.

Most of the constituents marked off in this fashion overlap. (One pair of constituents does not, which is the reason why row 5 of Table 1 seems incomplete; in fact, it is not complete, since one constituent is only half represented.) However, not all compounds or phrases have overlapping constituents. For phrases of a different structure, the relative positions of the brackets are different. For example, the pseudo-space phrase,

a program that orbits astronauts, makes modules, and embarrasses Russians

becomes the compound

a Russian embarrassing module making astronaut orbiting program.

As the bracketing shows, no constituents overlap. The cases of overlapping and nonoverlapping constituents, plus combinations of the two, appear to encompass all the situations in which long phrases can be transformed into single nominal compounds. Other phrase structures, such as the "self-embedding construction," in which a sentence is constructed like an onion (for example, "The race that the car that the people whom the man called sold won was held last summer"), cannot be transformed into nominal compounds. With allowable phrase structures, however, long compounds can be generated from long phrases through successive application of Lees's rules. Each rule produces only a two-word compound, but by applying the rules in a left-to-right direction throughout the phrase, one produces a right-to-left growth of the compound. The result is an orderly and predictable dependence of compounds on underlying phrases, a relation that is sufficient basis for use of the nominal compound as a source of technical terminology.

PSYCHOLINGUISTIC IMPLICATIONS

In the actual use of nominal compounds as technical terms, more is involved than the application of Lees's rules of transformation. One might suppose that the rules for forming compounds would work in two directions, from underlying phrase to compound and back again. In theory, of course, they do; it is always possible to retransform a compound into a phrase. But transformations in the two directions are not equally determined. Whereas transformation of a phrase is unique, retransformation of a compound is often ambiguous. *Mission suitability,* for example, could derive from either "suitability *for* the mission" or "suitability *of* the mission," which are quite different things. To NASA engineers, the term has the former meaning. Similarly, *time critical equipment* could mean "equipment for which there is a critical time [during which it is usable]" or "equipment for which there is a critical time [for performing a function]". Again, the former is the correct meaning.

Although such ambiguities exist, NASA engineers seem unaware of them. I interviewed four engineers at the Marshall Space Flight Center in Huntsville, Alabama; all were actively engaged in the design or testing of apparatus used in the Apollo program. They were alert and cooperative informants, but none was aware of ambiguities of the sort just mentioned. In view of the fact that nominal compounds are *constructed,* this is rather remarkable. One explanation is that these engineers had "recoded" certain of the nominal compounds into single units, quite as if they were simple nouns. Possibly, such recoding is due to a suspension of the process of transformation, and tends to occur in the case of nominal compounds that are used frequently. Presumably the status of these recoded compounds is similar to that of the nominal compounds of ordinary English. *Driveway* means "way *for* driving," but "way *of* driving" is equally possible. The fact seems to be that we do not disassemble *driveway* in order to understand it, and so we are, like the engineers, unaware of the ambiguity.

If we make the assumption that frequently occurring nominal compounds in engineering jargon are understood as unified nouns, we can see that it is for the encoder of terms, not the decoder, that this grammatical device is advantageous. Moreover, since an established nominal compound that is understood as a unit probably is produced as a unit as well, the advantages are not primarily for every encoder, but for the encoder who is producing a new term. The result is that the nominal compound is a device that mainly benefits the "culture," guaranteeing that new technical terms will be available when needed.

That frequently occurring nominal compounds can be recoded does not mean that the rules for foming nominal compounds are linguistic fictions. On the contrary, they conform to actual psychological processes. When asked to "unravel" nominal compounds, the engineers interviewed at Huntsville produced phrases in which the words of the compound appeared in reverse order. And, conversely, when the engineers were asked to create nominal compounds to go with definitions (which were unfamiliar to them but taken from a NASA dictionary), they selected two or more words in the definition, reversed their order, and placed them into a compound. Usually, in this latter experiment, the term the engineers created was not the term defined in the dictionary. But that does not alter the conclusion that, psychologically as well as linguistically, nominal compounds are transformed phrases.

Many people suspect that engineers use the nominal compound because of a careless lack of concern for the requirements of style. This seems to be a general opinion among nontechnical readers of engineering prose. It is an opinion, however, which overlooks the fact that nominal compounds are transformations, and so require the user to go at least one step beyond formulating an underlying phrase. Consider the following data. The proportion of all words in nominal compounds has already been given as 19 percent for several NASA technical reports. For some of the writers of these reports, samples of spoken language also were available (from written and oral testimony before a congressional committee). If the nominal compound is overused through carelessness, it should occur more often when an individual is speaking extempore than when he is writing. However, this is not the case; the nominal compound is a literary phenomenon.

Compared to the figure of 19 percent for written materials, only 7 percent of spoken words are in nominal compounds. The pressure of spontaneous speech thus has an effect quite opposite from the effect the hypothesis of carelessness would predict. Evidently, use of the nominal compound in technical writing reflects literary care, not lack of it. The nominal compounds that are used in speech are short and among the most common. In all probability, they are recoded compounds. If that is the case, the 12 percent comprised of compounds used in written language but not in speech would for the most part be newly created terms. There is psychological evidence (6) that speech containing many transformations is more difficult to understand than speech containing few transformations. Probably there is a similar difference in difficulty when speech is produced, so the nominal compound is used less frequently in spoken than in written language. It simply takes too much time and causes too much confusion to transform phrases as frequently when one is speaking as one does when writing.

INFLUENCE OF SPACE JARGON

There are at least two ways in which space jargon may influence the general language. One is through what may be called *specific* influence. In this case, a particular term passes into nontechnical language. There are numerous familiar examples: *countdown, astronaut, space probe*, and so on. Metaphors, metonyms, neologisms, and nominal compounds—all might be introduced into the general language as specific terms. The basis of specific influence is some knowledge, on the part of the speaker or writer, of the hardware or concept that the technical term names. Thus, specific influence is limited by the extent of the infusion of technical knowledge, but, by the same token, terms carried into the language through specific influence do not importantly change meaning in their passage from jargon to general language.

However, some of these terms appear to undergo a further development once they have been taken into the general language. For example, one hears people speak of starting something from a "launching pad of . . . ," by which they mean a "basis of. . . ." This is a metaphorical use of the space term *pad*. Some of the adopted terms that change in this way are already metaphors in space jargon, being adaptations of ordinary English words. *Pad* is an example. These new metaphors, then, actually are attachments of new meanings to old words, a process known to linguists as polysemy. Specific influence, therefore, can have two rather different effects. One derives from the simple introduction of technical terms; the consequences of this should be narrow for the general language. The other derives from the attachment of new meanings to old words, and it has more devastating possibilities. Polysemy is held to be a major force for change in language, and, through it, terms such as *pad* could conceivably lose their present meaning: our descendants may talk about the pad of our democracy being free speech.

Not all words that pass as "space speak" come from space technology. Indeed, some of the most popular specimens are spurious, having been invented by newsmen. Among the most notable of these are *A-OK, blast off,* and *spin off.* Nonetheless, many such words are examples of polysemy, and so are potential sources of change of meaning.

In contrast to specific influence, there is a second, more *generic* influence. In this case, elaborate use of the grammatical device of the nominal compound itself is adopted. Generic influence in no way depends on technical knowledge; it consists simply of extensive use of a construction already available in the general language. One way in which generic influence is mediated was suggested by some of the engineers whom I interviewed at Huntsville. On occasion, they said, engineers will deliberately overuse the nominal compound in order to impress their auditors. Apparently the nominal compound has about it an aura of technical sophistication. Such exploitation of the nominal compound could work also in the opposite direction, in that nontechnologists who desire to resemble technologists can use the nominal compound as a kind of poor man's engineering jargon. This would be an example of generic influence.

These considerations suggest computation of a measure, called here the "pretension index," for analyzing samples of prose for evidence of generic influence. The name pretension index is used to indicate that, by overusing the nominal compound, one can pretend to possess a degree of technical knowledgeability that, in fact, one does not have. There are two senses in which the nominal compound could be "overused," and the pretension index might measure either one of them. Overuse could be taken to mean simply increased frequency of use of these compounds. However, such an increase could occur simply because the content of a passage required it, and this would have nothing to do with generic influence. Because of this possibility, the pretension index measures overuse in the second sense—an increased use of the number of long compounds relative to the number of short compounds. The idea is that unnecessary use of the nominal compound would favor both increased frequency and increased length, but that where technical content requires unusually frequent use of some nominal compounds in a given passage, it would not ordinarily require, at the same time, an increase in their length. Greater length can come only from (1) a need to make technical terms more specific or from (2) use of the nominal compound without regard to technical terminology.

The pretension index is computed from the number of compounds of length 2, 3, 4, 5, . . . words that occur in a sample of prose. There is a simple relation between length and frequency, known as Zipf's law, that holds for a great variety of textual material. Zipf's law states that the logarithm of frequency and the logarithm of length are negatively related to each other by a straight line. In brief, the law states that the frequency of words (or compounds) is proportional to their shortness. The shorter the word or compound, the more frequent its occurrence. The slope of the line relating frequency and length, the "Zipf slope," depends on the relative number of long and short words or compounds. The pretension index is based on the "Zipf slope," but not directly, for it is necessary also to make some reference to a standard is the "Zipf slope" for the entries in a dictionary of space terminology. Such dictionaries contain only technical terms, and thus provide an estimate of the relative numbers of long and short compounds in the true technical vocabulary. The pretension index for a sample of speech, then, is computed by dividing the "Zipf slope" of the standard by the measured "Zipf slope" of the sample. The higher the index, the more "pretentious" the sample of speech.

Equipped with an index, we can now see whether there is any

Table 2.   Pretension Indices for Several Samples of Speech

Sample	Pretension index
NASA, written	1.00
NASA, spoken	0.79
Magazine on space technology, written	1.46
Congress, spoken	0.94

evidence for generic influence of space jargon. Pretension indices have been computed for samples of writing by NASA engineers (the same material that was used in the study cited above); for samples of spoken material by NASA personnel (oral testimony before a congressional committee); for samples of spoken material by some members of Congress; and for samples of writing from a popular magazine on space technology. In these computations NASA represents the engineering profession; the Congressmen and the space magazine represent laymen who deal a good bit with space technology. The results are given in Table 2.

The proper comparisons here are within modes of communication—written-to-written and spoken-to-spoken. Clearly, the space magazine uses relatively too many long compounds for all of them to be true technical terms. Since the pretension index is based on logarithms, small numerical differences reflect large differences in length of the compounds; expressed as percentages, these data are much more impressive. In the space magazine there are 220 percent more five-word compounds than there are in the NASA written reports, and 300 percent more six-word compounds. There is no reason to suppose that only the long compounds in the space magazine are nontechnical; no doubt many of the short compounds also result from generic influence.

The slopes for the two oral samples are both lower than those for the written samples—an effect that derives, in all probability, from the need to avoid complicated transformations in spontaneous speech. Nonetheless, Congressmen have an index nearly as high when speaking as NASA engineers have when writing, and possibly this too reflects generic influence.

Generic influence, of course, need not be limited to the non-engineer who attempts to appear knowledgeable about space technology. The nominal compound can be a source of borrowed dignity for any professional jargon. On the other hand, it would be a mistake to assume that every extensive use of the nominal compound by nonengineers is a case of generic influence. Other professional people may turn to it for the same reasons that engineers do, for technical terms. I know of no way to distinguish generic influence throughout the language from independent discovery of the nominal compound as a form of professional jargon. However, those who dread the influence of engineering jargon may be heartened to learn that newspapers, outside their science columns, show little indication of adopting the nominal compound.

ACRONYMS

As already indicated, Zipf's law asserts that the shorter compounds are the more frequent. The relation is often interpreted as showing causality: words (or compounds) become shorter because they are more frequently used. Indeed, Zipf concluded from his law that language users follow a principle of least effort. Whether or not Zipf's theory is correct, his law—which is a purely mathematical statement—implies that particular compounds should become shorter as their frequency of use increases. It is clear that such a shortening does take place in the case of individual words, as the erosion of *television* to *video* to *TV* illustrates. However, it is equally clear that compounds cannot be shortened in this way, for the reason that they have grammatical structure. When a word is shortened, the abbreviation appears to be made almost arbitrarily; it must remain pronounceable, but there are no other requirements. In England, for example, *television* has changed to *telly*. Comparable freedom does not exist with compounds. One cannot shorten *escape propulsion system* to *escape system*, *escape propulsion*, or *propulsion system* without changing the original meaning. The abbreviations correspond to new underlying phrases that are not identical with the original phrase. The solution to this problem, of course, is the acronym. Thus, *escape propulsion system* becomes *EPS*, while *propulsion system*, *escape system*, and *escape propulsion* become *PS*, *ES*, and *EP*, respectively. The original structural distinctions among the compounds are all represented among the acronyms. I suspect that most cases of "acronyming" can be explained as efforts to conform to Zipf's law without changing meaning at the same time. However, not all acronyms result from increased frequency of use of compounds. In some cases the sequence apparently is reversed: the acronym is devised first, then a compound is found to fit it. In these cases the acronym often spells a word whose meaning is somehow relevant to the meaning of the compound. This is a literary game, not the outcome of the natural linguistic development implied by Zipf's law. One such playful acronym is *EGADS*, which names the system used to destroy a malfunctioning missile after it has been launched, and "goes" with the compound *electronic ground automatic destruct sequencer.*

It is not possible, obviously, to disassemble an acronym into a kernel phrase. But, since frequently used compounds tend to be recoded and thus are not disassembled anyway, nothing is lost by reducing these compounds to acronyms. The ultimate outcome of compounding followed by "acronyming" is the creation of new vocabulary. In effect, acronyms are new words. However, they are words manufactured according to definite principles and so can be coined in abundance.

A CONCLUDING REMARK

Professional jargon is a topic that stands at the intersection of several academic fields. Sociology, anthropology, linguistics, and psychology, at least, can find something of interest in it. The emphasis here has been on the psycholinguistic aspects, not because they are the most notable in the study of jargon, but, on the contrary, because they have been the most neglected. However, it is not likely that psychologists or linguists will be entirely satisfied with the results. The psychologist will find the data scanty; the linguist will find the statement of rules informal. Both will be correct, for this psycholinguistic study of jargon should be regarded as preliminary. The purpose here has been merely to indicate some interesting lines of inquiry.

But until further work has been done, we can conclude that the following statement is probably true: space speak is an engineering technology concept expression manuscript sentence grammar device.

REFERENCES AND NOTES

1. "Short Glossary of Space Terms," *NASA (Nat. Aeron. Space Admin.) Publ. SP-1* (1962); "Apollo Terminology," *NASA (Nat. Aeron. Space Admin.) Publ. SP-6001* (1963).
2. *Destruct* is another neologism, which in many cases replaces the verb *destroy*; the reason for the neologism, I was told, is to avoid the warlike overtones of *destroy*.
3. T. S. Geisel (Dr. Seuss), *On Beyond Zebra!* (Random House, New York, 1955); I am indebted to Nobuko McNeill for bringing this example to my attention.
4. R. B. Lees, *Intern. J. Amer. Linguistics* 26, No. 3 (July 1960).
5. Actually, transformations do not operate on phrases, but operate on the abstract structure out of which phrases are built. The distinction is critical in most discussions of syntax. In the present case, however, the reader will not be seriously misled by thinking of phrases rather than structures. It should be borne in mind, nonetheless, that the term *underlying phrase* is really a loose figure of speech. For a complete discussion of the relation between phrases and underlying syntactic structures, see N. Chomsky, *Aspects of the Theory of Syntax* (M.I.T. Press, Cambridge, Mass., 1965).
6. G. A. Miller, *Amer. Psychologist* 17, 748 (1962).

13

DIFFERENCES IN EGOCENTRICITY BETWEEN SPOKEN AND WRITTEN EXPRESSION UNDER STRESS AND NON-STRESS CONDITIONS

Nancy J. Sunshine
Milton K. Horowitz

The nature of communication in the normal adult is generally believed to be balanced between diversification and repetition; there is a balance between the number of different words used and the frequency with which they are employed. When the communicator makes his objectives clear to his audience by using different words for each meaning, his orientation is considered sociocentric. Conversely, in the egocentric orientation there is greater repetition and less diversification; the speaker (or writer) endows his words with more different meanings than is normally the case and he continues to use the same words about an increasing diversity of things. The Zipf rank-frequency curve, which measures the balance between word repetition and diversification, represents mathematically the differences between egocentric and sociocentric expression and may be shown graphically. This is a plot of word frequencies on

Reprinted from *Language and Speech* 11, Part 3 (July-September 1968): 160–66.

the ordinate against rank on the abscissa graphed on log-log paper. In normal sociocentricity this shows up as a 45° angle and a slope of -1.00. A steeper slope is characteristic of egocentric language and typically a middle bulge shows up with this steepness.

Zipf found that the distribution of words in English approximates a harmonic series, i.e., the most frequent word in a sample will occur every 10 words, the nth most frequent word every $10n$ words, but he felt that the law of harmonic distribution would be valid only for written language, since in speech facial expressions and hand gestures would undoubtedly replace some words, thus distorting the form of the curve (Zipf, 1935). Studies have since been done to compare written and spoken expression. Spoken language has been found to be more redundant and prolific with a greater number of communicative signals and orientation signals. Speaking is physiologically easier and more efficient in that it produces more ideas in ratio to words used and time expended (Horowitz and Newman, 1964). When speaking, one has less time to think about words which may be more diverse and precise in articulation and more common words with broader meanings are used. Thus the greater repetition of speech in relation to the number of different words used makes it tend to the more egocentric repetitive orientation. On the other hand, writing is less natural, more artificial, more difficult, more stimulus bound, more inhibited and careful. There is more time for thought, and a resulting tendency to use more uncommon words in writing than in speech. Writing, therefore, ought to be more sociocentric and variegated because of fewer repetitions of words.

Studies of schizophrenic speech and writing have indicated an extremely egocentric orientation. The autist prefers the economy of the generic correlation to the expense of the specific correlation; that is, one word covers many different meanings. His verbalizations are understood, perhaps, by him, and hence are more for his own convenience than for meaningful communication (Zipf, 1949). The anxiety of schizophrenia which becomes manifest in this intellectual rigidity may also be evident in stress situations. The anxious person would become more concerned with maintaining his own emotional equilibrium than in communicating effectively; he would tend to repeat more common words, less precise in meaning and perhaps more affect-laden, in an effort to relieve his tension and restore internal balance.

To show the effects of stress on writing and speaking, Marcus (1965) did a study comparing written and spoken productions of children in an open-end task where children were asked to finish a story. Productions were compared under two different conditions, stress and non-stress. Four Zipf rank-frequency curves were plotted but not analysed. Visual inspection of the curves, however, suggested that stress speech was more egocentric than non-stress speech and writing in general was more sociocentric than speaking.

It is expected that if such variables as setting, time for thinking, topic, order for speaking or writing, and subjects are controlled that:

(1) Spoken expression is more egocentric than written expression.

(2) Expression elicited under stress conditions is more egocentric than that elicited under non-stress conditions.

METHOD

Forty students enrolled in the introductory course of Psychology during the summer session at Queens College were divided equally into "stress" and "non-stress" groups. The non-stress group was instructed to perform the task as though it were a game, while the stress group was told that what they produced would be analysed as a projective personality test. The exact instructions were read to the subjects. Two poems selected for stimulus material were both unpublished works of a comparable nature, obscure enough in meaning to elicit varied interpretations. Each subject was asked to speak on one of the two poems and write on the other. The order in which speaking or writing was required of each subject was varied identically in the two groups in "abba" fashion. The number of times each of the two poems was given for one mode or the other and the number of times each poem was presented first was controlled for. The experimenter was in the room while each subject wrote on one poem and spoke (into a portable tape recorder) on the remaining poem. After the experiment the true nature of the study was disclosed to the stress group to alleviate any anxiety. Both groups were asked to report their subjective anxiety feelings.

RESULTS

The results were obtained primarily in three ways: Zipf rank-frequency curves were compiled for each condition. Figure 1 shows the four superimposed.

Figure 1.   Superimposed Zipf Curves for All Conditions

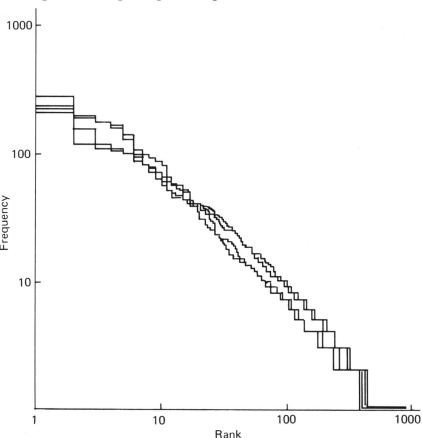

Since earlier studies utilizing the Zipf curves for the analysis of language samples have relied on visual inspection rather than rigorous statistical analysis, a mathematical analysis of it is used in the present study. On the premise that an egocentric bulge and greater verticality in the curve would show up in a correlation and slope analysis, correlation coefficients and slopes based on frequency logs plotted against average rank logs were computed for each curve. F ratios were found by taking the larger $1\text{-}r^2$ value and dividing it by the smaller one (each $1\text{-}r^2$ divided by its *d.f.*, $N\text{-}2$), and then checked for significance on the F table.[1] Slopes were computed and t tests were done on each to compare the curves with the ideal -1.00 slope value. Also, the percentage of words repeated less than five times was calculated for each condition. A summary of the results appears in Table 1.

Table 1.

A. Correlation Coefficients and Slopes of Zipf Curves

	r	*Slope*	σ *Slope*
N.S. Speech	−0.9881	−1.0242	0.01700
N.S. Writing	−0.9882	−1.0045	0.00721
S. Speech	−0.9900	−1.0140	0.01000
S. Writing	−0.9937	−1.0099	0.00098

Note: r is for all ranks; slopes are for curves after dropping ranks 1−10.

B. Significant F Ratios for Correlations

Non-stress speech versus stress writing: $F = 1.64$ p at 0.05
Non-stress writing versus stress writing: $F = 1.84$ $p < 0.05$

C. Comparing Slopes (omitting ranks 1−10) with Ideal −1.00 Slope : t Tests

	t	p
Non-stress speech	1.423	ns
Non-stress writing	1.00	ns
Stress speech	1.40	ns
Stress writing	10.05	<0.001

D. Comparing σ Slopes, Significant F Ratio

All speech versus all writing: $F = 3.29$ $p < 0.01$

The total numbers of words for each condition were: non-stress speech, 4662, non-stress writing, 3750, stress speech, 4996, and stress writing, 3979. 25 percent of speech and 32 percent of writing consisted of words repeated fewer than five times. Since a greater percentage of rare words were used in writing along with fewer total words, this suggests that writing is a more sociocentric mode of expression.

In comparing slopes, the steeper slope has the highest minus value. Slopes were taken of each curve after ranks 1−10 (more common words) were dropped because slopes were in a more consistent direction after rank 10. The slope values in order of least steep to most steep were: non-stress writing, stress writing, stress speech, and non-stress speech. Although these figures indicate greater egocentricity in speech, t tests discovered stress *writing* to have the only slope significantly steeper than −1.00. Since the smaller standard error in stress writing contributed to this finding, further comparisons were done on the variances. The variances for speech were significantly greater than those for writing at $p < 0.01$. Assuming that more variance reflects more egocentricity as shown in the egocentric bulge, this finding again supports the hypothesis that spoken expression is a more egocentric orientation than written expression.

For comparing correlations, r values obtained in this analysis were based on all the ranks, including 1–10. The values given are for the entire curve. Contrary to the hypothesis, both non-stress speaking and non-stress writing were significantly more egocentric at $p < 0.05$. Table 1 shows the results; non-stress speech was the most egocentric and stress writing the most sociocentric.

DISCUSSION

The results of this study suggest the following:

(1) The correlational method used to analyse the Zipf rank-frequency curve is a useful tool and flexible enough to analyse any portion of it.[2] Apparent differences in egocentricity of curves can be confirmed statistically by use of correlation coefficients. In this study, although visual inspection of the curves showed only possible differences, it remained for statistical analysis to disclose the significant differences.

(2) The findings on stress and non-stress conditions do not confirm earlier results (Marcus, 1965) from a study done on children which indicated stress conditions favored more egocentric expression. But in this present experiment, a major finding was the greater sociocentricity of expression under stress. This may be attributed to activation differences caused by different degrees of "felt stress" in children and in college students. Hebb (1955) stated in his arousal hypothesis that conditions maintaining a certain amount of neural activity in the individual act as an energizer or generalized drive, which leads to efficient performance of cognitive tasks when at an optimum level. There is a curvilinear relationship between degree of activation and quality of performance which looks like an inverted U; performance suffers with too much activation.

An explanation of the results of both this study and the aforementioned Marcus study is quite plausible in terms of the arousal hypothesis. In both experiments the subjects in the stress situation reported subjective anxiety feelings, and experimenter observation noted more nervous behavior here. The stress conditions did indeed induce more anxiety than the non-stress conditions. It is well known that children have a higher activation level than adults to begin with, and one may speculate that the stress that raised this activation brought that level past the point optimal for performance in the Marcus experiment. In the present study, environmental conditions were not conducive to any high degree of activation. During the two weeks in which the subjects were being tested, the weather was hot and sticky and the laboratory cubicle stuffy and poorly ventilated. Retrospectively, non-stress subjects were probably performing at the low end of the inverted U curve. They used a smaller vocabulary because their arousal was not high enough to bring the fullest range of words they knew to the threshold of awareness. Under stress, however, the resulting anxiety raised the activation level closer to, but not past, the optimum level for clear thought. More words became available.

(3) Significant differences in egocentricity between written and spoken expression, which showed up after the first ten ranks were dropped, supported the hypothesis of greater redundancy in speech and greater economy of words in writing. The results on the stress variable imply that egocentric verbal expression is not simply a function of mode of expression and stress alone; it is very likely also related to poor performance level in general, whether caused by too much or too little activation.

NOTES

[1]The formula used to compare the significance of these comparisons was derived from one commonly given to test the significance of one correlation, giving:

$$F = \frac{(n_1\text{-}2)\,(r_1)^2\,(1\text{-}r_2^2)}{(n_2\text{-}2)\,(r_2)^2\,(1\text{-}r_1^2)}$$

The formula was simplified by omitting the middle r^2 terms, giving the final formula used in this experiment, which was a more conservative test after this middle term was omitted. This formula is a simpler one than the Z transformation formula, especially when the r figures are carried out to more than two decimal places. The correlation ratio thus arrived at yielded slightly more significant results than the more commonly used Z transformation method with which it was checked. Comparing non-stress speech and stress writing, for example, give results significant at $p < 0.07$ in the Z method and at $p = 0.05$ in the correlational method.

[2]These correlations tend to be very high due to the monotonic function inherent in the structure of the curve; thus it is advantageous for the sake of comparison to use more than the normal two decimal places. Small differences between such high correlations tend to be more significant than between lower correlations. Because of this, extreme precision in calculating is essential.

REFERENCES

Hebb, D. O. 1955. Drives and the conceptual nervous system. *Psychol. Rev.*, 62: 243.

Horowitz, M. W. and Newman, J. B. 1964. Spoken and written expression: an experimental analysis. *J. abnorm. soc. Psychol.*, 68: 640.

Marcus, Sherry. 1965. Differences in spoken and written expression in children under neutral and stress conditions. N.I.M.H. Undergraduate Research Training in Psychology. Grant 2T2MH-7311-04.

Zipf, G. K. 1935. *The psycho-biology of language* (Boston).

Zipf, G. K. 1949. *Human behavior and the principle of least effort* (Cambridge, Mass.).

Part Four

STRUCTURING OF MESSAGES AS A FUNCTION OF DISTANCE TO THE REFERENTIAL OR TOPICAL MATERIAL

14

CHANGES IN REFERENCE PHRASES AS A FUNCTION OF FREQUENCY OF USAGE IN SOCIAL INTERACTION: A PRELIMINARY STUDY

Robert M. Krauss
Sidney Weinheimer

ABSTRACT

Pairs of subjects interacted in a problem-solving task which required them to communicate about ambiguous figures. The length of the reference phrase for each figure was calculated. A negative relationship was found between the frequency with which a figure was referred to and the mean length of its reference phrase.

Reprinted from *Psychonomic Science* 1 (1964): 113–14.
The authors gratefully acknowledge the aid of Mrs. Freda Zeiter, who devised the figures used in this experiment, and the technical advice and comments of P. D. Bricker.

PROBLEM

This paper reports a preliminary study in a program of research on the dynamics of linguistic changes which occur in the course of social interaction. The present study is concerned with the manner in which reference phrases (verbal labels) given to ambiguous figures change during interaction.

We hypothesized that subjects faced with the task of communicating about figures which are unique (in the sense that they do not evoke a common or "popular" reference phrase) would converge upon names for the figures. Further, it was hypothesized that these reference phrases would undergo modifications as a function of the frequency with which the subjects found it necessary to use them.

METHOD

The subjects' task was to match pairs of cards. Each subject had an identical set of six cards, each of which contained six ambiguous figures. In a given set, the same six figures appeared on every card. Three of the six figures (the "redundant figures") appeared in the same position on all cards. The remaining three (the "discriminating figures") appeared in permuted positions. An example of two cards from a set appears in Figure 1.

One subject's cards were labelled from A through F and the other's from 1 through 6. However, the letters and numbers were assigned randomly, so that subjects could not match cards simply on the basis of the identifying labels. Subjects were instructed to determine the correct letter-number matches for identical pairs of

Figure 1.   Two Cards from a Six-Card Set

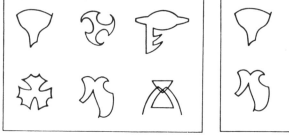
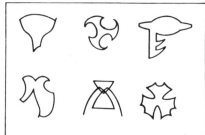

cards. Each pair of subjects worked on a total of 16 six-card sets and went through the sets in a different random order.

The six figures which appeared in a given set were drawn from a pool of 15 figures. Each figure had an assigned probability of appearing in a given set as a redundant or discriminating figure. These probabilities ranged from 1.0 to 0.125.

Three pairs of female and two of male college undergraduates were run. They worked in visually separated soundproof booths and communicated over a high-quality audio link. Their conversations were tape-recorded and later transcribed verbatim. The type script was coded by calculating the length (number of words) of each reference to each figure. Coder agreement was high, but because of the small sample size no systematic study of coding reliability was undertaken.

RESULTS

Figure 2 is a plot of the mean length of reference phrase for each figure as a function of the number of times that figure was referred

Figure 2. Mean Length of Reference Phrase as a Function of Frequency of Reference

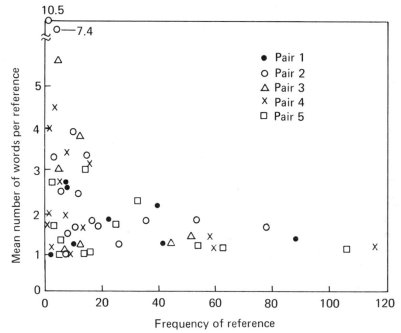

Figure 3.   Mean Length of Reference Phrase on Successive Repetitions

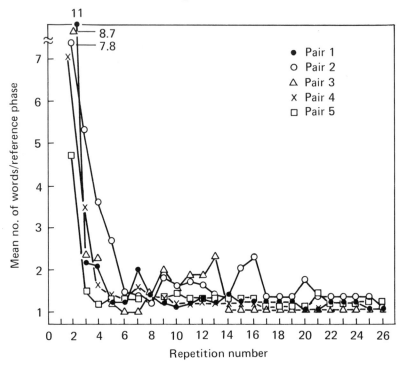

to. Data for all subjects are shown. Clearly there is a tendency for infrequently mentioned figures to be given reference phrases with long mean lengths and for frequently mentioned figures to be given relatively short reference phrases.

Some data suggesting the process which brings this relationship about appears in Figure 3. Here we have plotted the mean length of reference phrase for all figures on the first occasion they are mentioned, the second occasion, and so on, up to 25 repetitions. Curves for the five pairs are plotted individually. The first time a figure is referred to the reference phrase tends to be fairly lengthy. But over time with repetition the length rapidly decreases, approaching the lower limit of one word. As an example, one pair of subjects referred to a figure on the first mention as an "upside-down martini glass in a wire stand," then as an "inverted martini glass," then as a "martini glass," and then, after some time, simply as "martini."

DISCUSSION

Our results quite clearly indicate that the length of a reference phrase used to identify an ambiguous object diminishes as a function of its frequency of usage in the course of social interaction. Given the nature of our subjects' task and the strategy they employed, this result is not surprising. Essentially, the task required that they communicate about the location of the discriminating figures. To do this it was necessary that they develop a means of referring to these figures. The most commonly employed strategy was to assimilate the figures to variations of common objects (e.g., "an upside-down martini glass in a wire stand," "a boomerang with a notch in the blade"). Having identified the figure, it was then possible to "code" the figure's name into a shortened version of the initial reference phrase (e.g., "martini," "boomerang").

Similar processes may be observed in technical or other sorts of specialized vocabularies. Such shortenings as "hypo" from "hypothiosulfate of soda solution" (among photographers), "comps" from "comprehensive examinations" (among graduate students), and "dikes" from "diagonal cutting pliers" (among electronics technicians) are common examples.

Some similarity may be noted between Zipf's (1935) finding, that for natural languages a negative relationship exists between the size of a word and its frequency of usage, and the results of the present study. One would expect that the processes of linguistic change in a large linguistic community are both more subtle and more complex than those observed in our experimental situation. However, studies such as the present one may shed some light upon the dynamics which produce Zipf's findings.

Because of the small number of subjects employed and the preliminary nature of this study, these findings should be regarded as tentative. A full-scale study attempting to replicate these findings with a larger sample and some additional experimental variations is presently under way. We are concurrently running a study investigating the effect of types of feedback on changes of reference phrases.

REFERENCE

Zipf, G. K. The psycho-biology of language. Boston: Houghton Mifflin, 1935.

15

CHARACTERISTICS OF THE THREE-PERSON CONVERSATION

Julius Laffal

The three-person groups is the smallest social group, as distinct from the two-person pair, and it is of considerable interest to study the speech content of speakers in such a group. We have reported on content studies of single-word associations taken from a large number of Ss, continuous word associations taken from separate individuals, and the free speech of speakers in paired conversation (Laffal and Feldman, 1963). The present study deals with the language of three speakers in free conversation about a variety of topics. Its purpose was threefold: to determine to what extent the group influenced the speech content of the individual; to test the validity of grouping certain distinct content areas under a single content category on the basis of a psychological similarity between the areas; and to determine to what extent the topic overrode group or individual speech content characteristics.

Specific hypotheses were as follows:

(H1). The contents of each of three separate speakers in a particular conversation would be more like each other, than

Reprinted from *Journal of Verbal Learning and Verbal Behavior* 6 (1967): 555–59.

they would be like the contents of the same three speakers in another, different conversation.

(H2). In separate conversations, where the topics were related by some underlying psychological similarity, the contents of the three speakers would be more highly similar than in separate conversations where the topics had no such judged similarity.

(H3). That any particular speaker would be more highly correlated with himself in content, than with other speakers, across all conversations.

METHOD

Three summer students were given the task of talking before a tape recorder about two stimulus words (or phrases) per day, for one half hour per word. A total of 38 stimulus words were assigned. The words were selected to reflect 19 categories of a content dictionary which has been described in detail elsewhere (Laffal, 1965). There were two words per category, and each word reflected an area which had been judged to have a psychological affinity with the area of its similar word. The *S*s performed the experiment completely on their own. They were given a series of envelopes with numbers indicating on which of 19 succeeding days the two words contained in the envelopes should be discussed. They were to open the envelopes in sequence on each day that they held a discussion, discuss the first stimulus word for a half hour, then open the next envelope and discuss the second stimulus word for a half hour. No words belonging to the same category were discussed on the same day. Because of scheduling problems, several sets of words were discussed on the morning and afternoon of the same day rather than on succeeding days.

The instructions, in part, were:

"The idea is to talk about whatever comes to mind when you think of the word. Just talk as freely as possible about any thoughts or ideas that are brought up by the word. Each of you should try to contribute as much as you can to the discussion, while observing normal standards of politeness to one another. There are only two rules about what you should or should not say. First, your discussion about any word should center on the thoughts that word brings to mind. Some of the words are quite abstract. If you think of the word not so much as a single word, but as the key word of a concept or a broad area of subject matter, this might help the discussion. In your discussion try to keep the key word and the areas which it suggests in the center of your attention. The second rule is that you should try to approach each word independently of the others that you have discussed on previous days or in the first part of the session."

The students, who were employed during the summer to work as companions to patients on psychiatric wards, were two high school juniors and a college sophomore. The college sophomore was 24 years of age; the high school students were 17. The college student and one of the high school students were Negroes.

Although a total of 38 words were discussed by the students, the present study reports the analysis of only 12 of these words. This reduced analysis was made necessary by the vast amount of work involved in transcribing the tape recordings, and in hand scoring each word uttered by the speakers according to the category system employed. Further analysis of the remaining data has been deferred pending completion of a computer program for the automatic categorization of words.

The 12 stimulus words and their six categories, taken from the description of categories in Laffal (1965, pp. 189–216) were as follows: *waiting* and *resting* (from the category SLOW which includes references to waiting, immobility, standing still, sitting, quiescence, slow motion, gradualness, hesitation, pausing, laziness); *up* and *astronomy* (from the category UP which includes references to above, top, summit, height, tower and the direction up, as well as references to astronomical phenomena such as planet, stars, sky, space, heavens); *magic* and *fantasy* (from the category UNREAL, which includes references to the supernatural, magic, fortune-telling, conjuring, and seers, as well as references to visions, hallucinations, dreams, fantasies, imagined events, and illusions); *joining together* and *being related* (from the category JOIN, which includes references to coming together, meeting, visiting, joining, accompanying, associating, allying, and uniting, as well as references to family relationships); *comfort* and *pleasure* (from the category CALM, which includes references to ease, comfort, pacification, peace and quiet, as well as references to enjoyment, pleasure and happiness); and *sharpness* and *precision* (from the category SHARP, which includes references to sharp edges, points and cutting, as well as references to precision, unequivocality, directness, accuracy, definiteness and clarity).

The free discussions were transcribed from the tapes, and scorers assigned categories to each word in the transcripts, based on a category dictionary of approximately 25,000 root word-forms. The analysis is thus to all intents and purposes a total content analysis, and takes into account the frequency of occurrence of all categories in the speech of the various speakers. The system classifies all words except such interstitial words as articles, some prepositions, relative pronouns, auxiliary verbs and some other words which cannot be adequately categorized as to content.

RESULTS AND DISCUSSION

There were 12 words and 3 speakers, so that 36 content profiles were derived, reflecting each speaker's contribution in each of the 12 half-hour discussions. The profiles consisted of 114 categories of content, showing frequency of occurrence of a reference to each content. These profiles were compared to each other by means of Pearson product-moment correlations. Means were then taken of the correlations, and the mean correlations were compared by *t*-test. Where an *F* test indicated heterogeneity of variance of the distribution of correlations, a corrected *t* test was computed (Edwards, 1950, pp. 162–169).

Table 1 presents the mean correlations, and their comparison with each other, required by the hypotheses underlying the study. Thus the first comparison in Table 1 is between the mean corre-

Table 1. Comparisons of Mean Correlations Between Various Types of Speech Content Profiles[a]

Comparison of hypotheses	N_r	M_r	SD	t	F
H1 Intraconversation r's	36	.8662	.08	9.47[b]	
Similar word r's	54	.7241	.05	(8.94[b])[c]	1.94[b]
H1 Intraconversation r's	36	.8662	.08	13.07[b]	
Dissimilar word r's	54	.6531	.07		1.39
H2 Similar word r's	54	.7241	.05	5.73[b]	1.40
Dissimilar word r's	54	.6531	.07		
H3 Same speaker r's	51	.7011	.08	.83	1.04
Separate speaker r's	102	.6887	.08		

[a]The table shows the number of correlations of speech profiles (N_r), the means (M_r) | and SD's of these correlations, and tests of significance between the mean correlations. The hypotheses (H1, etc.) tested in each comparison is also indicated.

[b]Significant beyond the .05 level.

[c]The *t*-value in parentheses is *t* corrected to take into account the heterogeneity of variance indicated by the significant *F*.

lations of speakers within conversations (three speakers in con-versations about 12 separate words) and the mean correlation of their speech contents for each of six words correlated with speech contents for similar words (nine correlations in each of six pairs of similar words). The mean correlation between speakers within conversations was .8662; the mean correlation between speakers for similar words was .7241, the difference being significant. In the same way, the intraconversation mean correlation was compared with a random sample of between-speaker correlations in six dis-similar word pairs (nine correlations in each of six dissimilar word pairs). Here the difference is also significant. These two compari-sons support the first hypothesis.

In the comparison of similar (same category) and dissimilar (separate category) words, the conversations about similar words were significantly more highly correlated than the conversations about the dissimilar words. The second hypothesis was thus sup-ported. For the comparison of the same-speaker correlations with separate-speaker correlations, all similar word pairs and dis-similar word pairs employed in the tests of the first hypothesis, as well as five additional dissimilar word pairs not previously util-ized, were used. This provided 17 pairs of words (six similar and 11 dissimilar) with three speakers self-correlating across pairs, giving a total of 51 self-correlations. The same 17 pairs, with three speakers correlating with each other and not with self (six correla-tions per pair) provided 102 separate-speaker correlations. There was no significant difference between the mean same-speaker cor-relation across all conversations and the mean separate-speaker correlation. The third hypothesis must therefore be rejected.

In a previous study (Laffal and Feldman, 1963) it was found that subject matter is a more important determinant of content than individual differences, in the two-person conversation. The same finding appears to apply in the three-person conversation. Subjects correlate in content more highly with each other within conversations than they do with self across conversations. On the other hand, where topics judged psychologically similar are of-fered as stimuli for conversation, the contents are more similar to each other than for psychologically dissimilar topics.

The influence of topic of conversation on production of con-tent is thus quite clear. However, this may be seen itself as the product of two forces: a commonality of experience among the speakers which leads them to produce the same associations when faced with the same stimuli; and a social conformity factor in which each one submits to the suggestions entailed in the other's associations and shapes his associations accordingly. An interesting test of the implications of this idea would be a situation in which a speaker in a group conversation tended to deviate quite considerably in his associations from the others. Would the presence of the others, and their associations, bring the deviant individual's productions into line with the group? Such situations may occur where a psychotic individual participates in a group of normal or at least not seriously disturbed individuals.

In the present study, as in the previous one (Laffal and Feldman, 1963) individual differences in content seemed insignificant. A speaker correlated just as highly with another speaker in a separate conversation as he did with himself in the two conversations. It is difficult to interpret this absence of individual differences. It could be an accidental factor of similarity of interests and educations of the speakers, but this does not appear likely, since they differed in age and race. It may be due to an overriding commonality of words employed by speakers of the language. This is somewhat supported by the fact that all the correlations in the study are very high. Nevertheless, this commonality factor in the language, if it exists, is not strong enough to mask significant differences in content evoked by different stimuli. The most likely explanations are that on the one hand the speakers were influenced by each other in a given conversation to such an extent as to override their own internal consistency; and on the other hand, that speakers can shift to a relatively independent vocabulary when talking about distinctly different topics.

Of considerable significance for the technique of analysis, is the fact that words judged psychologically similar and categorized similarly in the system of analysis (Laffal, 1965) evoked contents which were significantly more similar to each other than did topics which were dissimilar. It is important to note, however, that although the differences were significant, they were not large. It will be worthwhile at some point to explore the possibility of focusing the analysis upon that middle range of frequencies which provides the most discrimination between separate profiles, by eliminating categories which occur universally in great frequency or in low frequency. Thus, in the present study, the categories SELF-REFERENCE, GO, INDIVIDUAL, NEGATION, REASON (COGNITION), and GENERAL TIME, occurred with very high frequency in almost all profiles where the categories ALL 3 (FREQUENT), ART, CLEAN, COLOR, CRIME, EASY, and ILLNESS had very little usage in any of the profiles. The inclusion of such high- and low-frequency categories tends to raise all correlations and so to make the differences between them smaller. The selective elimination of high- and low-frequency categories from the comparisons may also be a device for reducing the contribution of topic to the content, and may thus also reveal individual predilections for particular content no matter what the topic.

REFERENCES

Edwards, A. L. *Experimental design in psychological research.* New York: Rinehart & Co., Inc., 1950.
Laffal, J. *Pathological and normal language.* New York: Atherton Press, 1965.
Laffal, J., and Feldman, S. The structure of free speech. *J. verb. Learn. verb. Behav.,* 1963, 2: 498–503.

16

INTERVIEWER SPECIFICITY AND TOPICAL FOCUS IN RELATION TO INTERVIEWEE PRODUCTIVITY

Benjamin Pope
Aron W. Siegman

The present study is concerned with the relationship between *specificity* and *topical focus* in the interviewer's verbal behavior and interviewee verbal productivity. In a previous content analytic investigation Pope and Siegman (1962) found significant negative correlations between therapist specificity and patient clause units in immediately following responses. The present study differs from the previous one in two respects: it includes an additional independent variable, that of interviewer topical focus; and it is based on an experimental analogue of the initial interview, rather than on the content analytic study of naturalistic interviews.

The converse of *specificity*, ambiguity, has been investigated in a series of studies at the University of Michigan (Bordin, 1955; Dibner, 1953; Osburn, 1951), but prior to the work of Lennard, Bernstein, Palmore, and Hendin (1960) the concept lacked an adequate theoretical framework. Lennard *et al.* (1960) view the thera-

Reprinted from *Journal of Verbal Learning and Verbal Behavior* 4 (1965): 186–92.

peutic dyad as an informational exchange system and designate specificity as the crucial variable in therapist informational output. The more specific a therapist remark is, the more it limits the range or array of possible patient responses, and the greater is its informational stimulus value. The model of the therapeutic dyad as an informational exchange system, and the concept of therapist specificity as the crucial variable in therapist informational output are both accepted as theoretical bases of the present research. Moreover, the finding of Lennard and his group of an inverse relationship between therapist specificity and patient productivity (Lennard *et al.*, 1960) accords with Pope and Siegman's results in the study referred to above (1962).

Topical focus was included as a second interviewer variable in order to control for interview content, and to study its independent effect as well as its possible interaction with specificity. In spite of the great variability of personal meaning attributed to any given set of content categories by different *S*s, Kanfer (1960) has demonstrated the possibility of their successful manipulation when the subject population is kept homogeneous, and topical areas are selected to contrast in anxiety arousal effect with the *S*s chosen. In the present study, as in Kanfer's (1960), content areas are classified in terms of anxiety arousing potential with the selected *S*s.

The dependent variable in this study is interviewee productivity as reflected in number of words. Productivity is regarded as a basic measure of the efficacy of the interview, its success in evoking the verbal participation of the interviewee. It is recognized, of course, that in some instances verbose responses may be irrelevant to the purpose of the interview. Yet, it has been demonstrated that within the context of the initial interview (Howe and Pope, 1962) experienced clinicians tend to rate the more productive patient responses as more useful diagnostically than the less productive ones.

The following two hypotheses were proposed: (a) There is a negative relationship between interviewer specificity and interviewee productivity. (b) There is a positive relationship between topical anxiety arousal effect and productivity.

Although it was assumed that there would be some interaction between specificity and topical focus, there was no commitment to any particular hypothesis. Hypothesis (a) is consistent with the view of Lennard *et al.* (1960) that interviewee productivity decreases as interviewer specificity, i.e. informational output, increases. Hypothesis (b) derives from the view that aroused anxiety produces an activation effect (Duffy, 1962), and that such activation is positively correlated with verbal productivity.

METHOD

Subjects

The interview Ss were 50 junior and senior nursing students, all female, with ages ranging from 20 to 22, selected from the total membership of the junior and senior classes ($N = 104$) on the basis of the following criteria: (a) both parents living; (b) one or more siblings; (c) no report of school or college maladjustment or anxiety. The first two criteria were designed to fit each S into the content structure of the experimental interview. The third was used to eliminate all Ss who reported stressful experience in any period of past school history, and thus facilitate the use of school history as the low anxiety topic.

Procedure

The experimental interview is based on a planned manipulation of specificity and topical focus as the independent variables. It is divided into two content segments, including a *neutral topic* (past school history) and an *emotional* or anxiety-arousing topic (family relationships). In each topical area there is a "Low-High-Low" specificity order in which two low-specificity questions are followed by four high-specificity questions, and then again by two low. On an 11-point empirical specificity scale (Siegman and Pope, 1962), the low-specificity questions range from a scale value of 4.1 to 6.3; the high-specificity questions from 7.0 to 10.9. More than the required number of questions was prepared to give the interviewer some latitude in responding to the S. It will be seen that a partial control for a possible specificity order effect is built into the experimental design, in the LHL order within each topic. That this control is only partial is noted in the occurrence of high-specificity questions only in the middle portions of both topical segments. In order to evaluate a possible topical order effect, topic was alternated sequentially in the order in which Ss appeared for the interview.

One of the investigators (B.P.) conducted all the interviews. The apparatus consisted of two neck microphones, one worn by the interviewer and one by the S, and a tape recorder in the adjoining observation room. The length of the interview was determined entirely by the S, and was a consequence of her productivity, reaction time, articulation rate and silent pauses. As it turned out the median interview length was 26 min, with a range of 11 to 95 min. Immediately after the interview the second investigator (A.W.S.) administered a questionnaire to each S to determine whether she experienced greater discomfort when talking about the anxiety arousing topic (family relationships) or the neutral topic (school history). On this questionnaire the Ss reported feeling significantly more "uncomfortable" and "tense" during the *emotional* rather than the *neutral* topic, demonstrating that the topical manipulation had the intended effect.

RESULTS

The data consist of repeated measurements on the same Ss, who are randomly divided into two groups to control for a possible order effect on the topical manipulation. An analysis of variance for repeated measurements on two independent groups (Winer, 1962, pp. 324–330) is therefore appropriate. Such an analysis demonstrates that both independent variables have significant effects on interviewee productivity. For Specificity F (1, 48) is 217.93, $p <$ .001; for Topic, F (1, 48) = 5.85, $p <$ .05. As predicted, the low-specificity questions and the anxiety-arousing topic elicit greater productivity than the high-specificity questions and the neutral topic. Thus, the mean number of words per S in the high specificity-emotional topic and low specificity-emotional topic segments of the interview were 549.14 and 1684.66, respectively, and in the high specificity-neutral topic and low specificity-neutral topic segments, 478.26 and 1370.66, respectively. Although no precise predictions were made for a specificity by topical focus interaction, some form of interaction was anticipated. Actually, none occurs.

Since Matarazzo, Weitman, Saslow, and Wiens (1963) have demonstrated a strong association between duration of interviewer utterance and length of interviewee response, the possible confounding of duration with specificity and topical focus was assessed. There is, indeed, a significant difference in average duration of interviewer remarks between the two topical areas, with the neutral remarks being longer[1] than emotional ones, t(48) = 11.25, $p <$ .001. On the basis of the findings of Matarazzo, Weitman, Saslow, and Wiens (1963) one would therefore expect interviewee responses to be longer in the neutral-topical area; in fact they are significantly shorter. Thus the finding of a topical difference in productivity independent of the duration variable is sustained.

Specificity too is confounded with duration of interviewer utterance; interviewer remarks in the high-specificity segments are significantly shorter than those in the low-specificity segments, $t(48) = 25.57$, $p < .001$. An analysis of covariance for repeated measures therefore was carried out (Winer, 1962, pp. 606–615) to control for the effect of duration of interviewer remarks. As a result the original F-ratio for specificity changed from 217.93 to 46.01 ($p < .001$); the original F-ratio for topic from 5.85 to 7.64 ($p < .01$). The corresponding epsilon values are .49 and .30. It should be noted that these are the relationships that persist after the confounding with duration of utterance has been partialled out.

DISCUSSION

The finding of a negative relationship between interviewer specificity and interviewee productivity is consistent with the results of Lennard and his associates (1960), and with their analysis of the interview as an informational exchange system, in which a reciprocal relationship exists between the two participants. The possible mediating role of anxiety (Kenny and Bijou, 1953) in the specificity effect was considered in the previous study by Pope and Siegman (1962), i.e., the possibility that low specificity evokes high anxiety and consequently high productivity. However, the position is now taken that the Lennard *et al.* (1960) model is adequate, in itself, to deal with the results of the present study. It is postulated that low-interviewer specificity creates a condition of informational uncertainty which the interviewee strives to reduce through increased productivity.

On the other hand the arousal of anxiety through the topical manipulation was operational intended and confirmed by the post-interview ratings of the Ss. Its role as an activator (Duffy, 1962) is noted in the positive relationship between the anxiety arousing effect of topic and productivity. However, in this experiment topical focus is less efficacious than specificity in evoking productivity. Nevertheless the relationship is significant and consistent with the earlier results of Davids and Eriksen (1955), pointing to a positive correlation between anxiety and verbal productivity. In spite of the doubts raised by others (Matarazzo, Weitman, and Saslow, 1963) regarding the usefulness of a topical manipulation in the study of the interview, the present experiment demonstrates that such a manipulation can be effective if the interview Ss are selected with reference to relevant aspects of the topics used. In the present instance, the criteria for the selection of Ss ensured the contrast in anxiety arousal effect of the two topical areas.

The design of the present study, based on a dichotomous manipulation of anxiety, prevents the examination of a possible inverted U-relationship (Kenny and Bijou, 1953) between anxiety and productivity. Moreover, it is likely that even the emotional topic elicits only a moderate level of anxiety. However, the facilitating of interviewee verbal communication by an optimum level of anxiety and its possible inhibition by an excessively high level (Duffy, 1962, p. 194) deserve further investigation.

It may be asked to what extent the findings of the present study, based on an experimental analogue of the initial interview, can be generalized to a psychotherapy sequence. On this issue the authors have no information of their own. Lennard *et al.* (1960) have found interviewer-interviewee verbal contingencies similar to those reported here in a series of psychotherapy interviews. The limitation of the current research and the previous content analytic study (Pope and Siegman, 1962) to the initial interview was prompted by the wish to avoid the long-term vicissitudes of the doctor-patient relationship and the cumulative impact of previous therapeutic sessions, as possible confounding variables. Moreover, the initial interview is concerned primarily with facilitating the patient's communication of information desired by the therapist, and the present research is clearly relevant to this problem.

The concluding comment is prompted by the confounding of duration of interviewer remarks with the two independent variables. The efficacy of specificity, topical focus, and duration of interviewer's utterances as independent variables in the study of the interview is sufficiently well established now to warrant their further investigation in experiments designed to study them in controlled association with each other, so that their independent and interaction effects may be evaluated.

NOTE

[1]Although Matarazzo, Weitman, Saslow, and Wiens (1963) use duration of interviewee response as the dependent variable, and the present authors use numbers of words, the two are highly correlated.

REFERENCES

Bordin, E. S. Ambiguity as a therapeutic variable. *J. consult. Psychol.*, 1955, 19: 9–15.

Davids, A. H. and Eriksen, C. W. The relationship of manifest anxiety to association productivity and intellectual attainment. *J. consult. Psychol.*, 1955, 19: 219–222.

Dibner, A. S. *The relationship between ambiguity and anxiety in a clinical interview.* Unpublished doctoral dissertation, University of Michigan, 1953.

Duffy, Elizabeth. *Activation and behavior.* New York: Wiley, 1962.

Howe, E. S. and Pope, B. Therapist verbal activity level and diagnostic utility of patient verbal responses. *J. consult. Psychol.*, 1962, 26: 149–155.

Kanfer, F. H. Verbal rate, eyeblink and content in structured psychiatric interviews. *J. abnorm. soc. Psychol.*, 1960, 61: 341–347.

Kenny, D. T. and Bijou, S. W. Ambiguity of pictures and extent of personality factors in fantasy responses. *J. consult. Psychol.*, 1953, 17: 283–288.

Lennard, H. L., Bernstein, A., Palmore, E. G. and Hendin, Helen. *The anatomy of psychotherapy.* New York: Columbia University Press, 1960.

Matarazzo, J. D., Weitman, M., Saslow, G. and Wiens, A. N. Interviewer influence on duration of interviewee speech. *J. verb. Learn. verb. Behav.*, 1963, 1: 451–458.

Matarazzo, J. D., Weitman, M. and Saslow, G. Interview content and interviewer speech duration. *J. clin. Psychol.*, 1963, 19: 463–472.

Osburn, R. G. *An investigation of the ambiguity dimension.* Unpublished doctoral dissertation, University of Michigan, 1951.

Pope, B. and Siegman, A. W. The effect of therapist verbal activity and specificity on patient productivity and speech disturbance in the initial interview. *J. consult. Psychol.*, 1962, 26: 489.

Siegman, A. W. and Pope, B. An empirical scale for the measurement of therapist specificity in the initial psychiatric interview. *Psychol. Rep.*, 1962, 11: 515–520.

Winer, B. J. *Statistical principles in experimental design.* New York: McGraw-Hill, 1962.

Part Five

SOCIAL CLASS, HIERARCHY, AND LINGUISTIC HABITS

17

PERCEPTUAL AND VERBAL DISCRIMINATIONS OF "ELABORATED" AND "RESTRICTED" CODE USERS

W. P. Robinson
C. D. Creed

INTRODUCTION

Several investigations (Bernstein, 1962a, 1962b; Lawton, 1963, 1964; Robinson, 1965a, 1965b) have testified to the fruitfulness of Bernstein's distinction between "elaborated" and "restricted" codes in that they have revealed a number of grammatical, lexical, semantic, and paralinguistic differences in the language used by working and middle class subjects. While these studies have each controlled for intelligence test scores of their experimental subjects, allocation to different code groups has always been based upon social class.

As Bernstein (1961b) has argued, the association between membership of the working class and confinement to a restricted code is contingent rather than necessary, so that it is important to examine the possibility of using more direct measures of the elaboratedness of the code, either by the utilization of appropriate social

Reprinted from *Language and Speech* 11 (1968): 182–93.

psychological controls within social class or by a direct examination of appropriate language samples taken from children, again within class.

A second feature common to the previous studies referred to is their use of language samples obtained in the relatively unstructured situations of group discussions, essays, and letter-writing. The language produced was only constrained by the general topic offered, the mode of linguistic communication and the social psychology of the situation; there were no right or wrong brief answers for example. It has not yet been shown that confinement to a restricted code is associated with a reduced probability of efficient functioning in a task requiring a constrained precision of language.

It became possible and desirable to investigate both possibilities in the work undertaken by the Sociological Research Unit. Sub-samples of Infant School children could be selected from those being studied in at least two ways, each opposing elaborated and restricted code users; one basis of selection was dependent upon experimental manipulation and the other upon naturally occurring individual differences.

In some schools a language program[1] had been mounted, whose function was to encourage children towards the use of an elaborated code. The effectiveness of this program required assessment and this provided the first dichotomy of subjects into "elaborated" and "restricted" code users. The second variable was a direct control on the language of the children. At the commencement of the project, over a year earlier, samples of speech had been taken from each child, and it was possible to use linguistic criteria to divide these children in terms of code elaboration.

If the experimental situation selected showed no significant differences between the experimentally defined elaborated and restricted code users, the failure might be attributed to the unreliability or invalidity of the scores in the particular task used, so an additional subject variable was incorporated into the design, which would be almost certainly associated with the dependent variables. If this variable gave significant differences in performances, a failure to find differences between code users would then have to be assigned to faulty allocation of subjects to their respective groups or a faulty theoretical basis rather than to the performance scores obtained. Verbal intelligence test scores were selected as such a validating criterion (English Picture Vocabulary Test, Brimer and Dunn, 1962).

Three areas of interest were selected for study: (1) curiosity and attentiveness, (2) perceptual discrimination, and (3) verbal discrimination. Bernstein's (1961a, p. 164; 1961b, pp. 296–302) exposition of the consequences of a confinement to a restricted code enable the following predictions to be made. The elaborated code user should be higher than the restricted code user on the following three sets of variables:

(1) his greater facility for cognitive experience will lead him to spend more time studying and analyzing a new situation,

(2) as a further consequence he will see more relationships between objects in a new situation; he will notice more attributes, and similarly,

(3) these discriminations are more likely to have effective verbal correlates which can be used to communicate the discriminations to a second person.

The task chosen for an examination of the validity of these predictions required a child to look at a painting for as long as he wished and then report what was in the picture. He was then shown a second painting identical to the first except for a limited number of deliberately introduced differences and had to point to the differences. When this had been done, he had to say what the differences were.

It was predicted that children with either high intelligence test scores or elaborated codes would:

(1) study the first picture for a long time without seeking further instruction,

(2) point to more differences, and

(3) describe these differences more efficiently.

METHOD: CRITERIA FOR THE ALLOCATION OF SUBJECTS TO "RESTRICTED" AND "ELABORATED" CODE GROUPS

Language Program

The language program was initiated in three schools (E1), a second group of schools (C1) was given some intervention, while a third group of schools was used only for before and after measurements (C2). The extra control group C1 was used to control for such possibilities as the heightened motivation of teachers which may have affected E1 schools over and above the language program. The teachers in E1 schools met fortnightly with the Unit psychologists who were organizing the language program to discuss the techniques and materials to be used. The teachers implemented the program for at least twenty minutes a day and the Unit psychologists observed the teachers once a week to check that agreed procedures were being used. The teachers in C1 schools met fortnightly to discuss general problems arising in Infant School teaching and conducted a number of investigations to obtain information about possible improvements: language and speech did not arise as a substantive issue in these discussions.

The language program was designed with three general aims in mind: first to make speech and language more salient, second to improve and expand the range and type of grammatical, lexical, and semantic facility available to a child and third, arising out of the previous two, to give the child an increased awareness of new ways of describing and categorizing the perceptual world, both material and social. To achieve these aims the children performed a series of different tasks during the twenty minute period each day. Two or three of these tasks were performed in one session and variations in tasks were repeated with different materials. A few examples are given:

Variations of the O'Grady game were used ("O'Grady says all children to raise their left hands." Those who fail drop out of the game, etc.). This task was intended to enhance the ability to discriminate qualitative and quantitative physical and social differences and act upon them. To succeed, children had to analyze their own attributes and those of relatives and friends. In variations of "I-Spy" game, specified new vocabulary was introduced. For "The Surprise Box" the children had to describe and communicate to another child the nature of unseen objects. "The Five Minute Story" (listened to on tape recorders) offered new vocabulary, exposed the child to increasingly complex syntax and had a "Spot the mistake" in it. Telephones were used for children to describe familiar objects to each other without mentioning the usual name. "Question Time" and "New Time" were made use of to develop the vocabulary and syntax by questioning and reporting. "Picture stories" were frequently used. Children were given sets of pictures and had to discuss all possible features of the social and physical situation. Pictures were omitted and the order of presentation was reversed, so that the children could develop an inferential and hypothetical approach to the stories.

A general intention of the language program may be summarized by stating that the hope was that children participating in it would move towards the use of an elaborated code in appropriate circumstances, while their control counterparts would not. E1 children could be used as a sample for "elaborated" code users, while either C1 or C2 children could be used for the "restricted" code sample, but since the E1/C1 comparison is the tighter contrast, C1 girls were selected.

The program was introduced into E1 schools during the children's first term at school and had been running for some four terms (50 weeks) at the time of this experiment.

Direct Measure of Elaboration/Restriction

When the children first entered Infant School, a language sample was taken from each one. The child was interviewed in a permissive atmosphere and performed six tasks designed to provide a range of types of speech. First the child arranged a model room and answered questions about the activities and speech of the family. This was followed by three sets of pictures forming the basis of narrative stories. The child then talked about what was going on in postcard reproductions of three detailed paintings by Trotin. For the fourth task the child said what he might do in a completely free day. Fifth the child was asked how to play the game Hide and Seek, Musical Chairs, or Ring-a-ring o' roses, and finally he was required to describe and explain the actions of a mechanical elephant which made a number of movements when an attached rubber bulb was squeezed. This speech is being subjected to a grammatical analysis based upon Halliday's Scale and Category Grammar (Halliday *et al.*, 1964). (For a subsidiary analysis, see Rackstraw and Robinson, 1967.) Certain grammatical variables were selected as being likely to separate elaborated from restricted code users and, while a stronger justification of this selection must await later analyses, it seemed worthwhile to attempt a separation for experimental purposes. The criteria used for division were among those previously found to differentiate between social class groups. The precise selection followed discussions with linguists. The scores used were: (1) number of subordinate clauses, (2) number of rank-shifted clauses, (3) number of adverbial groups, and (4) number of verb tenses. These criteria were generally consistent in their ordering, ($W = 0.75$, $p < 0.001$) and summed unweighted rank-orders were used for the final allocation.

Subjects

Boys had been used in other experiments to evaluate the language program and to reduce the extent to which particular individuals were exploited for such comparisons, girls were chosen for this experiment. The experimental variables of language program participation, elaboration of code and intelligence test scores have already been described. Subjects were also matched as closely as possible on a 10-point social class scale. This scale compounded the occupation and education of both parents. Occupations were classified on the Hall-Jones scale (Hall and Jones, 1950), while the educational contrast was between basic secondary education and some extension of this. That the subjects were predominantly lower working class is shown by two examples: only five of the 48 parents left school after the age of 15 and 15 of the 24 fathers' occupations could be allocated unambiguously to the unskilled or semi-skilled categories of the Hall-Jones scale.

At the time of experiment the mean age of the girls was six years and eight months (standard deviation 1.5 months). Twenty-four girls were selected, 12 from the language program schools (E1) and 12 from the stricter control group (C1). In each group 4 were High IQ and 8 Low. Of the 8 Low IQ, 4 were labelled "elaborated code" users, 4, "restricted code" users. As far as possible a matched-pairs design was used. E1 and C1 were matched pairs on E.P.V.T. verbal intelligence test scores (mean discrepancy 1.42 points) (see Table 1) and on the 10-point social class (mean discrepancy 1.36, difference between group means 0.4). Elaborated and restricted code users were similarly matched (mean E.P.V.T. discrepancy 1.38 points) and social class (mean discrepancy 1.1, difference between group means 0.7), but the variances were so low in these groups that analyses of variance could be used. The subjects were predominantly lower working class.

Materials

Five pairs of pictures were painted of which four pairs were used for this analysis: Dock Scene, School Playground, Motor-Car/Bus, Living Room and Child Feeding Pet. Twenty-seven differences were intended, but thirty-two were subsequently categorized: 8 were omitted objects, 7 were differences of color, 7 involved shape or position, 8 were differences in the faces or clothes of boys and girls with one spelling and one number difference.

197

Table 1. Basic Data: Intelligence Test, Perceptual Discrimination and Verbalization Scores

	Language program group (E1)			Control group (C1)		
	E.P.V.T. IQ	Perceptual discrimination	Verbalization	E.P.V.T. IQ	Perceptual discrimination	Verbalization
HIGH IQ	125	28	21	127	28	16
	119	27	24	118	22	9
	118	22	19	118	24	14
	106	26	16	109	27	20
Mean scores	117.0	25.75	20.0	118.0	25.25	14.75
Low IQ Elaborated Code	85	18	10	86	8	0
	86	23	16	87	9	2
	91	19	8	91	15	9
	94	25	13	92	18	14
Mean scores	89.0	21.25	11.75	89.0	12.5	6.25
Restricted Code	86	20	1	86	26	14
	86	16	0	88	9	0
	91	18	9	86	16	0
	91	24	15	91	21	0
Mean scores	88.5	19.5	6.25	87.8	18.0	3.5

Two stop watches were used to measure relevant time intervals, all conversation was tape recorded, and a check was available for noting differences pointed to.

Procedure

Twelve randomly selected orders of presentation of the pictures were used, the order being the same for each E1/C1 pair. The order in which each member of a pair was offered was systematically varied. The experimenter was a quietly spoken young man of below average height. The atmosphere was friendly and relaxed.

The subject sat opposite the experimenter and the following instructions were given: Each girl was shown the first member of the first pair of pictures as the experimenter said:

"Here is a picture, I'd like you to look at it—for as long as you like."

The amount of time that the child spent looking was recorded from this moment until she had looked away from the picture for 15 seconds at one time. A cumulative stop-watch was switched on every time the child looked back at the picture. When a 15 second gap had been registered or after three minutes, the experimenter said,

"Now tell me what is in the picture."

(This instruction ensured that the child studied the picture with some care.) Each time the child stopped, she was asked, "What else is there?", and this was continued until she said, "Nothing." One extra probe was given: "Are you sure?" The child was then given the second picture of the pair and was told, "There are some differences between this picture and the one you've been looking at. I want you to point to all the differences you can see. I want you to point to them, but not to say anything." If the child only pointed to one of the pictures the experimenter said, "Now show me on the other picture." The "What else is there?" procedure was carried out as before. The experimenter then said, "Now you've pointed to the differences, can you *tell* me what they are?" and the "What else is there?" procedure was repeated. For two picture-pairs the child was also asked, "In what ways are these pictures alike?" and "Can you tell me if there is anything the same?"; but these data are not reported.

Finally the child was probed on those items where she had reported a difference, but had not made its essence explicit. "Now we're just going to look at this picture pair again. When we looked at these before, you said the X (name of objects) were different. Can you tell me how they are different?"

TREATMENT OF RESULTS

The Motor-Car/Bus pair of pictures was dropped from the analysis and no comments about similarities were included. Two scoring methods were used. For pointing there was no problem, but for the verbal description four gradations were common: (1) simple statement of difference, (2) recognition of relevant variable (shape, color, etc.), (3) recognition of variable plus a statement of the value of the variable in one picture (it's round there), (4) recognition of both values of variable (that is red and that is green). For one scoring system 0, 1, 2 and 3 were given for the four types of answer, if these were given without probing. If a probe was used, statements at levels (3) and (4) were both given a score of 1. A second scoring system coded (3) and (4) as 1 and all others as 0. The more complex scoring system involved dubious assumptions about the weighting of the parts of answers, and since it gave substantially similar results to the simple scoring, the results of only the latter are reported.

Times were measured in seconds.

Two main techniques of analysis were employed, analyses of variance and co-variance, the latter for E1/C1 and sometimes elaborated/restricted code comparisons, but because of the unequal numbers, High versus Low IQ comparisons were confined to analyses of variance. For E1/C1 comparisons all 24 subjects were used, but elaborated/restricted code differences could only be tested in the Low IQ sub-sample ($n = 16$).

RESULTS

Attentiveness and Curiosity

Three sets of scores were tabulated: (1) a D score: the amount of time in seconds for which the subject looked at the first of each pair of pictures, (2) a C score: the amount of time spent looking away and (3) a G score: the number of glances away from the pictures. All measures were only for the period prior to the beginning of the pointing instructions.

Two indices were obtained: D and the ratio G/C. Both were reliable estimates and rankings across the four pictures gave coefficients of concordance (W) of 0.88 for D ($p < 0.001$) and 0.69 for G/C ($p < 0.001$). The values of the middle two scores of each subject were summed for subsequent analyses, but neither measure gave significant differences between any comparison groups and no trends were indicated.

Errors

Some differences pointed to and described by subjects were not intended by the experimenters, but were in fact reasonable judgments, others were simply not there. Where there was no doubt that a mistake had been made, an error score was noted.

Pointing errors were not associated with IQ or language program in the analysis utilizing all subjects, but differences were suggested in the Low IQ sub-sample. An analysis for main effects showed the language program ($F = 4.21$, $df = 1$, 12, $p < 0.10$) to have a weak relevance and the subsequent analysis for simple effects showed two significant differences: E1 made fewer errors than C1 within the restricted code group ($F = 6.52$, $df = 1$, 12, $p < 0.05$) and elaborated code users made fewer errors than restricted code users in the C1 group ($F = 8.65$, $df = 1$, 12, $p < 0.025$). Verbal errors reflected a similar pattern at the same levels of significance.

Perceptual Discrimination Scores

Bartlett's test for homogeneity of variance gave an insignificant χ^2 and uncorrected scores were used (see Table 1). High IQ girls pointed to more differences than Low IQ girls ($p < 0.001$), and the analysis of simple effects (for the Low IQ sub-sample) showed that E1 girls pointed to more differences than C1 girls within the elaborated group ($p < 0.05$) (see Table 2).

Verbalization Scores

For the simple scoring technique Bartlett's test of homogeneity of variance permitted the use of untransformed scores and once more IQ was of considerable significance (see Table 3). When analyses of co-variance were used to eliminate the relevance of differing perceptual discrimination scores, IQ and language program were both significant, while in the Low IQ sub-sample the elaborated code users performed significantly more effectively (see Table 4).

Table 2. Perceptual Discrimination

(Variation of scores as a function of IQ, participation in the language program and elaboratedness of code)

Source of variation	df	Mean square	F ratio	p	Source of variation	df	Mean square	F ratio	p
		Total sample (n = 24)					Low IQ sample (n = 16)		
IQ	1	315.22	15.57	<0.001	Elab./restrict.	1	14.06	—	—
E1/C1	1	42.11	2.08	<0.2	E1/C1	1	105.06	4.27	<0.1
Interaction	1	28.41	1.40	—	Interaction	1	52.57	2.14	<0.2
Within cells	20	20.24			Within cells	12	24.56		

Table 3. Verbal Discrimination

(Variation of scores as a function of IQ, participation in the language program and elaboratedness of code)

Source of variation	df	Mean square	F ratio	p	Source of variation	df	Mean square	F ratio	p
		Total sample (n = 24)					Low IQ sample (n = 16)		
IQ	1	580.97	18.39	<0.001	Elab./restrict.	1	68.06	1.77	—
E1/E2	1	117.26	3.71	<0.1	E1/E2	1	68.06	1.77	—
Interaction	1	1.65	—	—	Interaction	1	7.57	—	—
Within cells	20	31.58			Within cells	12	38.27		

Table 4. Verbal Discrimination

(Variation of scores as a function of IQ, participation in the language program and elaboratedness of code, partialling out perceptual discrimination scores)

Source of variation	df	Mean square	F ratio	p	Source of variation	df	Mean square	F ratio	p
		Total sample (n = 24)					Low IQ sample (n = 16)		
IQ	1	567.85	15.57	<0.001	Elab./Restrict.	1	134.67	8.08	<0.05
E1/E2	1	163.38	5.08	<0.05	E1/E2	1	2.04	—	—
Interaction	1	0.95	—	—	Interaction	1	11.95	—	—
Within cells	19	29.26			Within cells	11	16.65		

DISCUSSION

The results generally confirmed expectations. For perceptual and verbal discriminations no differences were contrary to expectation and all differences were in the predicted directions, even though they were smaller and less stable than originally hoped, especially in the E1/C1 and elaborated/restricted comparisons.

Intelligence test scores gave clear and strong differentials, attesting to the reliability and validity of the materials used. These results have relevance also to the problem of how far the E.P.V.T. is a verbal rather than a non-verbal test. Efficiency of unverbalized perpetual discrimination is strongly associated with E.P.V.T. scores, but when pointing scores have been partialled out, the extra efficiency of verbalization remains significantly associated.

This strong association between the intelligence test scores and both perceptual and verbal discrimination was possibly responsible for the attenuation of E1/C1 differences when analyses of variance were used: the variance of discrimination scores within groups was probably increased by the small variation in the intelligence test scores.

No measure of attentiveness or curiosity bore a relationship to the dependent variables examined, although the measures of internal consistency suggested that the time periods recorded had satisfactory degrees of reliability. Either these measures are invalid or the original theoretical framework requires modification. Bernstein's comments about curiosity are general rather than specific. The implication of his viewpoint is that curiosity mediated through verbal communication will be lower in restricted code groups. The restricted code child will be discouraged from continuing to ask questions, because the answers he initially receives from his restricted code parents will have been unsatisfactory. This has now been supported empirically: asking questions of his mother, he is less likely to receive an answer, and any answer received is likely to contain less information of a less accurate nature and to be embedded in more "noisy" sentences (Robinson and Rackstraw, 1967). Similarly with attentiveness, it is the attentiveness to speech which may be lower in the restricted code child, so that the lack of differentiation with the measures of attentiveness and curiosity made here suggests that their proposed relevance should be restricted to situations involving verbal components.

The results with the error and pointing scores both support the prediction that elaborated code children perform more efficently than those confined to a restricted code. Both the language program and the direct measure of elaboration give significant differences on errors, but pointing differences are only significant between E1 and C1 for the elaborated code Low IQ group. Both measures of elaboration relate to verbalization, but only when perceptual discrimination scores are partialled out.

An examination of the verbalization scores (see Table 1) reveals one reason why the significance of E1/C1 and elaborated restricted differences are attenuated. One child in the restricted code C1 group made the third highest verbalization score of the sixteen Low IQ girls. Furthermore, for the analyses of co-variance in the E1/C1 comparison she was paired with the second to weakest E1 child. The elimination of this subject from the analyses left all predictions supported at high levels of significance. Are there good reasons for thinking that this C1 restricted code child was wrongly allocated? A check of his scores in the speech sample confirmed her assignment to the restricted code group. Her W.I.S.C. verbal score, taken six months before the experiment, was 97; this was 11 points higher than the earlier E.P.V.T. estimate, while the mean difference for the Low IQ C1 group was only 4. A further feature of possible relevance is social class. This subject was the highest in the Low IQ C1 group. Although her father had only basic secondary education and was a dock laborer, her mother had not left grammar school until she was 17 and had subsequently worked as a laboratory technician. Her matched pair in E1 achieved her higher social class by virtue of the father's self-employment. There are some special features differentiating this child from others in her group, but insufficient for dropping the child from the analysis. The case is mentioned in some detail because it illustrates the importance of a close examination of the bases of allocation when using small groups of subjects, and it seems that the use of the compound social class index may have been mistaken. In fields of inquiry such as this, the mother's education may be a more important index than father's occupation, and the true relevance of the variables examined may have been underestimated by this oversight. Nevertheless significant differences were found and these were not between extended samples of language in free situations.

The experimental situation constrained subjects severly. There were right and wrong answers, to be achieved by pointing and subsequent explicit verbal labelling of the different values of the relevant variable. For the verbalization an elaborated grammar was unnecessary: only a contextually appropriate range of adjectives or nouns was required for perfect answering. Whereas the characteristics of the working class language samples found in earlier studies could be attributed to a preference for certain modes of expression rather than an inability to use other grammatical structures or lexical elements, the results here support the view that group differences are more than matters of selective preferences. Further, this has been demonstrated with elaborated and restricted codes controlled more directly than heretofore.

Both indices proved satisfactory in spite of controls for verbal IQ and social class. The confirmation of the effectiveness of the language program is the more important result educationally, but the other has greater surprise value. The speech sample from which only four variables were used to classify the children was taken eighteen months before the experiment was conducted. This is a substantial proportion of the speaking life of the children tested and implies a high reliability of the original estimate, as well as its validity as an empirical basis for making predictions about behavior in other situations. As far as can be ascertained, this is the first demonstration that general differences in language samples, with IQ and social class controlled, are associated with perceptual and verbal discriminations. Since these results are consistent with Bernstein's distinction between elaborated and restricted codes, it would be of considerable theoretical and practical interest to examine the full range of behavioral differences in psychological and social psychological test situations between children whose major difference appears to be in speech code only.

NOTE

[1]This program was devised and administered by D. M. Gahagan and Georgina Gahagan.

REFERENCES

Bernstein, B. 1961a. Social structure, language, and learning. *Educational Res.*, 3: 163.

Bernstein, B. 1961b. Social class and linguistic development: a theory of social learning. In A. H. Halsey, J. Floud, and C. A. Anderson (eds.), *Education, economy and society* (New York).

Bernstein, B. 1962a. Linguistic codes, hesitation phenomena and intelligence. *Language and Speech*, 5:41.

Bernstein, B. 1962b. Social class, linguistic codes and grammatical elements. *Language and Speech*, 5: 221.

Brimer, M. A. and Dunn, L. M. 1962. *The English picture vocabulary tests* (London).

Hall, J. and Jones, D. C. 1950. Social grading of occupations. *Brit. J. Sociol.*, 1: 31.

Halliday, M. A. K., McIntosh, A. and Strevens, P. 1964. *The linguistic sciences and language teaching* (London).

Lawton, D. 1963. Social class differences in language development: a study of some samples of written work. *Language and Speech*, 6: 120.

Lawton, D. 1964. Social class differences in group discussion. *Language and Speech* 7: 102.

Rackstraw, S. J. and Robinson, W. P. 1967. Social and psychological factors related to variability of answering behaviour in five-year-old children. *Language and Speech*, 10: 88.

Robinson, W. P. 1965a. Cloze procedure as a technique for the investigation of social class differences in language usage. *Language and Speech*, 8: 42.

Robinson, W. P. 1965b. The elaborated code in working class language. *Language and Speech*, 8: 243.

Robinson, W. P. and Rackstraw, Susan J. 1967. Variations in mothers' answers to children's questions as a function of social class, verbal intelligence test scores, and sex. *Sociology*, 1: 259.

18

SOCIAL CLASS AND MODES OF COMMUNICATION

Leonard Schatzman
Anselm Strauss

Common assumptions suggest that there may be important differences in the thought and communication of social classes. Men live in an environment which is mediated through symbols. By naming, identifying, and classifying, the world's objects and events are perceived and handled. Order is imposed through conceptual organization, and this organization embodies not just anybody's rules but the grammatical, logical, and communicative canons of groups. Communication proceeds in terms of social requirements for comprehension, and so does "inner conversation" or thought. Both reasoning and speech meet requirements of criticism, judgment, appreciation, and control. Communication across group boundaries runs the danger—aside from sheer language difficulties —of being blocked by differential rules for the ordering of speech and thought.[1]

If these assumptions are correct, it follows that there should be observable differences in communication according to social class and that these differences should not be merely matters of degree of preciseness, elaboration, vocabulary, and literary style.

Reprinted from *The American Journal of Sociology* 60, No. 1 (January 1955): 329–38. Copyright © 1955 by The University of Chicago Press. Footnotes have been renumbered.

It follows also that the modes of thought should be revealed by modes of speaking.

Our data are the interview protocols gathered from participipants in a disaster. The documents, transcribed from tape, contain a wealth of local speech. Respondents had been given a relatively free hand in reporting their experiences, and the interviews averaged twenty-nine pages. These seemed admirably suited to a study of differences between social classes in modes of communication and in the organization of perception and thought. We used them also to explore the hypothesis that substantial intraclass differences in the organization of stories and accounts existed; hence low-class respondents might fail to satisfy the interviewer's canons of communication.

Approximately 340 interviews were available, representing random sampling of several communities ravaged by a tornado. Cases were selected by extreme position on educational and income continuums. Interviewees were designated as "lower" if education did not go beyond grammar school and if the annual family income was less than two thousand dollars. The "upper" group consisted of persons with one or more years of college education and annual incomes in excess of four thousand dollars. These extremes were purposely chosen for maximum socioeconomic contrast and because it seemed probable that nothing beyond formal or ritual communication would occur between these groups.

Cases were further limited by the following criteria: age (twenty-one to sixty-five years), race (white only), residence (native of Arkansas and more than three years in the community), proximity (either in the disaster area or close by), good co-operation in interview (as rated by interviewer), and less than eight probes per page (to avoid a rigid question-answer style with consequent structuring of interview by the interviewer's questions). The use of these criteria yielded ten upper-group cases, which were then matched randomly with ten from the lower group.[2]

DIFFERENCES BETWEEN CLASSES

Differences between the lower and upper groups were striking; and, once the nature of the difference was grasped, it was astonishing how quickly a characteristic organization of communication could be detected and described from a reading of even a few paragraphs of an interview. The difference is not simply the failure or success—

of lower and upper groups, respectively—in communicating clearly and in sufficient detail for the interviewer's purposes. Nor does the difference merely involve correctness or elaborateness of grammar or use of a more precise or colorful vocabulary. The difference is a considerable disparity in (*a*) the number and kinds of perspectives utilized in communication; (*b*) the ability to take the listener's role; (*c*) the handling of classifications; and (*d*) the frameworks and stylistic devices which order and implement the communication.

PERSPECTIVE OR CENTERING

By perspective or centering is meant the standpoint from which a description is made.[3] Perspectives may vary in number and scope. The flexibility with which one shifts from perspective to perspective during communication may vary also.

Lower class. Almost without exception any description offered by a lower-class respondent is a description as seen through his *own* eyes; he offers his own perceptions and images directly to the listener. His best performance is a straight, direct narrative of events as he saw and experienced them. He often locates himself clearly in time and place and indicates by various connective devices a rough progression of events in relation to his activities. But the developmental progression is only in relation to himself. Other persons and their acts come into his narrative more or less as he encountered them. In the clearest interviews other actors are given specific spatial and temporal location, and sometimes the relationships among them or between them and himself are clearly designated.

The speaker's images vary considerably in clarity but are always his own. Although he may occasionally repeat the stories of other persons, he does not tell the story as though he were the other person reconstructing events and feelings. He may describe another person's act and the motive for it, with regard to himself, but this is the extent of his role-taking—he does not assume the role of another toward still others, except occasionally in an implicit fashion: "Some people was helping other people who was hurt." This limitation is especially pronounced when the behavior of more than two or three persons is being described and related. Here the description becomes confused: At best the speaker reports some reactions, but no clear picture of interaction emerges.

The interaction either is not noticed or is implicitly present in the communication ("We run over there to see about them, and they was alright"). Even with careful probing the situation is not clarified much further. The most unintelligible speakers thoroughly confound the interviewer who tries to follow images, acts, persons, and events which seem to come out of nowhere and disappear without warning.

Middle class. The middle class can equal the best performance of the lower class in communicating and elaborating a direct description. However, description is not confined to so narrow a perspective. It may be given from any of several standpoints: for instance, another person, a class of persons, an organization, an organizational role, even the whole town. The middle-class speaker may describe the behavior of others, including classes of others, from their standpoints rather than from his, and he may include sequences of acts as others saw them. Even descriptions of the speaker's own behavior often are portrayed from other points of view.

CORRESPONDENCE OF IMAGERY BETWEEN SPEAKER AND LISTENER

Individuals vary in their ability to see the necessity for mediating linguistically between their own imagery and that of their listeners. The speaker must know the limits within which he may assume a correspondence of imagery. When the context of the item under discussion is in physical view of both, or is shared because of similarity of past experience, or is implicitly present by virtue of a history of former interaction, the problem of context is largely solved.[4] But when the context is neither so provided nor offered by the speaker, the listener is confronted with knotty problems of interpretation. In the accounts of the most unintelligible respondents we found dream-like sets of images with few connective, qualifying, explanatory, or other context-providing devices. Thus, the interviewer was hard pressed to make sense of the account and was forced to probe at every turn lest the speaker figuratively run away with the situation. The respondents were willing and often eager to tell their stories, but intention to communicate does not always bring about clear communication. The latter involves, among other requirements, an ability to hear one's words as others hear them.

Lower class. Lower-class persons displayed a relative insensitivity to disparities in perspective. At best, the respondent corrected himself on the exact time at which he performed an act or became aware that his listener was not present at the scene and so located objects and events for him. On occasion he reached a state of other-consciousness: "You can't imagine if you wasn't there what it was like." However, his assumption of a correspondence in imagery is notable. There is much surnaming of persons without genuine identification, and often terms like "we" and "they" are used without clear referents. The speaker seldom anticipates responses to his communication and seems to feel little need to explain particular features of his account. He seldom qualifies an utterance, presumably because he takes for granted that his perceptions represent reality and are shared by all who were present. Since he is apt to take so much for granted, his narrative lacks depth and richness and contains almost no qualifications and few genuine illustrations. The hearer very often is confronted with a descriptive fragment that supposedly represents a more complete story. The speaker may then add phrases like "and stuff like that" or "and everything." Such phrasing is not genuine summation but a substitute for detail and abstraction. Summary statements are virtually absent, since they signify that speakers are sensitive to the needs of listeners. Certain phrases that appear to be summaries—such as "That's all I know" and "That's the way it was"—merely indicate that the speaker's knowledge is exhausted. Other summary-like phraseologies, like "It was pitiful," appear to be asides, reflective of self-feeling or emotion rather than résumés of preceding detail.

Middle class. The middle-class respondent also makes certain assumptions about the correspondence of the other's images with his own. Nevertheless, in contrast with the lower group, he recognizes much more fully that imagery may be diverse and that context must be provided. Hence he uses many devices to supply context and to clarify meaning. He qualifies, summarizes, and sets the stage with rich introductory material, expands themes, frequently illustrates, anticipates disbelief, meticulously locates and identifies places and persons—all with great complexity of detail. He depends less on saying "You know"; he insists upon explaining if he realizes that a point lacks plausibility or force. Hence he rarely fails to locate an image, or series of images, in time or place. Frequent use of qualification is especially noteworthy. This indicates not only multiple centering but a very great sensitivity to listeners, actual and potential—including the speaker himself.

In short, the middle-class respondent has what might be called "communication control," at least in such a semiformal situation as the interview. Figuratively, he stands between his own images and the hearer and says, "Let me introduce you to what I saw and know." It is as though he were directing a movie, having at his command several cameras focused at different perspectives, shooting and carefully controlling the effect. By contrast, the lower-class respondent seems himself more like a single camera which unreels the scene to the audience. In the very telling of his story he is more apt to lose himself in his imagery. The middle-class person—by virtue, we would presume, of his greater sensitivity to his listener—stands more outside his experience. He does not so much tell you what he saw as fashion a story about what he saw. The story may be accurate in varying degrees, although, in so far as it is an organized account, it has both the virtues and the defects of organization. The comparative accuracies of middle- and lower-class accounts are not relevant here; the greater objectivity of the former merely reflects greater distance between narrator and event.[5]

In organizing his account, the middle-class respondent displays parallel conscousness of the other and himself. He can stop midstream, take another direction, and, in general, exert great control over the course of his communication. The lower-class respondent seems to have much less foresight, appearing to control only how much he will say to the interviewer, or whether he will say it at all, although presumably he must have some stylistic controls not readily observable by a middle-class reader.

CLASSIFICATIONS AND CLASSIFICATORY RELATIONS

Lower class. Respondents make reference mainly to the acts and persons of particular people, often designating them by proper or family names. This makes for fairly clear denotation and description, but only as long as the account is confined to the experiences of specific individuals. There comes a point when the interviewer wishes to obtain information about classes of persons and entire organizations as well as how they impinged upon the respondent, and here the lower-class respondent becomes relatively or even wholly inarticulate. At worst he cannot talk about categories of people or acts because, apparently, he does not think readily in terms of classes. Questions about organizations, such as the

Red Cross, are converted into concrete terms, and he talks about the Red Cross "helping people" and "people helping other people" with no more than the crudest awareness of how organizational activities interlock. At most the respondent categorizes only in a rudimentary fashion: "Some people were running; other people were looking in the houses." The interviewer receives a sketchy and impressionistic picture. Some idea is conveyed of the confusion that followed upon the tornado, but the organizing of description is very poor. The respondent may mention classes in contrasting juxtaposition (rich and poor, hurt and not-hurt), or list groups of easily perceived, contrasting actions, but he does not otherwise spell out relations between these classes. Neither does he describe a scene systematically in terms of classes that are explicitly or clearly related, a performance which would involve a shifting of viewpoint.

It is apparent that the speakers think mainly in particularistic or concrete terms. Certainly classificatory thought must exist among many or all the respondents; but, in communicating to the interviewer, class terms are rudimentary or absent and class relations implicit: relationships are not spelled out or are left vague. Genuine illustrations are almost totally lacking, either because these require classifications or because we—as middle-class observers—do not recognize that certain details are meant to imply classes.

Middle class. Middle-class speech is richly interlarded with classificatory terms, especially when the narrator is talking about what he saw rather than about himself. Typically, when he describes what other persons are doing, he classifies actions and persons and more often than not explicitly relates class to class. Often his descriptions are artistically organized around what various categories of persons were doing or experiencing. When an illustration is offered, it is clear that the speaker means it to stand for a general category. Relief and other civic organizations are conceived as sets or classes of co-ordinated roles and actions; some persons couch their whole account of the disaster events in organizational terms, hardly deigning to give proper names or personal accounts. In short, concrete imagery in middle-class communication is dwarfed or overshadowed by the prevalence and richness of conceptual terminology. Organization of speech around classifications comes readily, and undoubtedly the speaker is barely conscious of it. It is part and parcel of his formal and informal education. This is not to claim that middle-class persons always think with and use classificatory terms, for doubtless this is not true. Indeed, it may be that the interview exacts from them highly conceptualized descriptions. Nonetheless, we conclude that, in general, the thought and speech of middle-class persons is less concrete than that of the lower group.

ORGANIZING FRAMEWORKS AND STYLISTIC DEVICES

One of the requirements of communication is that utterances be organized. The principle of organization need not be stated explicitly by the speaker or recognized by the listener. Organizing frames can be of various sorts. Thus an ordering of the respondents' description is often set by the interviewer's question, or the speaker may set his own framework ("There is one thing you should know about this"). The frame can be established jointly by both interviewer and respondent, as when the former asks an open-ended question within whose very broad limits the respondent orders his description in ways that strike him as appropriate or interesting. The respondent, indeed, may organize his account much as though he were telling a special kind of story or drama, using the interviewer's questions as hardly more than general cues to what is required. The great number of events, incidents, and images which must be conveyed to the listener may be handled haphazardly, neatly, dramatically, or sequentially; but, if they are to be communicated at all, they must be ordered somehow. Stylistic devices accompany and implement these organizing frames, and the lower and upper groups use them in somewhat different ways.

Lower class. The interviewer's opening question, "Tell me your story of the tornado," invites the respondent to play an active role in organizing his account; and this he sometimes does. However, with the exception of one person who gave a headlong personal narrative, the respondents did not give long, well-organized, or tightly knit pictures of what happened to them during and after the tornado. This kind of general depiction either did not occur to them or did not strike them as appropriate.

The frames utilized are more segmental or limited in scope than those used by the middle class. They appear to be of several kinds and their centering is personal. One is the personal narrative, with events, acts, images, persons, and places receiving sequential ordering. Stylistic devices further this kind of organization: for instance, crude temporal connectives like "then," "and," and "so" and the reporting of images or events as they are recollected or as

they appear in the narrative progression. Asides may specify relationships of kinship or the individuals' location in space. But,
unless the line of narrative is compelling to the speaker, he is
likely to wander off into detail about a particular incident, where the
incident in turn then provides a framework for mentioning further
events. Likewise, when a question from the interviewer breaks
into the narrative, it may set the stage for an answer composed of
a number of images or an incident. Often one incident becomes the
trigger for another, and, although some logical or temporal connection between them may exist for the speaker, this can scarcely
be perceived by the interviewer. Hence the respondent is likely to
move out of frames quickly. The great danger of probes and requests for elaboration is that the speaker will get far away from the
life-line of his narrative—and frequently far away from the interviewer's question. As recompense the interviewer may garner useful and unexpectedly rich information from the digressions, although often he needs to probe this material further to bring it into
context. General questions are especially likely to divert the
speaker, since they suggest only loose frames; or he may answer
in general, diffuse, or blurred terms which assume either that the
listener was there too or that he will put meaningful content into
the words. If a question is asked that concerns abstract classes or
is "above" the respondent—a query, say, about relief organizations
—then very general answers or concrete listing of images or triggering of images are especially noticeable. When the interviewer
probes in an effort to get some elaboration of an occurrence or an
expansion of idea, he commonly meets with little more than repetition or with a kind of "buckshot" listing of images or incidents
which is supposed to fill out the desired picture. The lack of much
genuine elaboration is probably related to the inability to report
from multiple perspectives.

One requirement of the interview is that it yield a fairly comprehensive account of the respondent's actions and perceptions.
With the lower-class respondent the interviewer, as a rule, must
work very hard at building a comprehensive frame directly into
the interview. This he does by forcing many subframes upon the
respondent. He asks many questions about exact time sequence,
placement and identification of persons, expansion of detail, and
the like. Especially must he ask pointed questions about the relations of various personages appearing in the account. Left to
his own devices, the respondent may give a fairly straight-forward
narrative or competently reconstruct incidents that seem only

partially connected with each other or with his narrative. But the respondent seldom voluntarily gives both linear and cross-sectional pictures.

The devices used to implement communication are rather difficult to isolate, perhaps because we are middle class ourselves. Among the devices most readily observable are the use of crude chronological notations (e.g., "then, . . . and then"), the juxtaposing or direct contrasting of classes (e.g., rich and poor), and the serial locating of events. But the elaborate devices that characterize middle-class interviews are strikingly absent.

Middle class. Without exception middle-class respondents imposed over-all frames of their own upon the entire interview. Although very sensitive generally to the needs of the interviewer, they made the account their own. This is evidenced sometimes from the very outset; many respondents give a lengthy picture in answer to the interviewer's invitation, "Tell me your story." The organizing frame may yield a fluid narrative that engulfs self and others in dense detail; it may give a relatively static but rich picture of a community in distress; or, by dramatic and stage-setting devices, it may show a complicated web of relationships in dramatic motion. The entire town may be taken as the frame of reference and its story portrayed in time and space.

Besides the master-frame, the middle-class respondent utilizes many subsidiary frames. Like the lower-class person, he may take off from a question. But, in doing so—especially where the question gives latitude by its generality or abstractness—he is likely to give an answer organized around a sub-frame which orders his selection and arrangement of items. He may even shift from one image to another, but rarely are these left unrelated to the question which initially provoked them. He is much more likely also to elaborate than to repeat or merely to give a scattered series of percepts.

One prerequisite for the elaboration of a theme is an ability to depart from it while yet holding it in mind. Because he incorporates multiple perspectives, the respondent can add long asides, discuss the parallel acts of other persons in relation to himself, make varied comparisons for the enrichment of detail and comprehension—and then can return to the original point and proceed from there. Often he does this after first preparing his listener for the departure and concludes the circuit with a summary statement or a transitional phrase like "well—anyhow" that marks the end of the digression.

The stylistic devices utilized by any respondent are many and varied. But each speaker uses some devices more frequently than others, since certain ones are more or less appropriate to given frames. There is no point in spelling out the whole range of devices; they are of the sort used in any clear detailed narrative and effective exposition. If the respondent is pressed to the limit of his ability in explaining a complex point or describing a complicated scene, he calls into play resources that are of immensely high order. Sometimes a seemingly simple device will turn out on closer inspection to demand a sophisticated handling of communication —for instance, the frequent and orderly asides that break into exposition or narrative and serve with great economy to add pertinent detail.

INTRACLASS DIFFERENCES

Middle class.   Although all middle-class accounts were informative, there were considerable differences of construction among them. The frames utilized by any respondent are multiple, but respondents tend to use either a frame emphasizing sequence, human drama, and personal incident or one stressing interlocking classes of civic acts. Each orientation is implemented by somewhat different stylistic techniques. There are of course different ways of narrating; thus one can dwell more upon conditions for activity than upon the acts themselves. Similarly, accounts focused upon town organization vary in such matters as the scope of description and the degree of emphasis upon temporal sequence. Both frameworks are interchangeable, and their use is a function either of the speaker's habitual orientation or of his definition of the interview situation rather than of his ability to use one or the other mode.

Lower class.   Lower-class persons can best be distinguished in terms of ability to meet the minimum requirements of the interview. Some literally cannot tell a straight story or describe a simple incident coherently. At the other extreme we find an adequate self-focused narrative, with considerable detail tightly tied to sequential action, including retrospective observation about the narrator's facts as he develops them. Midway between these extremes are the people who can tell portions of narrative but are easily distracted: either an image suggests some other image, or the interviewer asks a question focusing interest and concentration elsewhere than upon the narrative or he calls for some expansion of detail. Then the interviewer must remind the speaker of the break in narrative. The interviewer constantly must be on the *qui vive* to keep the story going and to fill in gaps.

In the best accounts, also, competent description is handled by linking a variety of perceptions to the narrative. Images then appear to the listener to be in context and thus are fairly comprehensible. At the other extreme, images and incidents are free-floating. Probing improved the quality of this sort of interview but slightly. More frequently, the interviewer was confronted with fragments of the narrative and its related imagery. Then he had to piece together the general lineaments of the story by a barrage of probes: "Who?" "When?" "Where?" Even then the reader of these interviews will come across stray images and be hard pressed to fit them into the context. Competence in recounting narrative generally is accompanied by competence in making understandable departures from the narrative itself, and, lacking both skills, some lower-class respondents gave quite baffling and unintelligible reports. The best accounts are moderately clear, although subject to all the limitations already discussed.

DISCUSSION

Only if the situation in which the respondent spoke is carefully taken into account will we be on safe ground in interpreting class differences. Consider, first, the probable meaning of the interview for the middle-class respondents. Although the interviewer is a stranger, an outsider, he is a well-spoken, educated person. He is seeking information on behalf of some organization, hence his questioning not only has sanction but sets the stage for both a certain freedom of speech and an obligation to give fairly full information. The respondent may never before have been interviewed by a research organization, but he has often talked lengthily, fairly freely, and responsibly to organizational representatives. At the very least he has had some experience in talking to educated strangers. We may also suppose that the middle-class style of living often compels him to be very careful not to be misunderstood. So he becomes relatively sensitive to communication *per se* and to communication with others who may not exactly share his viewpoints or frames or reference.

Communication with such an audience requires alertness, no less to the meanings of one's own speech than to the possible intent of the other's. Role-taking may be inaccurate, often, but it is markedly active. Assessing and anticipating reactions to what he has said or is about to say, the individual develops flexible and ingenious ways of correcting, qualifying, making more plausible, explaining, rephrasing—in short, he assumes multiple perspectives and communicates in terms of them. A variety of perspectives implies a variety of ways of ordering or framing detail. Moreover, he is able to classify and to relate classes explicitly, which is but another way of saying that he is educated to assume multiple perspectives of rather wide scope.

It would certainly be too much to claim that middle-class persons always react so sensitively. Communication is often routinized, and much of it transpires between and among those who know each other so well or share so much in common that they need not be subtle. Nor is sensitive role-taking called forth in so-called "expressive behavior," as when hurling invective or yelling during a ball game. With the proviso that much middle-class speech is uttered under such conditions, it seems safe enough to say that people of this stratum can, if required, handle the more complex and consciously organized discourse. In addition to skill and perspicacity, this kind of discourse requires a person who can subtly keep a listener at a distance while yet keeping him in some degree informed.

Consider now, even at risk of overstating the case, how the interview appears to the lower group. The interviewer is of higher social class then the respondent, so that the interview is a "conversation between the classes." It is entirely probable that more effort and ability are demanded by cross-class conversation of this sort than between middle-class respondent and middle-class interviewer.[6] It is not surprising that the interviewer is often baffled and that the respondent frequently misinterprets what is wanted. But misunderstanding and misinterpretation are only part of the story.

Cross-class communication, while not rare, probably is fairly formalized or routinized. The communicants know the ritual steps by heart, and can assume much in the way of supporting context for phrase and gesture. The lower-class person in these Arkansas towns infrequently meets a middle-class person in a situation anything like the interview. Here he must talk at great length to a stranger about personal experiences, as well as recall for his listener a tremendous number of details. Presumably he is accustomed to talking about such matters and in such detail only to listeners with whom he shares a great deal of experience and symbolism, so that he need not be very self-conscious about communicative technique. He can, as a rule, safely assume that words, phrases, and gestures are assigned approximately similar meanings by his listeners. But this is not so in the interview or, indeed, in any situation where class converses with class in nontraditional modes.

There still remains the question of whether the descriptions of perceptions and experiences given by the lower-class respondent are merely inadequate or whether this is the way he truly saw and experienced. Does his speech accurately reflect customary "concrete" modes of thought and perception, or is it that he perceives in abstract and classificatory terms, and from multiple perspectives, but is unable to convey his perceptions?[7] Unless one assumes that, when talking in familiar vein to familiar audiences, speech and gesture incorporate multiple perspectives, which is, as we have already indicated, improbable, one concludes that speech does in some sense reflect thought. The reader is perhaps best left at this point to draw his own conclusions, although we shall press upon him certain additional evidence and interpretation arising from examination of the interviews.

In any situation calling for a description of human activities it is necessary to utilize motivational terminology, either explicitly or implicitly, in the very namings of acts.[8] In the speech of those who recognize few disparities of imagery between themselves and their listeners, explicit motivational terms are sparse. The frequent use among the lower class of the expression "of course" followed by something like "They went up to see about their folks" implies that it is almost needless to say what "they" did, much less to give the reason for the act. The motive ("to see about") is implicit and terminal, requiring neither elaboration nor explanation. Where motives are explicit ("They was needin' help, so we went on up there"), they are often gratuitous and could just as well have been omitted. All this is related to preceding discussions of single centering and assumed correspondence of imagery. To the speaker it was quite clear why people did what they did. There was no need to question or to elaborate on the grounds for acts. Under probing the respondent did very little better: he used motivational terms but within a quite narrow range. The terms he used ordinarily reflected kinship obligations, concern for property, humanitarian ("help") sentiments, and action from motives of curiosity ("We went down to see"). Such a phrase as "I suppose I went to her house because I wanted reassurance" would rarely occur.

Middle-class persons exhibit familiarity with a host of distinct "reasons" for performing particular acts. Their richness in thinking allows activities to be defined and described in a great variety of ways. Here, indeed, is an instrument for breaking down diffuse images ("They was runnin' all over") into classes of acts and events. The middle-class person is able to do this, for one thing, because he possesses an abstract motivational terminology. Then, too, the fine and subtle distinctions for rationalizing behavior require devices for insuring that they will be grasped by the hearer. In a real sense the need to explain behavior can be linked with the need to communicate well—to give a rational account as well as to be objective. Hence, there is a constant flow of qualifying and generalizing terms linked with motivational phraseology ("I don't know why, but it could be he felt there was no alternative . . .").

It is not surprising to find the middle class as familiar with elements of social structure as with individual behavior. Assuredly, this familiarity rests not only upon contact with institutions but upon the capacity to perceive and talk about abstract classes of acts. The lower-class person, on other hand, appears to have only rudimentary notions of organizational structure—at least of relief and emergency agencies. Extended contact with representatives of them, no doubt, would familiarize him not only with organizations but with thinking in organizational, or abstract, terms. The propensity of the lower class to state concretely the activities of relief organizations corroborates the observation of Warner that the lowest strata have little knowledge or "feel" for the social structures of their communities.[9] It also suggests the difficulty of conveying to them relatively abstract information through formal media of communication.

It may be that rural townspeople of the lower class are not typical of the national or urban low strata. This raises the question— vital to urban sociology but to which currently there is no adequate answer—of whether pockets of rural-minded folk cannot live encapsulated in the city[10] and, indeed, whether lower-class persons have much opportunity to absorb middle-class culture without themselves beginning the route upward, those remaining behind remaining less urban.

NOTES

[1]Cf. E. Cassirer, *An Essay on Man* (New Haven, 1944); S. Langer, *Philosophy in a New Key* (New York, 1948); A. R. Lindesmith and A. L. Strauss, *Social Psychology* (New York, 1949), pp. 237–52; G. Mead, *Mind, Self, and Society* (Chicago, 1934); C. W. Mills, "Language, Logic, and Culture," *American Sociological Review*, IV (1939), 670–80.

[2]Each document was scrutinized by both authors, and comprehensive notes were taken to help establish categories descriptive of the communicative style and devices of each respondent. From these notes profiles of respondents were constructed. From the notes and case profiles, there emerged the separate profiles for lower and upper groups that will be described. We had expected to code the documents to bring out the degree of overlap between groups, but it turned out that there was literally no overlap; nevertheless, each reader coded separately as he went along. Agreement upon coding scores between readers was virtually perfect.

[3]Cf. J. Piaget, *The Psychology of Intelligence* (London, 1950). See also a suggestive treatment of inadequate thinking analyzed in terms of centering in Max Wertheimer, *Productive Thinking* (New York, 1945), pp. 135–47.

[4]For a good discussion of this see B. Malinowski, "The Problem of Meaning in Primitive Language," in *Magic, Science and Religion and Other Essays* (Boston, 1948), pp. 228–76.

[5]Our discussion of objectivity and of mediation between self and image in communication is reminiscent of some of the literature on child, schizophrenic, and aphasic thought.

[6]Somewhat like this is the I.Q. testing session which involves a middle-class test (and tester) and a lower-class subject. The many and subtle difficulties in this situation are analyzed by Allison Davis in *Social Class Influences upon Learning* (Cambridge, Mass., 1951).

[7]The lower class is even more concrete in its outlook than the lower-middle class. For example, a question . . . where chewing gum is usually purchased will be answered by an upper-middle person: 'At a cashier's counter or in a grocery store.' By the lower-middle: 'At the National or the corner drugstore.' By the lower class: 'From Tony'" ("Marketing Chewing Gum in New England: A Research Study" [Chicago: Social Research, Inc., 1950]).

[8]Cf. K. Burke, *Grammar of Motives* (New York, 1945).

[9]W. L. Warner, *American Life: Dream and Reality* (Chicago: University of Chicago Press, 1953), pp. 193–94.

[10]David Riesman, "Urbanity and the Urban Personality," in *Proceedings of the Fourth Annual Symposium, The Human Development Bulletin* (Chicago: University of Chicago, 1953), p. 37.

19

SOCIAL CLASS, LANGUAGE, AND SOCIALIZATION

Basil B. Bernstein

It may be helpful to make explicit the theoretical origins of the thesis I have been developing over the past decade. Although initially the thesis appeared to be concerned with the problem of educability, this problem was imbedded in and was stimulated by the wider question of the relationships between symbolic orders and social structure. The basic theoretical question, which dictated the approach to the initially narrow but important empirical problem, was concerned with the fundamental structure and changes in the structure of cultural transmission. Indeed, any detailed examination of what superficially may seem to be a string of somewhat repetitive papers, I think would show three things:

1. The gradual emergence of the dominance of the major theoretical problem from the local, empirical problem of the social antecedents of the educability of different groups of children.

This article will also appear in *Current Trends in Linguistics* (The Hague, The Netherlands: Mouton Publishers), in press.

The work in this article was supported by grants from the Department of Education and Science, the Ford Foundation, and the Nuffield Foundation, to whom grateful acknowledgment is made. The author would also like to take the opportunity of acknowledging his debt to Professor Courtney Cazden, Dr. Mary Douglas, Professor John Gumperz, Professor Dell Hymes, and in particular to Professor Michael Haliiday. The author is also grateful for the constant constructive criticism he has received from members of the Sociological Research Unit, University of London Institute of Education.

2. Attempts to develop both the generality of the thesis and to develop increasing specificity at the contextual level.

3. Entailed in (2) were attempts to clarify both the logical and empirical status of the basic organizing concept, code. Unfortunately, until recently these attempts were more readily seen in the *planning* and *analysis* of the empirical research than available as formal statements.

Looking back, I think I would have created less misunderstanding if I had written about sociolinguistic codes rather than linguistic codes. Using only the latter concept gave the impression that I was reifying syntax at the cost of semantics, worse, suggesting that there was a one-to-one relation between meaning and a given syntax. Also, by defining the codes in a context-free fashion, I robbed myself of properly understanding, at a theoretical level, their significance. *I should point out that nearly all the empirical planning was directed at trying to find out the code realizations in different contexts.*

The concept of sociolinguistic code points to the social structuring of meanings *and* to their diverse but *related* contextual linguistic realizations. A careful reading of the papers shows the emphasis given to the form of the social relationship, that is, the structuring of relevant meanings. Indeed, role is defined as a complex coding activity controlling the creation and organization of specific meanings and the conditions for their transmission and reception. The general sociolinguistic thesis attempts to explore how symbolic systems are both realizations and regulators of the structure of social relationships. The particular symbolic system is that of speech *not* language.

It is pertinent, at this point, to make explicit earlier work in the social sciences that formed the implicit starting point of the thesis. It will then be seen, I hope, that the thesis is an integration of different streams of thought. The major starting points are Durkheim and Marx, and a small number of other thinkers have been drawn into the basic matrix. I shall very briefly, and so selectively, outline this matrix and some of the problems to which it gave rise.

Durkheim's work is a truly magnificent insight into the relationships between symbolic orders, social relationships, and the structuring of experience. In a sense, if Marx turned Hegel on his head, then Durkheim attempted to turn Kant on his head, for in *Primitive Classification* and in *The Elementary Forms of the Religious Life*, Durkheim attempted to derive the basic categories of thought from the structuring of the social relation. His success is beside the point. He raised the whole question of the relation between the classifications and frames of the symbolic order *and* the structuring of experience. In his study of different forms of social integration he pointed to the implicit, condensed, symbolic structure of mechanical solidarity and the more explicit and differentiated symbolic structures of organic solidarity. Cassirer, the early cultural anthropologists, and in particular Sapir (I was not aware of Von Humboldt until much later) sensitized me to the cultural properties of speech. Whorf, particularly where he refers to the fashions of speaking, frames of consistency, alerted me to the selective effect of the culture (acting through its patterning of social relationships) upon the *patterning* of grammar *together* with the pattern's semantic and thus cognitive significance. Whorf more than anyone, I think, opened up, at least for me, the question of the deep structure of linguistically regulated communication.

In all the above work I found two difficulties. If we grant the fundamental linkage of symbolic systems, social structure, and the shaping of experience, it is still unclear *how* such shaping takes place. The *processes* underlying the social structuring of experience are not explicit. The second difficulty is in dealing with the question of change of symbolic systems. Mead is of central importance in the solution of the first difficulty, the *how*. Mead outlined in general terms the relationships between role, reflexiveness, and speech, and in so doing provided the basis of the solution to the *how*. It is still the case that the Meadian solution does not allow us to deal with the problem of change. For the concept, which enables role to be related to a higher order concept, "the generalized other" is, itself, not subject to systematic enquiry. Even if "the generalized other" is placed within a Durkheimian framework, we are still left with the problem of change. Indeed, in Mead change is introduced only at the cost of the re-emergence of a traditional Western dichotomy in the concepts of the "I" and the "me." The "I" is both the indeterminate response to the "me" and yet at the same time shapes it. The Meadian "I" points to the voluntarism in the affairs of men, the fundamental creativity of man made possible by speech, a little before Chomsky.

Thus Meadian thought helps to solve the puzzle of the *how* but it does not help with the question of change in the structuring of experience; although both Mead implicitly and Durkheim explicitly pointed to the conditions that bring about pathological structuring of experience.

One major theory of the development of and change in symbolic structures is, of course, that of Marx. Although Marx is less concerned with the internal structure and the process of transmission of symbolic systems he does give us a key to their institutionalization and change. The key is given in terms of the social significance of society's productive system and the power relationships to which the productive system gives rise. Further, access to, control over, orientation of, and *change* in critical symbolic systems, according to the theory, is governed by these power relationships as these are embodied in the class structure. It is not only capital, in the strict economic sense, that is subject to appropriation, manipulation and exploitation, but also *cultural* capital in the form of the symbolic systems through which man can extend and change the boundaries of his experience.

I am not putting forward a matrix of thought necessary for the study of the basic structure and change in the structure of cultural transmission but *only* the specific matrix that underlies my own approach. Essentially and briefly I have used Durkheim and Marx at the macro level and Mead at the micro level, to realize a sociolinguistic thesis that could meet with a range of work in anthropology, linguistics, sociology, and psychology.

I want first of all to make clear what I am not concerned with. Chomsky, in "Aspects of the Theory of Syntax," neatly severs the study of the rule system of language from the study of the social rules that determine their contextual use. He does this by making a distinction between competence and performance. Competence refers to the child's tacit understanding of the rule system; performance relates to the essentially social use to which the rule system is put. Competence refers to man abstracted from contextual constraints. Performance refers to man in the grip of the contextual constraints that determine his speech acts. Competence refers to the Ideal; performance refers to the Fall. In this sense, Chomsky's notion of competence is Platonic. Competence has its source in the very biology of man. There is no difference between men in terms of their access to the linguistic rule system. Here Chomsky, like many other linguists before him, announces the communality of man; that all men have equal access to the creative act of language. On the other hand, performance is under the control of the social—performances are culturally specific acts, they refer to the choices that are made in specific speech encounters. Thus, from one point of view, Chomsky indicates the tragedy of man, the potentiality of competence, and the degeneration of performance.

Clearly, much is to be gained in rigor and explanatory power through the severing of the relationship between the formal properties of the grammar and the meanings that are realized in its use. But if we are to study speech la parole, we are inevitably involved in a study of a rather different rule system; we are involved in a study of rules, formal and informal, that regulate the options we take up in various contexts in which we find ourselves. This second rule system is the cultural system. This raises immediately the question of the relationship between the linguistic rule system and the cultural system. Clearly, specific linguistic rule systems are part of the cultural system, but it has been argued that the linguistic rule system in various ways shapes the cultural system. This very briefly is the view of those who hold a narrow form of the linguistic relativity hypothesis. I do not intend to get involved in that particular quagmire here. Instead, I shall take the view that the code the linguist invents to explain the formal properties of the grammar is capable of generating any number of speech codes, and there is no reason for believing that any one language code is better than another in this respect. On this argument, language is a set of rules to which all speech codes must comply, but these speech codes are realized as a function of the culture acting through social relationships in specific contexts. Different speech forms or codes symbolize the form of the social relationship, regulate the nature of the speech encounters, and create for the speakers different orders of relevance and relation. The experience of the speakers is then transformed by what is made significant or relevant by the speech form. This is a sociological argument because the speech form is taken as a consequence of the form of the social relation or, put more generally, is a quality of a social structure. Let me qualify this immediately. Because the speech form is initially a function of a given social arrangement, it does not mean that the speech form does not in turn modify or even change that social structure from which the speech form initially evolved. This formulation, indeed, invites the question—under what conditions does a given speech form free itself sufficiently from its embodiment in the social structure so that the system of meanings it realizes point to alternative realities, that is, alternative arrangements in the affairs of men. Here we become concerned immediately with the antecedents and consequences of the boundary maintaining principles of a culture or subculture. I am here suggesting a relationship between forms of boundary maintenance at the cultural level and forms of speech.

I am required to consider the relationship between language

and socialization. It should be clear from these opening remarks that I am not concerned with language but with speech, and concerned more specifically with the contextual constraints upon speech. Now what about socialization? I shall take the term to refer to the process whereby a child acquires a specific cultural identity *and* to his responses to such an identity. Socialization refers to the process whereby the biological is transformed into a specific cultural being. It follows from this that the process of socialization is a complex process of control, whereby a particular moral, cognitive, and affective awareness is evoked in the child and given a specific form and content. Socialization sensitizes the child to various orderings of society as these are made substantive in the various roles he is expected to play. In a sense then socialization is a process for making people safe. The process acts selectively on the possibilities of man by creating through time a sense of the inevitability of a given social arrangement, and through limiting the areas of permitted change. The basic agencies of socialization in contemporary societies are the family, the peer group, school, and work. It is through these agencies, and in particular through their relationship to each other, that the various orderings of society are made manifest.

Now it is quite clear that given this view of socialization it is necessary to limit the discussion. I shall limit our discussion to socialization within the family, but it should be obvious that the focusing and filtering of the child's experience within the family in a large measure is a microcosm of the microscopic orderings of society. Our question now becomes what are the sociological factors that affect linguistic performances within the family critical to the process of socialization?

Without a shadow of doubt the most formative influence upon the procedures of socialization, from a sociological viewpoint, is social class. The class structure influences work and educational roles and brings families into a special relationship with each other and deeply penetrates the structure of life experiences within the family. The class system has deeply marked the distribution of knowledge within society. It has given differential access to the sense that the world is permeable. It has sealed off communities from each other and has ranked these communities on a scale of individual worth. We have three components: knowledge, possiblity, and invidious insulation. It would be a little naive to believe that differences in knowledge, differences in the sense of the possible, combined with invidious insulation, rooted in differential *material* well-being would not affect the forms of control and in-novation in the socializing procedures of different social classes. I shall go on to argue that the deep structure of communication it-self is affected, but not in any final or irrevocable way.

As an approach to my argument, let me glance at the social distribution of knowledge. We can see that the class system has affected the distribution of knowledge. Historically and now, only a tiny percentage of the population has been socialized into knowl-edge at the level of the meta-languages of control and innovation, whereas the mass of the population has been socialized into knowl-edge at the level of context-tied operations.

A tiny percentage of the population has been given access to the principles of intellectual change whereas the rest have been denied such access. This suggests that we might be able to distin-guish between two orders of meaning. One we could call universal-istic, the other particularistic. Universalistic meanings are those in which principles and operations are made linguistically explicit, whereas particularistic orders of meaning are meanings in which principles and operation are relatively linguistically implicit. If orders of meaning are universalistic, then the meanings are less tied to a given context. The meta-languages of public forms of thought as these apply to objects and persons realize meanings of a universalistic type. Where meanings have this characteristic then individuals have access to the grounds of their experience and can change the grounds. Where orders of meaning are particularis-tic, where principles are linguistically implicit, then such meanings are less context independent and *more* context bound; that is, tied to a local relationship and to a local social structure. Where the meaning system is particularistic, much of the meaning is im-bedded in the context and may be restricted to those who share a similar contextual history. Where meanings are universalistic, they are in principle available to all because the principles and operations have been made explicit and so public.

I shall argue that forms of socialization orient the child towards speech codes that control access to relatively context-tied or relatively context-independent meanings. Thus I shall argue that elaborated codes orient their users towards universalistic meanings, whereas restricted codes orient or sensitize, their users to particu-laristic meanings: that the linguistic realization of the two orders are different, and so are the social relationships that realize them. Elaborated codes are less tied to a given or local structure and thus contain the potentiality of change in principles. In the case of elaborated codes the speech is freed from its evoking social structure and takes on an autonomy. A university is a place organized around talk. Restricted codes are more tied to a local social structure and have a reduced potential for change in principles. Where codes are elaborated, the socialized has more access to the grounds of his own socialization, and so can enter into a reflexive relationship to the social order he has taken over. Where codes are restricted, the socialized has less access to the grounds of his socialization, and thus reflexiveness may be limited in range. *One of the effects of the class system is to limit access to elaborated codes.*

I shall go on to suggest: that restricted codes have their basis in condensed symbols whereas elaborated codes have their basis in articulated symbols; that restricted codes draw upon metaphor whereas elaborated codes draw upon rationality; and that these codes constrain the contextual use of language in critical socializing contexts and in this way regulate the orders of relevance and relation that the socialized takes over. From this point of view, change in habitual speech codes involves changes in the means by which object and person relationships are realized.

I want first to start with the notions of elaborated and restricted speech variants. A variant can be considered as the contextual constraints upon grammatical-lexical choices.

Sapir, Malinowski, Firth, Vygotsky, Luria have all pointed out from different points of view that the closer the identifications of speakers the greater the range of shared interests and the more probable that the speech will take a specific form. The range of syntactic alternatives is likely to be reduced and the lexis to be drawn from a narrow range. Thus, the form of these social relations is acting selectively on the meanings to be verbally realized. In these relationships the intent of the other person can be taken for granted as the speech is played out against a backdrop of common assumptions, common history, and common interests. As a result, there is less need to raise meanings to the level of explicitness or elaboration. There is a reduced need to make explicit through syntactic choices the logical structure of the communication. Further, if the speaker wishes to individualize his communication, he is likely to do this by varying the expressive associates of the speech. Under these conditions, the speech is likely to have a strong metaphoric element. In these situations the speaker may be more concerned with how something is said when it is said, and silence takes on a variety of meanings. Often in these encounters the speech cannot be understood apart from the context and the context cannot be read by those who do not share the history of the relationships. Thus the form of the social relationship acts selectively in the meanings to be verbalized, which in turn affect the syntactic and lexical choices. The unspoken assumption underlying the relationship are not available to those who are outside the relationship. For these are limited, and restricted to the speakers. The symbolic form of the communication is condensed yet the specific cultural history of the relationship is alive in its form. We can say that the roles of the speakers are communalized roles. Thus, we can make a relationship between restricted social relationships based upon communalized roles and the verbal realization of their meaning. In the language of the earlier part of this talk, restricted social relationships based upon communalized roles evoke particularistic, that is, context tied meanings, realized through a restricted speech variant.

Imagine a husband and wife have just come out of the cinema and are talking about the film. "What do you think?" "It had a lot to say." "Yes, I thought so too—let's go to the Millers, there may be something going there." They arrive at the Millers, who ask about the film. An hour is spent in the complex, moral, political, aesthetic subtleties of the film and its place in the contemporary scene. Here we have an elaborated variant; the meanings now have to be made public to others who have not seen the film. The speech shows careful editing, at both the grammatical and lexical levels; it is no longer context tied. The meanings are explicit, elaborated, and individualized. While expressive channels are clearly relevant, the burden of meaning inheres predominantly in the verbal channel. The experience of the listeners cannot be taken for granted. Thus each member of the group is on his own as he offers his interpretation. Elaborated variants of this kind involve the speakers in particular role relationships, and *if you cannot manage the role, you cannot produce the appropriate speech.* For as the speaker proceeds to individualize his meanings, he is differentiated from others like a figure from its ground.

The roles receive less support from each other. There is a measure of isolation. *Difference* lies at the basis of the social relationship, and is made verbally active whereas in the other context it is *consensus.* The insides of the speaker have become psychologically active through the verbal aspect of the communication. Various defensive strategies may be used to decrease potential vulnerability of self and to increase the vulnerability of others. The verbal aspect of the communication becomes a vehicle for the transmission of individuated symbols. The "I" stands over the "we". Meanings that are discreet to the speaker must be offered so that they are intelligible to the listener. Communalized roles have given way to individualized roles, condensed symbols to articulated symbols. Elaborated speech variants of this type realize universalistic meanings in the sense that they are less context-tied. Thus individualized roles are realized through elaborated speech variants that involve complex editing at the grammatical and lexical levels and that point to universalistic meanings.

Let me give another example. Consider the two following stories that Peter Hawkins, Assistant Research Officer in the Sociological Research Unit of the University of London Institute of Education, constructed as a result of his analysis of the speech of middle-class and working-class five-year-old children. The children were given a series of four pictures that told a story and they were invited to tell the story. The first picture showed some boys playing football, in the second the ball goes through the window of a house, the third shows a woman looking out of the window and a man making an ominous gesture, and in the fourth the children are moving away.

Here are the two stories:

(1) Three boys are playing football and one boy kicks the ball and it goes through the window   the ball breaks the window   and the boys are looking at it   and a man comes out and shouts at them   because they've broken the window   so they run away   and then that lady looks out of her window   and she tells the boys off.

(2) They're playing football   and he kicks it   and it goes through there   it breaks the window and they're looking at it   and he comes out   and shouts at them   because they've broken it   so they run away   and then she looks out   and she tells them off.

With the first story the reader does not have to have the four pictures that were used as the basis for the story, whereas in the case of the second story the reader would require the initial pictures in order to make sense of the story. The first story is free of the context that generated it, whereas the second story is much more closely tied to its context. As a result the meanings of the second story are implicit, whereas the meanings of the first story are explicit. It is not that the working-class children do not have in their passive vocabulary the vocabulary used by the middle-class children. Nor is it the case that the children differ in their tacit understanding of the linguistic rule system. Rather, what we have here are differences in the use of language arising out of a specific context. One child makes explicit the meanings that he is realizing through language for the person he is telling the story to, whereas the second child does not to the same extent. The first child takes very little for granted, whereas the second child takes a great deal for granted. Thus for the first child the task was seen as a context in which his meanings were required to be made explicit, whereas the task for the second child was not seen as a task that required such explication of meaning. It would not be difficult to imagine a context where the first child would produce speech rather like the second. What we are dealing with here are differences between the children in the way they realize in language use apparently the same context. We could say that the speech of the first child generated universalistic meanings in the sense that the meanings are freed from the context and so understandable by all. Whereas the speech of the second child generated particularistic meanings, in the sense that the meanings are closely tied to the context and would be only fully understood by others if they had access to the context that originally generated the speech.

It is again important to stress that the second child has access to a more differentiated noun phrase, but there is a restriction on its *use*. Geoffrey Turner, Linguist in the Sociological Research Unit, shows that working-class, five-year-old children in the same contexts examined by Hawkins use fewer linguistic expressions of uncertainty when compared to the middle-class children. This does not mean that working class children do *not* have access to such expressions, but that the eliciting speech context did not provoke them. Telling a story from pictures, talking about scenes on cards, *formally framed* contexts, do not encourage working-class children to consider the possibilities of alternate meanings and so there is a reduction in the linguistic expressions of uncertainty. Again, working-class children have access to a wide range of syntactic choices that involve the use of logical operators: "because," "but," "either," "or," "only." The constraints exist on the conditions for their *use*. Formally framed contexts used for eliciting context independent universalistic meanings may evoke in the working-class child, relative to the middle-class child, restricted speech variants, because the working-class child has difficulty in managing the role relationships that such contexts require. This problem is further complicated when such contexts carry meanings very much removed from the child's cultural experience. In the same way we can show that there are constraints upon the middle-class child's use of language. Turner found that when middle-class children were asked to role play in the picture story series, a higher percentage of these children, when compared with working-class children, initially refused. When the middle-class children were asked "What is the man saying?" or linguistically equivalent questions, a relatively higher percentage said "I don't know." When this question was followed by the hypothetical question "What do you think the man might be saying?" they offered their interpretations. The working-class children role played without difficulty. It seems then that middle-class children at five need to have a very precise instruction to *hypothesize in that particular* context. This may be because they are more concerned here with getting their answers right or correct. When the children were invited to tell a story about some doll-like figures (a little boy, a little girl, a sailor, and a dog) the working-class children's stories were freer, longer, more imaginative than the stories of the middle-class children. The latter children's stories were tighter, constrained within a strong narrative frame. It was as if these children were dominated by what they took to be the *form* of a narrative and the content was secondary. This is an example of the concern of the middle-class child with the structure of the contextual frame. It may be worthwhile to amplify this further. A number of studies have shown that when working-class black children are asked to associate to a series of words, their responses show considerable diversity, both from the meaning and form-class of the stimulus word. In the analysis offered in the text this may be because the children for the following reasons are less constrained. The form-class of the stimulus word may have reduced associative significance and so would less constrain the selection of potential words *or* phrases. With such a weakening of the grammatical frame a greater range of alternatives are possible candidates for selection. Further, the closely controlled middle-class linguistic socialization of the young child may point the child towards both the grammatical significance of the stimulus word and towards a tight logical ordering of semantic space. Middle-class children may well have access to deep interpretive rules that regulate their linguistic responses in certain formalized contexts. The consequences may limit their imagination through the tightness of the frame these interpretive rules create. It may even be that with *five*-year-old children, the middle-class child will innovate *more* with the arrangements of objects (for example, bricks) than in his linguistic usage. His linguistic usage is under close supervision by adults. He has more *autonomy* in his play.

To return to our previous discussion, we can say briefly that as we move from communalized to individualized roles, so speech takes on an increasingly reflexive function. The unique selves of others become palpable through speech and enter into our own self, the grounds of our experience are made verbally explicit; the security of the condensed symbol is gone. It has been replaced by rationality. There is a change in the basis of our vulnerability.

So far, then, I have discussed certain types of speech variants and the role relationships that occasion them. I am now going to raise the generality of the discussion and focus upon the title of the paper. The socialization of the young in the family proceeds within a critical set of inter-related contexts. Analytically, we may distinguish four contexts.

1. *The regulative context.* These are authority relationships where the child is made aware of the rules of the moral order and their various backings.
2. *The instructional context,* where the child learns about the objective nature of objects and persons, and acquires skills of various kinds.
3. *The imaginative or innovating contexts,* where the child is encouraged to experiment and recreate his world on his own terms, and in his own way.
4. *The interpersonal context,* where the child is made aware of affective states, both his own and others.

I am suggesting that the critical orderings of a culture or subculture are made substantive—are made palpable—through the forms of its linguistic realizations of these four contexts—initially in the family and kin.

Now if the linguistic realization of these four contexts involves the predominant use of restricted speech variants, I shall postulate that the deep structure of the communication is a restricted code having its basis in communalized roles, realizing context bound meanings (for example, particularistic meaning orders). Clearly the specific grammatical and lexical choices will vary from one context to another.

If the linguistic realization of these four contexts involve the predominant usage of elaborated speech variants, I shall postulate that the deep structure of the communication is an elaborated code having its basis in individualized roles realizing context-free universalistic meanings.

In order to prevent misunderstanding, an expansion of the text is here necessary. It is likely that where the code is restricted, the speech in the regulative context may well be limited to command and simple rule-announcing statements. The latter statements are not context-dependent in the sense previously given for they announce general rules. We need to supplement the context-independent (universalistic) and context-dependent (particularistic) criteria with criteria that refer to the extent to which the speech in the regulative context varies in terms of its *contextual specificity*. If the speech is context-specific then the socializer cuts his meanings to the *specific* attributes/intentions of the socialized, the specific characteristics of the problem, the specific requirements of the context. Thus the general rule may be transmitted with degrees of *contextual specificity*. When this occurs the rule is individualized (fitted to the local circumstances) in the process of its transmission. Thus with code elaboration we should expect:

1. Some developed grounds for the rule
2. Some qualification of it in the light of the particular issue
3. Considerable *specificity* in terms of the socialized, the context, and the issue.

This does *not* mean that there would be an *absence* of command statements. It is also likely that with code elaboration the socialized would be *given* opportunities (role options) to question.

Bernstein and Cook (1965) and Cook (1970) have developed a semantic coding grid that sets out with considerable delicacy a general category system that has been applied to a limited regulative context. Turner, linguist to the Sociological Research Unit, is attempting a linguistic realization of the same grid.

We can express the two sets of criteria diagrammatically. A limited application is given by Henderson (1970)

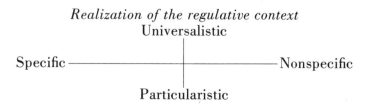

Realization of the regulative context
Universalistic

Specific —————————————————— Nonspecific

Particularistic

It may be necessary to utilize the two sets of criteria for *all* four socializing contexts. Bernstein (1967 published 1970) suggested that code realization would vary with context.

If we look at the linguistic realization of the regulative context in greater detail we may be able to clear up another source of possible misunderstanding. In this context it is very likely that syntactic markers of the logical distribution of meaning will be extensively used.

"If you do that, then . . . ."
"Either you . . . or . . . ."
"You can do that but if . . . ."
"You do that and you'll pay for it."

Thus it is very likely that young children may well in the *regulative* context have access to a range of syntactic markers that express the logical/hypothetical irrespective of code restriction or elaboration. However, where the code is restricted it is expected that there will be reduced specificity in the sense outlined earlier. Further, the speech in the control situation is likely to be well-organized in the sense that the sentences come as wholes. The child responds to the total *frame*. However, I would suggest that the informal *instructional* contexts within the family may well be limited in range and frequency. Thus the child, of course would have access to and so have *available*, the hypotheticals, conditionals, disjunctives, etc., but these might be rarely used in *instructional* contexts. In the same way, as we have suggested earlier, all children have access to linguistic expressions of uncertainty but they may differ in the context in which they receive and realize such expressions.

I must emphasize that because the code is restricted it does not mean that speakers will never use elaborated speech variants. Only that the use of such variants will be infrequent in the socialization of the child in his family.

Now, all children have access to restricted codes and their various systems of condensed meaning, because the roles the code presupposes are universal. But there may well be selective access to elaborated codes because there is selective access to the role system that evokes its use. Society is likely to evaluate differently the experiences realized through these two codes. I cannot here go into details, but the different focusing of experience through a restricted code creates a major problem of educability only where the school produces discontinuity between its symbolic orders and those of the child. Our schools are not made for these children; why should the children respond? To ask the child to switch to an elaborated code that presupposes different role relationships and systems of meaning without a sensitive understanding of the required contexts must create for the child a bewildering and potentially damaging experience.

So far, then, I have sketched out a relationship between speech codes and socialization through the organization of roles through which the culture is made psychologically active in persons. I have indicated that access to the roles and thus to the codes is broadly related to social class. However, it is clearly the case that social class groups today are by no means homogeneous groups. Further, the division between elaborated and restricted codes is too simple. Finally, I have not indicated in any detail how these codes are evoked by families, and how the family types may shape their focus.

What I shall do now is to introduce a distinction between family types and their communication structures. These family types can be found empirically within each social class, although any one type may be rather more modal at any given historical period.

I shall distinguish families according to the strength of their boundary-maintaining procedures. Let me first give some idea of what I mean by boundary-maintaining procedures. I shall first look at boundary maintenance as it is revealed in the symbolic ordering of space. Consider the lavatory. In one house, the room is pristine, bare, and sharp, containing only the necessities for which the room is dedicated. In the second there is a picture on the wall, in the third there are books, in the fourth all surfaces are covered with curious postcards. We have a continuum from a room celebrating the purity of categories to one celebrating the mixture of categories, from strong to weak boundary maintenance. Consider the kitchen. In one kitchen, shoes may not be placed on the table, nor the child's chamber pot—all objects and utensils have an assigned place. In another kitchen the boundaries separating the different classes of objects are weak. The symbolic ordering of space can give us indications of the relative strength of boundary-maintaining procedures. Let us now look at the relationship between family members. Where boundary procedures are strong, the differentiation of members and the authority structure is based upon clear-cut, unambiguous definitions of the status of each member of the family. The boundaries between the statuses are strong and the social identities of the members very much a function of their age, sex, and age-relation status. As a shorthand, we can characterize the family as *positional*.

On the other hand, where boundary procedures are weak or flexible, the differentiation between members and the authority relationships are less on the basis of position, because here the status boundaries are blurred. Where boundary procedures are weak, the differentiation between members is based more upon *differences between persons*. In such families the relationships become more egocentric and the unique attributes of family members more and more are made substantive in the communication structure. We will call these *person-centered* families. Such families do not reduce but increase the substantive expression of ambiguity and ambivalence. In person-centered families, the role system would be continuously evoking, accommodating, and assimilating the different interests and attributes of its members. In such families, unlike positional families, the members would be making their roles, rather than stepping into them. In a person-centered family, the child's developing self is differentiated by continuous adjustment to the verbally realized and elaborated intentions, qualifications, and motives of others. The boundary between self and other is blurred. In positional families, the child takes over and responds to the formal pattern of obligation and privilege. It should be possible to see, without going into detail, that the communication structure within these two types of family are somewhat differently focused. We might then expect that the reflexiveness induced by positional families is sensitized to the general attributes of persons, whereas the reflexiveness produced by person-centered families is more sensitive towards the particular aspects of persons. Think of the difference between Dartington Hall or Gordonstoun Public Schools in England, or the difference between West Point and a progressive school in the United States. Thus, in person-centered families, the insides of the members are made public through the communication structure, and thus more of the person has been invaded and subject to control. Speech in such families is a major media of control. In positional families of course, speech is relevant but it symbolizes the boundaries given by the formal structure of the relationships. So far as the child is concerned, in positional families he attains a strong sense of social identity at the cost of autonomy; in person-centered families the child attains a strong sense of autonomy but his social identity may be weak. Such ambiguity in the sense of identity, the lack of boundary, may move such children toward a radically closed value system.

If we now place these family types in the framework of the previous discussion, we can see that although the code may be elaborated, it may be differently focused according to the family type. Thus, we can have an elaborate code focusing upon persons or an elaborated code in a positional family focusing more upon objects. We can expect the same with a restricted code. Normally, with code restriction we should expect a positional family, however, if it showed signs of person-centered, then we might expect the children to be in a situation of potential code switch.

Where the code is elaborated and focused by a person-centered family, these children may well develop acute identity problems, concerned with authenticity, of limiting responsibility—they may come to see language as phony, a system of counterfeit masking the absence of belief. They may move towards the restricted codes of the various peer group subcultures, or seek the condensed symbols of affective experience, or both.

One of the difficulties of this approach is to avoid implicit value judgements about the relative worth of speech systems and the cultures they symbolize. Let it be said immediately that a restricted code gives access to a vast potential of meanings, of delicacy, subtlety, and diversity of cultural forms, to a unique aesthetic whose basis in condensed symbols may influence the form of the imagining. Yet, in complex industrialized societies its differently focused experience may be disvalued and humiliated within schools, or seen, at best, to be irrelevant to the educational endeavor. For the schools are predicated upon elaborated code and its system of social relationships. Although an elaborated code does not entail any specific value system, the value system of the middle class penetrates the texture of the very learning context itself.

Elaborated codes give access to alternative realities yet they carry the potential of alienation, of feeling from thought, of self from other, of private belief *from role obligation*.

Finally I should like to consider briefly the source of change of linguistic codes. The first major source of change I suggest is to be located in the division of labor. As the division of labor changes from simple to complex, then this changes the social and knowledge characteristics of occupational roles. In this process there is an extension of access, through education, to elaborated codes, but access is controlled by the class system. The focusing of the codes I have suggested is brought about by the boundary-maintaining procedures within the family. However, we can generalize and say that the focusing of the codes is related to the boundary-maintaining procedures as these affect the major socializing agencies; family, age group, education, and work. We need, therefore, to consider, together with the question of the degree and type of complexity of the division of labor, the value orientations of society that it is hypothesized affect the boundary-maintaining procedures. It is the case that we can have societies with a similar complexity in their division of labor but who differ in their boundary-maintaining procedures.

I suggest then that it is important to make a distinction between societies in terms of their boundary-maintaining procedures if we are to deal with this question of the focusing of codes. One possible way of examining the relative strength of boundary maintenance at a somewhat high level of abstraction is to consider the strength of the *constraints* upon the choice of values that legitimize authority/power relationships. Thus in societies where there is weak constraint upon such legitimizing values, that is, where there are a variety of formally permitted legitimizing values, we might expect a marked shift towards person type control. Whereas in societies with strong constraints upon legitimizing values, where there is a severe *restriction* upon the choice, we might expect a marked shift towards positional control.

I shall illustrate these relationships with reference to the family:

Division of labor	Constraints upon legitimizing values (Boundary maintenance)	
Simple → Complex	Strong	Weak
↓	↓	↓
Speech codes	*Positional*	*Personal*
Restricted code	Working class	Working class
↓		
Elaborated code	Middle class	Middle class

Thus the division of labor influences the availability of elaborated codes, the class system affects their distribution, and the focusing of codes can be related to the boundary-maintaining procedures, for example, the value system. I must point out that this is only a coarse interpretative framework.

CONCLUSION

I have tried to show how the class system acts upon the deep structure of communication in the process of socialization. I refined the crudity of the analysis by showing how speech codes may be differently focused through family types. Finally, it is conceivable that there are general aspects of the analysis that might provide a starting point for the consideration of symbolic orders other than languages. I must point out that there is more to socialization than the forms of its linguistic realization.

REFERENCES

Bernstein, B. Education cannot compensate for society. *New Society* No. 387, February, 1970.

Bernstein, B. Family role systems, socialization and communication. Manuscript, Sociological Research Unit, University of London Institute of Education, 1962; also in D. Hymes and J. J. Gumperz (eds.), "A socio-linguistic approach to socialization,"*Directions in socio-linguistics.* Holt, Rinehart & Winston, 1970.

Bernstein, B. & Cook, J. Coding grid for maternal control, 1965. Available from Department of Sociology, University of London Institute of Education.

Bernstein, B. & Henderson, D. Social class differences in the relevance of language to socialization. *Sociology* 3, No. 1, 1969.

Bright, N. (ed.) *Sociolinguistics.* Mouton, 1966.

Carroll, J. B. (ed.) *Language thought and reality: Selected writings of Benjamin Lee Whorf.* Wiley, 1956.

Cazden, C. B. Sub-cultural differences in child language: An interdisciplinary review. *Merrill-Palmer Quarterly* 12, 1969.

Chomsky, N. *Aspects of linguistic theory.* M.I.T., 1065.

Cook, J. An enquiry into patterns of communication and control between mothers and their children in different social classes. Ph.D. Thesis, awaiting submission to the University of London, 1970.

Coulthard, M. A discussion of restricted and elaborated codes. *Educational Review* 22, No. 1, 1969.

Douglas, M. *Natural Symbols.* Barrie & Rockliff, The Cresset Press, 1970.

Fishman, J. A. A systematisation of the Whorfian hypothesis. *Behavioural Science* 5, 1960.

Halliday, M. A. K. Relevant models of language. *Educational review* 22, No. 1, 1969.

Hawkins, P. R. Social class, the nominal group and reference. *Language and Speech* 12, No. 2, 1969.

Henderson, D. Contextual specificity, discretion and cognitive socialization: With special reference to language. *Sociology* 4, No. 3, Sept. 1970.

Hoijer, H. (ed.) Language in Culture, American Anthropological Association Memoir No. 79, 1954—also published by the University of Chicago Press.

Hymes, D. Models of the Interaction of Language and Social setting. *Journal of Social Issues* 23, 1967.

Hymes, D. & Gumperz, J. J. (eds.) *Directions in sociolinguistics.* Holt, Rinehart & Winston, 1970.

Hymes, D. On communicative competence. Research Planning Conference on Language Development among Disadvantaged Children. Ferkauf Graduate School, Yeshiva University, 1966.

Labov, W. Stages of the acquisition of standard English. In W. Shay (ed.), *Social dialects and language learning.* Champaign, Illinois National Council of Teachers of English, 1965.

Labov, W. The social stratification of English in New York City, Washington, D.C. Center for Applied Linguistics, 1966.

Mandelbaum, D. (ed.) *Selected writings of Edward Sapir.* University of California Press, 1949.

Parsons, T. & Shils, Edward (eds.) *Toward a general theory of action.* Harper Torchbooks (Chapter 1, especially).

Schatzman, L. & Strauss, A. L. Social class and modes of communication, *American Journal of Sociology* 60, 1955: 328–338.

Turner, G. & Pickvance, R. E. Social class differences in the expression of uncertainty in five-year-old children. *Language & Speech,* 1969.

Williams, F. & Naremore, R. C. On the functional analysis of social class differences in modes of speech. *Speech Monographs* XXXVL, No. 2, 1969.

20

ADDRESS IN AMERICAN ENGLISH

Roger Brown
Marguerite Ford

When one person speaks to another, the selection of certain linguistic forms is governed by the relation between the speaker and his addressee. The principal option of address in American English is the choice between use of the first name (hereafter abbreviated to FN) and use of a title with the last name (TLN). These linguistic forms follow a rule that is truly relational. Their use is not predictable from properties of the addressee alone and not predictable from properties of the speaker alone but only from properties of the dyad. Kinship terms of address (e.g., dad, mom, son) are also relational language, but they constitute a restricted language of relationship since most dyads that might be created in America would not call for any sort of kinship term. Proper names, on the other hand, constitute a nearly universal language of relationship; the semantic dimensions involved serve to relate to one another all of the members of the society.

Much of our knowledge of the dimensions that structure interaction has been obtained from paper-and-pencil performances such as the status ranking of acquaintances or the sociometric

Reprinted from *Journal of Abnormal and Social Psychology* 62, No. 2 (1961): 375–85. Copyright 1961 by the American Psychological Association, and reproduced by permission. Footnotes have been renumbered.

choice from among acquaintances. There can be no doubt that the dimensions revealed by such data are genuinely functional in ordinary life. However, performances elicited by the social scientist are not the everyday performances that reveal dimensions of social structure and cause each new generation to internalize such dimensions. It is always possible that a paper-and-pencil task imposes a dimension or encourages an unrepresentative consistency and delicacy of differentiation. It is desirable to study social structure in everyday life, but much of the everyday behavior that is governed by social dimensions is difficult to record and involves an uncertain number of significant contrasts (e.g., influencing decisions, smiling at someone, warmth of manner). Forms of address are speech and so there is a recording technique called writing which preserves most of the significant detail. English forms of address are reasonably well described by a single binary contrast: FN or TLN. These forms are ubiquitous and for any set of interacting persons it is possible to obtain a collection of address dyads from which the latent structuring dimensions can be inferred. This paper provides an example of the application of semantic analysis to the study of social structure. We begin by describing the norms of American address, then point out a certain pattern in these norms which is to be found in the forms of address of all languages known to us. This abstract speech pattern suggests a feature of social structure that may possibly be universal.

METHOD

Materials

To discover the norms of address in American English we require a large sample of usage. The range of the subject population is vast but the uniformity must be great. Some sensible compromise is required between the stratified national sample dictated by the scope of the problem and the unsystematic observation of one's friends dictated by the probable simplicity of its solution. Four kinds of data have been used.

Usage in modern American plays. There are more instances of address in plays than in any other form of literature. Thirty-eight plays written by American authors, performed since 1939, and anthologized in three volumes of *Best American Plays* (Gassner,

1947, 1952, 1958) were used. Of the plays in these volumes we omitted only those set in some remote time or in a country other than the United States. Without listing all titles it is possible to indicate the range of American usage that it represented. By geographic region we move from *The Philadelphia Story* to the Southland of *The Member of the Wedding* through the midwest of *Picnic* to the Far West of *The Time of Your Life*; by social class from *The Rose Tattoo* and *A View from the Bridge* through *Death of a Salesman* and *Tea and Sympathy* to *The Solid Gold Cadillac*. For military usage there are such plays as *Mister Roberts* and *No Time for Sergeants*. The speech of Jewish, Italian, and Negro minorities is represented and also that of such groups as politicians, corporation executives, narcotics addicts, college professors, and policemen.

Of course these materials are not a record of actual speech from the characters named but are the speech constructed for such characters by playwrights. Probably playwrights accurately reproduce the true norms of address, and it is possible to check one author against another. In addition, however, there are three other kinds of data to catch possible inaccuracies in this first set.

Actual usage in a Boston business firm.   For 2 months a man employed in a drafting firm took advantage of leisure moments to jot down for us instances of linguistic address overheard from his fellow workers. He collected address terms for 214 different dyads in which 82 different people are involved either as speaker or addressee. Each person is identified by full name, sex, age, and position in a 12-level occupational hierarchy. In addition, we benefited from our informant's good knowledge of friendship patterns among the dramatis personae.

Reported usage of business executives.   Each year there is at MIT a group of Alfred P. Sloan Fellows; these are business executives between 30 and 38 years of age, who are nominated by their respective employers to study for one year at the institute. The 34 Sloan Fellows designated for 1958–59 served as informants for this study. They had come from many different parts of the country, most of them from very large corporations but a few from small companies.

By the time the Sloan Fellows served as informants the general pattern of the norms had become sufficiently clear to make possible the writing of a questionnaire designed to elicit the most important information. Each man was asked to write down the full names and positions of four persons whom he was accustomed to see nearly every day at his place of business, and he was to distribute his selections so as to include: one person equal to himself in the organization hierarchy with whom he was on close or intimate terms, one person equal to himself with whom he was on distant or formal terms, one person superior to himself in the organization hierarchy, one person subordinate to himself in the hierarchy. After listing the names the informant was asked to write down for each person listed the exact words that he (the informant) would customarily speak in greeting that person for the first time each day. In addition, the Sloan Fellows were asked some other questions that will be described when they become relevant.

Recorded usage in Midwest. The Psychological Field Station of the University of Kansas directed by Roger G. Barker and Herbert F. Wright (1954) kindly allowed us to make an extended study of 10 "specimen records," each of which records the events and conversation in a full-day of the life of a child. The station has also allowed us to work with a set of brief "behavior settings observations" made on 56 children in the town called Midwest and on 56 children in Yoredale, England, matched with those in Midwest by sex and age. In these materials we have been primarily concerned with a grammatical analysis of the kinds of "mands" addressed to children (for another study of the language of social relationship) but have, in addition, taken the opportunity to check our conclusions about American address against the Midwest records.

Procedure

For each of the 38 plays every instance of address was recorded, together with an identification of the speaker and addressee. The method of study is a sort of controlled induction.[1] Approximately one-third of the plays were first examined in an effort to discover rules that would summarize all of the instances of address they contained. The resulting provisional rules were then tested against a second set of plays and underwent some revision. The revised rules proved adequate to the description of all instances of address in a third and final set of plays. The supplementary data from a business firm, from the Sloan Fellows, and from the Midwest records were used as additional checks on the rules induced from the plays and also to test several particular hypotheses.

MAJOR PATTERNS OF ADDRESS

If we consider only the FN and TLN there are just three logically possible dyadic patterns: the reciprocal exchange of FN, the reciprocal exchange of TLN, and the nonreciprocal pattern in which one person uses FN and the other TLN. All three patterns occur with high frequency and the problem is one of inducing the semantic factors invariably associated with a given pattern and serving to distinguish it from the others.

In classifying instances of address into the three classes, FN was taken to include full first names (e.g., Robert), familiar abbreviations (e.g., Bob), and diminutive forms (e.g., Bobbie). It may be said at once that male first names in American English very seldom occur in full form (Robert, James, or Gerald) but are almost always either abbreviated (Bob, Jim) or diminutized (Jerry) or both (Bobbie, Jimmy). Female first names are more often left unaltered. Titles for the purpose of this classification include, in addition to Mr., Mrs., and Miss, such occupational titles as Dr., Senator, Major, and the like.

Two Reciprocal Patterns

The vast majority of all dyads in the plays exchange FN (Mutual FN). Indeed, where the actual name is not known there occur sometimes what may be called generic first names; these include the Mack, Jack, and Buddy of taxi drivers. Mutual TLN is most commonly found between newly introduced adults. The distinction between the two patterns is primarily one of degree of acquaintance with the degree required for the Mutual FN being less for younger people than for older people and less where the members of the dyad are of the same sex than where they are of different sex.

It seems likely that the two reciprocal patterns are on a dimension that ranges from acquaintance to intimacy. However, in modern American English the distance between the two points is small with the Mutual FN usually representing only a very small increment of intimacy over the Mutual TLN; as small sometimes as 5 minutes of conversation. Because the segment of the line that lies between the two patterns is usually so very short, it is not easy to make out its exact character. However, in English of the past[2] and in cognate languages today the Mutual FN is farther displaced from the Mutual TLN, and from these cases and other materials later to be presented we can hazard a characterization of intimacy. Intimacy is the horizontal line between members of a dyad. The principal factors predisposing to intimacy seem to be shared values (which may derive from kinship, from identity of occupation, sex, nationality, etc., or from some common fate) and frequent contact. Among the behavioral manifestations of intimacy, a relatively complete and honest self-disclosure is important.

Nonreciprocal Pattern

In this case one member of the dyad says FN and the other TLN. There are two kinds of relation that can generate this pattern. The first is a difference of age: children say TLN to adults and receive FN; among adults an elder by approximately 15-or-more years receives TLN and gives FN to his junior. The second is a difference of occupational status: this may be a relation of direct and enduring subordination (e.g., master-servant, employer-employee, officer-enlisted man); it may be a relation of direct but temporary subordination, involving someone in a service occupation (e.g., waiter, bootblack) and a customer; it may be an enduring difference of occupational status that does not involve direct subordination (e.g., United States senators have higher status than firemen). If the intimacy dimension that governs reciprocal address is the horizontal of social relationship, then the status dimension that underlies the nonreciprocal pattern may be called the vertical of social relationship.[3]

Age and occupational status are correlated and most instances of nonreciprocal address involve congruent differences on the two dimensions. There is, however, proof that a difference on either dimension alone is able to generate the nonreciprocal dyads matched on one dimension but not on the other.

Because there are two criteria for the assignment of status and, in addition, the correlation between the two criteria is not perfect, we must ask what happens to address in dyads where the elder has the humbler occupation. There are in the plays numerous instances in which the criteria oppose one another: an adolescent girl and her family's middle-aged cook, a young navy ensign and a middle-aged enlisted man, a young executive and an elderly janitor. In all such cases address is in accordance with occupational status and so it would appear that there is a normative rule of priority for the two criteria. It is to be expected in a society whose values are more strongly linked to achieved personal attributes than to ascribed attributes (Parsons, 1951) that occupation would prevail over age in the determination of deference.

The three sets of data in addition to the plays confirm the generalizations made above. Sloan Fellows call almost all of their business acquaintances by FN and expect this address to be reciprocated. In the few cases where one of these men would say TLN and expect to receive FN the other member of the dyad was invariably an organizational superior and was also the elder. In the Boston drafting firm, also, most address is on the pattern of Mutual FN. The few cases of Mutual TLN involved persons who were scarcely acquainted and who were well matched by age and position. There were 40 different instances of nonreciprocal address. In 36 of these the recipient of TLN was the organizational superior and elder; in 28 cases he was a member of one of the four top executive ranks whereas the recipient of FN was a member of one of the eight unionized ranks. In three cases the organizational superior was younger than his subordinate and it was the superior, not the elder, who received TLN. The single remaining case involved a pair matched by rank but not by age and in this case the elder received TLN. Midwest children participate in nonreciprocal address dyads with parents and teachers and in Mutual FN dyads with other children.

VARIANT FORMS OF ADDRESS

In this section are offered tentative characterizations of the several common forms other than FN and TLN. At a later point in the paper we will return to these variants and suggest the nature of their relationship with the major patterns.

Title Without Name

Commonly used titles (T) include sir, madam, ma'am, and Miss. In general these forms are used like TLN; either reciprocally between new acquaintances or nonreciprocally by a person of lower status to a person of higher status. The address form T is probably a degree less intimate and a degree more deferential than TLN. It may, for instance, be used reciprocally where acquaintance is so slight that the last name is not known. In nonreciprocal military usage between ranks the TLN may be used to immediate superiors but the T to remote colonels, generals, commanders, and admirals even though the names of these superiors are well known.

Beyond this general characterization as a minimally intimate and maximally deferential form particular varieties of T have their specialized uses. The form ma'am is most commonly heard from young men to mature women. Schoolchildren in Yoredale, England preface almost all address to a teacher by saying: "Please, Miss . . . " In parallel circumstances Midwest children use TLN.

Last Name Alone

An occasional person is regularly addressed by LN. This seems usually to occur where the FN is polysyllabic and has no familiar abbreviation whereas the LN is either a monosyllable or readily transformed into a monosyllable. In these circumstances LN is simply a substitute for FN and patterns in identical fashion.

Where the LN is not the usual form for an addressee it represents a degree of intimacy greater than TLN but less than FN. In military usage enlisted men receive the LN from officers when they are little acquainted; increased familiarity leads to the FN downward thought not upward. Elderly and very distinguished professors sometimes begin letters to junior colleagues whom they know fairly well: "Dear Jones . . . " The form is not reciprocated in this case.

Reciprocal LN is common between enlisted men until they become acquainted. The enduring reciprocal LN seems always to go with a mutual antagonism that blocks progression to intimacy. In *The Caine Mutiny Court Martial*, for instance, Greenwald and Keefer exchange LN though the degree of acquaintance and their ages would normatively produce Mutual FN. In the climax of this play Greenwald dashes a drink in Keefer's face. In *The Philadelphia Story* Kittredge and Haven exchange LN; the former is the husband-to-be of Tracy Lord and the latter her former-but-still-interested husband.

Multiple Names

A speaker may use more than one form of the proper name for the same addressee, sometimes saying TLN, sometimes FN or LN or a nickname, sometimes creating phonetic variants of either FN or the nickname. We are not here interested in the business of temporal progression through the possible forms where earlier terms are dropped as new terms are taken up. The case of multiple names (MN) is the case in which two or more versions of the proper name are used in free variation with one another.

The instances of MN in the plays suggested that this form

represented a greater degree of intimacy than the FN, but degrees of intimacy are not easily judged and so we decided to put the hypothesis to a more direct test. The test involved individual interviews with 32 MIT male undergraduates. Each subject was asked to think of four men of about his own age all of whom he had met for the first time approximately one year ago. In addition, it was to be the case that the subject had had about equal opportunity to get to know all of these men and yet now was to find himself on close, friendly terms with some of them and on more distant terms with others. The subject was asked to write down the full names of the four men and then to record the name by which he usually addressed each one. When this had been done, the subject was asked, for each acquaintance, whether he ever addressed the man in any other way and all the names currently being used were noted down.

In an earlier paragraph it was suggested that one of the meanings of intimacy is a relatively complete and honest disclosure of the personality. Jourard and Lasakow (1958) have devised a Self-disclosure questionnaire which requires the subject to indicate whether or not he has discussed with a designated other person each of 60 topics classifiable under the headings: Attitudes and opinions, Tastes and interests, Work (or studies), Money, Personality, and Body. Our 32 subjects filled out this questionnaire for each acquaintance. For each subject, then, we ranked the four acquaintances in order of decreasing Self-disclosure and we take this to be an order of decreasing intimacy. It generally corresponds with the subjects' ordering of the four into friends and acquaintances.

Across all subjects we combined the 32 closest friends, those eliciting highest Self-disclosure scores (Self-disclosure 1) and also the 32 acquaintances with Self-disclosure rank orders 2, 3, and 4. For each rank group we determined the number of cases addressed by MN (2 or more proper names) and the number addressed by FN alone. The results appear in Table 1. The cases of MN decline as intimacy declines. Using the sign test and a one-tailed hypothesis it was determined that the Self-disclosure 1 group contained more cases of MN than did the next most intimate group (Self-disclosure 2) with $p = .020$. The difference between the most intimate and the least intimate (Self-disclosure 4) group shows more cases of MN in the former group with $p < .004$.

One informant addressed his closest friend whose name is Robert Williams as Williams or Robert or Bob or Willie and his next closest friend whose name is James Scoggin as Scoggin, James, Jim, or Scoggs. Many informants reported that they sometimes play-

Table 1.   Frequencies of Two Forms of Address to Acquaintances at Different Levels of Self-Disclosure

	Self-dis-closure 1	Self-dis-closure 2	Self-dis-closure 3	Self-dis-closure 4
Multiple names	18	10	7	3
First name	14	22	25	29

Note: Self-disclosure 1 versus Self-disclosure 2 by sign test, $p = .020$; Self-disclosure 1 versus Self-disclosure 4 by sign test, $p < .004$.

fully addressed a good friend by TLN. Others used playful, and usually pejorative, phonetic variations: Magoo for Magee, Katool for Katell, Lice for Leis.

The tendency to proliferate proper names in intimacy is interesting because it accords with a familiar semantic-psychological principle. For language communities the degree of lexical differentiation of a referent field increases with the importance of that field to the community. To cite a fresh example of this kind of thing, Conklin (1957) reports that the Hanunóo of the Philippine Islands have names for 92 varieties of rice which is their principal food. In naming ferns and orchids, with which they are little concerned, the Hanunóo combine numerous botanical species under one term whereas the rice they differentiate so finely is for the botanist a single species. Within a language community Brown (1958) has pointed out that a speaker more concerned with a given referent field will make finer lexical distinctions than a speaker less concerned with that field (botanists have more names for plants than do psychologists). In the referent field composed of other persons we have seen that where contact and concern are minimal and distance greatest, titles alone are likely to be used in address. To call someone Miss or sir is to address the person on a categorical level which does not establish the addressee's individual identity. The proper name constitutes the individual as a unique organism. Beyond the single proper name, however, where interest is still greater the individual is fragmented into a variety of names. Perhaps this differentiation beyond individuality expresses various manifestations or ways of regarding someone who is close (Brown, 1959).

A GENERAL SYSTEM OF ADDRESS

How are these various forms of address related to one another? Consider first only the three major patterns. The Mutual TLN goes with distance or formality and the Mutual FN with a slightly greater degree of intimacy. In nonreciprocal address the TLN is used to the person of higher status and the FN to the person of lower status. One form expresses both distance and deference; the other form expresses both intimacy and condescension. Within the limits of two dyadic address forms there is a formally or logically possible alternative pattern. The form used mutually between intimates could be used upward to superiors and the form used between distant acquaintances could be directed downward to subordinates. Because there is an alternative the pattern actually found is not a formal necessity but rather an empirical fact; a fact, we shall see, of great generality.

Several years ago we began our general studies of the language of social relationship with a selection point that does not occur in modern English but which does occur in the other Indo-European languages. In French, for example, a speaker must choose between two second person singular pronouns; his addressee may be addressed as *tu* or as *vous*. In German the comparable forms are *du* and *Sie*; in Italian *tu* and *Lei*. In English of the past, from about the 13th century until the 18th, there was a cognate option of address; the choice between *thou* and *ye*. We have studied the semantic rules governing these pronouns in 20 languages of Europe and India, comparing one language with another and the usage of earlier centuries with later (Brown & Gilman, 1960). For our present purposes the important point is that these pronouns in all the languages studied follow the same abstract pattern as the FN and TLN.

In discussing the pronouns of address let us use T as a generic designator for pronouns of the type of *tu* and *du* and V as a designator for pronouns of the type of *vous* and *Sie*. Mutual V is the form of address for adult new acquaintances; it begins where TLN begins—at the temporal point of origin of the dyad. Mutual T like Mutual FN is an expression of increased intimacy but it is, for most Europeans, much farther along the line than is the Mutual FN of Americans. From medieval times into the present century nonreciprocal T and V was the pattern for those unequal in status with the superior receiving the V and the subordinate the T. In recent times the nonreciprocal use of the pronouns has much declined because of a conscious egalitarianism. The important point is, however, that when the nonreciprocal pattern has been used anywhere from southern India to Scandinavia the downward directed form has been the intimate T and the upward directed the distant V.

It may be that the abstract linkage in personal address of intimacy and condescension, distance and deference is a linguistic universal, but we certainly do not know that as yet. We do know that the linkage occurs also in some non-Indo-European languages (e.g., Japanese second person pronouns). Indeed, in those few languages for which we have found adequate descriptions of the semantics of address, no violations of the abstract pattern have yet appeared.

It seems also that the pattern applies to more than names, titles, and pronouns. The Sloan Fellows' greetings to their business associates almost invariably used the FN. However, the greetings themselves were quite varied; including Hi, Morning, Good Morning, Hello, Howdy, etc. Only Hi and Good Morning occurred with sufficient frequency to make possible the discovery of a pattern. The Sloans reported on greetings to four classes of associate: Equal and Intimate, Equal and Distant, Superior, and Subordinate. In Table 2 appear the frequencies of Hi and Good Morning for these various categories. Hi is more common to intimates and to subordinates while Good Morning is for distant acquaintances and superiors. Using the McNemar test for the significance of changes in related samples with the Yates correction for continuity, the difference between intimates and acquaintances is significant with $p < .0025$ and the difference for subordinates and superiors with $p < .025$. In both cases a one-tailed test was used since the direction of the differences was predicted by the abstract pattern of address. The records of actual usage in a Boston firm accord with this finding. In one revealing instance a workman was greeted

Table 2.   Two Forms of Greeting for Four Classes of Associate

	Equal and intimate	
	Good Morning	Hi
Equal and distant		
Hi	0	4
Good Morning	4	10
	Subordinate	
	Good Morning	Hi
Superior		
Hi	1	3
Good Morning	13	8

Note: With McNemar test for the significance of changes in related samples (employing Yates correction) χ^2 for Intimate versus Distant $= 8.10$, $p < .0025$ and χ^2 for Subordinate versus Superior $= 4.00$, $p < .025$.

"Hi" and promptly answered "Hi," but as he turned and recognized the boss, he added "Good morning."

Why should the abstract pattern described govern address between two persons? A curious fact about contemporary use of T and V provides a clue. While the nonreciprocal pattern for pronouns has generally been abandoned in Europe, inequality of status continues to affect one aspect of usage. Dyads begin at the Mutual V and, with time, may advance to the intimacy of Mutual T. For many the shift from V to T is an important rite of passage. The Germans even have a little informal ceremony they call the *Bruderschaft*. One waits for a congenial mood, a mellow occasion, perhaps with a glass of wine, and says: "Why don't we say *du* to one another?" The new usage is, of course, to be reciprocal. However, there is one necessarily nonreciprocal aspect of the occasion— someone must make the suggestion. When there is a clear difference of status between the two the right to initiate the change unequivocally belongs to the superior—to the elder, the richer, the more distinguished of the two. The gate to linguistic intimacy is kept by the person of higher status.

The norms of English address also make a pattern in time. A dyad must, with time, either increase its total amount of contact or else dissolve. Since the Mutual TLN represents less contact than the Mutual FN if Mutual TLN is to occur in a given dyad it must occur at an earlier time than the Mutual FN. The place of the nonreciprocal pattern in time is between the other two and it may be understood as a step from Mutual TLN in the direction of Mutual FN; a step which, like the suggestion of the *Bruderschaft* is taken first by the superior. Many dyads will linger for a very long time—possibly the life of the dyad—in the nonreciprocal pattern. In this circumstance the pattern gives enduring expression to an inequality of status.

Consider a familiar sort of example. A prospective graduate student arrives at a university to meet some of the faculty of the psychology department and is interviewed by the chairman. Probably the two will initially exchange TLN. In the course of the day or, if not, shortly after the student enrolls, the chairman will begin to call him by FN. He extends the hand of friendship, but the student knows that it behooves him not to grasp it too quickly. The student will continue with the TLN for several years (4 is probably the mode) and in this period the nonreciprocality of speech will express the inequality of status. If the chairman is neither very elderly nor very august the student will eventually feel able to reciprocate the FN and the dyad will have advanced to Mutual FN. The three patterns may be described as a progression in time (see upper portion of Figure 1) if we add several important qualifications.

Not every dyad passes through all three steps. There are some that begin at each of the three points: adults of equal status with Mutual TLN, master and servant with nonreciprocality, young people with Mutual FN. In addition, not every dyad that continues to exist will necessarily advance to Mutual FN. In North Carolina until 1860 the Negro slave said TLN to his master and was told FN (Eliason, 1956), and there was no change with time. There is a final qualification concerning the progression of address in time. Even when relationships do develop in intimacy they will not necessarily pass through the intermediate nonreciprocal stage. When the members of a dyad are not of clearly unequal status, they will advance at the same time to Mutual FN.

Figure 1. Graphic Models of the Progression of Address in Time (from left to right).

(The upper portion of the figure represents the major progression; the lower portion represents the full progression.)

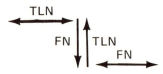

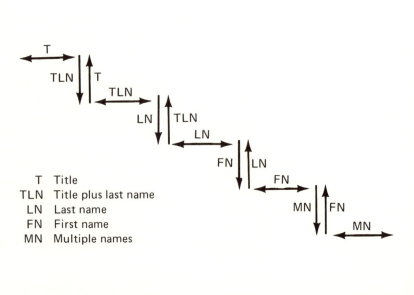

T   Title
TLN Title plus last name
LN   Last name
FN   First name
MN   Multiple names

The general statement that can be made is: if an address pattern changes in time it will change in the direction of Mutual TLN → nonreciprocal TLN and FN → Mutual FN though a step may be skipped. Even this statement cannot stand without a little more explanation. There are special circumstances in which the direction of movement of address can be reversed. If a person of lower status seems to move too fast to the reciprocation of the FN a superior may step back from his use of FN to TLN. The day after a convivial office party a breezy young clerk calls out to the president: "Morning, Jack!" and in icy tones the president replies: "Good morning, *Mr.* Jones." The person of lower status must never use a more familiar form of address than the person of higher status and the backstep by the superior puts the subordinate in just that position from which he will usually withdraw to the propriety of TLN.

The variant forms of address discussed at an earlier point in this paper seem to function as additional optional steps in the progression of address.[4] Title alone (T) probably is the formal extreme since we find in our data that dyads which begin as Mutual T often change with time to nonreciprocal TLN downwards and T upwards. The last name alone (LN) must be intercalated between TLN and FN since LN downwards is found in combination with TLN upwards and LN upwards is found in combination with FN downwards. The use of multiple names (MN), we have seen, represents the intimate extreme. Making these additions to the major three-step progression we arrive at the full progression of Figure 1 (lower portion) in which each new step towards intimacy is initiated by the superior who is, therefore, not just the gatekeeper to Mutual FN but the pacesetter for all linguistic advances in intimacy.

The qualifications that apply to the major progression apply also to the full progression. Dyads may begin at any point, need not move at all, and if they move may skip steps. There is an additional qualification that results from the multiplication of forms. Any less formal term may be used downwards in a nonreciprocal pattern with any more formal term being used upwards. Thus we find not only the TLN with the LN but also the T with LN or even with FN as when a captain calls an enlisted man *Jones* or *John* but is called *captain*.

Is there any way to test the accuracy of the full progression pictured in Figure 1? We have found no dyads that pass through the entire progression but only dyads moving in one or another limited region. By the time the third and final set of plays was ready for analysis, the full progression had been constructed. If the progression, with all its qualifications, is accurately descriptive of American English practice, one should find certain kinds of address combinations and not others. Any address form can be used mutually (5 possible combinations). When there is a clear difference of status we may have any nonreciprocal pattern that combines a less formal term downwards with a more formal term upwards (10 possible combinations). With a clear status difference we may not have any nonreciprocal pattern that combines a more formal term downwards with a less formal term upwards (10 impossible combinations). In the last set of plays instances of all the possible combinations occur and no instances of the impossible combinations. The static predictions of the model are validated.

The construction also generates a set of dynamic predictions. When address changes (if there is not either a reproving or a jocular intent) movement must be in the direction from left to right in the drawing of Figure 1 though it need not be to the immediately adjacent position. Changes of address in the plays are surprisingly infrequent and seldom involve more than two steps. Only seven different kinds of change occurred but all of these are included among those defined as possible by the model. One "impossible" change occurred in the play *Born Yesterday*. Billie Dawn, the junk dealer's mistress, in speaking with the wife of a United States Senator who is many years her senior initiates movement from Mutual TLN to a more intimate form. This violation of the norms is greeted with general shock and is a device that helps to establish Billie Dawn's ingenuous vulgarity. Insofar as the limited occurrences of change in address permit, then, the model is confirmed in its dynamic aspect.

STATUS AND INTIMACY IN SOCIAL RELATIONS

Two persons of unequal status may be conceived as two points on a generalized value scale of the sort used by Osgood and Tannenbaum (1955) for the congruity model which they have used to predict attitude change. The person of superior status has, of course, the greater value on such a scale. Movements towards intimacy of address in terms of the congruity model are acts of association. Such acts, the model predicts, will cause the objects of unequal value to move towards one another; in the case of address between persons this means that the value of the inferior is enhanced by intimate association with a superior while the value of the superior is diminished. The prediction is good intuitive sense. But now the interesting thing is that this model seems to call for the abstract pattern of address that does not occur. Since the person of lower status has a motive for initiating intimacy and the superior has none the intimate form ought, in nonreciprocal address, to be used upwards and the distant form to be used downwards. This is not the pattern which we have found in all of our materials but, is rather, the formal alternative to that pattern and we have nowhere found this alternative to be the operative norm.

The abstract design of address is not a direct expression of the realities of status and intimacy but is rather a denial of the realities. The pattern might have been designed to minimize the pain of invidious status distinctions. The person of lesser value may be presumed to be ever ready for association with a person of higher value must be presumed to be less ready. If the person of lesser value were to initiate associative acts, he would run the risk of rebuff; if the person of higher value initiates such acts there is no such risk. The superior, then, must be the pacesetter in progression to intimacy. If there is to be no progression but rather an enduring nonreciprocal expression of inequality, this expression is not so disagreeable as it might be since the superior offers intimate address and it is the inferior who demurs. The abstract pattern minimizes the pain that could be involved when persons are to be related on two dimensions: the horizontal of intimacy and the vertical of status.

The person of higher status is, we believe, the pacesetter not in linguistic address alone but in all acts that increase intimacy. The Sloan Fellows who served as informants for us responded to two questions that concern nonlinguistic moves towards intimacy. Each question was answered with reference to each of the four persons listed by the informant. One of these persons, you may remember, was a Superior, one a Subordinate, one Equal and Intimate, one Equal and Distant. The informant indicated on a scale from 1–5 how willing he would be to behave in the designated manner with reference to each person. The Number 1 represents maximal willingness ("Definitely would") and 5 minimal willingness ("Definitely would not"). The questions are:

1. In ordinary circumstances would you be willing to ask "X" for the loan of his comb?
2. Suppose "X" were feeling very unhappy about something or other. Would you put your hand on his shoulder in a reassuring way?

The results appear in Table 3 and show a familiar pattern. Informants were more willing to borrow a comb from, and to put a hand on the shoulder of, an associate who was Equal and Intimate than one Equal and Distant and also more willing to initiate these acts of intimacy with Subordinates than with Superiors. Using a sign test and a one-tailed hypothesis the comb question differentiates intimate from remote associates with a $p = .008$ and Subordinates from Superiors with a $p = .033$; the hand-on-shoulder question differentiates intimate from remote associates with a $p = .002$. These nonspeech acts follow the pattern of TLN and FN; of T and V; and of Hi and Good Morning. Perhaps all kinds of associative behavior can be placed on a rough scale of intimacy and in the progression over this scale of a dyad the superior may always be in advance.

With a good sized inequality of status the use of FN by the higher does not, of course, justify immediate reciprocation from the lower. The lower must wait for the initiation of additional acts of intimacy before taking a step on his own. It is very likely that the normative lag in intimacy increases with the degree of status inequality. However, the norms are not always perfectly clear; graduate students will sometimes be uncertain whether the time has come to say FN to a professor, employees will wonder whether they know their bosses well enough to use the familiar form. When someone is in this region of uncertainty, we find that he avoids the use of any sort of personal name and makes do with the uncommitted omnibus *you*.

Table 3. Comparative Willingness to Initiate Acts of Intimacy with Four Classes of Associate

	More willing with equal and intimate than with distant associate	More Willing with equal and distant than with intimate associate	More willing with subordinate than with superior	More willing with superior than with subordinate
Borrow comb	7	0	9	2
Hand on shoulder	11	3	24	1

Note. By sign test Intimate versus Distant on Borrow Comb, $p = .008$; on Hand on Shoulder, $p = .029$. Subordinate versus Superior on Borrow Comb, $p = .033$; on Hand on Shoulder, $p < .002$.

SUMMARY

The semantic rules governing address in American English are worked out from a varied collection of data that includes usage in American plays, actual usage in a Boston business firm, reported usage in a Boston business firm, reported usage of business executives from various cities in the United States, and usage recorded in a midwestern American town. The most common address forms are the first name (FN) and the title plus last name (TLN). These function in three sorts of dyadic pattern: the Mutual TLN, the Mutual FN, and the nonreciprocal use of TLN and FN. The semantic distinction between the two mutual patterns is on the intimacy dimension with Mutual FN being the more intimate of the two patterns. In the nonreciprocal pattern a distinction is made in terms of status with the higher saying FN and the lower TLN. The practice of using the intimate form to a subordinate and the distant form to a superior also governs the use of pronouns of address in many languages as well as the use of certain conventional greetings. It is suggested that this very general pattern prevails because in the progression towards intimacy of unequals the superior is always the pacesetter initiating new moves in that direction. The superior is the pacesetter because the willingness of the person of lower status to enter into association can be taken for granted and there is little risk that a superior will be rebuffed whereas the risk would be great if the inferior were to initiate acts of association. Such variant forms of address as the title alone, the last name alone, and the use of multiple names are fitted into a model that purports to describe the temporal progression of address from acquaintance to friendship. Each new step towards friendship is, in this model, initiated by the person of higher status.

NOTES

[1]Since address involves two persons and, very often, a choice between two linguistic forms, we believe it should be possible to treat the complete set of address dyads for any group of persons as a matrix of paired comparisons from which the dimensions structuring the group could be rigorously derived. We are at present trying to develop such a method.

[2]In six American plays (Quinn, 1917) written between 1830 and 1911 the reciprocal FN between adults clearly implies a much longer and closer acquaintance than it does in contemporary usage.

³Kinship terms of address in American English (Schneider & Homans, 1955) also show a nonreciprocality of status. Members of ascending generations are commonly addressed with kinship titles (mother, father, grandmother, grandfather, uncle, aunt) but respond by calling their children, grandchildren, nephews, and nieces by FN.

⁴This paper does not discuss all American English forms of address but only those that have clear positions in the intimacy and status pattern. There is, for instance, the use of the complete name (*John Jones* or even *John Montgomery Jones*) which is used as an intensifier and is particularly favored by mothers "manding" disobedient children.

REFERENCES

Barker, R. G., & Wright, H. F. *Midwest and its children.* Evanston, Ill.: Row, Peterson, 1954.

Brown, R. *Words and things.* Glencoe, Ill.: Free Press, 1958.

Brown, R. Humbert's idiography. *Contemp. Psychol.*, 1959, 4: 172–174.

Brown, R., & Gilman, A. The pronouns of power and solidarity. In T. Sebeok (ed)., *Style in language.* New York: Wiley, 1960.

Conklin, H. C. *Hanunóo agriculture.* Rome: Food and Agriculture Organization of the United Nations, 1957.

Eliason, N. E. *Tarheel talk: An historical study of the English language in North Carolina to 1860.* Chapel Hill: University of North Carolina Press, 1956.

Gassner, J. (ed.) *Best plays of the modern American theatre: Second series.* New York: Crown, 1947.

Gassner, J. (ed.) *Best American plays: Third series.* New York: Crown, 1952.

Gassner, J. (ed.) *Best American plays: Fourth series.* New York: Crown, 1958.

Jourard, S. M., & Lasakow, P. Some factors in self-disclosure. *J. abnorm. soc. Psychol.*, 1958, 56: 91–98.

Osgood, C. E., & Tannenbaum, P. H. The principle of congruity in attitude change. *Psychol. Rev.*, 1955, 62: 42–55.

Parsons, T. *The social system.* Glencoe, Ill.: Free Press, 1951.

Quinn, A. H. (ed.) *Representative American plays.* New York: Century, 1917.

Schneider, D. M., & Homans, G. C. Kinship terminology and the American kinship system. *Amer. Anthrop.*, 1955, 57: 1194–1208.

21

FORMS OF ADDRESS AND SOCIAL RELATIONS IN A BUSINESS ORGANIZATION

Dan I. Slobin
Stephen H. Miller
Lyman W. Porter

The form of address people use when speaking to each other is dictated by the nature of the relationship between them. Address is expressed linguistically by second-person pronouns, as the *tu* and *vous* of French, the *du* and *Sie* of German, etc., by the use of first name or title and last name, by the use of honorifics (as in Japanese), and so on. The variables governing address in some 20 languages have been extensively studied by Brown and Gilman (1960) and Brown and Ford (1961); additional data have been provided by Slobin (1963) for Yiddish, by Fischer (1964) and Befu and Norbeck (1958) for Japanese, by Howell (1967) for Korean, by Foster (1964) for Spanish, by Rubin (1962) for Spanish and Guaraní, and by Swartz (1960) for Truk. It is apparently a sociolinguistic universal that the address term exchanged between intimates ("familiar pronoun," first name, etc.) is the same term used in addressing social inferiors, and that the term exchanged between

Reprinted from *Journal of Personality and Social Psychology* 8, No. 3 (1968): 289–93. Copyright 1968 by the American Psychological Association, and reproduced by permission.

nonintimates ("polite pronoun," title and last name, etc.) is also used to address social superiors. Brown has observed that the relative positions of individuals on these two social dimensions of solidarity and status account for the forms of address used in any given dyad. Studies of address reveal the criteria employed by speakers for assigning addressees to positions on these dimensions. For example, Brown and Ford (1961) noted the importance of achieved status revealed in contemporary American address, and Slobin (1963) used address norms to reveal the importance of ascribed status in the social relations of prewar speakers of Yiddish in Eastern Europe.

In the present study we attempt to relate forms of address in American English (first name—FN, title and last name—TLN) to: (*a*) status (position in the formal hierarchy, age), (*b*) presumed familiarity (equality of status, time in organization), (*c*) intimacy (self-disclosure), and (*d*) personality (status seeking, self-assurance). The study is exploratory, and is intended to demonstrate that address behavior may reveal symptomatic and diagnostic aspects of the general nature of an organization, its structure, climate, and pattern of communications; conversely, comparative studies may demonstrate that these organizational variables influence the choice of address term.

In accordance with previous findings, it is expected that the greater the status difference between individuals the greater should be the probability of nonreciprocal address, the higher-status individual receiving TLN and the lower-status individual receiving FN. Given the dominance of achieved over ascribed status in determining forms of address in American English, the expected non-reciprocal address pattern should hold true even if the person of lower status is the elder.

In cases of mutual TLN or nonreciprocal address, the person of lower status should be more motivated to establish mutual FN address than should the person of higher status, for such an act of association enhances the value of the former while diminishing that of the latter (Brown, 1965). However, the former is presumed to hold back from directing FN upward, for, as Brown and Ford (1961) proposed:

> If the person of lesser value were to initiate associative acts, he would run the risk of rebuff; if the person of higher value initiates such acts there is no such risk. The superior, then, must be the pacesetter in progression to

intimacy. . . . The person of higher status is, we believe, the pacesetter not in linguistic address alone, but in all acts that increase intimacy [p. 383].

There is, however, one sort of relatively intimate associative act which a person of lower status might engage in without serious fear of rebuff—namely, limited disclosure of attitudes about his job, interests, opinions, and personal problems. It is predicted that an individual is relatively more self-disclosing to his boss than to his subordinates, in the hope of drawing the higher-status person into mutual self-disclosure, thereby increasing intimacy with the superior and enhancing status in the organization.

METHOD

Informants

Informants were drawn from a large state insurance company with central offices in San Francisco. Selection was made by the personnel director from two of the firm's largest divisions: administrative (underwriting, payroll auditing, data processing, and cashier departments) and program development (internal audit, safety services, district services, research and planning, and claims departments). Interviews were conducted with 57 male and 30 female informants, ranging in age from 20 to 59, with a mean age of 42.7. Informants were classed in four levels: (*a*) upper management (four division chiefs), (*b*) middle management (14 administrators or those reporting directly to division chiefs), (*c*) lower management (18 individuals one level above rank and file), and (*d*) nonmanagement employees (51 individuals at the lowest level in the hierarchy). Sampling in *d* was random, while all available individuals were interviewed at the three management levels (*a–c*).

Procedure

Interviews of 10–20 minutes each were conducted during a 2-week period in the spring of 1965. The interviewer (second author) introduced himself as a graduate research assistant from the Institute of Industrial Relations at the University of California, and told the informant that the Institute was interested in studying communications in organizations. The informant was assured of the complete confidentiality of the interview. At the end of the interview the informant was given a stamped, addressed envelope containing a Ghiselli Self-Description Inventory (Ghiselli, 1954). All but 7 of the 87 informants returned the Inventory.

Interview schedule. The basis of the first part of the interview was a chart in which the informant filled in the names which he used to address the following individuals, and the names he received from them in return: subordinate (S), subordinate's subordinate (SS), boss (B), boss's boss (BB), and fellow workers (FW). The second part of the interview followed a modified version of the Self-Disclosure Questionnaire developed by Jourard and Lasakow (1958). Each informant was asked if he had ever confided to SS, S, B, BB, or closest FW anything about: (*a*) aspects of his work, such as its problems, pressures, satisfactions; (*b*) his tastes in such areas as music, books, and food; (*c*) his opinions in such areas as politics, religion, and integration; and (*d*) his personal problems. In the case of negative answers, the informant was asked if he *would* confide such information if given the appropriate opportunity and, if not, why. Under each area of self-disclosure the informant was also asked if he received such information from SS, S, FW, B, or BB.

RESULTS

Forms of Address

Table 1 gives the percentages and frequencies (in parentheses) of forms of address used by the various organizational levels (columns) in addressing individuals of varying status relative to those levels (rows). The categories of middle and upper management have been combined, and the response category, "depends on situation," has been omitted. Since this response was generally infrequent, analyses are based only on the FN and TLN categories.

As expected, informants always reported using FN in addressing SS, S, and FW. Also as predicted, there is a slight (though not significant) decrease in use of FN from FW to B; and at every level there is a large decrease in first naming from B to BB (except in the case of upper management, who report universal FN address within the firm). There are no significant differences (using chi-square) among the levels in use of FN in addressing B. There is, however, a significant difference among levels in frequency of

Table 1. **Percentage and Frequency of Reported Forms of**
Address from Organizational Levels
to Individuals of Varying
Relative Status[a]

	Nonmanagement (N = 51)		Lower management (N = 18)		Middle and upper management (N = 18)	
	FN	*TLN*	*FN*	*TLN*	*FN*	*TLN*
BB	27.5	60.8	16.7	72.2	71.4	25.0
	(14)	(31)	(3)	(13)	(10)	(7)
B	84.3	9.8	72.2	11.1	78.6	17.9
	(43)	(5)	(13)	(2)	(12)	(5)
FW	100	0	100	0	100	0
	(51)	(0)	(18)	(0)	(18)	(0)
S	100	0	100	0	100	0
	(21)	(0)	(18)	(0)	(18)	(0)
SS	100	0	100	0	100	0
	(4)	(0)	(13)	(0)	(13)	(0)

[a]Percentages of FN and TLN do not sum to 100 percent because the "depends" category does not appear in the table.

addressing BB by FN, with the combined middle-upper-management level using FN most frequently and lower management using it relatively least frequently ($\chi^2 = 6.34$, $df = 2$, $p < .05$ for two-tailed test).

The expectation that B receives FN more frequently than BB is supported at both the staff and lower-management levels (for staff, Cochran Q distributed as $\chi^2 = 26.25$, with $df = 1$, $p < .01$; for lower management, Q = 10.00, $p < .01$). There is no significant difference at the middle-management level (Q = 1), and sample size is too small for statistical analysis at the upper-management level.

Note was taken of individual dyads, omitting "depends" and upper-management levels, in which address was other than mutual FN. A total of 11 out of 77 such dyads were of the type B-S, and 43 out of 67 of the type BB-S. Of these 54 dyads not using mutual FN only 4 used mutual TLN; in the remaining 50 the person of higher status reported receiving TLN and offering FN downwards. This picture is reinforced by interview responses which indicated that individuals of high status, such as the general manager, and strangers in the company would also receive TLN, and that the informant received TLN from individuals of relatively lower status, such as the "steno pool," or strangers from other departments. Thus Brown's "linguistic universal" is again supported: TLN is used in addressing persons of higher status or less intimacy, while FN is offered to those of lower or equal status. (In the latter case, the self-disclosure data reported below suggest that the use of mutual FN reflects a degree of intimacy between fellow workers. However, the possibility cannot be excluded that such address usage is simply determined by organizational norms.)

Table 2 gives the percentages and frequencies (in parentheses) of forms of address that the various levels (columns) report *receiving from* the various status individuals (rows). This gives a rough reliability check of Table 1, though not an exact one-to-one relationship, since the S and SS rows may refer to different individuals than those in Table 1 (because each superior has many subordinates, and the subordinates interviewed may not have been the same ones the superior had in mind when reporting his own use of names). The results discussed above are confirmed in Table 2. All informants reported receiving FN from B and BB (except for the four cases of mutual TLN mentioned above). In the case of nonreciprocal usage, TLN was received from below and FN from above. Individuals at a given level significantly reported receiving FN more frequently from S than from SS, confirming the findings from Table 1 that FN was reported to be used more frequently in addressing B than BB.

Table 2.   Percentage and Frequency of Forms of Address that Levels Report Receiving from Status Individuals[a]

	Nonmanagement		Lower management		Middle and upper management	
	FN	*TLN*	*FN*	*TLN*	*FN*	*TLN*
BB	84.3	0	88.9	11.1	92.9	3.6
	(43)[b]	(0)	(16)	(2)	(16)	(1)
B	96.0	2.0	100	0	96.5	0
	(49)	(1)	(18)	(0)	(17)	(0)
FW	100	0	100	0	100	0
	(51)	(0)	(18)	(0)	(18)	(0)
S	100	0	94.4	0	50.0	19.7
	(21)	(0)	(17)	(0)	(9)	(3)
SS	100	0	69.2	23.1	5.6	71.9
	(4)	(0)	(9)	(3)	(1)	(8)

[a]Percentages of FN and TLN do not sum to 100 percent because the "depends" category does not appear in the table.

[b]Five informants reported that BB did not know their name.

One additional interesting trend should be noted. The frequency of FN address reported as received from SS and S combined decreased with increasing level in the organization. Nonmanagement employees reported being called FN by SS and S 100 percent of the time; lower management reported 89 percent; middle management reported 57.1 percent; and upper management reported being called FN by only 38.5 percent of their SS and S. Thus it appears that the higher the level within the organization the less likely one is to report receiving FN from S and SS.

Address and age.   In 26 dyads the superior was younger than the subordinate, with a mean age difference of 10.4 years. In no dyad was nonreciprocal naming based on age as opposed to status—that is, there was no case in which the elder subordinate was TLN and the younger superior FN. In only two cases was the pattern of address mutual TLN. In five dyads the subordinate reported receiving FN and reported that the name addressed to his superior depended on the situation. The remaining 15 dyads reported using mutual FN.

Self-Disclosure

Regardless of level, individuals reported that they are relatively more self-disclosing to FW than to B and more self-disclosing to their immediate superior than to their immediate subordinates. Relative to the higher levels, the nonmanagement levels restricted its self-disclosure to FW.

Relationship between form of address and self-disclosure.   At zero status difference (FW) there was universal use of mutual FN and the highest percentage of frequency of disclosure. In dyads asymmetrical as to status, disclosure frequency was inversely related to status difference, but *self-disclosures were offered upwards even when FN was not.* This lends support to the suggestion that self-disclosure can be used as a means towards establishing the fuller intimacy reflected in mutual FN.

Reliability of self-disclosure.   In every case, individuals reported receiving least self-disclosure from BB and, where sample size was sufficiently large for analysis, least self-disclosure from SS. In every case but two, where the order of FW and S was reversed, informants reported most self-disclosure from FW followed by S and then B. (All of these findings are significant with $p < .01$, using the Cochran Q test.) These reports again indicate that individuals are most willing to disclose to equals, followed by frequent disclosures to superiors one level up, and least willing to disclose to individuals located at two hierarchical steps above or below.

Other Variables

The naming and self-disclosure patterns summarized above are not related to time with company or on job, or to status motivation and self-assurance as measured by the Ghiselli Self-Description Inventory.

DISCUSSION

The findings in regard to naming support those of Brown and Ford: where nonreciprocal address patterns occurred status was unequal, TLN offered upwards and FN downwards. The greater the status difference, the greater the tendency was for such nonreciprocal address.

The only naming difference found among organizational levels was in use of FN in addressing BB, the combined middle- and upper-management level using FN most often. Coupled with this was the fact that middle management most often responded "depends" when questioned about receiving FN from subordinates. These findings suggest an interesting pivotal and ambiguous role for middle management in the organization: their subordinates are uncertain as to whether they are entitled to FN or TLN address, while the middle managers themselves show and seek affiliation with higher managerial levels by addressing BB most frequently by FN and also by tending to disclose upward more than any other level. They seem to be "middle," both in formal organizational and psycholinguistic terms.

Along with Brown and Ford, we found age not to be a factor in determining form of address. Again, one may point to the importance of achieved rather than ascribed status in American society. It is interesting, however, that in most dyads in which the superior was the younger naming was symmetrical—either mutual TLN or, most commonly, mutual FN. In the few cases where nonreciprocal naming was reported, the elder subordinate stated that address to his superior depended upon the situation. Thus one may detect a residual feeling that age cannot be completely obliterated as a determinant of address. The data suggest that pairs of individuals (at least in the context of the firm investigated) feel uncomfortable with nonreciprocal naming when the elder is of lower status.

The findings in regard to self-disclosure indicate a modification in Brown and Ford's (1961) suggestion that "the person of higher status is . . . the pacesetter not in linguistic address alone, but in all acts that increase intimacy [p. 383]." It seems that the person of lower status is the pacesetter in *self-disclosure*, clearly an act that "increases intimacy." Our data are quite clear: Individuals disclose themselves more to superiors than to subordinates; but also, they sometimes perceive superiors to be more confiding to them, and themselves to be less confiding to subordinates, than would be indicated by other parts of the data. That self-disclosure can be used to influence intimacy when first naming cannot is revealed by the finding that self-disclosures were offered upwards even when the form of address was TLN. The fact that among fellow workers one finds mutual FN accompanied by the greatest willingness to self-disclose suggests that address usage at this level is based on a relatively high degree of intimacy as well as equal status.

Thus our findings are generally in accord with those of Brown and Ford, with additional suggestions about the role of self-disclosure to superiors in attempts to establish intimacy. We are convinced that a study of forms of address and other types of interpersonal communication can reveal a general picture of the climate and structure of an organization. A psycholinguistic approach would seem to be just as applicable to the analysis of organizations— especially in a comparative sense—as it is to the analysis of different cultures.

REFERENCES

Befu, H., & Norbeck, E. Japanese usage of terms of relationship. *Southwestern Journal of Anthropology*, 1958, 14: 66–86.

Brown, R. *Social psychology.* New York: Free Press, 1965.

Brown, R., & Ford, M. Address in American English. *Journal of Abnormal and Social Psychology*, 1961, 62: 375–385.

Brown, R., & Gilman, A. The pronouns of power and solidarity. In T. Sebeok (ed.), *Style in language.* New York: Wiley, 1960.

Fischer, J. L. Words for self and others in some Japanese families. *American Anthropologist*, 1964, 66(6), part 2: 115–126.

Foster, G. M. Speech forms and perception of social distance in a Spanish-speaking Mexican village. *Southwestern Journal of Anthropology*, 1964, 20: 107–122.

Ghiselli, E. E. The forced-choice technique in self-description. *Personnel Psychology*, 1954, 7: 201–208.

Howell, R. W. Linguistic choice as an index to social change. Unpublished doctoral dissertation, University of California, Berkeley, 1967.

Jourard, S. M., & Lasakow, P. Some factors in self-disclosure. *Journal of Abnormal and Social Psychology*, 1958, 56: 91–98.

Rubin, J. Bilingualism in Paraguay. *Anthropological Linguistics*, 1962, 4(1): 52–58.

Slobin, D. I. Some aspects of the use of pronouns of address in Yiddish. *Word*, 1963, 19: 193–202.

Swartz, M. Situational determinants of kinship terminology. *Southwestern Journal of Anthropology*, 1960, 16: 393–397.

Part Six

LANGUAGE AS AN INDEX IN SMALL GROUP INTERACTIONS

22

CHANNELS OF COMMUNICATION IN SMALL GROUPS

Robert F. Bales
Fred L. Strodtbeck
Theodore M. Mills
Mary E. Roseborough

The frequencies of communication between members participating in small face-to-face groups show certain striking regularities which have not previously been described. The observations reported here were made over a period of several years. Various sorts of small problem-solving groups were observed with a variety of primary hypotheses in mind. The method of analyzing the data reported here had not been developed at that time. The possibility of using the data for the present investigation grew from the fact that a uniform method of observation was used throughout.

A number of the groups were composed of students brought together in an experimental room to solve various contrived problems. Others were non-student committees or work groups in their natural settings. Two therapy groups through a series of sessions were included. A large number of groups were case-discussion meetings of diagnostic councils operating in a research-clinic setting. It is probably accurate to say that most of the groups could be called decision-making, or problem-solving, or discussion groups.

Reprinted from *American Sociological Review* (1951): 461–68. Copyright 1951 by The American Sociological Association, and reproduced by permission. Footnotes have been deleted.

The groups ranged in size from three to ten persons. The conversation generally proceeded so that one person talked at a time, and all members in the particular group were attending the same conversation. In this sense, these groups might be said to have a "single focus," that is, they did not involve a number of conversations proceeding at the same time, as one finds at a cocktail party or in a hotel lobby. The single focus is probably a limiting condition of fundamental importance in the generalizations reported here. Larger groups or other types of groups with multiple foci are probably somewhat different with regard to certain aspects of channel frequency.

HOW THE OBSERVATIONS WERE COLLECTED

Each act in the inter-communication process is recorded. If the act is verbal the unit is usually the simple subject-predicate combination. If the act is non-verbal, the unit is the smallest overt segment of behavior that has "meaning" to others in the group. With this method of recording, the number of units will be many for a lengthy speech given by one member of the group, and a laugh, a nod, or a fidget will each constitute a unit. We have found that the number of scores recorded for a given person bears a close direct relation to the total time he consumes in his overt participation. Thus it is quite probable that the relations we describe can be duplicated in terms of time-units alone. Several observation systems which have qualitative categories quite different from the system employed by the present investigators still produce information concerning who speaks, to whom he speaks, and the number of acts—the essential data involved in the present report. Our findings can probably be reproduced by other methods and checked by other investigators.

The originator of each act, as it occurs, is recorded. At the same time the recipient of the act or the "communication target" is recorded. For example, an act directed from person one to person two is recorded: 1-2. For convenience, a number is assigned to each member of the group, and the symbol 0 is used to designate the group as a whole without distinction as to separate persons. Any member of the group may be an originator or a target of a particular act, but the group as a whole may be only a target. The relation between any two members (including both directions, e.g., 1-2, 2-1) or between any member and the group as a whole (e.g., 1-0) we call a "channel of communication."

HOW THE OBSERVATIONS WERE ORDERED

When originators are placed so as to designate a series of rows of a matrix, and the possible targets are placed to designate a series of columns, a matrix with n rows and $n + 1$ columns results, where n = number of members in the group. The tabulation matrix for a three-man group is illustrated below:

Origi-nator	Target				Total initi-ated
	1	*2*	*3*	*0*	
1	–	1–2	1–3	1–0	
2	2–1	–	2–3	2–0	
3	3–1	3–2	–	3–0	
Total received					

The first ordering operation consists of tallying entries as scored by the observer in the appropriate cell in the tabulation matrix and finding the totals for each row and column.

The second ordering operation consists of ranking the members according to the frequency of their respective originations as indicated in the row totals for acts initiated. The person originating the greatest total number of acts is placed in the first row; the person originating the second largest total is placed in the second row, and so on for n members. The columns are then arranged so that the number of the row of an originator corresponds to his column number as target. In this operation the arrangement of columns is made regardless of the frequency of acts received. The identifying numbers of the members are then changed, so that 1 now represents the member initiating the highest total number of acts, 2 the second highest, and so on. We call the position obtained by this operation the *basic initiating rank* for each individual. A matrix ordered according to the basic initiating ranks of the members is called an *ordered interaction matrix*.

We prepared an ordered interaction matrix for each separate group or session observed. Then one further operation was performed on the collection of ordered matrices for groups of each size. Corresponding cells in each group were combined, that is, cell 1–2 for group 1 was added to cell 1–2 for group 2, group 3, . . . n; cell 1–3 for group 1 was added to cell 1–3 for group 2, . . . n, and so on for all cells. This addition resulted in a single composite matrix for each size of separate group matrices in this way we call an *aggregate interaction matrix*.

REPORT OF FINDINGS

The results of these operations for the 18 six-man groups in our sample are presented in Table 1. We use this aggregate matrix for illustration because it perfectly exemplifies the generalizations we wish to state. In this aggregate matrix it will be seen that *each* row and *each* column presents a rank order which is the same as the basic initiating rank of the members. These are the essential' uniformities we now wish to describe in more detail. In order to have a more exact notation for the statement of our findings, we present in Table 2 an ordered matrix paradigm suitable for groups of three or more persons with a generalized symbolic designation for each of the cells.

We may describe the basic ranking operation performed on each separate group in terms of the generalized notation in Table 2, and illustrate by concrete example from Table 1.

$$(0) \quad \Sigma a_{1j} + a_{10} > \Sigma a_{2j} + a_{20} > \ldots > \Sigma a_{nj} + a_{n0}$$
$$i \leq j \leq n; \, j \neq i$$

Example (0):

$$9167 > 3989 > 3027 > 2352 > 1584 > 1192$$

This ranking operation when performed on data for a single group provides the basic initiating rank for each individual. For convenience we shall speak of rank 1 as the "highest" rank of a series. When data for a given group are ranked in this manner, the following generalizations tend to hold.

(1) *Each row (acts directed by one individual to persons other than himself) tends to be ordered so that the cell for the person of the highest basic initiating rank receives the largest number, the cell for the person of the second highest basic initiating rank receives the second largest, and so forth.* This generalization is somewhat awkward to communicate accurately in words, because all individuals in the group have a basic initiating rank, and all are included in the target columns, yet the row of acts directed by any given person contains one empty cell—the cell indicating the given person as the target of his own acts. The generalization is thus understood with the restriction that the cell indicating the person originating the acts as target of his own acts is excluded. In the symbolic statement of the generalization, below, this difficulty is unequivocally resolved by the condition, $i \neq j$.

Table 1. Aggregate Matrix for Eighteen Sessions of Six-Man Groups

Person originating act	To individuals						Total to individuals	To group as a whole 0	Total initiated
	1	2	3	4	5	6			
1		1238	961	545	445	317	3506	5661	9167
2	1748		443	310	175	102	2778	1211	3989
3	1371	415		305	125	69	2285	742	3027
4	952	310	282		83	49	1676	676	2352
5	662	224	144	83		28	1141	443	1584
6	470	126	114	65	44		819	373	1192
Total received	5203	2313	1944	1308	872	565	12205	9106	21311

Table 2. The Paradigm for the Ordered Matrix

Person originating act	To individuals				Total to individuals	To group as a whole	Total initiated
	1	2	$\cdots$	n			
1	—	a_{12}	$\cdots$	a_{1n}	$\Sigma^{*}\ a_{1j}$	a_{10}	$\Sigma\ a_{1j} + a_{10}$
2	a_{21}	—	$\cdots$	a_{2n}	$\Sigma\ a_{2j}$	a_{20}	$\Sigma\ a_{2j} + a_{20}$
$\vdots$	$\cdots$	$\cdots$	$\cdots$	$\cdots$	$\cdots$	$\cdots$	$\cdots$
n	a_{n1}	a_{n2}	$\cdots$	—	$\Sigma\ a_{nj}$	a_{n0}	$\Sigma\ a_{nj} + a_{n0}$
Total received	$\Sigma\ a_{i1}$	$\Sigma\ a_{i2}$	$\cdots$	$\Sigma\ a_{in}$	$\Sigma\Sigma\ a_{ij}$	$\Sigma\ a_{i0}$	$\Sigma\Sigma\ a_{ij} + a_{i0}$

*All summations from $i, j = 1$ to $i, j = n$, $j \neq i$.

(1) $a_{i1} > a_{i2} > \ldots > a_{in}$ $1 \leq i \leq n;\ i \neq j$

Example (1):

$$1238 > 961 > 545 > 445 > 317$$
$$1748 > 443 > 310 > 175 > 102$$
$$\vdots$$
$$470 > 126 > 114 > 65 > 44$$

Since the *sums* of acts directed to participants tend to reflect the relationships described for each row, we may say somewhat more generally:

(1a) *The rank of the total number of acts received by an individual tends to correspond to his basic initiating rank.*

(1a) $\Sigma a_{i1} > \Sigma a_{i2} > \ldots > \Sigma a_{in}$ $1 \leq i \leq n;\ i \neq j$

Example (1a):

$$5203 > 2313 > 1944 > 1308 > 872 > 565$$

(2) *Each column (acts received by one individual from persons other than himself) tends to be ordered so that the values correspond to the basic initiating ranks of persons originating the acts.* Here again it is understood that the column representing acts received by the jth person omits the cell indicating this person as an initiator.

(2) $a_{1j} > a_{2j} > \ldots > a_{nj}$ $1 \leq j \leq n;\ i \neq j$

Example (2):

$$1748 > 1371 > 952 > 662 > 470$$
$$1238 > 415 > 310 > 224 > 126$$
$$\vdots$$
$$317 > 102 > 69 > 49 > 28$$

Again there is a summary statement which may be made in terms of totals:

(2a) *The rank of the number of acts directed by an originator to all other specific individuals tends to be ordered to correspond to the basic initiating rank of the originator.*

(2a) $\Sigma a_{1j} > \Sigma a_{2j} > \ldots > \Sigma a_{nj}$ $1 \leq j \leq n; i \neq j$

Example (2a):

$$3506 > 2778 > 2285 > 1676 > 1141 > 819$$

Finally, (3) *The rank of the number of acts directed by an individual to the group as a whole tends to correspond to his basic initiating rank.*

(3) $a_{10} > a_{20} > \ldots > a_{n0}$

Example (3):

$$5661 > 1211 > 742 > 676 > 443 > 373$$

With regard to generalizations (2a) and (3), it should be noted that even though the basic initiating rank is determined by the sum of acts directed to specific individuals and to the group as a whole, we have nevertheless gained an increment of precision in description by specifying that *each* of these columns tends to be ordered as the basic initiating rank.

HOW WELL DO THE GENERALIZATIONS REPRESENT THE DATA?

Our generalizations have been illustrated thus far with aggregate data for six-man groups. We now turn to the presentation of data which will illustrate the applicability of the generalizations (a) for the range of groups from three to ten persons, and (b) for individual sessions as well as for aggregates of individual sessions.

Our sample consists of 171 sessions in which approximately 138,000 acts were observed. The writers have included *all* cases available to them which have been observed by the uniform technique, but since the observations were carried out in terms of research designs which were quite independent of this paper, the cases are very unevenly distributed in terms of group size. For example only one nine- and three ten-man group sessions are available for analysis.

Each of the generalizations has been stated as a proposition predicting an expected order 1, 2, . . . *n*. It is desirable to compare the agreement between observed and expected for each of these propositions by a parallel technique. In order to express the correspondence in a uniform manner notwithstanding the variation in the size of the group, we define "d" as the difference between the expected and the observed rank. It may be shown that if all orders are equally likely

$$\overline{d}^2 = \frac{(n^3 - n)}{6}$$

and

$$\sigma_{\overline{d}^2} = \frac{\sqrt{n^2 (n + 1)^2 (n - 1)}}{N\,36}$$

In the tests we shall report we establish the ratio

$$\frac{\overline{d}_e^2 - \overline{d}_o^2}{\sigma_{\overline{d}^2}}$$

and make a one-sided test of the null hypothesis.

$$\overline{d}_o^2 \leq \overline{d}_e^2$$

The subscripts e and o refer to "expected" and "observed" in the formulae above.

When for any particular test we obtain a probability less than .05 we reject the null hypothesis and conclude that there is a significant departure from randomness in the direction of the ordering that we have predicted. For any particular hypothesis and for each group size two tests are made: one on the aggregate matrix and one on the full array of individual sessions.

In Table 3 we present the eighty probabilities derived from a systematic application of this test over the range of group sizes and hypotheses. The evidence overwhelmingly supports the generalizations presented. In all cases the probabilities observed are either less than .01, or the minimum probability theoretically attainable.

This degree of conformity with expectation is sufficiently unequivocal to lead us to believe that if we had done our basic ranking in terms of "acts received," "acts to individuals," or "acts to group as a whole" instead of "total acts initiated," substantially similar results would have been attained.

Table 3. Significance Levels by Size of Group and Hypothesis

Size of group	Number of sessions	Number of acts	Hypothesis				
			1	1a	2	2a	3
3	26	9,304	.000*	.000	.000	.000	.000
			.042	.079	.042	.079	.079
4	89	58,218	.000	.000	.000	.000	.000
			.002	.042	.002	.042	.042
5	9	10,714	.000	.000	.000	.000	.000
			.000	.036	.000	.036	.036
6	18	21,311	.000	.000	.000	.000	.000
			.000	.013	.000	.013	.013
7	15	22,044	.000	.000	.000	.000	.000
			.000	.007	.000	.007	.007
8	10	12,830	.000	.000	.000	.000	.000
			.000	.004	.000	.004	.006
9	1	1,422	.000	.008	.000	.002	.002
			.000	.008	.000	.002	.002
10	3	2,823	.000	.000	.000	.000	.000
			.000	.002	.000	.001	.009

*Cell values above represent the probability of the null hypothesis of random ordering. The nonitalicized values refer to the array of individual ordered matrices, and the italicized values refer to the ordered aggregate matrices.

DISCUSSION

We believe that the detection of these regularities represents a significant gain in our knowledge about the distribution of communications in small groups, and provides a basic framework of order within which many more detailed analyses of the interaction process may be made. We have noted other apparently typical features of the matrix which are probably sociologically significant, although they cannot be described systematically here. A few features can be illustrated, however, by reference to Table 1.

For example, it can be seen that the top man addresses considerably more remarks to the group as a whole than he addresses to specific individuals (5661 > 3506). All men of lower basic initiating rank address more of their remarks to specific individuals (and markedly more to the top man) than to the group as a whole (2778 > 1211, etc.). This seems to indicate that the top man is acting as a kind of communications center, and in this sense is performing a leadership function.

When the amounts each man gives out to the sum of specific individuals is compared to the amounts he receives, a still more suggestive picture is obtained. The top man receives more from particular others in total than he gives out to them specifically (5203 > 3506). His contributions tend to be addressed more frequently to the group as a whole than to the specific persons who address him. All other men, however, tend to receive less from particular others than they give out to them (e.g., for Rank 6 man, 565 > 819.

In our exploratory analyses of data we have constructed matrices for particular categories of activity, such as agreement, disagreement, asking for information, etc., as defined in the system of observational categories we use. The matrices are constructed according to the basic initiating rank of the individuals (based on totals of all types of activity) as the ordering principle. Matrices of these kinds which have been examined so far tend to show the top man giving out more information and opinion to specific individuals than he receives, while, on the contrary, low men give out more agreement, disagreement, and requests for information than they receive. The analysis of the quality of the communications in terms of general theory regarding the properties of social systems appears at present to be the most promising approach to the understanding and rationalization of the generalizations we present here. It is expected that an approach of this kind will provide a fundamental basis for accounting for differences between matrices and exceptions to the generalizations we have made, as well as the typical features of the matrices.

The relative magnitudes of the number of acts falling in each cell of the ordered matrix can probably be expressed and predicted with much greater precision than a rank order description permits. This will require the development of mathematical models, but there is some doubt that appropriate models will be simple. One model often suggested for data like our series of rank orders of total acts initiated is the harmonic distribution. We are inclined to believe that no simple mathematical function of this type, which does not at least include more parameters than the size of the group, will really fit our data. However, because of the general interest in this model, we compare its predictions with our data below.

To obtain expected values in terms of the harmonic distribution we have employed the following formula:

$$X_{(i,n)} = \frac{S}{i\left(\sum_{j=1}^{n} \frac{1}{j}\right)}$$

where,

$X_{(i,n)}$ is the expected number of acts by the person with the ith rank in a group of n persons, and

S is the sum of acts in the set of data under consideration.

In Figure 1 we have plotted a series of curves derived from the harmonic distribution model. Shown against the curves are a series of points representing data drawn from the "total initiated" column of our aggregate matrices. It may be seen by inspection that

Figure 1. Rank Ordered Series of Total Acts Initiated, Compared with Harmonic Distribution, for Groups of Sizes Three to Eight

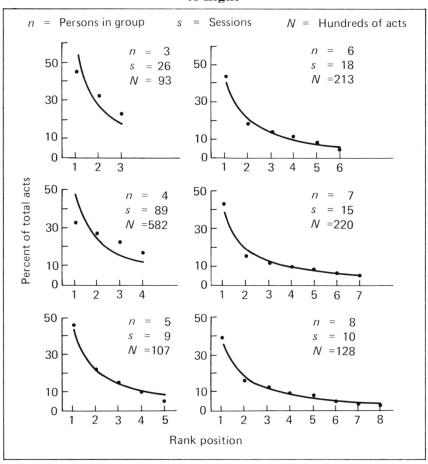

the empirical curves for the groups under size 5 are flatter than expected, while those for size 5 and above are steeper. The top man in the larger group sizes initiates more activity than predicted by the model. Our groups of size 4 show a particularly poor fit. A large number of homogeneous sessions are included here, of groups working on a particular type of problem (making series of clinical ratings of personalities from case material). There was a formal allocation of reporting and recording roles, and systematic rotation of members between the roles. It seems reasonable to believe that conditions of this kind could affect the participation gradients in an atypical way.

The fit for groups of size 6 is the best obtained by this model. The observed data for their aggregate matrix have previously been presented in Table 1. The deviations between observed and expected values are presented in Table 4. In terms of chi square we may quickly determine that the fit is not sufficiently good to permit us to believe that the deviations have arisen as random fluctuation. With values of this magnitude, the chi-square criterion would require correspondence between the first two places of each value. By similar tests it can be shown that none of the fits is acceptable.

In assessing the importance of the findings reported in this paper there is one point which deserves great emphasis. The generalizations presented are average empirical tendencies. They are assumed to be the result of certain general conditions which we are not yet able to specify. But we assume that as conditions vary, the matrices will vary. Any specific group, or some particular types of groups, may present exceptions to the generalizations we describe, in one or more particulars, depending on the conditions

Table 4. Number of Acts, by Rank Position, for Aggregate of Eighteen Six-Man Groups Compared with Expected Number of Acts by Harmonic Assumption

Rank position	Theoretical values	Expected*	Observed
1	.4082	8698	9167
2	.2041	4349	3989
3	.1361	2900	3027
4	.1020	2174	2352
5	.0816	1740	1584
6	.0680	1450	1192
Total	1.0000	21311	21311

*Expected values represent the product of the total acts observed times the theoretical values.

operating. For example, we have often found particular exceptions to predicted rank positions in cases where one of the members disagrees with the others persistently, and so tends to attract or receive a disporportionate amount of communication. And we have also found exceptions when two highly interactive and agreeing members form a sub-group vis-a-vis a third neglected or rejected member. The average empirical tendencies described constitute a base-line expectation for the detection of discrepancies or exceptions which we believe will be useful in diagnostic and comparative analysis of particular groups. There are many sorts of experimental predictions that can now be made with an increased degree of accuracy through the use of the ordered matrix. The importance of the generalizations will be much increased as we are better able to identify and measure the effects of various kinds of conditions on them.

SUMMARY

The findings reported indicate that if participants in a small group are ranked by the total number of acts they initiate, they will also tend to be ranked:

(1) by the number of acts they receive,
(2) by the number of acts they address to specific other individuals, and
(3) by the number of acts they address to the group as a whole.

Exceptions to these general tendencies are expected to be diagnostic of special features of the social relationships in the group, of interest in the comparison of a given group with others.

More refined ways of analyzing the interaction matrix promise to yield further generalizations. The harmonic distribution model of total amounts of participation is found to be a very rough approximation, but probably too simple. However, mathematical models taking into account more variables may be possible. In general, the most promising approach to an understanding of the matrix regularities seems to be through a sociological analysis of the nature of small social systems. This approach does not preclude, but rather invites formulation in terms of mathematical or statistical models.

23

THE DISTRIBUTION OF PARTICIPATION IN SMALL GROUPS: AN EXPONENTIAL APPROXIMATION

Frederick F. Stephan
Elliot G. Mishler

In contemporary sociological and social psychological theory and research an increasing amount of attention has been given to the functioning of small groups. Many attempts have been made to analyze the interaction that takes place in small group meetings and to discover general principles that appear to determine, or at least influence, the pattern of participation by the various members of the group. The research reported here is devoted to one of the basic aspects of small group research, namely the relative frequency of participation. Specifically, this study concerns the application of relatively simple mathematical function that appears to express quite well the distribution of participation within a particular type of small discussion group.

In a recent paper[1] Bales suggested that a harmonic distribution might serve to approximate the relative frequency of acts of participation among members of small problem-solving groups. The

Reprinted from *American Sociological Review* 17 (1952): 598–608. Copyright 1952 by The American Sociological Association, and reproduced by permission.

results he obtained, however, indicated that this approximation is not close enough to be fully satisfactory and, for this reason, he concluded that a more complicated model may be necessary for greater precision.[2]

The proven inadequacy of the harmonic model, however, does not necessitate the use of models of great complexity. A model of comparable simplicity is available which appears to provide a very good representation of data obtained from a variety of small discussion groups. It is a simple exponential model, that had previously been applied by one of the authors to another study of group participation. When it was applied to Bales' published data, it provided a good fit.[3] This paper is primarily concerned with the general adequacy of this exponential model for representing other sets of participation data.

METHODOLOGY

The data presented here are drawn from a project[4] which is part of a general study of the educational process.[5] The findings are based on observations of a total of 81 separate meetings, held by 36 distinct groups, ranging in attendance from four to twelve participants.

The group meetings have certain formal characteristics in common which serve to distinguish them from the problem-solving groups that were studied by Bales. Since the generality of the model is the important consideration, it seems advisable to list these characteristics as specifically as possible. (A more abstract formulation of these conditions, as they affect the applicability of the model, is presented later in the discussion of results.) These common features are:

(1) *Social context of the meetings.* The weekly, 50-minute meetings are held at a prescribed time and place in connection with certain courses at Princeton University. The usual expectations, associated with college courses, governing attendance and the fulfillment of assigned work are thus operative here.

(2) *Composition of the group.* The members of the group are relatively homogeneous in regard to age, educational training, social background, etc. In addition, membership tends to be restricted to junior and seniors, increasing the homogeneity within each group in terms of interest and special knowledge.

(3) *Role of the leader.* The leader of the group is an instructor in the course. He differs from the other members in his relationship to the group along those social dimensions which are involved in a student's orientation toward a teacher as compared with his orientation toward a fellow student. Although he receives his power ultimately from the outside structure, the leader has considerable freedom to do what he wants in the way he wants. In general, the norms hold that he should be friendly, sociable, and democratic.

(4) *Norms regarding student participation.* The meetings are conducted under the influence of strong traditional attitudes that emphasize discussion by the students and de-emphasize the dominance of the faculty leader in contrast to the usual patterns of lecture, class, and quiz section meetings. They are regarded as an especially valuable part of the education of students. It is expected (by both students and faculty) that all the students will participate actively during each meeting. The leader is expected to stimulate discussion (although specific devices to this end are not prescribed) or at least not to discourage the students from participating. Active participation is regarded as instrumental to the major goal of the meetings.

(5) *Goal of the meetings.* The institutionally defined objective of the meetings is an increase in the members' understanding of assigned course materials. There is a further goal, considered a function of the cumulative effect of many of these meetings in a variety of courses, of an improvement in the general analytical ability of students. It is understood that neither consensus nor action is to be taken as a specific end, although it is recognized that either may occasionally occur as by-products.

The 36 groups whose meetings were observed were a stratified random sample drawn to represent the more than 500 groups that met weekly in the Fall term of 1950. Two variables were used to stratify the population: the department of instruction and the time (day and hour) at which the group met. An additional restriction provided that no single leader (instructor) was represented more than once in the sample. It is assumed that there was no important systematic bias in the types of content discussed, styles of leadership exercised, or kinds of student members in the sample groups.

There are two important methodological differences between the procedure for recording participation and that developed by Bales.[6] The basic unit of participation tallied by the observers is the word, sentence, or longer statement of an individual that follows such a participation by one member and continues until it is terminated by an appreciable pause or by the participation of another member. In other words, an individual's uninterrupted contribution is taken to be one participation. However, if there was a clear change of content during the course of a lengthy contribution, it was taken to be the beginning of a new unit of participation. If Bales' procedure had been used, these units of participation would have been divided into elementary "acts" each consisting of a simple sentence or equivalent meaningful expression. What is recorded here as one unit of participation would be recorded by Bales as many times as the number of "acts" it contained.

In the present study, the observers interrupted their recording of participation periodically to make other observations. They did this after each series of participations that totalled 50 units or covered a period of 15 minutes, whichever limit was reached first. This interruption of the recording lasted for less than five minutes, and was devoted to rating certain general aspects of group activity.[7] As soon as the ratings were completed the observers resumed the regular recording of participation. This sequence continued throughout the meeting. The participation records are, therefore, a sample rather than a full record of the meeting. Although systematic evidence was not collected, informal reports by the observers and certain other data indicate that this sampling procedure did not present a distorted picture of the distribution of the participation of members of the group during the entire period.

The differences between this approach and that of Bales have been cited in some detail. If results of both approaches can be described by the same simple model, these differences lend added significance to this finding.

Participation in the discussion groups was observed and recorded by 18 student observers. Each of them had minimum of about 15 hours of experience in the development and use of the procedure before he started the regular observation of the sample groups. The reliability among observers was investigated by having pairs of observers record the same discussion meeting.

The reliability of the observers may be gauged from Table 1 which shows the distributions of differences between observers

Table 1. Differences Between Pairs of Observers Recording at the Same Meeting Participation by and Participation to, Each Member*

	Difference between percentages recorded for the same individual by two observers							
Percentage of participation†	*0.0–0.9*	*1.0–1.9*	*2.0–2.9*	*3.0–3.9*	*4.0–4.9*	*5.0–5.9*	*6 or more*	*Total*
by the member								
0–9.9	25	12	5	4	1	0	1	48
10 or more	5	10	5	4	1	0	2	27
Total	30	22	10	8	2	0	3	75
to the member								
0–9.9	33	9	9	5	2	0	0	58
10 or more	1	1	4	1	1	2	7	17
Total	34	10	13	6	3	2	7	75

*An individual might direct his remarks to the whole group as well as to another individual. The percentage of participations directed to the group is excluded from this table and the later analysis.

†The mean of the percentages given by the two sets of observations was used to define the individual's percentage of participation.

through nine such jointly-observed meetings for the two variables with which this paper is concerned, namely, the proportion of the total participations that was contributed *by* an individual and the proportion that was directed *to* an individual.

The observers recorded a full session. They started at approximately the same time but did not synchronize their periods of observation. Hence if one of them interrupted his observations for a longer time when he made his general ratings of the discussion, he started each subsequent period of observation later than the other observer in the pair and recorded a somewhat different sample of the discussion. The differences in Table 1 reflect the effects of the observers being a little out of phase as well as their omissions and mistakes in observation and recording. Variations of judgment in determining to which member, if any, the participation was directed also contributed to the differences. This is apparent in the lower half of the table.

The differences are those found between the percentages that were recorded at one session. They are composed of systematic components associated with each observer and more or less random components. The latter are reduced when several sessions are averaged. Some of the systematic components are reduced by the consolidation of data produced by different observers. However, any consistent bias that is common to all observers persists in totals and averages and tends to escape attention because it is not revealed by comparisons of observers such as those in Table 1.

The observation of participation was complicated in some of the sessions by persistent difficulty in determining when remarks were addressed to a particular individual and when to the group as a whole. The largest differences appeared to stem from this difficulty. It affected the percentages that were computed for individuals as well as the percentage computed for the group. In Table 1 and in the subsequent analysis the percentages computed for the group have been omitted since it appeared that they had substantially lower reliability than the other percentages and they constituted a somewhat distinct aspect of group interaction.

The number of participations recorded at a session varied from fewer than 100 to more than 200. Consequently, a difference of one percentage point corresponded to a net difference of one or two participations in the number recorded for a given member.

All differences were taken as positive since they were computed for two observers presumably both subject to error, not for one observer in comparison with a standard. For participation *by* a member, the average difference was 1.7 percentage points and 70 out of 75 pairs of percentages agreed within 4 points. For participation *to* a member, the average difference was 3.2 percentage points and 63 out of 75 differences were less than 4 points. The differences tend to increase with percentages. If it is reasonable to assume that errors of the observers in each pair were not correlated, half the mean square difference can be taken to be an estimate of variance of individual observers, apart from the common observation biases of the entire group of observers. The square root of half the mean square difference is an estimate of the standard error of observation for a single observer. The data from which Table 1 was tabulated provide the following estimates of standard errors:

	Standard error, in percentage points	
Percentage of participations	*Participations by the member*	*Participations to the member*
Less than 10 percent	1.5	1.2
10 or more	2.7	5.3

These reliability tests were part of the training program. The observers had the benefit of a review of their differences as well as the experience of the recording itself and consequently their subsequent work may have had a higher degree of reliability than the test revealed.

PARTICIPATION DATA AND THE EXPONENTIAL FUNCTION

The data recorded by the observers were tabulated for each individual at a meeting and then the individuals were ranked according to the number of units of participation that were contributed by them. The tabulations for all meetings of the same size were then combined by adding the counts of units of participation for the members that had the same ranking. The result is given in column 3 of Table 2. Each individual was also ranked according to the number of units of participation that were directed to him. The tabulations of these units for all groups of the same size were combined according to this second ranking and appear in column 7 of Table 2.

Table 2. Distribution of Participation by and to Members of Small Discussion Groups*

(Data combined for all meetings of the same size, participations to the group omitted)

Size and number of meetings (1)	Rank of the member (2)	Participations originated by the member				Participations directed to the member			
		Partici-pations (3)	Per-cent (4)	Estimated percentage (5)	Differ-ence (6)	Partici-pations (7)	Per-cent (8)	Estimated percentage (9)	Differ-ence (10)
Four (6)		755		50.3		755		36.0	
	L	323	42.7	42.6	−0.1	333	44.1	44.1	0.0
	1	212	28.0	29.6	+1.6	151	19.9	20.4	+0.5
	2	155	20.5	17.5	−3.0	95	12.5	11.5	−1.0
	3	65	8.5	10.3	+1.8	46	6.0	6.5	+0.5
Five (7)		856		41.3		856		26.2	
	L	380	44.4	44.1	−0.3	410	47.9	47.5	−0.4
	1	214	25.0	25.3	+0.3	143	16.7	16.7	0.0
	2	126	14.6	15.4	+0.8	83	9.6	10.6	+1.0
	3	100	11.6	9.4	−2.2	72	8.4	6.8	−1.6
	4	36	4.2	5.8	+1.6	28	3.3	4.3	+1.0
Six (17)		2951		36.9		2951		28.8	
	L	1261	42.8	44.8	+2.0	1402	47.5	47.5	0.0
	1	704	23.8	23.0	−0.8	471	15.9	16.2	+0.3
	2	455	15.4	14.3	−1.1	272	9.2	9.1	−0.1
	3	297	10.0	8.9	−1.1	162	5.5	5.1	−0.4
	4	175	5.9	5.6	−0.3	90	3.0	2.9	−0.1
	5	59	2.0	3.5	+1.5	39	1.3	1.6	+0.3
Seven (15)		1999		30.3		1999		21.9	
	L	912	45.6	45.8	+0.2	933	46.6	46.5	−0.1
	1	416	20.8	20.1	−0.7	287	14.5	14.1	−0.4

Table 2. (cont.)

Size and number of meetings (1)	Rank of the member (2)	Participations originated by the member				Participations directed to the member			
		Participations (3)	Per cent (4)	Estimated percentage (5)	Difference (6)	Participations (7)	Per cent (8)	Estimated percentage (9)	Difference (10)
	2	245	12.2	13.2	+1.0	167	8.3	9.1	+0.8
	3	175	8.6	8.8	+0.2	118	5.9	5.8	−0.1
	4	119	5.9	5.8	−0.1	82	4.1	3.8	−0.3
	5	86	4.2	3.8	−0.4	55	2.6	2.4	−0.2
	6	46	2.4	2.5	+0.1	27	1.3	1.6	+0.3
		2042		31.9		2042		22.0	
Eight (14)	L	803	39.2	39.9	+0.7	946	46.3	46.0	−0.3
	1	434	21.2	21.3	+0.1	266	12.9	14.1	+1.2
	2	294	14.3	14.2	−0.1	218	10.6	9.0	−1.6
	3	184	8.9	9.5	+0.6	105	5.1	5.8	+0.7
	4	140	6.6	6.3	−0.3	87	4.1	3.7	−0.4
	5	98	4.8	4.2	−0.6	49	2.3	2.4	+0.1
	6	55	2.6	2.8	+0.2	32	1.5	1.5	0.0
	7	34	1.6	1.9	+0.3	17	0.7	1.0	+0.3
		1269		28.9		1269		19.2	
Nine (10)	L	571	44.9	44.1	−0.8	602	47.3	47.0	−0.3
	1	238	18.9	19.3	+0.4	148	11.7	12.6	+0.9
	2	157	12.4	12.9	+0.5	109	8.7	8.3	−0.4
	3	113	9.0	8.6	−0.4	72	5.7	5.4	−0.3
	4	79	6.2	5.8	−0.4	52	4.1	3.6	−0.5
	5	56	4.5	3.8	−0.7	31	2.5	2.3	−0.2
	6	35	2.8	2.6	−0.2	17	1.4	1.5	+0.1

Table 2. (cont.)

Size and number of meetings (1)	Rank of the member (2)	Participations originated by the member				Participations directed to the member			
		Partici-pations (3)	Per-cent (4)	Estimated percentage (5)	Differ-ence (6)	Partici-pations (7)	Per-cent (8)	Estimated percentage (9)	Differ-ence (10)
	7	13	1.1	1.7	+0.6	9	0.8	1.0	+0.2
	8	7	0.6	1.2	+0.6	4	0.3	0.7	+0.4
Ten (4)	L	481		23.8		481		17.4	
	1	236	48.9	48.1	-0.8	240	49.8	48.9	-0.9
	2	83	17.2	16.5	-0.7	63	13.1	11.6	-1.5
	3	51	10.6	11.4	+0.8	28	5.8	7.8	+2.0
	4	36	7.5	7.9	+0.4	25	5.2	5.2	0.0
	5	31	6.4	5.5	-0.9	15	3.1	3.4	+0.3
	6	15	3.1	3.8	+0.7	12	2.5	2.3	-0.2
	7	13	2.7	2.6	-0.1	7	1.4	1.5	+0.1
	8	9	1.9	1.8	-0.1	5	1.0	1.0	0.0
	9	7	1.4	1.3	-0.1	5	1.0	0.7	-0.3
		0	0.0	0.9	+0.9	0	0.0	0.4	+0.4
Eleven (3)	L	437		20.6		437		14.1	
	1	224	51.2	51.3	+0.1	206	47.0	45.9	-1.1
	2	62	14.1	14.6	+0.5	39	8.9	9.6	+0.7
	3	43	9.8	10.4	+0.6	34	7.8	6.6	-1.2
	4	36	8.2	7.4	-0.8	22	5.0	4.5	-0.5
	5	24	5.4	5.2	-0.2	7	1.6	3.0	+1.4
	6	17	3.9	3.7	-0.2	7	1.6	2.1	+0.5
	7	11	2.5	2.6	+0.1	5	1.1	1.4	+0.3
		10	2.3	1.9	-0.4	5	1.1	1.0	-0.1

Table 2. (cont.)

Size and number of meetings (1)	Rank of the member (2)	Participations originated by the member				Participations directed to the member			
		Partici-pations (3)	Per-cent (4)	Estimated percentage (5)	Differ-ence (6)	Partici-pations (7)	Per-cent (8)	Estimated percentage (9)	Differ-ence (10)
	8	5	1.1	1.3	+0.2	3	0.7	0.7	0.0
	9	3	0.7	0.9	+0.2	3	0.7	0.4	−0.3
	10	2	0.4	0.7	+0.3	0	0.0	0.3	+0.3
		525		*20.6*		*525*		*15.3*	
Twelve (5)	1	256	48.8	48.4	−0.4	259	49.3	47.8	−1.5
	2	76	14.5	14.9	+0.4	59	11.2	10.5	−0.7
	3	55	10.5	10.9	+0.4	33	6.3	7.6	+1.3
	4	42	8.0	7.9	−0.1	27	5.2	5.4	+0.2
	5	33	6.3	5.7	−0.6	23	4.4	3.9	−0.5
	6	25	4.8	4.2	−0.6	14	2.7	2.8	+0.1
	7	17	3.2	3.0	−0.2	14	2.7	2.0	−0.7
	8	9	1.7	2.2	+0.5	7	1.3	1.5	+0.2
	9	9	1.7	1.6	−0.1	5	1.0	1.0	0.0
	10	3	0.6	1.2	+0.6	1	0.2	0.8	+0.6
	11	0	0.0	0.8	+0.8	0	0.0	0.5	+0.5
				0.6	+0.6			0.4	+0.4

*a. The percentages for participations *to* within each size of meeting (columns 8 and 9) do not total 100. This is due to the fact, noted previously, that the percentage of participation *to* the group has been omitted.

b. The numbers in *italics* in columns 3 and 7 are the total number of participation units recorded. The totals in column 7 include participations directed *to* the group as a whole. These totals were the basis on which the percentages of total in columns 4 and 8 were calculated.

c. The numbers in *italics* in columns 5 and 9 are the percentages that would be estimated for the leader by extrapolation from the exponential model.

Graphs of relative participation plotted against rank are similar to those reported by Bales[8] and are therefore omitted from the present paper. The decrease in rate from the leader to the highest ranking student becomes somewhat sharper as one goes from smaller to larger groups. It was found that the percentage distributions could be approximated by an exponential function,

(1) $$p_i = ar^{i-1},$$

where p_i is the estimated percentage for students ranked i, r is the ratio of the percentage for any rank to the percentage for the next higher rank, and a is the estimate for students ranked 1. The variation of r and a with the size of the group will be discussed later.

In the fitting of this function, the percentages by and to the leaders and to the group were omitted from the distributions. There were several reasons for this step. First, they differed from the students in knowledge of the subjects under discussion, experience in discussion, etc. Second, they had different functions to perform in the meeting, a different role to play. Third, it was deemed a sufficient first step to find a function that fitted the student members' participation rates, without the addition of another function for the leaders' roles.

In order to give what was judged to be appropriate weight to the fit for large and for small percentages, the function was fitted to the data by minimizing the sum of squares of deviations of the logarithms of the estimated percentages from the logarithms of the observed percentages, each square being weighted by the observed percentage. That is, the quantity to be minimized was:

$$\Sigma\, p_i[\log p_i - \log(ar^{i-1}).^2$$

where p_i is the percentage observed for the members ranked i. It was not possible to establish a defensible probability model for maximum likelihood estimates or a more rational formulation of least squares procedure. The selection of this basis for fitting was to a degree arbitrary but it appears to be justified by the closeness of fit that was attained. It led to the following equations:

(2) $$\log a = \frac{CD - BE}{AC - B^2}$$ (3) $$\log r = \frac{AE - BD}{AC - B^2}$$

where $A = \Sigma\, p_i$, $B = \Sigma\, ip_i$, $C = \Sigma\, i^2 p_i$,
$$D = \Sigma\,(p_i \log p_i),\ E = \Sigma\,(ip_i \log p_i)$$

These equations were solved for each distribution of percentages. Then estimates were computed from equation (1) and entered in columns 5 and 9 of Table 2.

To complete the estimates, a percentage was added for the leaders in each distribution that brings the total to 100 percent. It may be compared with the figure above it, in italics, which is the percentage that would be estimated for the leader according to the exponential function, when he is assigned rank 0.

The percentages computed from the exponential function agree remarkably well with the actual percentages, except for the estimates for the leader. Considering participation *by* a member, 62 of the 72 differences in column 6 are less than one percentage point, positive or negative. For participation *to* a member, 59 differences are less than one percentage point, either way. There is a little evidence of systematic error, primarily a tendency toward negative errors in the middle rankings and positive errors for the very lowest ranks.

Table 3 presents the ratios (r in equation 1) that were used for computing the percentages and an approximation to them by two linear functions of the size of the meeting.

The ratios appear to increase with the size of the meeting in fairly close conformity to the linear functions. Thus, men of ad-

**Table 3. Ratios r_n Used in Estimating Partici-
pations and Approximations by Linear
Functions of the Size of the Meeting**

Size of meeting, n, including leader	Participation by a member*		Participation to a member†	
4	.589	(.590)	.566	(.582)
5	.611	(.607)	.638	(.596)
6	.623	(.624)	.563	(.610)
7	.661	(.641)	.643	(.624)
8	.667	(.658)	.640	(.638)
9	.668	(.676)	.656	(.652)
10	.694	(.693)	.667	(.666)
11	.710	(.710)	.682	(.680)
12	.727	(.727)	.686	(.694)

*Approximation using $r_n = .522 + .0172\, n$ is shown in parentheses.
†Approximation using $r_n = .526 + .0140\, n$ is shown in parentheses.

joining rank tend to have more nearly equal rates of participation as the size of the meeting increased.

The parameter, a, also changes in a fairly regular way with the size of the meeting. It can be represented by such an empirical function as $a_n = 234/(n + 4)$, for participations by the member, and $a_n = 157/(n + 4)$, for participations to the member.

DISCUSSION OF RESULTS

The findings presented above suggest that the simple exponential model may be applicable for describing the distribution of participation in other types of small groups. The problem now becomes one of discovering the conditions under which the model may be expected to remain applicable (i.e., of "explaining" this empirical law). Such an analysis should also be helpful in specifying those factors which influence the size of the ratio in the exponential equation. A great deal of research may be necessary before this problem can be solved. As a step toward formulating hypotheses, the authors will set forth some of their thoughts about the essential conditions.

It would appear that, within the general context of a face-to-face group oriented toward some common problem or content, the fit of the model to the data may be a consequence of the following conditions:

(1) There is a distribution of what might be labeled "verbal participation potential" among the participants present at a meeting. The genesis of this potential, i.e., whether it is a personality characteristic or situationally induced, is not relevant here although it would seem to be a fruitful area for investigation. The inequality among the participants in this respect is the important factor rather than the reasons for this inequality. One qualification should be suggested, although it will not be elaborated in this paper. That is, that the differences among the participants should not be of such a nature as to divide them into two or more distinct groups characterized by markedly different systems of participation relationships. If this restriction does not hold, the variation involved in the distribution of participation may be more abrupt than the model can handle. The potential of a given member of the group may vary during the meeting and be

affected by the influences to which he is subjected, but it is essentially a compounded resultant of individual factors. The data that are yielded by observation of participation reflect average differences in potential.

(2) There is not systematic regulation of the "free competitive expression" of "verbal participation potentials." For example, neither the leader nor the group attempts to control the rates of participation by specifying when an individual may participate or by regulating the distribution of relevant information.

(3) The members are relatively undifferentiated in regard to the roles they play in the discussion, except for the differentiation that results from the relative strength of their verbal participation potentials. There is no set of structured differentiated roles that has a major effect on the distribution of participation. In the groups described above there was always present, of course, a clearly differentiated leader role. This is not an exception to the general rule, however, since the leader's participation was calculated residually and not directly by the formulae. This device permits one to use the model in concrete instances where there is such a well-differentiated role.

It is believed that the groups from which the data were drawn fulfilled these conditions. The evidence is, however, inferential rather than direct. The controls which were exercised in drawing a sample, the manner in which the group discussions were conducted, and the processes of observing and tabulating the data operated to ensure that there was no systematic selection in terms of "verbal participation potential" or the possibilities for the "free expression" of this potential. The general norms for student behavior also served to mitigate against any well-defined role structure among the members.

The results presented in Table 3 suggest that under these conditions the size of the group is a major determinant of the ratio, r_n, in the exponential function that fits the participation relationships of the members.

In groups of a given size it might be expected that the ratio will vary with changes in some of the conditions noted above. For example, the effect of selecting members on the basis of factors closely associated with their verbal participation potentials is revealed by an experiment conducted by the Study of Education.[9] Two groups were formed from students who had been observed in discussion groups during the preceding term. One of the groups consisted of individuals who had shown high rates of participation and the other of individuals who had shown low rates. This selection not only established a substantial difference between the two experimental groups in their average previous rate of participation, but it narrowed the range of verbal participation potential within each group. The results of applying the model to data drawn from two meetings of each of these groups are shown in Table 4.[10]

The exponential model is found to hold for these data also. Although one might have expected the homogeneity within each of the groups to have the same effect on the ratio, i.e., to increase it in both instances, it appears that there have been opposite effects. Members of adjacent ranks in high-participator groups seem to be more like each other; those in low-participator groups to be less like each other.

One source for this difference lies in the original selection of members. The members of the high-participator group were more homogeneous with regard to their previous rankings than were the members of the low-participator group. It was possible to recruit the former group from men who had been in the first to the fourth rank in their prior meetings; for the latter group it was necessary to select from men in a broader range of prior ranking that extended from the sixth to the fourteenth.

While the range of previous ranking was reduced for both groups by the process of selection, it was compressed to one-quarter of the original range for the high-participator group, while for the low-participator group it was compressed only one-half. This difference in the degree of homogeneity in prior ranking is assumed to have produced a corresponding difference between the two groups in their range of verbal participation potentials and hence in their respective ratios, r, in the subsequent meetings. On this assumption the ratio for the low group should be roughly the square of the ratio for the high group and it is nearly so.

This explanation is by far the simplest one but does not sufficiently account for the fact that the low-participator ratio is also lower than that found in non-selected groups of the same size where one would normally expect to have even greater initial variation among the members. It may be that the nature of the participation pattern among those with low verbal participation potentials is such that a low ratio would result even though homogeneity were increased. It may be that here one finds some evidence that the fit of the exponential is defective beyond a certain degree of ap-

Table 4. Participation by Individuals in High- and Low-Participator Groups

Rank of member	Meetings of high-participator group			Meetings of low-participator group		
	Percent of total	Estimated percentage	Difference	Percent of total	Estimated percentage	Difference
L	30.1	30.0	-0.1	42.3	40.3	-2.0
1	19.1	19.0	-0.1	28.3	26.7	-1.6
2	14.9	15.2	+0.3	12.9	15.1	+2.2
3	11.7	12.1	+0.4	8.9	8.6	-0.3
4	10.1	9.7	-0.4	4.0	4.9	+0.9
5	9.3	7.8	-1.5	3.6	2.8	-0.8
6	4.7	6.2	+1.5	0.0	1.6	+1.6
Ratio, r_i		.799			.567	

Table 5. Participation by Members of Discussion Groups Under Passive and Active Leadership

Rank of member	Group with passive leader			Rank of member	Group with active leader		
	Percent of total	Estimated percentage	Difference		Percent of total	Estimated percentage	Difference
1	34.3	33.0	-1.3	L	52.8	52.5	-0.3
2	23.3	22.9	-0.4	1	16.3	15.6	-0.7
3	14.3	15.9	+1.6	2	8.9	11.2	+2.3
4	9.9	11.1	+1.2	3	8.8	8.0	-0.8
L*	7.8	7.7	-0.1	4	6.8	5.7	-1.1
6	6.1	5.4	-0.7	5	4.4	4.1	-0.3
7	4.2	3.8	-0.4	6	2.0	2.9	+0.9
Ratio, r_7		.696				.717	

*In this instance, inasmuch as the leader did not have a role which differentiated him markedly from the other members, his participation was computed directly rather than residually.

proximation. Further research is needed to separate out the effects of homogeneity from the effects of average strength of verbal participation potential, and to bring to light other factors that should be incorporated into the model.

One further illustration of the effect of various factors on the ratio in the exponential function is provided by a study of experimental groups at another university that compared two situations in which the behavior of the leader was markedly different.[11] For present purposes, the two styles of leader behavior might be described as active and passive. In the former instance the leader played a major role in the discussion through his own contributions. In the latter, the leader merely introduced the subject for discussion and permitted the group to function with a minimum of interference. The members within each group were heterogeneous in regard to a personality dimension usually labeled "ascendance-submission." That is, within each group the members represented a range of scores from high to low on personality tests considered to measure this variable. The groups under different leaders had similar membership in terms of this variable. They were not selected on any other variable. "Ascendance-submission" is not equivalent to "verbal participation potential," but it was found to have consistent though low correlations with actual participation.

In comparison to the groups in the last illustration, these groups appear to be relatively heterogeneous in regard to verbal participation potential and functioned under two different leader styles. Table 5 shows the results of applying the model to data drawn from three meetings of passive-leader groups and four meetings of active-leader groups.[12]

The ratios for the two styles of leadership are higher than the ratio for the seven-man groups in Table 3 but differ very little between themselves. The different leadership styles did, of course, produce different effects. There was, quite obviously, a large difference between the proportions of total participation contributed by the members in each of the groups. The leadership styles did not differentially affect the participation relationships among the members. (Nor were these relationships significantly different from those holding among members in groups where leader styles were not altered in any systematic way.)

To understand why a difference, which might have been expected, failed to appear, one may refer back to the previously listed conditions which were considered responsible for the fit of the model and for the derived ratios.

It would appear that in both the active- and passive-leader groups, the three required conditions were fulfilled. To the extent that the personality dimension of ascendance bears some relationship to participation (and as a minimum it may be said with assurance that heterogeneity in the former is not likely to produce homogeneity in the latter), the groups were heterogeneous in regard to verbal participation potential. Second, there were no clearly differentiated roles by which the members were distinguished from each other.

Third, although the active leader was indeed active, none of his activity was directed towards controlling "who" spoke during the time when he himself was not speaking. Although he controlled the content and contributed over half the total number of participations, he recognized whomever wanted to speak and neither attempted to stimulate non-participators nor ignore over-participators. There was, therefore, no systematic regulation of the "free competitive expression" of the "verbal participation potentials" present in the active-leader groups; and most certainly not in the passive-leader groups.

The last discussion raises an important point which should be borne in mind in research with different styles of leadership (whether autocratic versus democratic, or directive versus non-directive, etc.). The areas of group functioning to which the leader is to be systematically oriented (whether content, distribution of participation, etc.) must be specified if one is to understand the effects of alternations in leader styles. As has been pointed to above, marked differences in certain aspects of leadership behavior do not produce differences in the participation relationships of members when the leaders have not also been differentially oriented to the latter dimension.

Finally, it may be said that the usefulness of the model extends beyond its utility for describing the distribution of participation in small groups. Its fit in these cases is a function of certain theoretically postulated conditions. These conditions all refer essentially to groups which are unstructured, i.e., where a pattern of interaction is permitted to develop spontaneously.

Where the data do not fit or where the ratios are considerably different from what might be expected, this is a cue to search for the conditions which are responsible for these alterations. One cannot, with this model alone, develop a full theory of group functioning. The results of applying it, however, may stimulate work of this kind in other areas and so serve to further the development of a more complete and more adequate theory.

SUMMARY

A simple exponential model is fitted and is found to describe adequately the distribution of participation among the members of small groups. Where three conditions are fulfilled: a range of verbal participation potential among the members, no systematic interference with the "free competitive expression" of these potentials, and a lack of well-differentiated roles among the members—then the size of the group is found to be an important parameter affecting the size of the ratio in the basic equation. That is, as groups increase in size members of adjacent ranks become more like each other in their relative rates of participation.

The model is applied to other data where the conditions appear to vary from those required. Its fit in these cases is discussed along with suggestions for further research which develop out of these new applications.

NOTES

[1]Bales, R. F., *et al.*, "Channels of Communication in Small Groups," *American Sociological Review*, 16 (August, 1951), pp. 461–68.

[2]*Op. cit.*, pp. 466–68.

[3]Stephan, Frederick F., "The Relative Rate of Communication Between Members of Small Groups," *American Sociological Review*, 17 (August, 1952).

[4]Mishler, Elliot G., "The Princeton Preceptorial System," in preparation.

[5]The Study of Education at Princeton.

[6]Bales, Robert F., *Interaction Process Analysis*. Cambridge: Addison-Wesley Press, 1950.

[7]These ratings are related to the larger study noted above and will not be reported here. Cf. Elliot G. Mishler, *op. cit.*

[8]"Channels of Communication in Small Groups," *op cit.*

[9]The data on high and low participating groups are drawn from unpublished work by Douglas W. Bray: "A Comparison of Precepts Composed of Low and High Participating Students," Study of Education, 1950.

[10]These meetings were chosen because they permitted comparison of meetings at which the size of the group was the same. Other meetings were observed at which the attendance was greater or less than seven. Some of them did not conform as closely as these to the exponential function, usually because of definite factors that tended to structure the discussion, such as assignment of reports to be presented by one or more members.

[11]These data are drawn from an unpublished study in which the distribution of participation was an important but not primary focus. Cf. Elliot G. Mishler, "Ascendant and Submissive Members and Leaders: Their Interaction in Group Discussion," Occasional Paper of the Conference Research Project, University of Michigan, 1950.

[12]The unit of participation counted in these groups differs from that used for the other groups reported in this paper. Briefly, a contribution could be assigned to from one to twelve separate problem-solving categories. Each assignment to a category constituted a unit of participation.

24

THE EFFECT OF TALKATIVENESS ON ABILITY TO INFLUENCE GROUP SOLUTIONS OF PROBLEMS

Henry W. Riecken

On the basis of his studies of five-man groups discussing human relations problems and deciding on solutions for them, Bales (1) has reported a clear tendency for the member who does the most talking to be credited by his fellow-members with having contributed most to the solution of the problem. Other investigators (2, 5) have obtained substantially the same result in different situations with different problems.

Several points about Bales' finding are worth noting. First, the obtained relationship is between quality of ideas and sheer quantity of interactive behavior (almost entirely verbal behavior). Second, the relationship is established by subjects' ratings of quality rather than by any objective assessment of the worth of the ideas; and, it is the subjects' perceptions of which member contributed the best ideas rather than some objective procedure for identifying their source. It could readily be argued that the active participants are neither the best possible judges of the intrinsic merit of an idea expressed during a meeting, nor the most accurate observers

Reprinted from *Sociometry* 21 (1958): 309–21. Copyright 1958 by the American Sociological Association, and reproduced by permission. Footnotes have been renumbered.

of who said what during a discussion. Finally, it is clear that the problems to be solved by the subjects in the several studies cited above did not have uniquely "best" solutions, and hence, that it might be hard to make dependable objective judgments of the quality of any person's contributions.

These ambiguities make it difficult to interpret Bales' finding. In particular, one would like to know whether the relationship is an artifact of the procedure for assessing quality and source of contributions; whether, perhaps, it is found only when there is no unique best solution for the problem; or whether it is indeed true that the best ideas for solving the problem come from the member who does the greatest amount of talking.

One way to answer these questions is to arrange a problem-solving discussion in which the most frequent interactor in the group (or the least frequent interactor in the alternative treatment) is equipped with the best solution to a problem, and then to observe whether groups in which great talkers have the best solution are more likely to agree upon that solution than are groups in which infrequent interactors have it. The experiment reported below was designed to fit this purpose.

PROCEDURE

Groups of four members were formed from voluntary subjects enrolled in elementary psychology courses. In general, subjects were previously unacquainted with each other, although no special effort was made to ensure that the members of any group were complete strangers.

Instructions to Subjects

Subjects were told that the experimenter was interested in how groups solved "human relations problems," and that they would be given several such problems. Each member would be given a written description of the problem and a chance to read it. Then the group would discuss the problem and try to reach a solution.

Subjects were further told that each of these problems had actually occurred in some industry or business and had been successfully solved, so a proven solution was known. They were instructed that when they had reached a solution that all or a majority could agree upon, they were to write it out on a sheet of paper.

Further instructions explained that E would observe the discussion from behind a one-way screen and set the time limits— 3 minutes of silence for reading the problem-statement, and 25 minutes for discussion, with a warning signal 5 minutes before the end of the discussion period. Finally, E informed the subjects that he would distribute a questionnaire at the end of each problem discussion in order to secure some additional data.

Discussion Problems

Three human relations problems were presented to the subjects for discussion, the first two of which were used simply to develop an ordering of quantity of interaction among group members. The first two problems had the same general form as the third, namely: a situation in a business or industry in which the behavior of an employee was interfering with the task of the organization.

The third problem was superficially similar to the first two but actually did have a uniquely best solution that was not likely to be discovered by student Ss. Furthermore, the essential nature of this solution depended on an insight that could be communicated easily and quickly to an individual. By secretly giving one member of the group the "insight" solution, the experimenter could be sure that the "best idea" would be initially suggested by only one person in each group and thus the *actual* (rather than the perceived) source of "the best idea" could be unequivocally determined.

This third problem was an adaptation of Maier's (4) "parasol assembly problem." It concerns an assembly line on which one worker is substantially slower than his fellows so that pieces pile up at his station while those behind him are idle or working at less than full speed. The slow man suffers from lack of manual dexterity but, for various reasons, it seems undesirable to discharge him. The question put to the subjects is: What should be done to increase the production of the line?

Hint. All four subjects in each experimental group were given a detailed, two-page statement of the foregoing problem at the start of the third discussion period. One member of each group, however, found the following additional matter typed at the bottom of the second page of his problem description:

> You are the only one in this group to whom the hint below is given. You may use the information in any way you wish but *you must not reveal that you have been given special information.*

Hint: The best solution to the problem is to have the men exchange places periodically, progressing from one position to the next in the direction of the flow of work. In this manner, the fast workers would reduce work piled up in positions occupied by slow workers, thus making production dependent upon the ability of the average man rather than on the ability of the slowest worker.

The hint contains compactly all the essential elements of what Maier calls the "elegant solution" for the parasol assembly problem. Presumably, since he was equipped by the hint with the requisite insight, a reasonably intelligent subject should be able to present a dramatically novel solution for the problem, and be able to argue convincingly for his proposal.

Measurement Techniques

As mentioned above, the first two problems for discussion provided an estimate of the amount of talking each member of a group usually did in that group, so that E could decide which member was to receive the hint. A simple measure of total elapsed time of speaking was used to determine interaction rank since it gives the same ordering of group members in groups of the size used in this experiment as does Bales' more complicated method.

The total time talked on the first two problems was used to decide which member of the group would receive the hint on the third problem. In half the groups the hint was given to the member who had done the greatest amount of talking (the "High" treatment); in the remaining groups, it went to the least frequent interactor (the "Low" treatment). A chance procedure was used for deciding the treatment for each group. There were a few groups in which the criteria could not be met. In two groups, one man out-talked other members on the first problem but was himself out-talked on the second. In one group one man talked least on the second problem but next-to-least on the first. In these three groups the strict criteria were violated and the hint assigned to the man whose *total* interaction on *both* problems was greatest (or least) when compared with his fellow members'.

A second observer joined the timing observer behind the one-way screen for the third problem discussion. The second observer's job was to keep a record of the occasions on which the holder of the hint mentioned any of the essential facts or arguments of the elegant solution. The second observer recorded the time, the item mentioned, and the response that *other* members of the groups made to the hint-holder's statement. Responses were classified as *supportive* (+) when they indicated agreement, interest, or desire for elaboration; or as *rejective* (−) when they showed disagreement, disbelief, or consisted of counterarguments.

Questionnaire

The questionnaire distributed at the end of each problem provided data about the participants' perception of each other and their activities. Each subject ranked his fellow members on: "Who contributed most to the solution of the problem?" and "Who did the greatest amount of talking?" Another question asked whether there was "any single idea or suggestion that formed the basis for the solution which the group chose," and, if there was, to identify the contributor of the suggestion and to state briefly what it was. Finally, one question concerned the respondent's satisfaction with the solution achieved by the group.

OBJECTIVES OF THE EXPERIMENT

The specific questions the present experiment was designed to answer are:

First, will the group member who characteristically does the greatest amount of talking be perceived as having contributed the most to the solution of the problem?

Second, is the "top man's" contribution to the solution a result simply of his position in the interaction hierarchy, or is it due to the superiority of his information, opinions, or suggestions as such? If a "bottom man" is equipped with superior information— the hint—will he be as able as a top man to get the elegant solution accepted?

Third, how accurate are group members in judging who contributed most to a solution? Do they more readily recognize a contribution if it comes from a top man than from a bottom man?

Finally, what insight can be gained as to the processes that help a top man or hinder a bottom man in contributing to group problem-solving, if indeed that turns out to be the case? This question is exploratory in nature, and we shall be less concerned with the statistical significance of findings than with their power to suggest explanations for what we observe.

RESULTS

The first question is readily answered and the answer confirms the findings of earlier studies. Figure 1 reproduces the graph Bales (1) used to present his data and, alongside the data from the present experiment. It is clear that the higher the individual ranks in amount of interaction initiated, the higher he is ranked in terms of his contribution to the solution of the problem. The results of the present experiment exhibit an even clearer relationship between these variables than Bales found, although the increased sharpness of the differences between men may be attributable in part to the smaller size of groups used in the Minnesota experiment.

Table 1 provides the data relevant to the second question. The top man is more often able to get the elegant solution accepted by his fellows than is the bottom man, even though the latter is, by design, equally well equipped with information and suggestions. When the top man has the insight needed to solve the problem elegantly, the group accepts this solution more than two thirds of the time; when the bottom man has the same information, the elegant solution is rejected in more than two thirds of the groups. This result does not achieve the conventional level of significance (by Fisher's exact test $p = .08$), but it is consistent with Bales' earlier finding. It seems reasonable to conclude, therefore, that it is probably not the superiority of the top man's information, suggestions, or opinions as such that lead him to be seen as having contributed most to the solution. Rather, his influentiality seems to be the result of his status as the most frequent talker in the group or of some personal attribute associated with this status.

Our third question concerns the accuracy of group members in identifying the source of a contribution to the solution of a problem. Since our attention will be given principally to the relationship between talkativeness and perceived contribution, it is worth while to point out initially that group members are fairly accurate in identifying the individuals who did the greatest and the least amount of talking during a discussion. Combining all groups on all problems, and excluding self-ratings, subjects' rankings of the most talkative member were accurate 68 percent of the time and their rankings of the least talkative member were correct 72 percent of the time. (Interestingly enough, subjects did not improve in accuracy from Problem 1 to Problem 3).

Proceeding now to the heart of the question, Figure 1 has already shown there is a distinct tendency to identify quality of con-

Figure 1. "Total Number of Votes Received"* in Answer to Question About Who Contributed Most to the Solution of the Problem

(Data from Bales is approximate from (1), p. 146.)

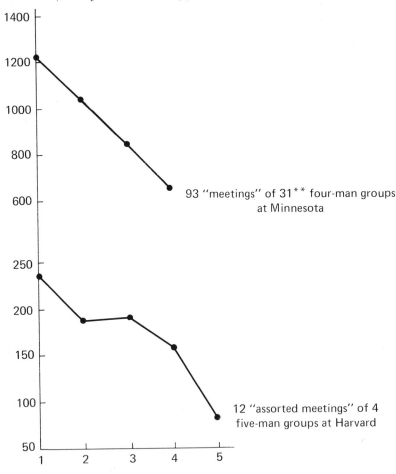

All men of each basic initiating rank

*"Total Number of Votes Received" calculated by summing scores derived from ranks assigned by each member to every member (including self-ranking) on each problem in answer to "Who Contributed Most to the Solution of the Problem?", and pooling scores for all men of each basic initiating rank. Thus, a man receiving rank 1 on the question gets a score of 4; a man receiving a rank of 2 gets a score of 3, etc. This procedure appears to be the one used by Bales to derive his Chart III (p. 146 in (1)).

**Data for one group are incomplete on this question.

Table 1.   Number of Groups Accepting or Rejecting the "Elegant Solution" by Status of Hint-holder

Acceptance of "*elegant solution*"	*Hint-holder's interaction status*	
	High	*Low*
Accept	11	5
Reject	5	11
Total	16	16

tribution with amount of talking. Even when the possible effect of having the hint is eliminated by considering only Problems 1 and 2, it turns out that 59 percent of all the first-place rankings in answer to the "contribution" question were assigned to the member who had actually done the greatest amount of talking. Table 2 makes this tendency quite clear.

The data on Problem 3 (in Table 2) suggest strongly that subjects do not simply and completely confound amount of talking and quality of contribution. At the end of Problem 3 other members of the group rate the hint-holder high in amount of contribution when the group accepts his elegant solution, and accurately rate him down when it is rejected. Thus, having the hint tends to boost the ranking that the low-talking hint-holder receives from others on contribution, *provided that he is able to get his proposed solution accepted.*

On the other hand, it is not entirely clear that group members can distinguish between quality and quantity of contribution, for there is some tendency to rate a high-talking hint-holder as having contributed more than a low-talking one even when the group accepts the elegant solution. Further analysis shows that in the High Accept cell, 82 percent of the subjects correctly attribute the source of the greatest contribution to the hint-holder; whereas, in the Low Accept groups, only 60 percent make the correct attribution. It may well be that there is a general tendency toward accuracy in

Table 2.   Mean Rank* Assigned to Hint-holder in Reply to Question: "Who Contributed Most to the Solution of the Problem?" (Self-ratings Excluded)

		Problem 1	*Problem 2*	*Problem 3*
High	Accept	1.27	1.73	1.27
	Reject	1.80	1.93	2.53
Low	Accept	3.53	3.20	1.80
	Reject	3.73	3.24	3.45

*1 = Contributed most

Table 3.   Number of Nominations of the Hint-Holder in Reply to Question: "Was There Any Single Idea or Suggestion that Formed the Basis for the Solution? If So, Who Contributed the Idea?" (Self-Ratings Excluded)

	High Accept groups	Low Accept groups
Hint-holder nominated	25	7
Other person or no nomination	8	8

recognizing the personal source of a good suggestion, but group members appear to be more accurate, so to speak, in recognizing an identically good contribution when it comes from a more talkative rather than from a less talkative member.

Finally, the replies to the question: Was there any single idea or suggestion that formed the basis for the solution? tend to support the other findings on attribution. As Table 3 shows, in the High Accept groups most members (excluding the hint-holder himself, of course) correctly identify some element of the hint and correctly attribute it to the hint-holder. But in the Low Accept groups fewer than half the members recognize the suggestion of the hint-holder and credit him with it; slightly more than half of the subjects in these groups fail to identify the hint, or say there was no single suggestion on which the solution was based, or attribute the hint to someone in the group other than the hint-holder.

These findings tentatively suggest two possible relationships between talkativeness and perceived contribution. Perhaps the participants in a discussion confound quantity with quality in such a way that the greatest talker is also seen as making the best contributions. Such a generalization could hold even if the members of the group made no mistakes in attribution of the source of a particular idea or suggestion. On the other hand, perhaps inherently good ideas are recognized as such but not incorrectly attributed to the wrong person when these ideas are produced by an untalkative member. This latter possibility suggests some perceptual principle of congruence and is almost reminiscent of the findings of Horowitz, Lyons, and Perlmutter (3) regarding the tendency of group members to attribute liked statements made during a meeting to persons whom the attributor likes.

To be sure neither of these two possibilities is unequivocally demonstrated in the present data, but they suggest that subjects' reports of the quality of contribution to discussion tend to underestimate the contributions of those who characteristically have relatively little to say.

The fourth question to which the present experiment was addressed asked what factors might help to account for the relative success of the top man and the relative failure of the bottom man to get the elegant solution to Problem 3 accepted, and it is to this exploratory question that we now turn.

One rather obvious possibility for explaining differential acceptance invokes the intelligence of the hint-holder: more intelligent men in this position have their suggestions accepted, less intelligent ones fail. This plausible explanation was investigated by comparing the scores of hint-holders and nonhint-holders on a standard test of measured intelligence, the A.C.E.[1] Since the explanation places its reliance on relative intelligence, the comparison was made by ranking the percentile scores of the four men in each discussion group and comparing the relative ranks of hint-holders in each of the four conditions of the experiment. The distribution of ranks when assessed by the median test yields a chi-square value of 0.282, which has a probability of occurrence by chance of between .95 and .98. Thus there is every reason to believe that there are no significant differences in relative intelligence among the various categories of hint-holders and, in fact, that they are remarkably similar. Differences in intelligence appear to play no part in accounting for the differential acceptance of the elegant solution, nor in the differential talkativeness of the various hint-holders. Finally, there is no evidence of interaction between intelligence and talkativeness in relation to acceptance.

A second possible explanation of differences in acceptance of the elegant solution revolves around the fluency, persuasiveness, and skill of the hint-holder—that is, the extent to which he uses available information, offers convincing arguments, and pushes the elegant solution. Table 4 presents data on the number of elements of the hint that its holder brought out in discussion and the number of times he mentioned some element or offered rebuttals to counterarguments. These findings are inconclusive in that the

Table 4. Activity of Hint-Holder on Problem 3

Condition	Number of elements of hint mentioned at least once		Total number of times any element of hint or argument for elegant solution was mentioned	
	Mean	SD	Mean	SD
High Accept	5.73	1.41	25.18	8.07
High Reject	2.80	1.47	12.80	8.98
Low Accept	4.00	2.28	17.00	9.82
Low Reject	3.73	0.85	19.09	10.16

only statistically significant differences (at the .05 level or better) are between High Accept and High Reject hint-holders on both measures; and between High Accepts and Low Rejects on number of elements mentioned. The direction of some of these differences, however, is suggestive.

First, it appears that High Accept hint-holders are more differentiated from others by the number of hint elements they mention than by the total number of mentions they make. In other words, it may be that High Accepts are using a superior strategy, namely: more varied arguments and a broader range of suggestions and information. In this sense, the High Accepts are more fluent and skillful persuaders.

On the other hand, there is virtually no difference between the successful and the unsuccessful Low hint-holders on either measure. They are remarkably alike in activity, and fluency or skill of the hint-holder does not seem to distinguish acceptance from rejection in this group.

Finally, the differences in activity between the successful and unsuccessful High talkers engages our attention. Successful high-talking hint-holders mention more than twice as many elements of the hint and speak in favor of it twice as often as their unsuccessful counterparts. The explanation of this curious state of affairs can only be conjectural at this point, but perhaps it is that the unsuccessful high-talkers failed because they personally were not convinced that the hint was an elegant solution and therefore did not push it very hard. Rather, perhaps, they took the stance of an instructed delegate who is not in sympathy with his party's position and thus advocates it weakly—only enough to pay lip service to his role.

Some support for such an interpretation comes from the data on the participants' ratings of their satisfaction with the solution the group reached on Problem 3. Understandably, the successful hint-holders in both High and Low treatments were most satisfied with the solution, their average ratings being 3.73 and 3.60 (on a 4-point scale ranging from 1. "Dissatisfied" to 4. "Quite Satisfied"). Equally understandable is the average rating of 1.91 by unsuccessful hint-holders in the Low condition, since their groups had rejected the elegant solution. But the unsuccessful hint-holders in the High condition returned an average satisfaction rating of 3.00. It seems reasonable to conclude that these subjects were unconvinced of the values of the hint, did not try hard to push it, and were rather relieved when it was rejected. If this explanation is correct, we are forced to add a restriction to the hypothesis that a high-talker can exercise greater influence on the deliberations of a group: he can do so only if he is convinced of the validity of what he advocates. But, under such a restriction, the evidence for a positive relationship between talking and influence would probably be stronger. If all the high-talkers had been convinced as well as equipped with the elegant solution, there might have been no cases in the High Reject cell.

If we now turn our attention away from the hint-holder's behavior and look at the responses of the rest of his group to him, we find sharp differences between conditions of the experiment. Table 5 presents data obtained by scoring the responses made by other group members to each mention, by the hint-holder, of some element of the hint. It is immediately apparent that the chief difference in response to successful (as compared to unsuccessful) hint-holders is the relatively large amount of support the former receive. All comparisons between successful and unsuccessful hint-holders in amount of support are significant at the .01 level. On the other hand, the amount of opposition, or rejection of the hint-holder's remarks, shows surprisingly little variation among conditions. None of the comparisons between groups of hint-holders on the measure of opposition even approaches statistical significance. In short, success in gaining acceptance for the elegant solution seems to depend not on amount of opposition aroused, but on amount of support the hint-holder musters. The suggestions and opinions of unsuccessful hint-holders are not opposed so much as they are ignored. Perhaps one part of the explanation as to why a highly talkative member is able to influence a group is that his fellows pay attention to him, whereas they ignore an untalkative person.

Yet this last generalization does not explain the success of hint-holders in the Low Accept condition, for these men apparently do not succeed through becoming more talkative. Among the Low

Table 5. **Amount of Support and Rejection Received by the Hint-Holder on Problem 3**

Condition	*Number of supportive remarks made to hint-holder*		*Number of rejective remarks made to hint-holder*	
	Mean	*SD*	*Mean*	*SD*
High Accept	10.55	4.03	14.82	8.22
High Reject	2.60	1.36	11.00	8.25
Low Accept	10.20	2.93	19.00	11.08
Low Reject	2.36	2.10	19.91	11.38

hint-holders as a whole, possession of the crucial information appears to have an inflationary effect on the amount of talking they do: 6 out of 16 of them move up to third place or higher in the interaction hierarchy. But only one of these six is successful in getting the elegant solution accepted. The combination of increased activity and superior information is not a guarantee of success.

If, instead of looking at the activity of the hint-holder in the Low Accept condition, we examine more carefully the responses of his co-members, we find an interesting and suggestive fact. In all five of the Low Accept groups there is at least one member whose response pattern shows more support of than opposition to the hint-holder's arguments for the elegant solution. (Interestingly, in four of these five groups it is the "second man"—to use Bales' phrase—not the top man who takes this role of providing support.) On the other hand, the parallel data for the Low Reject condition show that in none of the eleven groups was there a single co-member whose response pattern showed a predominance of support over opposition. In short, these findings suggest that, when an untalkative hint-holder does succeed in getting the elegant solution accepted, he does so because he has the support of a more talkative member—usually the "second man" whom Bales has characterized as frequently a specialist in social-emotional activity in the group.

SUMMARY

An experiment in which 32 four-man groups discussed "human relations problems" provided an opportunity to test a finding of Bales and others that the discussant who talked the most contributed most to the solution of the problem. By providing a hint about a uniquely good, insight solution to one problem, and by differentially locating that hint in the hands of either the highest or the lowest talker in the group, an opportunity was afforded to assess both the perceived and the actual contribution of the top man compared to the bottom man. The results show that top men are almost uniformly perceived as contributing more, and that they are in fact more influential in getting the elegant solution (contained in the hint) accepted by the group. Further data suggest that the differential ability of top men to exert influence is related more to their ability to win attention and support from the group than it is to their ability to reduce opposition. Neither measured intelligence nor fluency and skill in persuasion seem to be important factors in determining the hint-holder's influentiality. Finally, it appears that when highly talkative hint-holders fail to get the elegant solution accepted, it is probably because they are unconvinced of its value and do not advocate it strongly. When untalkative hint-holders succeed in getting acceptance, they do so with the support of one of the more talkative members of the group.

NOTE

[1]The American Council on Education Psychological Examination for College Freshmen is ordinarily administered to entering students at the University of Minnesota and percentile scores based on national norms were available for all the subjects except for one hint-holder in a High Reject group and one in a High Accept group. These two groups had to be dropped out of the analysis of the intelligence test scores and these results are therefore based on any N of 30.

REFERENCES

1. Bales, R. F., "The Equilibrium Problem in Small Groups." In T. Parsons, R. F. Bales, and E. A. Shils, *Working Papers in the Theory of Action*, Glencoe, Ill.: The Free Press, 1953.
2. Bass, B. H., "An Analysis of Leaderless Group Discussion," *Journal of Applied Psychology*, 1949, 33: 527–533.
3. Horowitz, M. W., J. Lyons, and H. V. Perlmutter, "Induction of Forces in a Discussion Group," *Human Relations*, 1951, 4: 57–76.
4. Maier, R. F., "The Quality of Group Decisions as Influenced by the Discussion Leader," *Human Relations*, 1950, 3: 155–174.
5. Norfleet, B., "Interpersonal Relations and Group Productivity," *Journal of Social Issues*, 1948, 4, (2): 66–69.

25

SOME FACTORS IN THE SELECTION OF LEADERS BY MEMBERS OF SMALL GROUPS

John P. Kirscht
Thomas M. Lodahl
Mason Haire

Several studies have reported the relationship between leadership and the rate of participation. Bass (1949) found a correlation of .93 between ratings on leadership and the amount of participation time in ten-person groups. However, the size of this correlation may be partially the effect of using the subjects as raters and of the prior acquaintance of the subjects in a class. A study by Borgatta and Bales (1956) reports that high ratings on leadership by group members tends to be associated with high rates of interaction-initiation. Moderate but consistently positive correlations between amount of participation and sociometric scores were found by Peterman (1950).

Although such findings are not unexpected because of the generally task-oriented behavior of laboratory discussion groups, participation, by itself, may not be very predictive of leadership. Slater (1955) reports that leadership as rated by other group mem-

Reprinted from *Journal of Abnormal and Social Psychology* 58 (1959): 406–08. Copyright 1959 by The American Psychological Association, and reproduced by permission.

bers coincided with highest participation in only 11 of 20 discussion groups.

Other researchers have attempted to specify the particular kinds of interaction that differentiate the leaders of small groups. Carter, Haythorn, Shiver, and Lanzetta (1951), using four-person groups, examined the interaction in 53 scoring categories. Two of these categories consistently differentiated leaders in three kinds of tasks: "diagnoses situation—makes interpretation" and "gives information on carrying out action." Other categories that showed differences but not as reliably were: "proposes course of action for others," "intiates action toward problem-solving which is continued," and "integrates group behavior." It was also found that in the reasoning rask, leaders ask for information or facts significantly more often than nonleaders. Furthermore, Shaw and Gilchrist (1956) found that leader rank and the number of written communications sent were positively related and that the major source of the difference for leaders was communications about organizing the group and giving factual information.

Thus it seems that leaders are persons who organize the group, solicit and integrate contributions, and propose courses of action. A high rate of participation would not necessarily be associated with these behaviors.

The present study was designed to investigate the relationship between amount of participation, frequency of task- and group-oriented interaction, and the selection of leaders by other group members. The general hypothesis was that amount of participation and organizational-integrative interaction are both associated with leader selection but that each may reflect different aspects of the criterion.

METHOD

Two three-person groups met simultaneously in separate rooms and were given identical instructions by the experimenters. Each group discussed a human relations problem for about 20 minutes, reaching a group consensus in that time. The groups were then told that a second meeting would take place immediately in which one person from each group would act as a representative; the two representatives would discuss a concrete problem related to the previously discussed topic. Each group then selected one of the members to act as representative.

Tape recordings of the meetings were scored for the amount of time each participant talked. Also, each meeting was scored with a system of eight categories based on Bales' (1950) system. In general, the unit of analysis was one simple statement. The three relevant categories and their definitions follow:

D. Gives suggestion (any statement which proposes a course of procedure but is *not* simply an expression of opinion, e.g., "Let's have each person give his solution"—not, "I think teachers should unionize").

E. Asks for suggestion, opinion, fact, (any request which is not for repetition or rhetorical purposes, e.g., "What do you think?" or "Would you agree that . . .").

F. Sums up, integrates (any statement attempting to organize the points covered in the discussion, or to bring together diverging opinions, or to re-word or make explicit opinions of others, e.g., "We seem to agree that strikes are bad"; "These restrictions would qualify what we said earlier").

These three categories will be referred to as "DEF." They define group-oriented, organizational kinds of interaction and are similar to the categories that differentiated leaders in the Carter et al. (1951) study. It was hypothesized that the interaction scored in these categories would distinguish those members who would be chosen by the group as representatives from those not chosen. Data were obtained on 26 three-person groups. Two of the groups were discarded because of incomplete interaction records and two were also discarded because they used random devices (flipping coins, etc.) to select the representative.

RESULTS

For the total sample of 66 Ss, data on time-talked were put into percentage form for each meeting. Those members who were chosen as representatives talked an average of 44.8 percent of the meeting time; nonrepresentatives talked an average of 27.6 percent of the time. This difference yields a t of 5.2, significant beyond the .001 level. The average number of DEF interactions per meeting was 12.6 for representatives and 6.1 for nonrepresentatives. However, the variances are heterogeneous in this case, so a median test was used, yielding a chi square of 8.79, significant beyond the .01 level. Thus, both on measures of amount of participation and DEF interaction, those members chosen as representatives were higher.

The time-talked measure correlated with DEF scores +.39, *p* less than .01. Although a moderate, positive relationship exists between participation and DEF, the two variables do not measure the same thing. When the DEF scores were put into percentage of total DEF per group, the correlation between DEF and time-talked is +.44, not significantly higher than the former correlation.

Since the measure of leadership was a discrete variable, point-biserial correlations were computed to determine the amount of relationship between leader choice and the two interaction measures. It was found that the time-talked measure correlated with leadership +.543; for DEF scores, the point-biserial correlation coefficient was +.527. Both of these correlations are significant beyond the .01 level.

A weighted combination of the two interaction variables was made up using the discriminant function (McNemar, 1955, pp. 210−211). The relative weights were .26 for time-talked and .16 for DEF. This combination yields the best discrimination between the distributions of scores for representatives versus nonrepresentatives. When composite scores were made up using these weights, they correlated with leadership +.632.

If the selection of leader is examined group by group, the predictive power of the interaction measures can be determined and compared. That person who talked the most was chosen as representative in 14 of the 22 groups. Since the chance level of selection is one out of three, this represents a highly significant ($\chi^2 = 9.15$, $p < .01$) prediction, if not too reliable in a practical sense. In those groups where one person dominated the discussion, i.e., talked over 50 percent of the time ($N = 8$), time-talked accounts for the representative in seven of the eight cases.

In 14 of the 22 cases, the person with the highest DEF score was chosen as representative. In two of the negative cases, two members were tied in DEF score, and one of the two was chosen. There are 10 cases in which the highest DEF score does not coincide with the highest time-talked. Thus, it is apparent that the two variables do not account for the same thing.

If the dominant person is predicted in those cases in which one person talks over 50 percent of the time, and where this is not applicable, DEF scores are used, 16 of the 22 cases are accounted for. This method of combining the two variables yields the best practical prediction that can be made from the data.

Although one of the DEF categories may be more crucial than the others, none of the three was found to predict as well by itself as the combined score. It may be that there are particular kinds

of groups or situations in which different types of integrative behaviors are particularly appropriate, but these refinements are not
possible with the present data.

The other categories used in scoring the interaction yielded
no significant differences between representatives and nonrepresentatives. These categories included agreement, positive social
interaction, tension release, disagreement, and hostility.

DISCUSSION

The major problem in this experiment is the isolation of variables
that can be used to account for the perception of leadership by
group members. The data show that amount of participation and
DEF interaction are significantly related to leadership choice.

Participation and DEF interaction are neither independent
nor highly correlated. They show a moderate, positive relationship.
Conceptually, we might think of the group discussion situation in
functional terms. The task set by the experimenter defines the goal
of the group. Analytically, the process of reaching this goal can be
broken down into several components, as is done by Bales (1950).
One set of problems involves the production of relevant ideas by
the group members; a second set is concerned with the organization and integration of these ideas into a solution that is acceptable
to the group. It it can be assumed that the perceptions of the group
members of each other with respect to leadership center around the
group's functioning, then it appears that the relationship between
these two aspects of problem-solving is not a simple one. Within
the area of perceived leadership are two subregions: amount of
participation and organizational behavior. In general, these two
overlap partially, but it appears from our data that the relative
importance and the amount of overlap varies from group to group.
In some groups, it appears that any person who takes over the task
and produces something will be chosen as leader. In other groups,
ideas may be plentiful and the problem is to work out a mutually
acceptable result. While this scheme makes difficult a simple
prediction of leader choice, it appears to do more justice to the
data than a monolithic concept of leadership in small groups.

Another way to state this interpretation is in terms of the
differentiation of roles in small groups. Where one member talks
a great deal, he is perceived as an appropriate representative, but
in a more equal participation situation, group-centered, integrative
behavior is relatively more important. In the latter case, persons

are differentiated with respect to functioning in synthesizing the group. Even in this case, however, there is undoubtedly a minimum amount of participation necessary before the group-oriented behavior is noticed.

It must be remembered that these groups met only once and that the members were unacquainted with each other prior to the meeting. The representatives are leaders only in the narrow sense that they are empowered to act for the group. While these results may not pertain to a wide range of leadership situations, many short term, problem-solving groups are found that are similar to the experimental situation. Furthermore, the results with respect to DEF interaction seem to corroborate the findings of Carter et al. (1951) regarding the types of interaction which are important in leader behavior. This confirmation includes Carter's negative findings also: the expression of agreement, "personal feelings," and disagreement did not reliably differentiate emergent leaders from nonleaders. In addition, the results on amount of participation tend to confirm the importance of this variable, as has been found by other experimenters.

In summary, the general picture of a small group leader which appears to be common to various researches shows a group member who tends to have a high rate of participation in the discussion; he is task-oriented, attempts to specify the problem, to suggest courses of action, to seek out the members' contribution, to integrate these and to propose solutions in the attempt to secure consensus in the group.

REFERENCES

Bales, R. F. *Interaction process analysis.* Cambridge: Addison-Wesley, 1950.

Bass, B. M. An analysis of the leaderless group discussion, *J. appl. Psychol.*, 1949, 33: 527–533.

Borgatta, E. F., & Bales, R. F. Sociometric status patterns and characteristics of interaction. *J. soc. Psychol.*, 1956, 43: 289–297.

Carter, L., Haythorn, W., Shriver, B., & Lanzetta, J. The behavior of leaders and other group members, *J. abnorm. soc. Psychol.*, 1951, 46: 589–595.

McNemar, Q. *Psychological statistics.* New York: Wiley, 1955.

Peterman, J. N. Verbal participation, its relation to decision satisfaction and the leader function in decision making groups. Ann Arbor: Univer. of Michigan Conference Research Project, 1950.

Shaw, M. E., & Gilchrist, J. C. Intra-group communication and leader choice. *J. soc. Psychol.*, 1956, 43: 133–138.

Slater, P. E. Role differentiation in small groups. *Amer. Sociol. Rev.*, 1955, 20; 300–310.

26

PROBLEM SOLVING BY SMALL GROUPS USING VARIOUS COMMUNICATION NETS

George A. Heise
George A. Miller

A trend can be discerned in the history of the experimental studies of small groups. Early studies determined that the presence of other people has an effect upon individual performance. Competitive and noncompetitive situations were compared, but social inter-action and cooperation was slight (2). More recently the small group has been studied as a unit. The group is given a problem to solve; the discussions of the group are recorded (1), or the efficiency of the group is compared to that of a single individual (6). From Lewin and his followers have come studies of interaction in dif-ferently organized groups and of the effectiveness of these groups in coping with various situations. The trend seems to be toward more detailed analysis of the group structure and more interest in the processes of interaction among the members of the group.

Still more precise specification of the group structure and of the kind of interaction has been achieved by Bavelas and his as-sociates. These workers control the channels of communication among the members. Components of the solution are given to each

Reprinted from *Journal of Abnormal and Social Psychology* 46 (1951): 327–35. Copyright 1951 by The American Psychological Association, and reproduced by permission.

person, but all members of the group must cooperate to reach the correct solution.

In Leavitt's experiment (4), for example, five Ss were seated around a table, but separated from one another by vertical partitions. Written notes could be passed through slots in the partitions. By varying the slots that were open, the channels among the five could be manipulated into any desired pattern. Four patterns were tested: (1) In the *circle* each person could pass notes to the person to his right or to his left; (2) the *chain* was identical to the circle except that one more slot was closed, so the Ss on either side of this closed slot found themselves at the two ends of a chain; (3) the Y was a four-member chain, and the fifth S could exchange notes only with one of the inner members of this chain; and (4) the *wheel* (or X) put one S at the center of the net in such a way that he could exchange messages with all the other members, and the other four could not exchange information without passing it through the central member.

Each S was given five different symbols out of a possible set of six. The task was for the entire group to discover the one symbol held in common by all five members. Records were kept of speed, errors, and number of messages. At the end of the experimental session the Ss were given a questionnaire before they talked to each other.

The circle was the most active, erratic, unorganized, and leaderless, but was most satisfying to its members. The wheel was least erratic, required relatively few messages to solve the task, was organized with a definite leader, but was less satisfying to most of its members. The chain and the Y were more like the wheel than like the circle. The member in the central position became the leader, and was more satisfied with his job than were the occupants of peripheral positions. The different communication nets did not differ significantly in the average time it took to solve the problem.

The present experiment is similar in many respects to Leavitt's, although the control of the situation is carried still further. Each S is required to reach a solution of the problem. The necessary information is divided equally among the Ss. Speech, instead of written messages, is the method of communication between group members. However, the content of the messages an S can send is restricted and suitable for quantification. The intelligibility of the speech was controlled during a test by controlling the relative intensitites of the speech and the noise. These controls permit determination of the dependent variable, group performance, as a function of the independent variables: (1) group organization, (2) intelligibility of the message, and (3) type of problem.

APPARATUS AND PROCEDURE

Nets

The communication nets were set up as follows. Three Ss were located in three adjoining rooms. Each S had a microphone, amplifier, and earphones. Listening was binaural except when a listener heard one talker in one earphone and one in the other. The five nets tested are shown schematically in Figure 1. The direction of the arrows indicates the channel from talker to listener. A two-headed arrow signifies two-way communication. The nets will be referred to by number, 1 to 5. The subjects will be referred to by letter, A, B, or C, according to the positions indicated in Figure 1. All the channels were free of distortion, and passed frequencies from 200 to 7000 cps.

Noise

Random noise is a shishing sound that has all frequencies of vibration present at equal intensities. Because of the similarity to a white light that has all wave lengths present, such a sound is often called white noise. White noise is a very effective masking sound. This noise was introduced in equal amounts into all the channels. Some noise was always present during the tests in order to mask any airborne sounds that passed directly through the walls.

The intelligibility of speech in the presence of noise is a function of the relative intensities of the speech and the noise, and is independent of their absolute levels over a wide range (3). In order to control the amount of external stress introduced, the speech-

Figure 1.   The Five Nets

(The arrows indicate the direction of communication from talker to listener.)

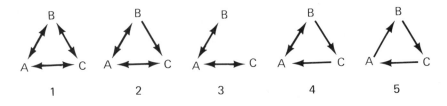

to-noise ratio was set to a given value by adjusting the intensity of the noise. Each *S* was given a voltmeter that indicated the intensity of the electrical signal generated by his voice. This meter was used to monitor the speech signal at a constant level (approximately 80 db re 0.0002 dyne/cm^2 at the listener's earphones). Use of the meter counteracted the natural tendency of talkers to raise their voices as more noise is introduced. In this way the likelihood of errors could be controlled by the experimenter. Preliminary tests showed that 85 percent of the monosyllabic words (from a memorized list of 256) could be received correctly at a speech-to-noise ratio of +6 db, 66 percent at −2 db, and 24 percent at −10 db.

Problems

The problems were of three kinds. Problems used in Experiment I called for a comparatively stereotyped and unimaginative exchange of isolated words. The problems in Experiment II provided more opportunity for initiative in the construction of sentences. Experiment III was based on a kind of anagram problem. These problems are described in more detail in the discussions of the three experiments.

Subjects

The three *S*s in the word tests were undergraduates in Harvard College. They had been *S*s for 15 hours of articulation testing during the preceding month. These *S*s had become thoroughly familiar with a master list of 256 common monosyllables. Two of these three *S*s continued through Experiment II; the third was replaced by a graduate student who quickly mastered the procedure under the tutelage of the other two. After the first few trials the new member performed as well as the others. Two groups of three naive *S*s, all graduate students, were recruited for the anagram tests of Experiment III.

EXPERIMENT I: TESTS WITH WORD PROBLEMS

Method

In order to explain the construction of the word problems, the following terms are defined. (1) The *master list* is a set of 256 monosyllables from which all test words were drawn. These 256 words, arranged according to vowel sounds, were placed in easy view of each *S* throughout the word tests. (2) The *test list* is a list of 25 words selected at random from the master list. (3) The *subject's list* is a list of pairs of words selected at random from the test list. The first step in the construction of a word problem is to assemble a test list of 25 words. Then the pairs of consecutive words from the test list are collected in three sets to form three sub-lists, one for each *S*. Part of a sample test list and the three *S*s' lists derived randomly from it are shown in Table 1. The word pairs are given to the *S*s in their correct order as they appear on the test list.

The problem is to reconstruct the test list in its entirety. Since each *S* has only a part of the information needed for the reconstruction, he is forced to communicate over the net provided. In the example of Table 1, *C* begins by saying "You will write 'south.'"

Table 1.   Sample of Test Material

(The three subjects received their lists in this form, and attempted to re-construct the test list cooperatively.)

Test list	Subject A's List	Subject B's List	Subject C's List
south	though	south	south
though	off	though	
off			plod
quiz	off	grade	sniff
grade	quiz	act	
act			pounce
dwarf	quiz	sin	rash
plod	grade	whiff	
sniff			rash
pounce	act	range	gun
rash	dwarf	sledge	
gun			gun
coast	dwarf	wire	coast
pig	plod	nine	
sin			coast
whiff	sniff	raid	pig
pent	pounce	jug	
cook			whiff
range	pig	shaft	pent
sledge	sin	fake	
comes			sledge
fort	pent	fake	comes
wire	cook	by	
nine			etc.
etc.	etc.	etc.	

(The carrier phrase "you will write . . ." makes it possible to warn the listeners and to monitor the speech level before the test word occurs.) The word "south" travels through the net until it reaches *B*, who then introduces "though." When "though" reaches *A* he introduces "off," "quiz," "grade." The details of the process are evolved by the *S*s themselves during the preliminary testing, but in this general manner the test list can be patched together. Every *S* must get the entire test list of 25 words before the problem is completed.

Before each test the *S*s were carefully informed about the pattern of channels. They knew that the speech-to-noise ratio was always the same in all channels. Discussion of the roles of members located at different points in the net was discouraged. No suggestions were made about the strategy that the group might employ in solving the problem. The *S*s were not instructed to solve the problem in the shortest possible time; they were told to proceed at a reasonable rate consistent with the accurate reconstruction of the test list by all three participants. The *S*s were permitted to speak only the carrier phrase followed by any number of the words on the master list. A talker was not allowed to indicate to whom he was speaking. These restrictions on the group's vocabulary maintained the intelligibility of their speech at a known, constant level. The order for testing the nets and the positions of the *S*s in the nets was determined by a pre-arranged plan.

Four three-hour experimental sessions were required before the group performance stabilized enough to permit satisfactory comparisons of different trials. The times required for completion of the problems decreased steadily during the preliminary period as the *S*s became familiar with the problem and the best procedure on the various nets. The rate of learning was too rapid for accurate assessment of the influence of the experimental variables, although the same general relations obtained as in the later trials that are reported in detail.

The *S*s found the problem an interesting one. Post mortems were a common occurrence after a trial was over, especially when a persistent error had hampered progress. During the trial several spontaneous expressions of agitation were noted. Frustration and irritation were evident on net 5 at the lower signal-to-noise ratios, where correction of errors was difficult and progress was slow. Once, in net 1, an *S* complained that the other two were monopolizing the conversation. In net 3 both subjects *B* and *C* occasionally talked at the same time to a harried subject *A*. Frequent reminders were necessary to prevent the Ss from raising their voices, thus improving the signal-to-noise ratio, when attempting to correct errors.

By the end of the preliminary period of rapid improvement the group was a smoothly functioning unit within the limits imposed by the three signal-to-noise ratios and the five nets. The Ss evolved the practice of reporting both members of the word pairs in the same message, which tended to keep all Ss "up to date" and the words in their proper context.

Results

The results reported in Table 2 and Figure 2 were obtained in two three-hour experimental sessions. Three kinds of measures are reported. (1) The *time* required to complete the task was measured from the first "You will write . . .," spoken by the S who had the first word, to the point when each S had compiled his 25-word list. (2) The *accuracy* of the completed list was scored by comparing the S's written record with the test list. (3) The *number of words*

Figure 2.   Performance of the Group on the Word Problems (Experiment I) as a Function of the Communication Net

(Nets are numbered as in Figure 1. Performance is measured in terms of (A) total words spoken and (B) time required to finish the task. Parameter is signal-to-noise ratio.)

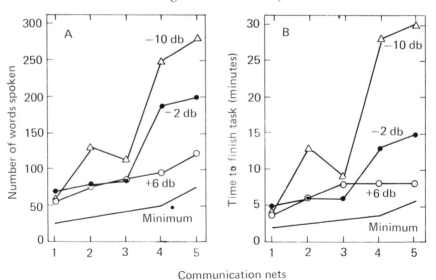

Table 2. Group Scores for Word Problems

Net	Theoretical minimum no. of words	Theoretical minimum time (in minutes)	Percent words correct			Total words required			Time to finish task (in minutes)		
			+6db	−2db	−10db	+6db	−2db	−10db	+6db	−2db	−10db
1	25	1.9	97.5	94.7	80.0	56	68	58	4	5	4
2	33	2.5	97.5	94.7	86.7	75	77	128	6	6	13
3	42	3.2	98.7	85.4	96.0	86	85	112	8	6	9
4	50	3.8	96.0	94.7	84.0	94	186	248	8	13	28
5	75	5.8	96.0	90.7	82.7	122	198	279	8	15	30

spoken by each *S* was recorded by him as he said them. The totals for all three gave the number of words the group had spoken in order to solve the problem.

A reconstruction of the course of solution would have been possible if the *S*s had written down all the words they said. It proved impossible to write out all the words spoken without destroying the tempo and spontaneity of the group interaction. Hence the *S* was asked to record only the *number* of words he said, rather than the actual words themselves.

The minimum curve plotted in Figure 2A represents the minimum total number of words that the group could say for each *S* to conclude with a reconstruction of the 25-word test list. The calculation assumes no articulation errors by any *S*, and no deviations from the maximally efficient procedure for a particular system. The minimum times of Figure 2B are obtained by dividing the minimum word scores by 13, the average number of words spoken per minute. The similarity between Figure 2A and Figure 2B indicates that the *S*s tended to talk at an approximately constant number of words per minute under all conditions.

It will be noted that the results for a signal-to-noise ratio of +6 are strikingly similar to the minimum curve except for a displacement upwards. Few errors in communication occur at this favorable signal-to-noise ratio. Consequently the difference between minimum and empirical curves indicates a consistent use of surplus words. Unnecessary repetitions and the habit of saying both the words of a pair provided the surplus. The *S*s were not instructed to be economical with words or time.

Figure 2 shows that raising the noise level, with the consequent introduction of errors, accentuates the differences between the systems. The comparative inefficiency of net 5, the one-way closed chain, becomes clear when the noise is introduced. In this net one person's failure to hear correctly a particular word stalls the group's progress; locating the culprit is difficult and correcting him harder still. The same message, containing an error stubbornly introduced by one member and as stubbornly corrected by another may go round and round net 5 before the mistake is finally corrected. Short periods of silence, extremely unusual in other systems, occurred often enough to decrease appreciably the average number of words per minute. The deficiencies of net 5 are present in a less extreme form in net 4, where only one of the *S*s was in the semi-isolated position.

The resistance of net 1 to the deleterious effects of noise is readily explained. Each *S* starts the problem with more than a third of the total information required for solution. He is provided with the words he must contribute and also the words that precede them. Thus in net 1, one of the two listeners to every word must have the word (if it is correct) written down in front of him. Each listener makes what is essentially a two-alternative decision. He decides whether the word he hears is the one on his paper, in which case he introduces the second word of his pair, or whether it is some other word. The articulation score for a two-alternative vocabulary is quite high (5). The listener in this situation is likely to make the correct decision. Incorrect decisions are immediately detected when neither, or both, of the Ss introduces a next word.

The number of words spoken by a member of the group is determined by his position in the net. The proportional partici- pation of each member is approximately the same as the propor- tions that can be calculated by considering the most efficient pos- sible solution.

Casual observations indicated that Ss in different positions in the nets play different roles. The man in position A of net 3 is forced by his central position to become a coordinator. He usu- ally warns the other two members at the beginning of a trial, and takes charge of any procedural matters that arise during the trial. When asked at the conclusion of the experiment which position in the network they preferred, all Ss chose this central position. Iso- lated positions, of which the clearest example is C in net 4, were un- popular with the Ss, who reported that in these positions they felt left out and unsure of themselves.

A stereotyped procedure, in which the S waits passively until he hears the first word of a pair on his list before introducing the second word of his pair, is quite appropriate for the solution of these word problems. The correspondence of the empirical results to the predictions of group performance—predictions based upon the assumption of such machine-like behavior—shows that the word problems did not provide a real challenge for the group's abilities.

EXPERIMENT II: TESTS WITH SENTENCE PROBLEMS

Method

The sentence problems relied upon verbal context, rather than the repetition of word pairs, to link the contributions of the three mem- bers. These problems were less rigidly structured and provided more scope for initiative. The test materials consisted of sentences of 25 words, as simple in thought and expression as possible. For example, "The picture we saw was painted by an old woman who had been taught how to mix the colors by one of the native artists." All sentences used were of approximately equal difficulty and were designed (1) to minimize punctuation, common phrases, and clichés, and (2) to express thoughts unrelated to any particular knowledge possessed by the Ss. The words in the sentences were common-place; no proper names and no words longer than three syllables were used.

The words in the sentences were divided into three parts with the aid of a table of random numbers. At the beginning of a trial each S received his portion of the words. The words were listed vertically in the order in which they occurred in the test sentence. As before, the task of the group was to reconstruct the original sequence of words in their correct order; each member had to conclude with the complete sentence.

The same five networks and three speech-to-noise ratios were investigated as for the word problems, but more attention was paid to nets 1, 3, and 5, and more data are available for them. The Ss received the same instructions; they could say as many words as they wished, preceded always by the warning "You will write . . ." The messages actually sent were somewhat longer than they had been for the word problems, because the intelligibility could be raised by placing the words in the context of the sentence.

Sentence building provided a problem that held the S's interest. Each sentence posed a novel problem. Discussions, in which the correct sentence was disclosed and jocular recriminations passed among the Ss, were unavoidable after trials that were difficult or delayed by errors.

Records were kept of (1) the time required to complete the problem, and (2) the number of words spoken by each S. Accuracy scores were not useful. An S could tell when he had the correct sentence by observing that he had 25 words strung together in a reasonable sequence that included, in the proper order, the words he had been given at the outset. The Ss seldom missed more than one or two words of the test sentence.

Results

Time and total word scores are given in Table 3 and plotted in Figure 3. The results indicate that net 3 is superior to net 1. This superiority is most marked for the unfavorable speech-to-noise ratios,

Table 3. Group Scores for Sentence Problems

Net	Theoretical minimum no. of words	Theoretical minimum time (in minutes)	Total words required			Time to finish task (in minutes)		
			+6db	−2db	−10db	+6db	−2db	−10db
1	25	1.4	76	99	186*	4	5	15*
2	33	1.8	117		121	8		7
3	42	2.3	101*	96	154*	6*	4	7*
4	50	2.8	112		287	4		17
5	75	4.2	112	315	446*	7	15	30*

*Averages for two problems.

which shows once more that the stress of noise exaggerates differences among the nets.

In net 1 everyone always talks to everyone else. In net 3 a
man in the middle is the go-between for the other two. Why is net
1 superior for word problems but inferior for sentence problems?
Apparently the reconstruction of sentences requires more integration of group activity; the central man can coordinate and place in
the proper context the words that the S s contribute. He is in a posi-

**Figure 3. Performance of the Group on the Sentence Problems
(Experiment II) as a Function of the Communication Net**

*(Nets are numbered as in Figure 1. Performance is measured in terms of
(A) total words spoken and (B) time required to finish the task. Parameter
is signal-to-noise ratio.)*

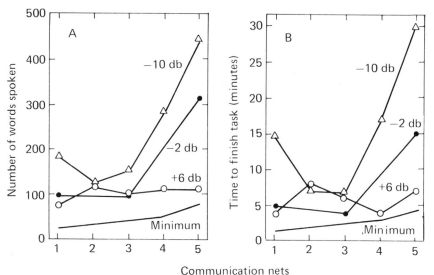

tion to detect and correct mistaken words and incorrect hypotheses. Conversely, the situation can become chaotic in net 1, for no one organizes the individual contributions. These considerations could mean that the proportional participation of the central man in system three is higher for the sentence problem, where he plays a more significant role, than for the word problem. The individuals' data show, however, that the proportional contributions for the central man are approximately equal for both kind of problem.

EXPERIMENT III: TEST WITH ANAGRAM PROBLEM

Method

The anagram problem was taken from a study by Watson (7). The group was given a word and instructed to form as many anagrams as possible. The test words were *abolished, courtesan, educators, neurotics, secondary,* and *universal.* All had nine letters, four vowels, and the consonant *s.* The words formed had to be at least three letters long; singular and plural did not count as separate words; proper nouns and slang were not permitted. The group's goal was to get the largest possible number of words on all three papers; a word could count three times toward the group total if it appeared on all three papers. Communication was not essential for carrying out the task. The extent to which *S*s communicated the words they made up, or heard from other *S*s, was left completely to their own discretion.

The instructions in the use of the equipment were the same as before. Only three nets were tried with anagram problems, nets 1, 3, and 5. Two speech-to-noise ratios, −10 and +6 db, were tested. The group was allowed ten minutes to work on each word. Three practice tests, one with each net, accustomed the *S*s to monitoring their voices and to constructing anagrams.

Results

The results for the last six tests are summarized in Table 4. These figures are the average values obtained for two groups of three subjects.

It is clear from Table 4 that the differences among the nets were small, and that the introduction of noise did not emphasize the differences among the nets. For this kind of problem, there-fore, the pattern of channels among the members of the group has

Table 4.   Average Group Scores for Anagram Problems

Net	Total words constructed		Words spoken	
	+6db	−10db	+6db	−10db
1	165.5	149.5	61.5	64.0
3	167.0	142.5	93.0	81.0
5	176.0	141.0	135.5	99.0

little effect upon the efficiency of the group's performance. The unfavorable speech-to-noise ratio interfered with the group's performance in about the same degree for all nets.

The *S*s marked on their score sheets all the words that they spoke aloud. The total number of words (average for the two groups) that were spoken during the 10-minute tests are shown in Table 4. Fewer words were spoken over the multi-connected net 1 than over the minimally-connected net 5. Intense noise decreased the amount of talking.

In the word and sentence problems of Experiment I and Experiment II, the efficiency of the group depended upon the pattern of channels available for communication among the group members. In the anagram problem, the type of net apparently made no systematic difference in the efficiency of the group. This difference can be explained on the basis of two principal ways in which the word and sentence problems differ from the anagram problems.

(1) The information necessary to solve the anagram problem was nonconsecutive and was not divided among the group members. All group members began the problem with identical information which was adequate for the assigned task. In contrast to the word and sentence problems, where the *S* had to wait for the contribution of another group member before he could proceed, the *S* in the anagram problem could work at the task in his own preferred order, at his own optimum speed. Consequently errors and delays in the transmission of words did not appreciably hinder an individual's productivity. The correction of errors, a procedure much easier in some nets than in others, was unnecessary in the anagram problem for keeping the group at work. Errors in the transmission of words frequently stalled progress on the word and sentence problems, however, because an *S* often could not introduce the next word until he had correctly heard the preceding word.

(2) The task assigned an *S* in the word and sentence problems was primarily to communicate to the other group members the information that had been presented to him at the beginning of the problem. Consequently, the performance of the group depended

in large measure upon the ease of communication. In the anagram problem, however, the S himself had to make up the words he sent out. Table 4 shows that S s made up about five anagrams per minute, and that not all of these were sent over the communication net. Even the most inefficient system was adequate for this slow rate of output; it is not surprising that no significant differences were observed for the various nets.

DISCUSSION

A few generalizations can be drawn from these experiments. The relative efficiency of a communication net depends upon the kind of problem the group is trying to solve. The nature of the group's task is the most important variable that remains to be explored. Exposing a group to unfavorable conditions can exaggerate differences in the relative efficiency of different nets. However, if the problem does not require successful communication, the efficiency of the group may be little affected by the net pattern or by noise.

The experimental situation investigated here is considerably more restricted than most of the group situations studied in the laboratory or in the social interaction of day-to-day life. To what extent does this artificiality limit the generality of the results? Some of the limitations of the method can be overcome by modification or enlargement of the equipment. Additional persons, and additional group organizations, can be introduced by adding microphone, loudspeaker, amplifier, and separate room for each person. The size of the group is an important variable that we have not considered here. A switching system can easily be installed that would allow the S s themselves to determine the group organization and the recipients of particular messages. Differential noise conditions in the channels can be used to force some of the group members into relatively insignificant roles and to give relative prominence to others. Wire recording can be used for a more thorough analysis of each individual's contribution, the origin of errors, and the progress of problem solution.

Less easily overcome are the limitations imposed by the range of problems appropriate for this experimental situation. Quantification of results is greatly facilitated by restriction of vocabulary and standardized procedure. Since the problem material must all be expressed verbally, the results are perhaps unduly influenced by factors such as verbal context and intelligibility, with a reduction in general applicability to the less restricted life situation.

One thing that is needed is a classification of group problems. What are the significant dimensions of a problem? One obvious dimension is the degree to which the problem is structured. A continuum, based on the degree of structure of the problem, would run from problems so highly restricted that an individual group member could be replaced by a fairly simple robot to the problem faced by a town council deciding whether to raise taxes. The problems devised for these experiments are far toward the structured end of the continuum. At the other end of the scale are problems investigated by the Lewin group, where factors such as the role played by various group members and their personalities, attitudes, and needs were involved explicitly. Many of these factors could be introduced systematically into the intercommunication system employed in this work by a relaxation of curbs on the members' activities, and the setting of more broadly defined tasks.

Other dimensions include such possibilities as the uniqueness of the solution, the initial distribution of information, the number of decisions that someone must make, the rate at which a participant can narrow the range of possible solutions, the position along a competition-cooperation continuum, etc. With a reasonable classification of problems we can begin to relate the problem, the net, and the stress in a systematic way.

It is possible that stress may act as a microscope to magnify differences that otherwise are difficult to measure. How general is the stressful effect of noise? Do other kinds of stress have comparable effects? To what extent can the activity of one member be regarded as a source of stress to another member of the net?

By their careful controls of the conditions under which a group must work, Bavelas and his co-workers have extended the precision of research with small groups. If this precision does not cost too much in validity, we may have a powerful experiment method.

SUMMARY

The performance of a three-man group was studied for five different communication nets, three signal-to-noise ratios, and three kinds of tasks. The first type of problem was a simple reassembling of a list of standard words. The second type consisted in the construction of a sentence, the words of which had been distributed among the group members. The third type required the group to form anagrams.

For the first type of problem, comparative group efficiency, measured in terms of time or number of words required to complete the task, could be predicted from the net structure. A closed chain in which only one-way communication was possible between any two persons was by far the least efficient; an open chain, which allowed two-way communication between any two adjacent individuals, was intermediate; a closed chain where all members talked and listened to all other members was most efficient. The second type of problem was less rigidly structured and placed a higher premium on the coordination of the group activity. The results were generally similar to those for the first type of problem, except that the open chain, which had a man in a central coordinating position, replaced the two-way closed chain as most efficient. The anagram problem did not require communication; under these conditions there was no large difference among the nets.

Lowering the signal-to-noise ratio introduced errors and increased the time and number of words required to complete the task. For the first two types of problems the stress of noise accentuated the differences between the systems and emphasized the inefficiency of the one-way closed chain. The third problem, where communication was a luxury, was solved equally well over all nets; noise did not accentuate differences.

The performance of a small group depends upon the channels of communication open to its members, the task the group must handle, and the stress under which they work.

REFERENCES

1. Bales, F. *Interaction process analysis.* Cambridge. Mass.: Addison-Wesley Press, 1950.
2. Dashiell, J. F. Experimental studies of the influence of social situations on the behavior of individual human adults. In C. Murchison (Ed.), *Handbook of social psychology.* Worchester, Mass.: Clark Univ. Press, 1935.
3. Egan, J. P. Articulation testing methods. *Laryngoscope*, 1948, 58: 955–991.
4. Leavitt, H. J. Some effects of certain communication patterns on group performance. *J. abnorm. soc. Psychol.*, 1951, 46: 38–50.
5. Miller, G. A., Heise, G. A., and Lichten, W. The intelligibility of speech as a function of the context of the test materials. *J. exp. Psychol.* In press.
6. Shaw, M. E. A comparison of individuals and small groups in the rational solution of complex problems. *Amer. J. Psychol.*, 1932, 44: 491–504.
7. Watson, G. B. Do groups think more efficiently than individuals? *J. abnorm. soc. Psychol.*, 1928, 23: 328–336.

27

COMMUNICATION AND THE PROCESS OF WORK

Tatiana Slama-Cazacu

1. Communication and work activity are two processes in which the "social" is inherent to a high degree, and which greatly concern social psychology. The relationship between these two processes has been, however, only a minor object of study for psychology and social psychology in general, and for socio- and psycholinguistics in particular.[1]

1.1. Data recorded by ethnographers or linguists provide factual argument, important in supporting the fundamental thesis concerning the relationship between language and labor. Various linguistic monographs, however, rarely arrive at theoretic interpretations and rarely are based on records or analyses of the *entire* ensembles of linguistic facts that appear in the communication proper, *at the very moment of work activity.*

1.2. In psychology, and especially in psycholinguistics, even the *formulation* of this problem is quite rare. Does any link exist between language behavior and work, in the present stage of human development (representing a transitory one as to technique, with prevailing forms of work by mechanized means, but also with elementary manual forms as well as a superior automated technique)? Also, what does this link consist of? What are its consequences for the two processes?

The hypotheses to be corroborated by the research that will be presented are: (a) that in the present stage labor has a strong

345

influence upon communication and upon language itself, the signals (choice of signal systems and of signals as such) varying in accordance with the diverse conditions of work; and (b) that language—and communication as a whole—plays, in its turn, a very important part in the process of work carried on as a collective activity. A corollary of hypothesis (b) is that even under the conditions of automated technique this relation has consequences for both processes (See Slama-Cazacu, 1964B and 1964c.)

2. The research method[2] was devised to gather relevant material in order to reach conclusions bases on evidence alone. Field observation was the first important step in this research, providing direct contact with reality in natural conditions before construction of some experimental models. *Observation* was the principal method: *noting* protocols throughout the situation, *recording* speech during work, and *photographing* other means of communication. *Conversation* (for explaining certain terms, and so forth), and preliminary or control *experiments* in work situations were used only as subsidiary methods. Observation was performed *during work,* in wholly natural circumstances, and mostly when work was performed in teams.

The author collected this material during 1961 and 1962 from more than seventy units. Over twenty occupations from various regions of Romania comprised these units. Some major occupational categories are: forestry work (especially handling the raftsman's pick or "tapina"); brigade fishing at sea and on lakes; agricultural work at various technical levels; construction-related labor; industrial labor; factory labor such as machine fabrication, metallurgy, steel works, boiler forges, rolling mills, wood processing, and the food industry); transportation and communications labor (such as radio, television, cinematography, and telephone).

3. In *analysing* and interpreting the material, we will first refer to the *part played by communication in the process of work* (schematically, *communication → work*), and then to *the influence of work upon communication (work → communication). Language$_2$* and psycholinguistic implications will be emphasized.[3]

3.1 Why is communication *necessary?* Under what circumstances is it necessary during work?

Communication is linked to the necessities of working in a team. Even when a person appears involved in a work activity by himself, work is done independently for only certain moments, because everyone belongs in a complex social network. For example, although the worker who is operating the elevator in a mine is alone in his extraction tower, he is linked to other workers by a communication system, receiving information to direct his actions and transmitting information needed by other workers.

Communication during work is necessary when information must be transmitted or retransmitted because other members lack knowledge necessary to their work. For example, these situations occur: when a person's physical view is restricted as is the crane driver's on a building site); when a person has knowledge concerning the whole work process (as a controller of railway traffic); when a person has certain theoretical, technical, or practical knowledge and an exchange of information becomes necessary; when action must be not only coordinated but synchronized; when an action must be accomplished with a certain tempo or intensity; or when mobilization of attention or motor effort is needed.

3.2. *Communication → work.* A discussion of the necessity of communication directly concerns the effects of communication. This evidence led to the conclusion that communication during work plays a role: (a) in *learning* or *instructing* showing how to act); (b) in labor *planning* (from the individual mental planning of every action, up to the complex planning of group activity; (c) in *coordinating* the work process, with special effort in *synchronizing* movements (for instance, when lifting or shoving certain big, long, or heavy objects—as in cable setting, trawl fishing, oil worker's labor, or a team of forest workers handling big logs by means of raftsman picks—but also for setting a train in motion, for television transmission, or for launching spaceships; consequently, showing *when* to act, that is, the moment for every element of a sequence of actions, but also the intensity of every movement); (d) in *appreciating* the results of labor (from a mere encouraging appreciation, to the information concerning complicated laboratory analyses of the product).

These various aspects may be included in the general role of *regulating* (socially, psychologically, physiologically) the *activity* in the work process. During work, the cognitive-active aspect of communication appears very clearly, with a marked stress upon activity adaptation, that is, upon communication as a determinant of the action and of its regulation. Reciprocal adjustment—so necessary to the work process—is achieved, to a great extent, through mediated communication.

4. *Work → communication.* This study of the influence of work on communication will be centered around the discussion of two essential aspects. The choice of modality of communication in the work process implies: (1) selection of a *certain system* of expression-reception and of an appropriate type of *distribution*; and (2) *formal modifications* of messages within the frame of the chosen system, as well as adaptation of the receptor to this system. This second aspect can also be reduced to a *choice* of certain modalities existing within a system.

4.1.1.   The work process dictates the choice of a system. In the selection of a communication system, the characters of the work and the conditions under which it is carried on determine which system will be most appropriate (awareness of the system and of the work process is an essential condition for the efficiency of the communication system).

The fundamental means of communication in the work process, as well as in all human activities, is the articulated language—a certain *language₂* in its concreteness and in the messages. Other means of communication are used during the process of work, such as: *mimico-gesticulation* (which is important, not only as speech auxiliary but, very frequently, also as the only system used); some vocal means (such as *whistling* or *"yodeling"*); various acoustic signals (from the *bell*, or *hammering* or *striking* of a pipe, for instance, to the *horn, bell,* or *hooter*); or visual signals (from the shaking of a lantern or a flag, to diverse *graphic* signs and *electric* light signals).

4.1.2.   Communication presupposes not only a choice of signals, but also of a way of message *distribution*; that is, a choice of *networks* which include the emitters of messages and receivers during communication. There are two forms of networks: the *linear* form, with "threads" directly linking two or more persons; or the net form, with *emission centres* (an emitter-receiver of "dispatch" or retransmission"). The net form also comprises the special form—common in certain work situations—of simple "relay," or "retransmission," in which the message is distributed "in chains," "from man to man," and "from mouth to mouth." In the practical reality of work (contrary to laboratory occurrences based on artificially "restricted" modalities), these forms are very complicated because of the interference of diverse factors, of new partners, of sudden changes in the route of a message, or of mixtures of "linear" and "dispatch" nets.

4.2.   The *choice* of both *signal systems* and *communication networks* in the work process is determined primarily by the conditions under which work is performed, by the specific circumstances, and by the immediate environment. These facts reveal a field that has practical importance, in which psycholinguistic studies (in connection with social psychology and sociolinguistics) are needed.

Even within the *same* type of work—or within one and the *same stage* of work—one specific signal system is sometimes selected, depending upon environmental conditions. People resort to gestures during conditions of intense *noise* (in boiler forges, during mechanized agricultural work, or in truck circulation outside the mines), or when *silence* must be maintained in the television studio or when work partners are separated by considerable distance. *Distance* is a compelling factor. For instance, an increase of speech intensity—shouts—determines the eventual of gesticulation.

4.3. Once a certain system and distribution of communication has been chosen, certain *formal modifications* occur because of the manner in which the work process is performed.

Quantitative modifications are one aspect of communication (the general frequency of messages during work, the rate of verbal flow, the length of a verbal sentence, or the amplitude of a gesture). The rate of communication may vary because of existence of a well-established and well-learned code, knowledge of the activity, previous instructions, or well-established habits, and because of environmental or work conditions. Maintaining a swift pace during a certain work provides little time for communication and at the same time makes short and economic messages—based upon ellipsis—a necessity.

Qualitative modifications represent another aspect of communication regarding *vocabulary,* and *phonetic* and *morphologic-syntactical*[4] peculiarities (used only in reference to the spoken language, which, because of its importance, has been more thoroughly analysed.) Many of these features pertain to *language₂*. These features were selected for the necessities of work, but many of them were (or are) also created during work activities and afterwards entered into the system of *language₂*.

4.3.1. As technique develops, a *special terminology* appears and evolves because it is necessary for distinguishing reality and fixing experience in the cognitive activity. Consequently, this terminology is essential in the communication process for a clear discrimination of the tools and of their component parts and properties, as well as for differentiating actions in their various components and shades.

The modification of terminology in connection with the *evolution of technique* has been studied very little in linguistics (and almost never in psycholinguistics). It would be interesting to compile terminological inventories from the viewpoint of technical evolution, considering its dynamic process of discarding or of replacing ancient terminology, for instance. Still more interesting perhaps, would be psycholinguistic studies establishing present use of a term corresponding to a more ancient technique, and also describing transfer to the superior technique. For instance, names of ancient tools or operations are slowly *forgotten*, even by persons who once used them very frequently. On the other hand, one can also note the *conservation* of ancient terms—some of them polysemic—by an analogous transposition of ancient terms that are now used for naming new devices or parts proper to modern technology.

4.3.2. *Phonetic modifications* have developed because of the requirements of rapid information exchange, the necessity of certain aspects, distance between interlocutors, a speaker's effort in performing an action, and a speaker's emotion. These modifications generally concern tempo and intensity of speech, intonation, and general melody of the sentence; they provoke certain features in the phonemic units. One example is the disappearance, lengthening, or stressing or particular sounds. *Agata si trageee!* "Hoop up and draaag!", shouts a brakeman to the miner's trolley driver in the Petrila mine. Or *Joos!* "Down!", calling to a craner on a building site in Bucharest.

4.3.3. Nouns, adverbs, or adjectives may be used as imperatives within *morphologic alterations. Prafuu!* "The powder!" (lift up the hydrophobic powder), calls a builder from the floor of a building on a site in Bucharest. Numerals or adjectives may also be used as nouns. Verbs, adverbs, imperatives, and vocatives are used frequently to name actions or to give details about actions.

4.3.4. One *syntactic peculiarity* is the selection, because of work conditions, of strict necessary elements, so that sentences are generally short. These short sentences do not contain, in most cases, all the "classical" elements but are incomplete, or elliptical. For instance, "∫ Vin ∫ saizeci ∫ de vagonete ∫ la ∫ putul ∫ noua!" "∫ There are coming ∫ sixty ∫ trolleys ∫ to the ninth ∫ pit ∫!", is being communicated in the Petrila mine. Or, "*Patru!*" "The fourth! ∫" —"The operator of camera number four come to action! ∫," announces assistant director in a television studio. Although the sentences verbally have an elliptical aspect, they are, in fact, more ample, and are completed by an implicit reference to the situation, by a gesture, or by an action.

In the work process more than in other activities, perhaps, some grammatical categories of the verbal linguistic system are replaced by other means of communication. Gestures and appeals to objects existing in the real situation are most prevalent. These phenomena, little studied by linguists or psycholinguists, are extremely important for a correct understanding of the *langage du travail*, for interpreting some of the facts mentioned above (such as morphologic alterations), and especially for constructing an appropriate image (far from the traditional one) of grammar. In oral communication during work, as in general communication, human beings frequently use not only the verbal system, but a mixture of verbal and nonverbal cues. At the same time, in the sequential flow of messages, there are verbal components addressed to an auditive reception, and nonverbal or visual ones addressed to the optical channel of reception (a device we have called "indication ad oculos"). The latter is a substitute for some verbal-oral components that the author calls "a mixed syntax." (See Slama-Cazacu 1968c and 1969.)

4.3.5. We may even say that there is a certain "style" of communication during the work, characterized by: (a) *peculiarities* of a *motion-engendering (dynamogenic) nature* (using verbs and adverbs, transforming noun values, shortening messages in relation to the rhythm of an action, stimulating intonation, mobilizing supplementary gestures, or modifying word order); and (b) peculiarities conspicuously arising from the common circumstances under which collective work is being carried on.

The special syntactic peculiarities observed in the work process occur mainly during rapid dialogue related to the work activity. *Dialogue* is based, at the same time, upon *common context*. This, in turn, leads to elliptic replies, reciprocal completions, and, in general, to the characteristic syntax of dialogue, as well as to situational-contextual indications.

In addition to these features of dialogue, other features result directly from the *common situation* of the partners and generally from context.[5] The partners resort to implicit knowledge or to existing cues to facilitate communication, saving time and also allowing a better understanding of the messages. This is also an origin of "mixed syntax" or parallel gestures, with partners resorting directly to the situational context by frequently using verbal or plain gestural deictics. The syntactic peculiarities mentioned above are thus determined not only by dialogue relation but also by the common situation in which communication occurs.

Generally speaking, expression during labor is governed by the principle of *economy* as well as that of *necessary redundancy*, or the useful "plus." (See also Slama-Cazacu 1962a.) In the work process, the problem of distinguishing what has been termed—despite the paradox—*necessary redundancy* (which has an especially important role under conditions of noise or peril and, generally, whenever a strengthening of communication is necessary) from *superfluous* or even noxious *redundancy*. Superabundant communication is a consequence of disorganized work. This situation has, in its turn, negative consequences upon work because attention is diverted from necessary action or from actually important messages.

5. Conclusions.
   5.1. The *relationship* between language and work implies: (a) *reciprocal relations of interaction between the two processes*; and (b) at the same time, an *evolutional change* of the details of this relationship, according to the development of concrete circumstances the social-historical ones and, as a subsidiary, the restricted situation in which the work is being carried on.
   (a) The principle of *selection stemming from a certain work situation* constitutes one fundamental conclusion of this study.
   (b) The relationship between labor and language varies in its diverse details, in accordance with the evolution of work—with the development of the social organization and technical conditions of the latter—and also with the general evolution of the human mind, which entails a development of language as such.
   Our assumption—based upon observations that will also be verified by forthcoming experimental investigations—is that *language*$_2$ will continue to play an important part under the conditions of automation, both in the formation of interhuman communication and communication between man and "machine." An important task of future technique will be the achievement of proper conditions for the specific human method of reception.
   5.2. A methodological conclusion that may be of interest for linguistics, psycholinguistics, and psychosociology of language, is the necessity of studying details in this field that have not been thoroughly explored.
   It must also be taken into account that the relationship between work and language is not static. This relationship appears only during direct contact with the work situation and dynamic work

activity, by recording *during the work activity, all contextual ensemble* (such as verbal context, gestures, and behavior of the total situation), as well as by analysing all the aspects of *language$_2$* (lexical, phonetical, morphological, and syntactical), and by *interpreting every fact of communication* in connection with the conditions of activity. This last method could be called "*a dynamic-contextual method*," because it requires the recording of linguistic facts in the contextual ensemble and during the activity.

5.3. *Language$_1$*, as communication, plays an important inter-regulating part in the work process as part of the partners' reciprocal action and in close connection with the autoregulator one. Hence the link between *language* (in its communicative aspect) and *activity* is evident.

Another thesis confirmed by the present investigation is that a close *link* exists *between function of communication and the cognitive aspect of language$_1$*, between communication as a determinant of action and communication as a vehicle of items of information, but also between communication and the directly cognitive aspect of *language$_1$*.

Finally, it is necessary to draw the conclusion that, in studying the *language$_1$*, psychology and psycholinguistics must not omit the important part nonverbal means of communication may play in the work process. First and foremost is the mimical-gesticulatory system, which has witnessed a great development and a marked expressive fineness, and whose meanings are sometimes at a certain level of abstraction.

5.4. In close connection with both social and industrial psychology is that of *practical consequences* of our investigation (improvement of communication, establishing the optimal messages, and so forth).

NOTES

[1]For a more comprehensive presentation of these topics, results, and discussions, see Slama-Cazacu, 1964a. The book also contains an extensive bibliography. Except for some works used for a critical discussion in the book's introduction, the material proper and further comments were based entirely on the author's research; the actual presentation may also be taken as such and needs no other references.

[2]See reference list, 1962a to 1970.

[3]The English term *language* is ambiguous. Further, there is no specific or adequate English term corresponding to the French *langage* (found also in other

Romance languages). The difference between the French *langage* and *langue* will be indicated by: *language*₁ (*langage*—the ensemble of psychical processes), and *language*₂ (*langue*—the system of signs).

⁴In the present synthesis we it is impossible to make a minute analysis. See, for details, Slama-Cazacu, 1962a, 1962b, 1963b, and 1964a.

⁵See Slama-Cazacu, 1961.

REFERENCES

Slama-Cazacu, Tatiana. 1970. Les éléments de la communication, niveaux du code et la triade langage-langue-parole. *Linguistique contemporaine* (volume dedicated to E. Buyssens). Bruxelles: Ed. Inst. de Sociologie.

———. 1969. Communication levels, interdisciplinary approach, and the object of psycholinguistics. Paper presented at the Conference on Psycholinguistics, Bressanone, July.

———. 1968a. Psiholingvistică şi aplicarea metodei dinamic-contextuale în dialectologie. *Studii şi cercetări lingvistice*, no. 2: 83−96.

———. 1968b. *Introducere în psiholingvistică*. Bucuresti: Ed. Stiintifică.

———. 1968c. L'étude du roumain parlé: Un aspect négligé—"l'indicatio ad oculos." Abstract of the paper presented at the XIIth International Congress of Romance Linguistics and Philogy. In XIIᵉ Congrès International de Linguistique et Philogie Romanes—Rapports et Communications. Résumés. Bucuresti.

———. 1966. La méthodologie psycholinguistique et quelques-unes de ses applications. *Linguistics*, no. 24: 51−72. (Also in *Revue roumaine de linguistique*, 1965, nos. 1−3: 309−16.

———. 1964a. *Communicarea in procesul muncii (Communication in the process of work)*. Bucuresti: Ed. Stiintifică, (English and Russian abstracts).

———. 1964b. Verbal signals in automation. *Revue roumaine des sciences sociales—Psychologie*, no. 1: 89−99. (In Romanian, in *Revista de psihologie*, 1963, no. 4: 519−45.)

———. 1964c. Problèmes psycholinguistiques posés par les messages verbaux employés dans l'automation. *Revue roumaine de linguistique*, no. 2: 119−30.

———. 1963a. Bemerkungen zür Sprachlichen Kommunikation im Arbeitsprozess. *Forze-Briefe*, no. 3: 110−34. (Also in *Magyar pzsichologiai szemfe*, 1963, no. 2: 225−32.)

———. 1963b. Remarques sur quelques particularities du message verbal determinees par le travial. *Linguistics*, no. 2: 60−84.

———. 1963c. Observations concerning language communication in the process of work. *Revue des sciences sociales—Serie pshilosophie-psychologie*, no. 1: 63−89. (In Romanian, in *Revista de psihologie*, 1962, no. 2: 183−212.)

———. 1962a. L'économie et la redondance dans la communication. *Cahiers de linguistique théorique et appliquée*, vol. I. Bucuresti: Ed. Academiei R. P. R. Pp. 17−25.

———. 1962b. Sprachliches über die Kommunikation im Arbeitsprozess. *Revue de linguistique*, no. 2: 269−88.

———. 1961. *Langage et contexte*. 'S-Gravenhage. (Romanian edition, Bucuresti: Ed. Stiintifică, 1959.)

Part Seven

MEANING IN THE PSYCHOLOGICAL STUDY OF LANGUAGE

28

LINGUISTIC AND NONLINGUISTIC COMPONENTS OF COMMUNICATION: NOTES ON THE INTERSECTION OF PSYCHOLINGUISTIC AND SOCIAL PSYCHOLOGICAL THEORY

Ragnar Rommetveit

1. INTRODUCTION

The primary aim of the present paper is to suggest how *a cognitive social psychology* may provide a framework for integration of linguistics and psychology. I want, more specifically, to explore the act of speech in the setting of person-to-person communication and show how messages are mediated by the linguistic utterance, by nonlinguistic features of the communication setting, and by an articulation between linguistic and nonlinguistic features of the communication process.[1]

Let us first explore a case in which the fusion of linguistic and nonlinguistic components is fairly transparent. An American friend of mine enters my office and he is looking at the empty table where my typewriter is usually located with an expression of inquiry and curiosity. As I am watching him at that very instant, I say: "Under repair." My two-word utterance is under this particular condition

357

Figure 1. Linguistics and Nonlinguistic Constituents of Messages

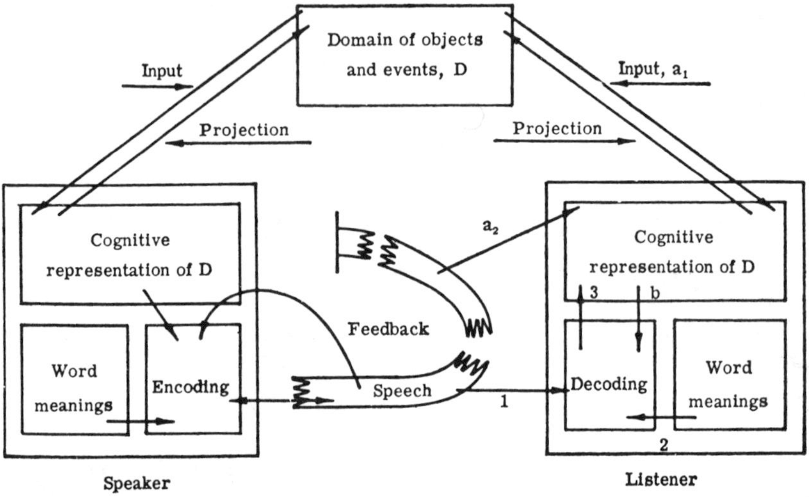

Source: Ragnar Rommetveit, *Words, Meanings and Messages* (New York: Academic Press, and Oslo: Universitetsforlaget, 1968), p. 193. Copyright © 1968 by Academic Press Inc. and Universitetsforlaget.

sufficient to convey the message that the typewriter is presently being repaired. And let us now make use of this very simple case to explicate a very complicated diagram (Figure 1).

The message has obviously only in part been mediated via encoding and decoding of word meanings. The spoken words constitute merely a fragment of some sort of frame of assertion whose initial slot is inequivocally filled by a nonlinguistic feature. And this nonlinguistic constituent of the message must be established by convergence of cognitive orientations on the part of my friend and me. The typewriter has attracted our joint attention and is hence at the center of external *domain of objects and events* toward which both of us are oriented during my act of speech.

This is not a simple case of quasi-predication (Mowrer, 1963) in which a physically present object replaces the subject of the complete sentence. We are jointly oriented toward the typewriter because of its *absence* from the actual scene of communication. The nonlinguistic constituents of the message can therefore not be explained in terms of stimulus input from the unmentioned object but rather in terms of shared *cognitive representations*.

Imagine, next, the simple utterance: "There are too few seats," inserted in two different settings. The speaker is a political candidate who has rented a room in a public building for a political campaign meeting, and the utterance occurs immediately before he starts his speech. The listener, however, is in one case the janitor of the building who is standing in front of the closet where extra chairs are stored. In the other case, the utterance is made in response to a telephone call from the candidate's wife who shares his political ambitions and hopes for election.

The janitor understands immediately that the speaker wants him to bring some more chairs. The master-to-servant relationship between the two participants in the communicative act, the particular location of the janitor at the moment he is addressed, etc. —these are pre-established features of the communication setting that constitute the situational frame for the utterance. Linguistic and nonlinguistic constituents may therefore fuse in such a way that the receiver can hardly disentangle them. If we ask the janitor what the speaker said, he may very well respond: "He asked me to bring some more chairs." The wife, on the other hand, may rush from the telephone and tell her children: "Daddy has attracted a large crowd tonight." Such spontaneous recodings confirm our suspicion *that the same linguistic fragment has conveyed distinctively different messages in the two situational frames.*

2.   NOTES ON SOME DESIGN FEATURES OF SPEECH

So far we have merely shown that a cognitive social psychology is required in order to explicate *unmentioned constituents, presuppositions,* and implications of otherwise verbally mediated messages. We may hence postpone our efforts, it may be argued, until linguistics and psycholinguists who are studying semantic and syntactic processing can tell us more about what is being conveyed by the utterance itself. Linguistic and nonlinguistic constituents do *not* fuse in any simple, additive fashion, however. A social psychological perspective seems to be required even in an analysis of purely linguistic fragments of the communicative act.

The vocal-auditory channel of transmission of speech signals first of all, imposes particular constraints upon the communication process (Hockett, 1963). Because of the rapid fading of the signals, encoding and decoding have to take place in extremely close temporal contiguity. The audibility of the human voice is such, furthermore, that reception is restricted *to a very narrow area.* The listener will hence, under normal conditions, immediately identify the speaker and vice versa.

Whenever messages are mediated by speech signals, we have

thus, as a rule, a well-defined temporal-spatial-social framework for the communicative act. The proximity of the speaker and the listener provides an unequivocal *here* of message transmission and the act of speech itself establishes an equally distinctive *now*. The direction of transmission furthermore defines the *sender* (the I) and the *receiver* (the you) of the message. And every known language is tagged onto this temporal-spatial-social framework by the linguistic tools of *deixis* (Weinreich, 1963). The term *deixis* stems from the greek word for *pointing* and the specific deictic tools of English are such words as personal and demonstrative pronouns, place and time adverbs, and suffixes for tense of verbs.

Notice that such linguistic tools are not tagged directly onto the proper names of the speaker and hearer nor the moment and location of speech as physically defined. Consider, for instance, the Norwegian sentence *"Horn gjekk no."* ("He left now.") The past tense of the verb and the time adverb are apparently in this case at variance: the former demands a projection onto a point of time *before* the act of speech, the latter to an immediate *now*. The fact that none of us would consider the utterance contradictory, however, indicated the subtle psychological processes involved in establishing the deictic temporal-spatial-social coordinates of communications. The past tense of *left* maps the event onto the temporal axis *before* the instant of speech, whereas the time adverb *now* further restricts its temporal location to the *vicinity of the act of speech*. The extension of the vicinity will vary with the temporal segmentation required by the domain of objects and events toward which speaker and listener are oriented. If the message concerns a professor leaving his office for the day, it may only include a few minutes of measured time. If it concerns his leaving the university to take over another job, on the other hand, a rounding of the *now* to the nearer semester or academic year may actually be presupposed by the speaker and the listener. Decoding of deictic elements will thus usually involve a temporarily established shared cognitive representation of spatial-temporal-social relationships (arrow b in Figure 1). The specific contributions of words such as *now* and *here* will vary with the particular domain of objects and events toward which the listener is oriented during the act of speech.

It is also a design feature of language that every speaker—except for pathological cases—is a listener to himself and that members of a speech community are interchangeable as encoders and decoders of speech signals. The speaker's capacity as an encoder *and* the complete feedback therefore provide him with an opportunity for anticipatory decoding *before* and at *successive stages* of the act of speech. Let us now examine to what extent and in which ways this opportunity is actually made use of.

Consider once more, the utterance *under repair*, in the particular communication setting described earlier. My particular choice of words is determined by my intention to convey a message to my friend *and* the expectation *that he will not comprehend Norwegian* (he is an American colleague). Anticipatory decoding may hence be said to be involved in choice of linguistic medium. Such problems of choice do not arise in an ordinary unilingual setting. Appropriate anticipatory decoding is a sine qua non, however we "leave out" words (ellipsis). When uttering only "Under repair," I am temporarily *taking the role of the other.* I correctly assume that my friend at that very moment is oriented toward the typewriter and concerned with its whereabouts. And such a *taking the role of the listener* constitutes a central theme in the perspectives on linguistic communication developed by G. H. Mead (1950), Vygotsky (1962), and Piaget (1926).

Piaget found in his analysis of small children's storytellings that their language was particulary deficient with respect to *deixis.* Personal pronouns (he, she,), demonstrative pronouns (this, that) and time adverbs (then) will in storytelling serve the general function of linking some component of the immediate utterance to a particular fragment of preceding speech (see arrows a and b in Figure 1). The *he* and *that* being uttered at any particular stage of a discourse must be tagged onto persons and events in a shared designative domain and the small child apparently does not yet have the capacity for the sustained role-taking required for such successful deixis. The apparently egocentric and noncommunicative utterance of the child is thus not egocentric with respect to *intention,* but primarily because his capacity for anticipatory decoding fails. This is perhaps more clearly revealed when a demonstrative pronoun such as "this" is tagged onto some concrete object that constitutes the focus of the child's attention but is invisible to the listener.

3. MESSAGE, UTTERANCE, AND TRANSMISSION OF INFORMATION

What is the locus—if any—of the *message* in our diagram of the communication process?

Our introductory example shows that there is no one-to-one

correspondance between messages and utterances by which they are conveyed. This holds true even if we were to expand the utterance into a full-fledged and apparently self-sufficient sentence. The message that my typewriter is under repair may obviously be mediated by a variety of nonlinguistic and linguistic tools. I may, for instance, put some particular sign outside my door whenever it is under repair in order to save my friend the trouble of entering the room and looking for it. I may rephrase the sentence and I may translate it into languages other than English. What remains invariant across such diverse linguistic tools may possibly be explicated as the *deep syntactic structure* of sentence (Chomsky, 1965). The fact that it also remains the same across nonlinguistic media of communication, however, makes it equally clear that the message is not of a narrowly defined linguistic nature, not even when it seems to be extremely portrayed by a well-formed sentence and can be made intuitively accessible in no better way than by linguistic tools.

Let us therefore return to the cognitive representations, the processes of encoding and decoding, and the projection onto the domain of objects and events as depicted in Figure 1. A *sent message* may now be conceived of as an act of encoding by which the sender intends to initiate (in the receiver) a particular projection onto the designative domain. A *received message* may be tentatively defined as an act of decoding by which the receiver projects from the utterance and features of the situation to that domain. And the *transmitted message*, finally, may possibly be assessed in terms of correspondance or "intersecting elements" between sent and received message and respect to projections onto a shared word.

Notice that nothing has been said about the relationship between the sender's beliefs and the sent message. I may lie, for instance, when I say that the typewriter is under repair, but the truth value of the message is as such of no immediate significance for message transmission. Notice furthermore that there is no unequivocal relationship between *message transmission* and transmission of information as the latter term in defined within the framework of information theory (Attneave, 1959). My friend may already know that my typewriter is being repaired, or he may be very much surprised when he is informed about it.

The inference from received message to information transmission will thus require a comparison on the receiver's beliefs and expectations *before* and *after* decoding. If we disregard actual and assume credibility of the sender and other complicating factors, we may then conclude that transmission of information takes place whenever the receiver's projection to the domain of objects and events is at variance with his pre-established beliefs.

4. FURTHER ILLUSTRATIONS AND SOME IMPLICATIONS OF A SOCIAL-PSYCHOLOGICAL PERSPECTIVE

It seems reasonable to assume that the relative contributions of linguistic and nonlinguistic constituents to the message will largely depend upon the state of pre-established cognitive convergence of speaker and listener. Let us therefore examine what happens in communication settings that are clearly different in that respect.

Imagine the utterance "He is in the cafeteria," imbedded in two somewhat different situational frames. In one case, I am knocking at Bill's office door, but nobody answers. Fred, watching me standing there, says, "He is in the cafeteria."

Consider, next, the very same utterance in a different setting. A friend of mine wants me to listen to a short story he has written and he starts out reading, "He is in the cafeteria . . . ."

Fred and I are colleagues. Both of us know Bill and we lunch together daily in a cafeteria nearby. The deictic word *he* and the construction *the cafeteria* are hence immediately tagged onto the particular person Bill and a particular location we both know (arrow b in Figure 1). The message is thus *mediated* by words. Its content, however, stems exclusively from an already established convergence of cognitive orientation, a shared social word.

In the other case, we have to search in vain for a pre-established, shared denotative domain. The *he* of the short story has at the early stage of the story hardly any deictic anchorage outside the act of speech. Its contribution to the *received message* must therefore reside in its reference to some imagined male human being who happens to be at the focus of the speaker's intention at the moment. The construction *the cafeteria* serves to reduce my ignorance concerning the whereabouts of the unknown man by excluding locations other than those encompassed by the referential possibilities of that phrase. In addition, there is *"eine Als-bekannt selzung"* (Reichling, 1963): the definite article signals further specification, that is, the storyteller indicates that he has a particular cafeteria in mind, and that he is going to introduce me into an imagined world, in which I am going to be familiar with that cafeteria. Until my friend tells me more, however, my cognitive representation of the scene of action will remain, approximately as diffuse as the sphere of reference of *cafeteria* with its fringe of associative and emotive potentialities.

Subtle individual differences with respect to word meanings that were of absolutely no significance in the office-door setting may hence in the short-story setting produce a discrepancy between intended and received message. My friend the author may, by the word *cafeteria*, want to convey an image of the scene of action, the distinctive feature of which is an unpleasant atmosphere of cheap food, smoke, and juke boxes. My associative fringe, on the other hand, may be of a peaceful place, intimacy, and pleasant conversations with colleagues. Subtle—and partly idiosyncratic—components of acquired word meanings may thus fill that slot of the message that in the other setting was occupied by a shared representation of a unique and very familiar location.

When no shared designative domain has been induced by present behavioral setting and/or preceding speech (arrows a_1 and a_2 in Figure 1), then message transmission depends primarily upon shared word meanings and commonality with respect to syntactic competence. The process of decoding can in such cases be indicated by arrows 1, 2, and 3. Cognitions introduced by features of the situation and preceding speech, however, will usually change this pattern. Decoding will, then, be more appropriately indicated by arrows a_1 (or a_2), 1, 2b, and 3. The major outcome of such a process will frequently be the insertion, into some slot of the message, a cognitive element that was already available perceptually, intentionally, or in immediate memory prior to the act of speech.

Situational features and preceding linguistic context may therefore affect decoding in very similar ways. This is not only so in deixis, but also when contexts induce particular contraints upon word meanings. Imagine, for instance, how different men may emerge from the same word *man* in the two situations:

In one case, my wife and I are looking at a photograph of a deceased friend of ours, and she says, "He was a man." In the other case, we have been wondering whether the boy who delivers our daily newspaper has quit the job. As we hear the newspaper being dropped outside the door, my wife therefore goes to the window to find out. As she turns toward me again, she says, "He was a man."

Distinctively different referential, associative, and emotive potentialities of the word *man* are obviously involved in its decoding in the two cases. Since its linguistic context did *not* differ, such marked differences in decoding can only be explained in terms of the impact of nonlinguistic features. The psychological process involved, however—even though far more complex and less well understood—may resemble the mechanism underlying semantic transfer features of words (Weinreich, 1966). Such transfer features are inferred when one constituent of a phrase restricts the reference of another constituent in specific and predictable ways.

Our notion of a situationally induced designative domain may also be useful when we try to explore problems of *self-reference* and *pragmatic modes* that attract the attention of philosophers and linguists. Some of the problems arise in connection with utterances such as "I believe the weather is nice," and one of the issues is whether the utterance portrays a statement about the *speaker's belief* or about *the weather*.

This issue cannot, according to our preceding consideration, be settled for the utterance *in vacuo*.

Consider, first, a situation in which my integrity has been challenged in some way. I have tried to persuade a friend to spend the vacation with me in a particular recreation area. He has the suspicion, however, that I am actually *lying* about the wonderful conditions there. This insinuation and my own concern with his distrust produce a shift of topic—from *weather conditions and vacationing* to *my beliefs and sincerity*. My own person is thereby being included in the designative domain, and the fragment *I believe* will in this particular setting be self-referring.

In most other situations, however, no self-reference is involved in such as "I guess," "I suppose," inserted, parenthetically in various slots. I may say, "I believe the weather is nice," or "the weather, I believe, is nice," or "the weather is nice, I believe." And in no case will the fragment "I believe," as such, produce a shift of topic (from *weather conditions* to *beliefs*). Urmson (1963) has therefore labelled verbs like *believe*, *guess*, or *suppose*, in such ordinary contexts, "parenthetical verbs." He suggests that the insertions function as signals guiding the hearer to a proper appreciation of the statement in its context.

Linguistic *form* alone cannot, therefore, tell us whether an utterance is self-referring. A social-psychological analysis of denotative orientations in the communication setting is required. Fragments such as "I believe" or "I suppose," may—when no self-reference is involved—hence be conceived of as *pragmatic operators* (Weinreich, 1966). They do not constitute parts of the received message as such, yet *contribute* (like symptoms of credibility on the part of the speaker, the conviction revealed in his tone of voice and facial expression etc.) to the pattern of information exchange and social influence in which the message is embedded. The so-called parenthetical verbs are therefore linguistic tools by which the speaker may propose a communicative frame for the utterance, and hence similar to the major pragmatic modes such as *interrogation* and *assertion*.

The interrogative mode ("Is the weather nice?") implies a speaker-to-hearer for information and a plea for continuation of the discourse with a reversal of the speaker and hearer roles. The assertive mode ("The weather is nice.") provides a frame of speaker to listener transmission of information, with no presupposition concerning continuation of the communication process. A parenthetical fragment such as "I know," "I believe" or "I suppose" in a given assertive sentence frame may then modify the frame such that successively less transmission of information and correspondingly more of a request for information is being presupposed (or proposed).

Let me add, finally, that a social-psychological analysis of the situational frame and designative domain to the message seem to complicate the issue of what constitutes the *topic* and what is the *comment* of an utterance. Osgood proposes, in agreement with Chomsky's early analysis of *deep structure*, that the topic can be identified by a purely linguistic analysis. He uses as an illustration the following sentence (1963, p. 479).

The clever young thief was severely sentenced by the rather grim-faced judge.

The subject of the assumed underlying kernel sentence is *judge*. The letter word provides, therefore, according to Osgood, the *topic*. Comprehension of the sentence is then by means of a very elaborate analysis of the hypothesized semantic and syntactic processing involved, finally explicated as a uniquely modified meaning of the word *judge*.

Such an identification of the *topic* of an utterance *in vacuo* and *on the basis of a word's assumed status in the deep syntactic structure*, stems from the perspective I have tried to outline in this paper to be of greater purely linguistic than psychological relevance. As far as the potential *message* convoyed by such an utterance is concerned, no single word or word meaning can constitute the topic. If the listener happens to be the mother of the clever young thief, she may be so overwhelmed by the message conveyed by the first seven words of the utterance that she actually fails to hear that a grim-faced judge was involved.

5. CONCLUDING REMARKS

I have tried to outline a tentative framework for social-psychological contribution to the field of psycholinguistics. My presentation has largely consisted of general statements and casuistic analysis. Empirical psychological evidence of relevance can hardly be established until social psychologists invade the area of psycholinguistic research.[2]

Linguists who work on problems of semantics and deictic tools, however, will probably welcome such an invasion. The Dutch linguists Reichling (1963) and Uhlenbeck (1963) have, in their purely linguistic analysis, explicitly emphasized the imbeddedness of the utterance in the situation. The very structure of language is founded on the assumption that it will not be used *in vacuo*, they maintain.

The same general perspective is adopted by Mounin, in a theoretical analysis of the problems of translation. He writes (1963, p. 38), "*La semantique est la partie de la linguistique où la formule de Saussure est fausse, la partie où la langue ne peut pas être envisagée en elle-même, parce que c'est la partie par où l'on passe incessamment de la langue au monde et du monde à la langue.*"

The primary aim of this paper has been to suggest how social-psychological inquiries may contribute to a better understanding of this subtle and continuous oscillation between linguistic and non-linguistic mediators of messages.

NOTES

[1]Many of the problems raised in this paper are discussed in far more detail in a more comprehensive work (Rommetveit, 1968).

²Since this paper was written, however, we have witnessed considerable progress in terms of systematic theoretical explorations as well as exploratory empirical research. See, for instance, Moscovici (1971), and Carswell and Rommetveit (1970).

REFERENCES

1. Attneave, F. *Applications of information theory to psychology.* New York: Holt, 1959.
2. Carswell, E. A. and Rommetveit R. *Aspects of language in context.* London: Academic Press, 1970.
3. Chomsky, N. *Aspects of the theory of syntax.* Cambridge: M.I.T. Press, 1965.
4. Hockett, C. F. The problems of universals of language. In J. H. Greenberg (ed.), *Universals of language.* Cambridge M.I.T. Press, 1963.
5. Mead, G. H.. *Mind, self and society from the standpoint of a behaviorist.* Chicago: University of Chicago Press, 1950.
6. Moscovici, S. Communication processes and the properties of language. In L. Burkowitz, (ed.), *Advances in experimental social psychology,* Vol. 3. New York: Academic Press, 1967.
7. Mounin, G. *Les problèmes théoriques de la traduction.* Paris: Gallimard, 1963.
8. Mowrer, O. H.. *Learning theory and the symbolic processes.* New York: Wiley, 1960.
9. Osgood, C. E.. On understanding and creating sentences. *Am. Psychologist* 18 (1963): 735-51.
10. Piaget, J. *The language and thought of the child.* New York: Harcourt, Brace, 1926.
11. Reichling, A. Das Problem der Bedeutung in der Sprachwissenschaft. Innsbruckker—Beiträge zur Kulturwissenschaft. Sonderheft 19, Innsbruck, 1963.
12. Rommetveit, R. *Words, meanings and messages.* New York: Academic Press, and Oslo: Universitetsforlaget, 1968.
13. Rommetveit, R. Language games, deep syntactic structures and hermenentic circles. In F. Israël and H. Tajfel (ed.), in press.
14. Uhlenbeck, E. M. An appraisal of transformation theory. *Lingua* 12 (1963): 1-18.
15. Urmson, J. C., Parenthetical verbs. In C. E. Caton (ed.). *Philosophy and ordinary language.* Urbana: University of Illinois Press, 1963.
16. Vygotsky, L. S. *Thought and language.* Cambridge: M.I.T. Press, 1962.
17. Weinreich, U. On the semantic structure of language. In J. H. Greenberg (ed.), *Universals of language.* Cambridge: M.I.T. Press, 1963.
18. Weinreich, U. Explorations in semantic theory. In T. Sebeok (ed.), *Current Trends in linguistics,* Vol. III.

29

LANGUAGE AND TAT CONTENT IN BILINGUALS

Susan M. Ervin

Spoken language is, almost without exception, learned in a social setting. This setting includes material and behavioral referents for speech, rewards for speaking in a certain way about specific topics, and feelings towards those who hear and towards those who provide models of speech. Speakers in different language communities will have different things to say, and we may expect that learning a language carries with it learning of content.

Bilinguals provide a natural control for the investigation of content differences. Lambert, Havelka, and Crosby (1958) have shown that for "house," "drink," "poor," and "me," semantic-differential meanings differed for French-Canadian bilinguals. The pooled differences were significant only for those who learned the two languages in different physical settings. Since different social surroundings may occur in the same region, it is possible that the meanings of emotion or social-role terms might differ even for childhood bilinguals who learn two languages in the same physical surroundings.

With the purpose of studying content differences in speech, the present study compared two sets of Thematic Apperception Test (TAT) stories told by bilinguals about the same pictures at

Reprinted from *Journal of Abnormal and Social Psychology* 68, No. 5 (1964): 500–7. Copyright 1964 by The American Psychological Association, and reproduced by permission. Footnotes have been renumbered.

a French session and at an English session. The choice of languages was dictated by necessity (the author's ability to speak English and French) but it should be recognized that the languages and language community chosen were in some respects poor for testing the hypothesis of systematic content difference. The relationship of French and English makes generalization between them more likely; middle-class French and American cultures have many similarities; many of the bilinguals in the Washington, D. C., French community speak both languages with the same interlocutors. For all of these reasons content differences would be minimal.

Since economy precluded testing appropriate monolingual control groups, predictions regarding TAT differences were based on data about culture differences made available by Maccoby (1952) and by Métraux and Mead (1954), corroborated by other informants. Since that time, Wylie (1958) has confirmed some of the generalizations. A set of assumptions regarding the relation between TAT content and culture permitted specific predictions.

These assumptions were derived principally from Sanford's (Sanford, Adkins, Miller, Cobb, et al., 1943) study of the relation between school children's TAT stories and ratings of their behavior. In interpreting his findings, he proposed that: behavior that does not conflict with social sanctions appears in fantasy only if there is insufficient ability or opportunity for overt expression (e.g., achievement and dominance); behavior conflicting with social sanctions appears more often in fantasy expression; ambivalent cultural prescriptions lead to more primitivism in fantasy than in nonfantasy expression.

Because of the possibility, suggested by experimental work with the TAT, that the testing conditions might influence the extent to which content conflicted with social sanctions, it was decided to conduct testing individually, orally, and face-to-face. In these conditions, while socially prohibited needs might be expressed, it seemed that the form of expression might be governed by cultural differences in preferred modes. Otherwise there was the risk that a greater prohibition of a certain form of behavior in one of the two cultures would have ambiguous implications for predicting TAT thematic differences.

Specific predictions of differences were these:

1. For women, greater achievement need in English. This difference was based on the ambivalence of American education for women toward the role of housewife, in contrast with the French view, and on the greater sex-role difference in France.

2. More emphasis on recognition by others in English. This prediction was based on Kluckhohn's (1949) remark that emphasis is less on fulfillment and more on external success in America than in Europe. Riesman (1950) has made a statement which implies the contrary: he states that other-directed persons (such as Americans) want to "cut everyone down to size who stands up or stands out in any direction." The hypothesis of culture difference between France and America is thus a weak one.

3. More domination by elders in French stories. Parents were said to be more influential in selection of wives and jobs in France.

4. More withdrawal and autonomy in French stories. A characteristic mode of aggression reported within French families was silent withdrawal to do as one wished perhaps contrary to the wishes of another. Wylie (1958) reported that both children and adults after a disagreement tended to withdraw, and quoted a French child: "What we really do when we're angry is to go away from each other and not speak anymore [p. 199]."

5. More verbal aggression toward parents in English stories. Verbal attacks on elders are more strictly prohibited in France than in the United States, though Wylie reported considerable variation between families in the extent to which threats of punishment for verbal disrespect were carried out.

6. More verbal aggression toward peers in French stories. There is considerable admiration for verbal prowess in France. Wylie (1958) reports that this was true even in a rural village. French education emphasizes skill in oral argument, and children "are allowed to threaten and insult each other as much as they like [p. 50]."

7. More physical aggression in English stories. In France, children are immediately separated by adults if they begin to fight, and both are punished, according to Wylie, regardless of the culprit (p. 81). Presumably the culture difference would be greater for men than for women, since physical aggression is prohibited for American as well as French girls. However, there were too few men in the sample to permit a breakdown by sex.

8. More guilt in French stories and more frequent attempts to escape blame in English stories. This prediction was based in part on the age difference for acquisition of the two languages, on the assumption that a language learned in childhood would be more strongly associated with internalized values than one learned during adult life. Further, Métraux and Mead's (1954) informants reported greater emphasis in France on internal control of behavior

by adults, rejection of social pressure as a legitimate basis for action, and more strictness and consistency in child rearing.

In terms of the evidence of culture difference, the strongest evidence, most widely confirmed, concerns the forms of aggression preferred. The weakest evidence concerns the difference in the need for recognition.

METHOD

Subjects

Sixty-four adult French persons, raised in metropolitan France in middle-class families, were found in Washington, D. C. All had lived in the United States for more than 4 years and had learned English primarily from Americans. All of them spoke both languages fluently, the average number of years in the United States being 12. Forty were or had been married to Americans. The mean age was 38 years. Two-thirds were women.

Background Interview

An extensive interview determined how English was learned, how often and to whom both languages were spoken, and how much contact there had been with Americans. Scores from this interview were used to evaluate contact, amount of mixture, or switching of languages with the same interlocutors, degree of current French usage, education, and attitude toward linguistic interference. Details of this interview and other methodological information can be found in Ervin (1955).

Language Dominance Test

As a test of relative skill in French and English, a tape-recorded word-association test was constructed. The language of the stimulus word was varied at random in a list of words in various semantic domains, with frequency of the words in the respective languages matched. The subjects were instructed to offer orally an association to each word in the same language as the stimulus word. The score consisted of the median French reaction time in log seconds minus the median English time, when corrections had been made for translation responses and other language switches. The average subject, according to this test, was slightly French dominant.[1]

Materials and Procedure

Nine standard TAT pictures which elicit themes related to the hypotheses were selected: 1, 2, 3BM, 8BM, 6BM, 4, 13 MF, 7BM, and 18GF. They were presented in the above order. Subjects were given instructions to tell what was happening, what had happened in the past, what would happen in the future, and what the characters were thinking and feeling. In addition, at the second session, they were instructed to tell a different story if they recalled the first. Stories were to be 3 minutes long; a 3-minute glass was turned before the subject as he began each story.

The same examiner appeared at both sessions, speaking only French at the French session from the moment the subject appeared. The instructions were tape recorded in the appropriate language, and all responses were tape recorded. Analysis of content and of linguistic features was based on a verbatim typescript.

Design

Two groups were matched on the basis of sex, age, education, and language dominance. In addition, it was found that they were matched, on the average, in years in the United States, age at which English was learned, amount of contact with Americans, and amount of language switching. One group was instructed to tell French stories at the first session, and the other group told stories in English. There was a 6-week interval between the sessions for each subject.

Content Analysis

A quantitative system of analysis was adapted from those devised by McClelland, Atkinson, Clark, and Lowell (1953) and by Aron (1949). Each time a theme appeared in a story with a new actor (hero) and target of action, it was given a quantitative score. Thus a theme might be scored several times if in a given story the actor or object changed. If a picture "pulled" a particular theme—e.g., physical aggression in 18GF—each occurrence of the theme received a lower base score than if it was a rare theme for that picture. If there was more than a simple occurrence of the theme—

if there was adjectival or adverbial elaboration, addition of details, or repetition of the theme—the value might be increased by one or two points.

The reliability scores reported are product-moment correlations based on scores by picture for each theme. In the abbreviated category definitions below, reliabilities are presented in parentheses. The first is the reliability (product-moment correlation) of scores by two different coders, and the second the intracoder reliability with a 2-month interval. Since all coding in both languages was done by the author, the intracoder reliability is important.

Achievement (.77, .88). The hero is industrious. He fantasies hard work, studiousness, invention, attainment, accomplishment, reaching a career goal. He wants to accomplish great things. He prepares for or has achieved a profession, or a skilled occupation.

Recognition (.90, .81). The hero fantasies greatness, public acclaim, recognition by others, applause, prestige, renown. He seeks approval, boasts, performs in public, competes, strives to rise in status as a primary goal. He is a master; he is great.

Dominance (.84, .84). The hero tries to influence another by pleading or persuasion. He leads, directs, guides, advises, cajoles, but does not bring undue pressure, threaten withdrawal, or argue.

Withdrawal and autonomy (.69, .74). The hero does something bad, violates moral standards, or acts in a way contrary to the wishes of love objects. He makes them suffer or knowingly disappoints them. He expresses anger or dislike by turning away from, snubbing, or rejecting a love object.

Verbal aggression (.88, .87). The hero verbally expresses scorn, contempt, disdain. He quarrels, is involved in a misunderstanding or discussion (a more disputatious term in French than in English, but scored as verbal aggression in both languages).

Physical aggression (.81, .93). The hero fights, attacks physically, or injures, or kills another human being.

Guilt (.44, .73). The hero evaluates on the basis of moral principle. He avoids or regrets out of duty, moral standards, religious scruples. He resists temptation, or experiences anguish or regret. (The results will not be reported for this category because of the low reliability.)

Escaping blame (.70, .99). The hero seeks to avoid external censure or punishment by refraining from reprehensible acts, or by resorting to denial, deceit, or flight. He verbally defends himself against censure, proclaims his innocence, justifies his action.

Translation Control

Since there was a possibility of systematic bias in the scoring in the two languages, one of each subject's stories in each language was translated. These translations were given the appearance and style of originals, and were indistinguishable except by checking a code number. In the first phase of coding, the originals were removed, and the translations were mixed with the untranslated versions of each story for coding. In the second phase, 2 months later, the originals of the translated stories were mixed with other copies of previously coded stories for the intracoder reliability check.

Three kinds of checks were used to test coder bias. First, the intracoder reliabilities were compared for stories scored in the same language twice, and for stories scored in the original and in translation. It was found that achievement was scored more reliably when the story was in the same language both times. Reliability correlations differed at the .05 level. Escaping blame was scored more reliably in the same language at the .01 level. Thus it appeared that changing language might have led to different scoring standards. Such a difference might not be significant if it was unrelated to the hypotheses.

The total amount of each variable found in the originals and in the translations of the same stories were then compared to see if the differences in reliability were systematic. There were no significant differences.

Finally, the frequencies of the variables in all the stories coded in the first phase were compared to see if the stories coded in translation differed from those coded in the original language. There were no significant differences for any of the variables.

RESULTS

Content frequencies for each subject were weighted by the reciprocal of the total length in each language, since the stories in French were usually longer. The distributions of the variables were very skewed, medians of zero occurring for all but three variables. These distributions reflected the fact that some themes were readily elicited by the pictures, others not so readily. One might characterize the pictures as differing in their power to bring out thematic material above a threshold of overt speech. Presumably other pictures might have elicited responses from all subjects, and allowed a measure of session differences for all subjects for each theme. In order to make an analysis of variance possible in spite of the skewed distributions, the assumption was made that subjects who gave no responses relevant to a given theme at either session were randomly distributed as to session differences. Since the relative strength of their responses was in effect not measured, there was no way of knowing whether appropriate pictures would have elicited more thematic material in French or in English. In calculation of the analysis of variance, for each theme, subjects were removed who never used the theme at either session. For Physical Aggression and Withdrawal-Autonomy this adjustment was not necessary, and all subjects were included. The remaining frequencies were transformed to the logarithm of $X + 1$.

The analysis of variance was a Lindquist (1956) Type I design, with the group to which the subject was assigned a between-subject effect, and the session and language as within-subject effects. Because of the four-celled Latin-square design, there was con- founding of certain types of interaction. The effects of language in this design appear as an interaction of session with group, since Session I is in French for one group and in English for the other. There is likely to be an interaction of language with session for certain variables, however, and this interaction cannot be isolated.

With these limitations, three variables showed significant language effects in the predicted direction: Verbal Aggression to Peers, Withdrawal-Autonomy, and Achievement. In addition, there was a significant group difference in Recognition, with no effect of language at all.

The following stories will illustrate the difference between the French and English versions by the same subject, a 27-year-old Frenchwoman, married to an American, who spoke English with her husband and child. Most of her friends were Americans. She was a full-time clerk, using English for the most part in her work. The stories were told for Picture 4 in the Murray series.

[French, first session] She seems to beg him, to plead with him. I don't know if he wants to leave her for another woman or what, or if it's her who has . . . but she seems to press against him. I think he wants to leave her because he's found another woman he loves more, and that he really wants to go, or maybe it's because she . . . she's deceived him with another man. I don't know

Table 1. Weighted Content Differences in TAT Stories

Content variable	N^a	32 French-first M[b]		32 English-first M		df	F for language[c]
		F_1	E_2	F_2	E_1		
Achievement (women)	21	14.3	26.6	21.1	25.1	1/40	6.148*
Recognition	24	4.7	4.8	7.3	8.3	1/46	—[d]
Dominance to younger	27	5.3	4.4	4.8	3.2	1/52	2.051
Withdrawal-autonomy	32	30.5	24.8	25.5	21.0	1/62	9.234**
Verbal							
Aggression to elders	17	3.6	4.4	1.5	2.2	1/32	1.682
Aggression to peers	20	5.1	4.9	4.7	3.2	1/38	5.333*
Physical agression	32	10.8	15.3	12.3	11.0	1/62	1.709
Escaping blame	16	2.3	3.2	2.3	3.8	1/30	3.926

[a]N in each group after cases with zero in both sessions had been removed.
[b]Means for the weighted raw scores of the total sample of 32 in each group.
[c]Lindquist's Type I analysis, with Language as a within-subject effect, and a within-subject error term derived from the within-subject sum of squares minus Session and Language.
[d]The Group effect here had an F of 5.503, $p < .025$.
*$p < .05$.
**$p < .01$.

whose fault it is but they certainly seem angry. Unless it's in his work, and he wants to go see someone and he wants to get in a fight with someone, and she holds him back and doesn't like him to get angry. I don't know, it could be many things. . . .

[English, second session] Oh, that one. In the past, well I think it was a married couple, average, and he got out of the Army and got himself a job or something like that or has decided he would go to college. He's decided to get a good education and maybe after he would have a better job and be able to support his wife much better, and everything would come out for the best. He keeps on working and going to college at night some of the time. Now let me see. He finally decided that was too much. He found he was too tired, he was discouraged and something went wrong with his work. The boss told him that, well, his production had decreased or something like that, that he didn't get enough sleep or something like that, that he couldn't carry on studies and working at the same time. He'd have to give something up, and he's very discouraged and his wife tries to cheer him up. Now, let me see. And eventually he'll probably keep on working his way through and finally get his diploma and get a better job and they will be much happier and . . . well, his wife will have helped him along too and as he was discouraged and all and was willing to give up everything, she boosted him up. That's all.

In French the picture elicited a variety of themes of aggression and striving for autonomy. In English the heroine supports the husband in his achievement strivings.

The subject below was a 33-year-old bachelor, with higher education in both countries. Most of his friends were Americans, but he used French in his work. The picture was 13MF.

[English, first session] Now this is a horrible story. This is one of those, one of those things that happen in married life when the husband suddenly finds out his own intelligence, his own way of living, his own . . . life altogether has gone to pieces. There is no weapon around in the room. But there is the hand which have murdered. There is the guilt of having in a moment of horrible passion, of aberration of mind when she was telling him that she loved the other, that he was more intelligent, that he was more beautiful, that he let himself go and put his fingers around her neck. And her laughter became more and more raucous. He had pressed down his thumbs and then he has gotten up, has dressed. The horror of the moment becomes entirely obvious to him. He knows that the next thing he will have to do is to go to the police and report it—maybe to flee, maybe to take his car and drive away. What kind of a life that will be. Constantly this thing in front of him. A dead body in the bed half-naked. Over the sheets. Police. Discovery. Warrants. Sirens. Shame. Flight. And perhaps prison and perhaps death. All this goes through his mind as he wonders where to go.

[French, second session] That's not a scene of a household but of a false household. There are sometimes false households with love, and there are those with hatred. This is a false household with hatred. They detest each other, and cannot separate. They are held together by physical attraction as much as by their quarrels, quarrels which change their life from an everyday life, a life which becomes infernal and at the same time different. If they had no quarrels they would be nearly dead with boredom, and when they are separated they desire only to see each other. He is still young, she already older, and it is she basically who holds him. He, too young, doesn't want to marry. She, older, wants only one thing, a home. Then, to oblige this man to live with her, to found this home she wants, she tries to hold him, to live with him at any price even if it is torture for both. Their joy, their only joy is physical contact, and even this joy has dangers of torture, of horror because for them this physical life is a bond, a terrible bond, of which he particularly is aware. This is how the woman holds him. He detests her and yet cannot detach himself. What we see here is the night when he has slept with her another, time, dressed, and while she sleeps, he wants to leave, to leave forever, to forget this inhuman life, tear the bonds which . . . one becomes enslaved to this woman. He hides his eyes still, an instant of reflection, then takes his two books and goes out the door forever.

The last two stories contrast aggression by physical assault with aggression by quarreling and escape. Certain characteristics of the English story reflect mass media models.

DISCUSSION

There are several alternative explanations for the differences in content, none of which can as yet be excluded. One explanation is that the subjects interpreted the instructions to speak a particular language as an instruction to tell a story appropriate to that language. Such an alternative could be tested by giving instructions to give appropriate stories, while the language is held constant. No such control was used.

A second possibility is that language affects classification of stimuli (Ervin, 1961b) and presumably recall of experience through the classification (Brown & Lenneberg, 1954), and that bilinguals have systematically different recall of past experience in two languages. If we extrapolate findings from recall of simple pictured objects (Ervin, 1961a), we would expect that use of the weaker language would have a strong biasing tendency toward recall of experiences originally codified in that language and appropriate to its culture.

Third, the thematic differences may reflect the respective mass media. Those who use projective tests to assess individual differences usually dismiss this explanation and point out that selective reading, viewing, and recall are pertinent to differences usually dismiss this explanation and point out that selective reading, viewing, and recall are pertinent to differences. But such an argument cannot be used when cross-cultural comparisons are at issue, since exposure is not then entirely self-selected but is culturally imposed, and there is little doubt that there are systematic differences in thematic frequencies in the mass media in different countries.

A fourth alternative is that the differences are not due merely to contrasts in the mass media, but to more pervasive differences in the verbal preoccupations and values expressed verbally in the two cultures. Thus it may be said that story themes may reflect the gossip, verbalized personal experiences, and verbal evaluations of the behavior of oneself and others which have been experienced in the two cultural settings.

It should be noted that much value learning comes from verbal sources; condemnation of murder is learned not by punishment for murder, but by verbal learning of what is classified as murder (not killing in war, for instance), and by learning emotional attitudes toward verbal descriptions of murder and what happens to murderers; only in part is it learned by generalization of punishment for committed aggressive acts. Nobody concerned with education, propaganda, advertising, or the study of opinion change through role playing would dismiss the possibility that verbal sequences may affect other behavior as well, and thus create consistency with nonverbal behavior. Some of the effect of verbal sequences on other behavior may come through what has come to be known as verbal mediation. Self-control through verbal mediation has been studied in relatively few situations (e.g., Luria, 1961). Since the origins of such mediation may lie in verbal training conditions in early childhood, which vary widely, we can expect significant group and individual differences in the extent to which verbal training affects nonverbal behavior.

Finally, quite aside from such mediational effects, it is possible that a shift in language is associated with a shift in social roles and emotional attitudes. Since each language is learned and usually employed with different persons and in a different context, the use of each language may come to be associated with shift in a large array of behavior. Presumably such changes would have to be assessed nonverbally, at least in part through physiological measures, to separate changes in emotional state from the verbal statements by which attitudes are usually judged.

The above explanations can be summarized as attributing content changes with language to different interpretation of instructions, differences in perception and in recall of experience, to the effects of mass media; to differences in verbally expressed values; and to role or attitude shifts associated with contacts with the respective language communities.

Do these findings mean that our subjects have two personalities? The answer seems to be yes, at least to the extent that personality involves verbal behavior and perhaps further. This is a result no more surprising than any other shift in behavior with social context. It happens that bilinguals have available an additional dimension of potential variation in behavior in comparison with the alternative roles available to monolinguals.

But language is a very important dimension. It is not yet clear whether the differences found in bilinguals are merely a special case of biculturalism, or whether the fact that language is a medium not only for social behavior but for internal storage of information and self-control implies that bilinguals have a means of insulating sets of alternative behavior more pervasive than mere contrasts in behavior for different social situations or audiences.

Our basis for choosing between these explanations is at present slight. The fact that certain variables yielded stronger content differences than others may provide a clue. For this purpose, we may exclude Recognition, for which the evidence for an actual culture contrast on which to base a prediction was from the start precarious. The largest differences appeared in Autonomy, Verbal Aggression against Peers, and Achievement in Women. The smallest appeared in Physical Aggression, Domination by Elders, and Verbal Aggression against Parents. One feature that the first three share is that they are likely to be the preoccupations of adults, in contrast with the second three. Quite simply, adults who move to the United States from France may observe cultural contrasts in those domains of interpersonal relations that they observe directly in consequence of the roles into which they are cast as adults. If some of this learning is second hand, from the mass media, then it selectively reflects adult concerns. Physical aggression is certainly a common feature of the mass media in this country, yet the contrast in the amount mentioned in the French and English stories was not significant.

Not all of the subjects displayed content differences of the sort found in the averages. Too little data on individual acculturative experiences were available to account for the individual differences. Presumably some people are attracted to a second culture because they are already deviant in their own; others never adapt to a new culture but merely translate the familiar into a new language. Ervin and Osgood (1954) had suggested earlier that "coordinate" bilinguals who learned both languages in distinct settings should display these differences more than those who learn in one setting. All of the bilinguals in this study were coordinate bilinguals by this criterion but there was a wide range in their actual learning. Of all the variables measured—amount of switching with interlocutors, amount of linguistic interference in the stories from the other language, contact with Americans, attitude towards assimilation, having children reared here—none correlated markedly with the degree of contrast found. Thus the clarification of both the nature of the contrast we observed grossly and the indivdual process by which the differences develop must await later research.

NOTE

[1]Superior language dominance tests have since been constructed. Literate subjects may use a machine devised by Lambert (1955) which measures reactions to printed words. A pictorial test, measuring time in naming simple objects, was used by Ervin (1961a).

REFERENCES

Aron, Betty. *A manual for analysis of the Thematic Apperception Test.* Berkeley, Calif.: Willis E. Berg, 1949.

Brown, R. W., & Lenneberg, E. H. A study in language and cognition. *J. abnorm. soc. Psychol.*, 1954, 49: 454–462.

Ervin, Susan M. *The verbal behavior of bilinguals: The effect of language of report upon the Thematic Apperception Test stories of adult French bilinguals.* (Doctoral dissertation, University of Michigan) Ann Arbor, Mich.: University Microfilms, 1955, MicA 55-2228.

Ervin, Susan M. Learning and recall in bilinguals. *Amer. J. Psychol.*, 1961, 74: 446–451. (a)

Ervin, Susan M. Semantic shift in bilingualism. *Amer. J. Psychol.*, 1961, 74: 233–241. (b)

Ervin, Susan M., & Osgood, C. E. Second language learning and bilingualism. *J. abnorm. soc. Psychol.*, 1954, 49(Pt. 2): 139–146.

Kluckhohn, C. *Mirror for man.* New York: McGraw-Hill, 1949.

Lambert, W. E. Measurement of the linguistic dominance of bilinguals. *J. abnorm. soc. Psychol.*, 1955, 50: 197–200.

Lambert, W. E., Havelka, J., & Crosby, C. The influence of language-acquisition contexts on bilingualism. *J. abnorm. soc. Psychol.*, 1958, 56: 239–244.

Lindquist, E. F. *Design and analysis of experiments in psychology and education.* Boston: Houghton Mifflin, 1956.

Luria, A. R. *The role of speech in the regulation of normal and abnormal behavior.* New York: Liveright, 1961.

McClelland, D. C., Atkinson, J. W., Clark, R. A., & Lowell, E. L. *The achievement motive.* New York: Appleton-Century-Crofts, 1953.

Maccoby, Eleanor. Some notes on French childrearing among the Parisian middle class. Cambridge: Harvard Laboratory of Human Development, 1952. (Ditto)

Métraux, Rhoda, & Mead, Margaret. *Themes in French culture.* Stanford: Stanford University Press, 1954.

Riesman, D. *The lonely crowd.* New Haven: Yale University Press, 1950.

Sanford, R. N., Adkins, M. M., Miller, R. B., Cobb, E. A., et al. Physique, personality, and scholarship: A cooperative study of school children. *Monogr. Soc. Res. Child Develpm.*, 1943, 8.

Wylie, L. *Village in the Vaucluse.* Cambridge: Harvard University Press, 1958.

30

REASONING AND SPATIAL REPRESENTATIONS

Stephen Handel
Clinton B. DeSoto
Marvin London

Psychologists of such widely different theoretical orientations as Lashley (1961) and Inhelder and Piaget (1964) have noted that ordering elements in thinking is so commonplace that it is easy to overlook the question of how it is accomplished. These researchers have suggested that spatial representations subserve even nonspatial orderings in thinking; even in abstract reasoning tasks people rely on internal spatial constructions as thought models.

The widespread use of spatial metaphors to describe nonspatial ordering relations—*higher* status, *upper* crust, etc.—seems to provide glimpses of the inner constructions of which Lashley and Piaget wrote. However, they might reveal nothing more than fortuitous linguistic conventions. In one attempt to provide another kind of evidence, DeSoto, London, and Handel (1965) developed a model for a spatial paralogic which asserts that individuals construct spatial representations in solving linear syllogisms.

Reprinted from *Journal of Verbal Learning and Verbal Behavior* 7 (1968): 351–57.

SPATIAL PARALOGIC THEORY

Spatial Representations

The degree to which relations are tied to spatial axes was evaluated by DeSoto *et al.* (1965) and in the present study by giving *S*s statements like *Tom is better than Bill* and asking them to position the names in two-dimensional space. DeSoto *et al.* (1965) found that the better-worse relation is oriented vertically with the "better" man placed on top whether the premise is *Tom is better than Bill* or *Bill is worse than Tom.* "Better" and "worse" are tied to spatial axes, have a hierarchical organization, and are called consistent relation words. Inconsistent relation words are not consistently placed on axes and do not have a hierarchical organization. The relation lighter hair-darker hair does not have a consistent spatial assignment. The same *S* may visualize the "lighter haired" person on top if the premise is *Tom has lighter hair than Bill*, but may visualize the "darker haired" person on top if the premise is *Bill has darker hair than Tom.* These spatial representations merely reflect the position of the elements in the premise statement.

Linear Syllogisms

A linear syllogism consists of two premises specifying order relations among three elements followed by a question: e.g., *Tom is better than Bill, Mike is worse than Bill, Is Tom worse than Mike?.* The difficulty of solving a linear syllogism is measured by the percentage of *S*s able to answer the question. The eight possible combinations of premises which can be constructed from a pair of opposite relation words are shown in Table 3; R represents one relation and R' represents the opposite relation. There are four possible questions for each syllogism: *Is Tom better than Mike?, Is Mike better than Tom?, Is Tom worse than Mike?, Is Mike worse than Tom?.*

Paralogic of Spatially Tied Relations

DeSoto *et al.* (1965) demonstrated that two principles could be used to explain the difficulty of the premise combinations shown in Table 3.

    Directionality. In our culture, people think downward or rightward more easily than upward or leftward. Thus *Tom is above Bill* or *Tom is to the left of Bill* is more easily apprehended than *Bill is below Tom* or *Bill is to the right of Tom.* In applying this principle to novel relation words, we must first determine their preferred spatial representation. For example, the premise *John is cleaner than Carl* proceeds downward if the "cleaner" person is visualized at the top of the vertical axis, but it proceeds upward (and is harder to apprehend) if the "dirtier" person is visualized at the top.

This principle can be applied to premise combinations in two ways: within premises and between premises. In Table 3, Combination 1 proceeds downward within premises since for each premise, the top element is the first element in the premise. Combination 1 proceeds downward between premises since the pair of people in the first premise are in the top and middle positions and the pair of people in the second premise are in the middle and bottom positions. Combinations 2 and 3 are of intermediate difficulty because in one sense the premises go downward, and in the second sense they proceed upward. Combination 4 is difficult to solve because the premises proceed upward both within and between premises. The difficulty of Combinations 5 through 8 cannot be explained by within-premise direction since they have one downward and one upward premise statement. However, Combination 5 should be easier than 6 and Combination 7 easier than 8 due to downward between-premise direction. The same pattern of difficulty would occur for relations represented along the horizontal axis if we substitute rightward for downward.

If, however, *S* visualized the "worse" person at the top of the vertical axis or the left of the horizontal axis, the predictions for premise combination difficulty would be reversed. Combination 4 now proceeds downward both within and between premises, while Combination 1 proceeds upward in both senses so that Combination 4 should be easier than Combination 1.

End-Anchoring. The second principle, used when different relation words appear in the two premises, is end anchoring: premises are more easily understood when they proceed from the ends of the ordering to the middle. Therefore Combination 5 should be easier than 7, and Combination 6 should be easier than 8.

Paralogic of Nonspatially Tied Relations

The above analysis applies only to relations which have preferred directions of reasoning. For inconsistent relations, the relation word used in the first premise determines the spatial assignment. For instance, if the first premise is *John has lighter hair than Bill,* then John will be visualized either at the top or at the left and the representation proceeds downward or rightward from "lighter hair" to "darker hair." In the previous study, 88 percent of Ss placed the first name in the left or top position. If the relation of the second premise is "lighter hair," then the second premise dovetails with the spatial representation given to the first premise and the premise combination should be easy. But, if the relation of the second premise is "darker-hair," the premise combination should be harder since S can't readily transform the second premise to match the assignment already given to the first premise. Only 46 percent of Ss transformed the second premise in the previous study. Syllogisms using relations which are not spatially tied should be easy when the premises have identical relation words (Combinations 1, 2, 3, 4) and difficult when the premises have different relation words (Combinations 5, 6, 7, 8).

Present Experiment

One goal of the present experiment is to determine whether the spatial paralogic theory developed by DeSoto *et al.* (1965) from a small set of ordering words can be applied to different words. If spatial representations underlie syllogistic reasoning, then relations with the same spatial representation should show the same order of premise-combination difficulty. For example, since the descent relation, father-son, has always been diagrammed and thought of spatially on a vertical axis (Davis and Warner, 1937), the difficulty of premise combinations using father-son should be analogous to the difficulty of premise combinations using different relation words which are also spatially represented from top to bottom. Better-worse was found to be represented from top to bottom by DeSoto *et al.* (1965) and can serve as a model.

The second goal is to attempt to predict each S's performance on the syllogism-reasoning task from the S's own spatial representation. This was impossible in the previous study since different Ss were used for each task.

METHOD

Subjects

The Ss were 122 evening students enrolled in psychology classes at Johns Hopkins University. They were run in classes of about 30.

Task and Procedure

Each *S* was given two booklets, one for the linear syllogism-reasoning task and one for the spatial assignment task.

Reasoning task.   The *S*s first solved the reasoning task consisting of 68 different linear syllogisms printed on separate sheets of paper. There were 32 syllogisms using the father-son relation representing the 32 possible arrangements from eight premise combinations, each with four questions. The other 36 syllogisms used the relations more-less, earlier-later, farther-nearer, cause-effect and faster-slower in Premise Combinations 1, 4, 5, and 7, and two additional combinations in which the information given was insufficient to solve the syllogism (e.g., *Jack has more than Doug, Bill has more than Doug, Does Jack have more than Bill?*). Two questions were used for the cause-effect relation and one question was used for the other relations. The two additional premise combinations in which the information was insufficient showed essentially no variation in difficulty across the relation words and are not included in the results.

The two premise statements and the question were typed in three rows and under the question were three possible answers: "Yes," "No," or "?". The *S*s were told to circle "Yes" if the syllogism was correct, "No" if the syllogism was incorrect, "?" if there was insufficient information, and not to circle any answer if they did not know the answer. The *S*s had 10-seconds to solve each syllogism, and the syllogisms were presented in random order, with the restriction that syllogisms with the same relation words were kept apart.

Spatial Assignment Task.   There were 12 sheets, one sheet for each relation word in the second booklet. Each sheet had a premise statement on the left side and a horizontal and a vertical line crossing at 90° on the right side. At both ends of each line was a box. The *S* was asked to write the premise names in whatever boxes seemed most appropriate in view of the relation. The sheets were arranged in random order. The task was self-paced, and *S*s were not allowed to look back at previous responses.

RESULTS AND DISCUSSION

Spatial Assignments

Table 1 shows the percentages of *S*s making given spatial assignments of the relation words. The first (Top to Bottom) row of Table

Table 1. Percentages of Types of Spatial Assignments for All Relation Words

Spatial assignment	Better-worse*	Father-son	More-less	Earlier-later	Cause-effect	Faster-slower	Farther-nearer	Lighter hair-darker hair*
Top to bottom	78	74	71	21	32	25	9	12
Left to right	2	6	4	39	25	16	4	14
Bottom to top	0	1	1	3	2	0	6	4
Right to left	2	2	5	14	1	34	38	16
Inconsistent	18	18	20	24	41	25	43	54

*The spatial assignments for *Better-worse* and *Lighter hair-darker hair* are reported by DeSoto et al. (1965).

Table 2. Percentages of Correct Answers for Certain Premise Combinations of All Relation Words

Premise combination	Better-worse*	Father-son	More-less	Earlier-later	Cause-effect	Faster-slower	Farther-nearer	Lighter hair-darker hair*
1	61	67	77	71	62	76	63	63
4	43	53	56	53	42	69	57	64
5	62	69	65	51	38	60	34	40
7	42	52	33	38	32	41	29	25

*The percentages of correct answers for *Better-worse* and *Lighter hair-darker hair* are reported by DeSoto et al. (1965).

1 indicates the percentage of times the first word of the pair of relation words was placed at the top of the vertical axis. For example, 21 percent of the time the "earlier" person was placed on top. Similarily, the right-to-left spatial assignments can represent the percentage of time the "earlier" person was placed on the right. The inconsistent row represents the percentage of Ss who did not have a consistent spatial assignment for the relation words. The relations in Table 1 demonstrate patterns ranging from the highly consistent top-to-bottom assignment of better-worse, father-son, and more-less to the inconsistent assignment of lighter hair-darker hair.

Syllogistic Reasoning

The percentages correct for Premise Combinations 1, 4, 5, and 7 for all the relation words are shown in Table 2. The patterns of difficulty are generally quite different but certain similarities exist. For example, the relation words farther-nearer, faster-slower, and cause-effect seem to have a similar pattern of difficulty.

Spatial Assignment and Syllogistic Reasoning

The major hypothesis of this study was that spatial representations underlies the ability to solve linear syllogisms. Several approaches were used to test this hypothesis.

The first approach was to demonstrate that the pattern of premise-combination difficulty when using father-son and better-worse is similar. Table 3 shows the percentage correct of all premise combinations for father-son and better-worse. The relative difficulty of the premise combinations is essentially the same, with a rank order correlation of .99 ($df = 7$, $p < .01$). Since father-son and better-worse have nearly identical spatial assignments, the prediction that relations with the same spatial representation should show the same ordering of premise-combination difficulty is confirmed. Not only are descent relations generally thought of as going from father to son, but Ss appear to use this representation in solving linear syllogisms involving descent.

The second approach was to demonstrate that relations having similar patterns of spatial assignments also have similar patterns of premise-combination difficulty. An eight-by-eight intercorrelation matrix of the relation words was constructed from Table 1 by correlating across the spatial assignments. By rearranging the rows and columns of the matrix, three distinct groups of relation words

Table 3. Percentages of Correct Answer for All Premise Combinations Based on *Better-worse* and *Father-son*

Premise combinations	Premise combination based on *Better-worse**	Percent correct	Premise combination based on *Father-son*	Percent correct	Analysis	
1. ARB	A is better than B	61	A is the father of B	67	Within premise	Down
BRC	B is better than C		B is the father of C		Between premise	Down
2. BRC	B is better than C	53	B is the father of C	57	Within premise	Down
ARB	A is better than C		A is the father of B		Between premise	Up
3. BR'A	B is worse than A	50	B is the son of A	53	Within premise	Up
CR'B	C is worse than B		C is the son of B		Between premise	Down
4. CR'B	C is worse than B	43	C is the son of B	53	Within premise	Up
BR'A	B is worse than A		B is the son of A		Between premise	Up
5. ARB	A is better than B	62	A is the father of B	69	Within premise	Ends to middle
CR'B	C is worse than B		C is the son of B		Between premise	Down
6. CR'B	C is worse than B	57	C is the son of B	61	Within premise	Ends to middle
ARB	A is better than B		A is the father of B		Between premise	Up
7. BR'A	B is worse than A	42	B is the son of A	52	Within premise	Middle to ends
BRC	B is better than C		B is the father of C		Between premise	Down
8. BRC	B is better than C	38	B is the father of C	50	Within premise	Middle to ends
BR'A	B is worse than A		B is the son of A		Between premise	Up

*The data for *Better-worse* are reported in DeSoto *et al.* (1965). Since that study found only a small premise-combination by question interaction, only the mean percent correct averaged over all questions is shown.

emerged. Each group represents relation words that show similar patterns in their spatial assignments; i.e., their intercorrelations are high. Alternatively, a second eight-by-eight intercorrelation matrix of the relation words was formed from Table 2 by correlating across premise combinations. The same three groups emerged in this matrix. These similar patterns of intercorrelations are strong support for the relation between spatial representations and premise-combination difficulty.

The first group (Better-worse, Father-son, More-less) consists of relation words which proceed from the top to the bottom and therefore show a pattern of difficulty with Premise Combinations 1 and 5 easy, and 4 and 7 difficult. The second group (Farther-nearer, Faster-slower, Lighter hair-darker hair) is not consistently tied to any spatial representation; for these, the syllogisms should be easy when the relation words are identical in both premises, and hard when the relation words are different. The spatial assignments for the third group (earlier-later, cause-effect) are of three types: top to bottom, left to right, and inconsistent. The top-to-bottom and left-to-right assignments lead to the prediction that Premise Combination 1 should be easier than 4. Although end anchoring should make Combination 5 easier than 7, the inconsistent assignments should tend to make both 5 and 7 difficult. All of these predictions are borne out.

In summary, the patterns of similarity in Table 1 and Table 2 are closely matched. The same groups of relation words are derived from the similarity of patterns of spatial assignments or from the similarity of patterns of premise-combination difficulty. In addition, it is possible to use the average spatial assignments of each of the three groups to predict premise-combination difficulty.

The third approach is to use directly the spatial assignments to predict premise-combination difficulty. The rank-order correlation of each row in the spatial-assignment table with each row in the premise-combination table tests whether increasing the proportion of Ss using one type of spatial assignment results in increasing or decreasing the probability of correctly solving one type of premise combination. Since some relation words are easier overall, it is possible to correlate the spatial assignments with the actual percentage of Ss solving a syllogism or with a normalized value (x or z). The correlations based on each of these measures was averaged to get an overall index of correlation, and these are shown in Table 4 (see Cronbach and Gleser, 1953, for a discussion of this problem).

Table 4. Average Rank-Order Correlations Between Premise Combinations and Spatial Assignments

| | Spatial assignments | | | | | |
| | Top to bottom Left to right | | Bottom to top Right to left | | Inconsistent | |
Premise combinations	Predicted correlation	Actual correlation	Predicted correlation	Actual correlation	Predicted correlation	Actual correlation
1	+	+.25	−	−.10		−.11
4	−	−.76*	+	+.88*		+.68
5	+	+.89**	−	−.63	−	−.92**
7	+	+.26	−	−.22	−	−.29

*$p < .05$.
**$p < .01$.

Paralogic theory would predict no difference in the rank order of premise-combination difficulty if either the top-to-bottom or left-to-right spatial assignments were used. Therefore these two assignments were averaged and used as one of the variables in the correlation matrix. Similarly, the bottom-to-top and right-to-left assignments were averaged.

The predicted directions of all the correlations are also shown in Table 4. For example, paralogic theory predicts that the top-to-bottom and left-to-right assignments should aid the solution of Combinations 1, 5, and 7 (positive correlation) and hinder the solution of Combination 4 (negative correlation). The reverse predictions are made for the bottom-to-top and right-to-left spatial assignments. Inconsistent assignments should hinder the solution of Combinations 5 and 6 but no predictions can be made for the correlation between inconsistent assignments and Combinations 1 and 4.

All predictions are in the correct direction although the correlations are significant only for Combinations 4 and 5. One possible reason that Combinations 1 and 7 do not correlate significantly with spatial assignment is that these premise combinations show a very restricted range of difficulty, so that the rank order of difficulty probably suffers from sampling fluctuations.

Individual Assignments

Each S solved the syllogisms and gave spatial assignments. It is possible to get the pattern of premise-combination difficulty for each type of spatial assignment and see if the pattern of difficulty conforms to that hypothesized for each type of spatial assignment. The results of this analysis are ambiguous. Most predictions are in the proper direction although predictions of absolute magnitudes are not fulfilled. For example, paralogic theory would predict that Ss giving a right-to-left spatial assignment would find Combination 4 easier than Combination 1. However, these Ss still solved Combination 1 more readily than Combination 4, although the difference in difficulty between these two premise combinations was least for these Ss. It is clear that using S's spatial representations alone does not adequately tap the reasoning process.

CONCLUSIONS

The present experiment has generalized the results found by DeSoto *et al.* (1965) and has further substantiated the view that spatial representations underlie the solution of linear syllogisms. People have the ability to order elements in a cognitive space, of at least two dimensions, which has properties not found in geometric space. It is easier to represent relationships vertically in this cognitive space and to order from the top element to the bottom element. In addition, the highest and the lowest elements are used as anchors to aid in organizing the middle elements. Further research is needed to trace the development of this cognitive space and to evaluate the effect of certain motor stereotypes, such as reading direction, on spatial representations.

REFERENCES

Cronbach, L. J., and Gleser, G. C. Assessing similarity between profiles, *Psychol. Bull.*, 1953, 50; 456–474.

Davis, K., and Warner, W. L. Structural analysis of kinship, *Amer. Anthrop.*, 1937, 39: 291–313.

DeSoto, C. B., London, M., and Handel, S. Social reasoning and spatial paralogic. *J. Pers. soc. Psychol.*, 1965, 2: 513–521.

Inhelder, B., and Piaget, J. *The early growth of logic in the child*, New York: Harper, 1964.

Lashley, K. S. The problem of serial order in behavior. In L. A. Jeffress (ed.), *Cerebral mechanisms in behavior*. New York: Wiley, 1951. Pp. 112–136.

31

MOTIVATION AND LANGUAGE BEHAVIOR: A CONTENT ANALYSIS OF SUICIDE NOTES

Charles E. Osgood
Evelyn G. Walker

Whenever a person produces a message, whether it be conversation, an ordinary letter to a relative, or a suicide note, he employs a complex set of encoding habits. It seems reasonable to assume that these language habits are organized in much the same way as the habits underlying nonlanguage behavior and that the general principles of learning and performance therefore apply equivalently in both cases. This paper is concerned with the effects of motivation upon language behavior. It is assumed that the author of a suicide note—presumably written shortly before he takes his own life—is functioning under heightened motivation. Therefore, the structure and content of suicide notes should differ from both ordinary letters and from simulated suicide notes in certain ways predictable from a general theory of behavior. Following a brief theoretical discussion, we describe the application of a number of relevant content measures to a comparison, first, of suicide notes with ordinary letters to relatives and, second, of suicide notes with

Reprinted from *Journal of Abnormal and Social Psychology* 59 (1959): 58–67. Copyright 1959 by The American Psychological Association, and reproduced by permission.

faked notes. Many of these measures differentiate in predicted ways suicide notes from normal control notes; a smaller number differentiate suicide from simulated suicide notes, suggesting that nonsuicidal individuals are able to adopt the state of the suicidal person in some respects but not in others.

Language habits, like habits in general, appear to be organized into hierarchies of alternatives. We shall assume that increased drive has two distinct effects upon selection within such hierarchies: generalized energizing effects and specific cue effects (cf., Osgood, 1957, for a more complete analysis).

The generalized energizing effects of drives are characterized by a nonspecific facilitation of all habits. Following the views expressed by Hebb (1955), one may identify the generalized energizing effects of drives with arousal of a neural system in the brainstem from which there is diffuse, nonspecific projection into the cortex, these impulses having a summative, "tuning-up" function. Assuming a multiplicative relation between habit strength and drive in producing reaction potential (cf., Spence, Farber, & McFann, 1956), the effect of increasing drive should be to make the dominant alternatives within all hierarchies even more probable relatively. Our first prediction, therefore: (A) *Suicide notes will be characterized by greater stereotypy than messages produced under lower degrees of motivation.* Suicide notes should therefore be more repetitious, less diversified in lexical content, use fewer adjectival and adverbial qualifiers, more familiar words and phrases, and so on. However, since the maximum strengths of habits are assumed to be asymptotic, extreme increase in drive should force many competing habits toward a common maximum and hence produce interference and blocking. Therefore: (B) *If extremely high levels of drive can be assumed, suicide notes should display greater disorganization of language behavior.* This would include various kinds of errors, breaking up of messages into shorter units, and similar phenomena.

To the extent that drive states are accompanied by distinctive sensations—e.g., thirst sensations, feelings of anxiety, sensations of pain—these distinctive cues can become associated with certain alternatives within habit hierarchies through the operation of ordinary learning principles. The presence of such cues, as directive states, will have the effect of modifying the probability structure of behavioral hierarchies, increasing the probability of some alternatives, decreasing the probability of others. This leads to the following prediction: (C) *Suicide notes should be characterized by increased frequency of those grammatical and lexical choices associated with the motives leading to self-destruction.* On a rather mundane level, this means that suicide notes should contain a relatively high frequency of self- and other-critical statements. Less obviously, they should contain a high frequency of what Skinner (1957) calls "mands"—constructions of the demand, command, request type that express needs of the speaker and require some behavior on the part of the listener for their satisfaction. Finally, if two or more motives are operating, and their cues are associated with selection of different alternatives within hierarchies, one may expect oscillation between the responses associated with each state. Since it seems reasonable to assume that suicidal people will often be functioning under competing motives, e.g., self-criticism versus self-protection, spouse-aggression versus spouse-affection, etc., we may predict that: (D) *Suicide notes should be characterized by more evidence of conflict than messages produced under nonsuicidal states.* Among indices of conflict would be use of constructions with *but, however, if,* and the like, qualification of verb phrases, and ambivalence in the assertions made about significant persons.

METHOD

The suicide materials for this study consisted of two samples. The first was a set of 100 genuine suicide notes, 50 written by men and 50 written by women just prior to taking their own lives. These were obtained from Edwin S. Shneidman from his Los Angeles files. For comparison purposes, we obtained a sample of ordinary letters written to 100 members of a panel of *S*s in the Champaign-Urbana area; this panel had been used for other purposes in connection with research on the communication of mental health information. Since many of the quantitative measures we wished to make made it desirable that the messages include at least 100 words or so, the total sample was reduced to the following: 40 male suicide; 29 female suicide; 13 male control; 59 female control. The second set of materials received from Edwin S. Shneidman consisted of 33 paired notes, one of each pair being a genuine suicide note and the other a simulated suicide note; a key to which was which accompanied this set in a sealed envelope. We decided to use this set as a final test of our measures, after trying them out against the known suicide and normal letters. It was expected, however, that certain measures that would discriminate between suicide notes and ordinary letters probably would not do so between genuine and deliberately faked suicide notes—particularly measures reflecting the specific content of the message.

Quantitative measures designed to test the four general predictions—intended indices of *sterotypy*, of *disorganization*, of *directive state*, and of *conflict*—were devised and applied to the samples of known suicide notes and control letters. Sixteen measures were applied, along with certain additional analyses. Some of the measures are standard and well known in content analysis work; others were developed by us for this purpose. These were probably not the best measures that could have been devised, and they certainly do not exhaust the possibilities, but they do represent a considerable variety of quantitative estimates. The two investigators worked together in devising the measures, stabilizing the rules, and applying them to a small sample of notes. Each measure was then applied as consistently as possible to the total materials by one of us, not by both. We therefore have no direct evidence on the reliability of our measures across coders. For some of the measures, the objectivity of what was counted (e.g., *number of repetitions, number of syllables per word*) reduced the seriousness of this problem. Several of the less objective measures (e.g., *evaluative assertion analysis, distress-relief quotient, type/token ratios, cloze procedure*) have been checked for reliability by their authors, and these reports are in our references. To avoid redundancy, the detailed description of the measures will be given in connection with the results obtained with them.

RESULTS

Suicide Notes vs. Ordinary Letters to Friends and Relatives

The differences between scores of males and females were tested for statistical significance separately within suicide and control groups. If no sex difference was found, the male and female letters within groups were combined and the total suicide versus control samples were then compared statistically. If a sex difference did appear, separate analyses for differences between suicide notes and controls were made for each sex. Nonparametric tests of significance were used, generally the median test, and occasionally chi square. In the former case, levels of significance were evaluated by reference to the Mainland and Murray tables (1952). Conservative estimates of the significance of the differences are given since a two-sided hypothesis was tested in spite of the fact that the direction of the difference was predicted in all cases.

Stereotypy Measures

1. Average number of syllables per word. We would expect a person functioning under high drive to select words in terms of his strongest habits, i.e., familiar high frequency words. Since, as Zipf (1949) has shown, there is an inverse relation between length of words and their frequency, and since longer, rarer words typically have more syllables, it follows that ordinary letters should have more syllables per word on the average than suicide notes. The total number of syllables per message, as estimated from breath pulses, was divided by the total number of words per message to obtain this index. There were no sex differences on this measure. Differences between suicide notes and control letters did not reach statistical significance but were in the expected direction.

2. Type/token ratio (TTR). This measure is obtained by dividing the number of *different* words by the total number of words in each message. It has been shown to be a good index of lexical diversity, differentiating between educational levels, telephone vs. ordinary conversation, and so on (cf. Johnson, Fairbanks, Mann, & Chotlos, 1944). If high drive increases stereotypy, we would expect suicide notes to display lower TTRs than ordinary letters to friends and relatives. There were no sex differences on this measure, and differences between suicides and controls were significant at the .01 level in the predicted direction.

3. Repetitions. Another index of stereotypy in messages is redundancy in what is talked about. We would expect people under high drive to repeat phrases more often than people under low drive. Here repetition of single words did not count (cf. TTR above), but phrases and parts of phrases of more than one word did. For example, in ". . . I really love you very much . . . and *I really* do *love you* . . .," the part phrase *I really love you* would count as repetition of 4 words. For each message, the number of words repeated in this fashion was divided by the total number of words as an index of repetitiousness. Here, again, there were no differences between sexes, but the differences between suicide notes and ordinary letters was significant at the .01 level.

4. *Noun-verb/adjective-adverb ratio.* This measure—a modification of the familiar verb/adjective ratio (Boder, 1940)—was obtained by dividing the total number of nouns and verbs contained in the message by the total number of adjectives and adverbs. Definition of nouns, verbs, adjectives, and adverbs was done on the basis of whether the words could be substituted in linguistic test frames characteristic of the particular grammatical form. The rationale for the analysis is that under high drive states there should be less tendency to ward modification of noun and verb forms, toward discriminative qualification of simple assertions, in line with our assumptions about the generalized energizing effects of drives. The prediction therefore follows that the ratio should be higher in the suicide than in the normal letters. The results bore out this prediction at the .01 level of confidence.

5. *Cloze measures.* Taylor (1956) has devised a method of estimating redundancy or stereotypy in which a message is "mutilated" by substituting a blank for every *n*th word (say, every fifth word, as used here) and Ss try to fill in these missing items. Presumably, the more predictable the message as a whole, the more accurately Ss can perform this task and, hence, the higher will be the cloze score. It follows that suicide notes should generate higher cloze scores than control notes. Sub-samples of 10 male suicide, 10 male control, 10 female suicide, and 10 female control notes were multilated by substituting blanks for every fifth word. Because sex differences in content might be significant here, we had 34 male Ss fill in the male notes and 31 female Ss fill in the female notes; suicide and control letters were alternated in order of presentation. Each S's mean cloze score for the 10 suicide notes and the 10 control letters was computed. A chi square test was used to determine whether the proportion of Ss having mean suicide cloze scores higher than their control scores deviated significantly from chance. For male Ss completing male materials, differences were significant at the .01 level in the expected direction; for females completing female material, however, there were no differences whatsoever.

6. *Allness terms.* People speaking or writing under high drive or emotion could be expected to be more extreme or polarized in their assertions. They should use more terms that permit no exception, e.g., *always, never, forever, no one, no more, everything, everyone, completely, perfectly,* and so on. Strictly speaking, this is not a measure of stereotypy, but it should be affected by gen-

eralized drive level. The number of such terms in each message was divided by total words and expressed as a rate per 100 words. Suicide notes yielded significantly more allness terms (.01 level), and there were no sex differences.

Disorganization Measures

1. Structural disturbances.   Extremely high levels of drive should result in disruption of the myriad of delicately balanced language encoding habits, according to theoretical analysis. To obtain a disturbance measure, the coder took the attitude of an English composition teacher, noting all grammatical, syntactical, spelling, and punctuation errors, and even clearly awkward constructions. Points where material was obviously omitted, e.g., "I don't ( ) him any more," were also counted. The index was the number of such errors expressed as a rate per 100 words. There were no sex differences here and no significant differences between suicide and control notes, although the latter difference was clearly in the expected direction.

2. Average length of independent segments.   We assume that people encoding under stress will tend to break their utterances into short, explosive units. Here we are interested in sentence length, but must correct for compound sentences joined together by conjunctions like *and* and *but*. The coder divided each message into the number of segments that could stand by themselves as sentences. The index was the total number of words in each message divided by the number of such segments, yielding the average number of words per independent segment. Although there were no sex differences for control letters, there were for suicide notes, male suicides using significantly longer segments (.05 level). Comparing suicides with normals, we find no differences for females but a difference significant at the .05 level for males—male suicide notes used significantly *longer* independent segments than ordinary letters written by males, a finding that is contrary to the direction predicted.

Directive State Measures

1. Distress/Relief Quotient (DRQ).   This well-known measure developed by Dollard and Mowrer (1947) is the ratio of distress-expressing phrases to the sum of these plus relief-expressing phrases, the former being indicative of disturbing drive states and the latter of the reduction of such states. This measure obviously depends to a considerable degree on the judgment of the coder. Here we found definite sex differences for both control and suicide messages; females yielded higher ratios (more distress-expression), in both cases significant at the .05 level. This difference may reflect a trait of masculine reticence in our culture. And, as might be expected from the nature of the suicide situation, both male and female suicide notes displayed higher DRQs than ordinary letters to friends and relatives (.01 level in both cases).

2. *Number of evaluative common-meaning terms.* Common-meaning terms in a language are those upon whose denotation and connotation people must agree if they are to understand one another. Examples would be *sweet, round, table, thunder, run, eat,* and so on. They are in contrast to attitude objects, like *labor union* and *ex-Senator McCarthy,* upon whose connotative meanings, at least, communicators need not agree. *Evaluative* common-meaning terms are those, like *unfair, dangerous, sweetheart,* and *drunkard,* which can be judged as clearly related to either *good* or *bad.* Our index here is simply the total number of such terms in each message divided by the total number of words in the message. There are no differences between sexes for either suicides or normals in the simple *number* of evaluative common-meaning terms (in contrast to the distress/relief measure above and percentage of positive evaluative assertions below), but differences between suicides and normals are significant at the .01 level, with suicides having more evaluative terms.

3. *Positive   evaluative   assertions.* Evaluative   Assertion Analysis has been described in detail elsewhere (Osgood, Saporta, & Nunnally, 1956; Pool, 1959). In essence, it involves the linguistic isolation of statements that assert a relation between an attitude object and either another attitude object or an evaluative common-meaning term. Examples: *I* (EGO)/*have always respected/ you* (FATHER); *You* (SPOUSE)/*could never stand being/simply a loyal helpmate.* Assertive relations can be either associative (*have always respected*) or dissociative (*could never stand being*). For present purposes, analysis was restricted to those attitude objects representing the significant persons in Ego's life and their relation to Ego; e.g., EGO, ALTER (person written to when not spouse, parent, or child), SPOUSE, CHILD, MOTHER, FATHER. The index with which we are presently concerned was obtained by dividing the number of positive evaluative assertions by the total number of evaluative assertions, positive and negative, i.e., the proportion

of positive evaluations. It would be expected that this measure would correlate highly and negatively with the Distress/Relief Quotient, and it does. Although sex differences were not significant, they were in the direction of greater negative evaluation by females in both suicide and normal letters. Differences between suicide and ordinary letters home were significant at the .01 level and in the expected direction.

4. *Time orientation.* It was expected that the motivational state characteristic of suicide might direct interest of the writer away from the present toward the past. Therefore, suicide notes should contain fewer statements referring to the present and the future but more referring to the past. Examples: present reference —*I love you, I'm afraid that* . . .; past references—*I have tried . . . Everything you've done* . . .; future reference— *. . . who will always love you, Tell my parents.* . . . We measured both the proportion of total references which were to present time and the imbalance of nonpresent references toward past vs. future. Contrary to our expectations, there were neither significant differences between sexes nor between suicides and controls.

5. *Mands.* According to Skinner (1957), a *mand* is an utterance which (*a*) expresses a need of the speaker and which (*b*) requires some reaction from another person for its satisfaction. It is usually expressed in the form of an imperative, where the verb comes early in the utterance (e.g., *Don't feel too bad about this* or *Please understand me*), but is not restricted to this form (e.g., *I wish I could see you, I hope you understand,* or *May God forgive me*). Our index was the number of such constructions, expressed as a rate per hundred words. This proved to be one of the most useful measures in our arsenal. In the present test situation, differences between sexes were not significant, but differences between suicide notes and ordinary letters to friends and relatives were significant at the .01 level in the predicted direction.

Conflict Measures

1. *Qualification of verb phrases.* When a speaker or writer is in conflict about the topics being discussed, it seems likely that he will modify or qualify his assertions away from the flat, direct present or past tense, e.g., from *I was good to you* to something like *I used to be good to you*, or *I tried to be good to you*. To quantify this characteristic of messages, the coder first bracketed each complete verb phrase for which a single verb could be substituted e.g., for *I (could have helped) you more* we can substitute *I (loved)*

you more, where the one word *loved* substitutes structurally for the three words *could have helped*; then the coder totaled the number of words in these brackets and divided by the number of such brackets. The larger this ratio, the greater the amount of excess, qualifying material. There were no sex differences on this measure, but differences between suicide and normal letters were significant at the .01 level in the expected direction.

2. *Ambivalence constructions.* There are a number of syntactical constructions in English that may directly express ambivalence, conflict, and doubt on the part of the speaker: *but, if, would, should, because (for, since), well, however, maybe, probably, possibly, seems, appears, guess, surely, really, except*, etc. Certain question forms also express the same indecisive state, e.g., *Must I do it? Why do I try at all?* The coder determined the number of such forms in each message and expressed it as a rate per 100 words. Differences between sexes were not significant; differences between suicide notes and ordinary letters were significant at the .01 level.

3. *Percentage of ambivalent evaluative assertions.* The essential nature of evaluative assertion analysis has already been described (see Directive State Measures numbered 2 and 3). If a speaker displays perfect consistency or lack of ambivalence, then all of the assertions relating to each attitude object or association between each pair of attitude objects will have the same sign. For example, assertions concerning the self would be either consistently positive or consistently negative—*I am no good; I have been a failure; Luck has not been on my side*; or for the relation of Ego to Spouse, *I have always loved you; You relied on me; I tried to help you; My Darling Wife.* Ambivalence, on the other hand, is indicated by assertions of different signs in the same set, e.g., *I love you, Honey; You never trusted me; I quarreled with you; You stuck by our marriage, though.* Our index of assertion ambivalence was the total number of deviant assertions (i.e., the number of least frequent signs in each set, summing over sets) expressed as a proportion of total assertions. For this conflict measure, also, there were no sex differences, but suicide vs. control differences were significant at the .01 level and in the predicted direction.

Genuine vs. Simulated Suicide Notes

We had originally planned to apply the measures that had successfully differentiated suicide from control letters blindly to the entire set of 33 paired suicide and simulated notes. Unfortunately only

13 of these pairs included both suicide and faked notes of sufficient length to make most of our measures meaningful. In attempting to predict which of these 13 pairs were the genuine suicide notes, we eliminated those measures which had failed to differentiate suicides from normal controls (*structural disturbances, average length of independent segments, time orientation*), those which obviously and nonsubtly reflected the suicide topic and hence would be readily faked (*distress-relief quotient, evaluative terms, positive evaluative assertions*), and the *cloze procedure* (too few messages of sufficient length). A prediction of suicide vs. simulated was made for each of the 13 paired notes on the basis of each of the remaining nine measures, and the final prediction was based on which note in each pair garnered the most suicide votes. Our quantitative predictions proved to be correct in 10 out of 13 cases, a value significant at the .05 level.

However, before checking the accuracy of these quantitative predictions against the key in the sealed envelope, both authors independently assigned all 33 pairs to suicide or fake categories on an intuitive basis. One of us got 31/33 correct and the other 26/33. To check on the possibility that we had actually been employing cues derived from our previous quantitative coding, we had eight graduate students with no prior experience with these notes assign the pairs to genuine suicide and fake categories. They were successful on the average in 16.5/33 cases, exactly chance. So it would appear that familiarity with a large sample of known suicide vs. nonsuicide notes, or sensitivity to cues derived from quantitative measures, or both, contributes to successful identification of genuine suicide notes.

Knowing which of the 33 pairs are genuine suicide notes, we may now ask which of our quantitative measures, successful in differentiating suicide from ordinary letters home, are also succussful in differentiating genuine suicide from pseudo notes. This analysis should indicate which encoding characteristics of the suicidal individual can be intuited and, hence, faked by the nonsuicidal person, and which cannot. We may look first at the very small sample of 13 pairs where both genuine and pseudo notes could be coded.

Stereotypy Measures: Of these measures, three (*syllables per word, repetitions,* and *allness terms*) were clearly in the expected direction but not significantly so. One, *noun-verb/adjective-adverb ratio* was significant at the .05 level in the predicted direction.

Directive State Measures: Of the directive state measures,

DRQ, frequency of evaluative terms, and *proportion of positive evaluative assertions* did not differentiate (as expected), but *mands* did differentiate significantly at the .05 level.

Conflict Measures: Of the three conflict measures, one was not significant (*qualification of verb phrases*), one was significant at the .05 level, but in *the wrong direction (ambivalence constructions)* and one was barely significant in the predicted direction at the .10 level (*proportion of ambivalent assertions*).

If we enlarge our sample to 24 suicide and 18 faked notes by scoring all notes of sufficient length, regardless of their pairing, about the same results appear: *Stereotypy measures* tend in the right direction, but only the *noun-verb/adjective-adverb ratio* significantly so; *mands* just miss significance at the .05 level; *proportion of ambivalent assertions* approaches significance in the expected direction, but the other *conflict measures* are either non-differential or significant in the wrong direction. Interestingly, the two disorganization measures, which were computed for this larger sample, approach (*structural disturbances*) or reach (*length of independent segments*) significance at the .05 level and in the predicted direction.

Although gross measures of "what is talked about" like the DRQ and negative evaluative assertions may not differentiate genuine from pseudo suicide notes, we may ask if a more detailed content analysis might reveal differences. Accordingly, the frequency with which lexical words (nouns, verbs, adjectives, and adverbs) were used in the 33 genuine and facsimile suicide notes was analyzed. Since the sample of *S*s was small, and hence liable to bias by discussion of a particular topic by a single *S*, subject-frequencies rather than word-frequencies per se were counted, i.e., the use of a given word by a given *S* was only counted once no matter how often he used it.

Table 1 gives the words included in five or more of the 33 suicide notes and in five or more of the simulated notes. Again, we note evidence for greater stereotypy in the suicide group; in every category, suicide notes display a greater sharing of common lexical items than do simulated notes. Some of the differences in choice of most frequently used lexical items are interesting: Suicide notes are more heavily loaded with terms of endearment (*darling, dear, honey*) and references to *mother*, whereas faked notes have more abstractions (*life, way, all*) and references to *insurance*. Whereas genuine suicide notes are replete with verbs referring to simple action (*tell, do, get, say, take, give*), faked suicide notes

Table 1. Words Included in Five or More of the Genuine and Simulated Suicide Notes

Nouns		Verbs		Adjectives and adverbs	
Genuine	Simulated	Genuine	Simulated	Genuine	Simulated
everything (9)	life (13)	love (19)	know (10)	good (15)	good (9)
way (out) (9)	way (11)	tell (13)	leave (9)	sorry (11)	sorry (8)
wife (9)	way (out) (8)	know (12)	think (9)	only (7)	happy (6)
love (8)	thing (8)	hope (11)	have (8)	dear (6)	all (5)
mother (8)	wife (7)	please (11)	please (8)	bad (5)	
thing (8)	all (8)	think (11)	love (7)		
God (6)	love (5)	do (10)	forgive (6)		
time(s) (6)	insurance (5)	get (9)	hope (5)		
darling (5)		say (9)	seem (5)		
dear (5)		take (9)	see (5)		
honey (5)		give (8)	tell (5)		
life (5)		want (8)			
one (5)		feel (7)			
person (5)		goodbye (7)			
something (5)		have (7)			
trouble (5)		make (7)			
way (5)		go (6)			
year(s) (5)		help (6)			
		see (6)			
		forgive (5)			
		try (5)			
		take care of (5)			

include relatively more verbs referring to mental states (*know, think, seem, see*). The genuine suicides have more stress on positive states (*love* 19 and *hope* 12 versus 7 and 5 for the same words in pseudo notes), whereas the simulated notes have 9 references to *leave* versus only 3 for suicides. To summarize this rough content comparison, genuine suicide notes reflect ambivalence toward loved ones through higher frequency of *positive evaluative terms* (cf., *ambivalent assertions* above) and they reflect greater *concreteness*.

Finally, a contingency analysis[1] of some of the major content categories in suicide and pseudocide notes was made in an attempt to get at the association structures characteristic of the two groups. The content categories given in Table 2 were used. Before discussing the results of the contingency analysis, some of the differences in relative frequency of reference to these categories in the genuine and spurious suicide notes are worth noting: Suicide notes have relatively higher frequencies of reference to *self praise and defense*,

Table 2. Relative Frequency of Cases Reflecting Various Content Categories

Categories	Genuine	Simulated
Spouse praise, defense, love	.69	.42
Self criticism	.48	.39
I'm sorry; forgive me	.45	.36
Self praise, defense	.39	.06
Children	.36	.33
Goodbye, farewell, etc.	.30	.12
Feelings of confusion, being tired, etc.	.27	.42
Spouse criticism	.24	.03
"Way out"	.24	.39
Physical disabilities, symptoms	.21	.18
Parents	.21	.06
God and religion	.21	.06
Material possessions	.21	.00
Reference to suicidal act	.18	.33
Money, bills, debts	.15	.06
Notify, tell someone	.15	.03
Isolation, loneliness	.15	.00
Insurance, etc.	.12	.21
Reference to suicide note	.12	.06
Instructions about own remains	.12	.03
Job	.09	.03
Love triangles (other man, woman)	.09	.06
"Fate," "Life," "World," etc.	.03	.33
Sex relations	.03	.00

goodbyes and *farewells, criticism of the spouse,* references to *parents, God and religion,* and *material possessions;* simulated notes refer relatively more frequently to *feelings of confusion, being tired,* and the like, to the *suicidal act* itself, to *insurance,* and to abstractions like *Fate, Life,* and *The World.*

Expected and obtained contingencies among these categories (for genuine suicide and simulated notes separately) were obtained in the following way: Letting A and B represent two content categories, the *expected contingency* is p_{AB}, i.e., the probability of both A and B being present in notes of a given type, based on their separate rates of occurrence. The *obtained contingency* is simply the relative frequency of actual co-occurrence, i.e., the percentage of notes of a given type in which contents A and B are actually both present. The obtained contingency may be either greater than (association) or less than (dissociation) the expected or chance contingencies. Significances of deviations from chance expectancies are estimated in terms of the standard error of the expected percentage. Because of the crude nature of this analysis and the rather small N, significances at the .10 level or better were used as the basis for the following summary statements; they should be considered to be merely suggestive.

In the genuine suicide notes we find *criticism of the spouse* associated with references to *insurance, money, bills and debts,* and *requests to notify* someone of his death. As might be expected, *requests to notify* are associated with references to the *suicide note* itself and with *instructions about handling one's remains.* Expressions of feeling *isolated and lonesome* are associated with references to *money, bills and debts,* and to *love triangles.* References to the *parents* appear with statements about taking a *"way out"* and with references to *material possessions.* References to *own children* appear with *instructions about handling remains.* Again as would be expected, references to *money, bills and debts* co-occur with references to *material possessions.* Less obviously, references to *the job* are contingent upon references to the *suicide note* itself; *self praise* is contingent upon references to *insurance.*

In the simulated notes, references to *own children* are associated with references to *God and religion,* while references to *parents* are associated with stereotyped abstractions, *Fate, Life, the World.* When people write "make-believe" suicide notes, references to *the suicide act* itself tend to be accompanied by references to *God and religion,* and talking about a *"way out"* appears with comments about *money, bills and debts.* Expressions of *sorrow, regret, and asking for forgiveness* appear with saying *good-bye* and *farewell* in these faked notes. There are also two significant dissociations (co-occurrence *less* than chance at the .10 level)—faked notes that speak of *physical disabilities* do not express *feelings of confusion and being tired,* and the notes which refer to *insurance* do not include expressions of *sorrow, regret, and asking for forgiveness.*

In viewing the total evidence on association structures, one gets the following general impression: When people produce fake suicide notes "on demand," they generally embroider a few standard themes available in our folklore—taking a "way out" of financial and other problems, asking forgiveness and saying "farewell," pondering on the moral and religious implications of taking one's own life, and so on. The patterns of association in genuine suicide notes suggest more mundane connections—for example, criticism of the spouse being connected in the suicidal person's mind with his financial problems, with being insured and the like, or references to being insured being coupled with self-praise.

DISCUSSION

Of the four general predictions about the effects of heightened motivation upon encoding, three are borne out clearly in the comparison of suicide notes with ordinary letters to friends and relatives. Suicide notes display greater *stereotypy*—the writer of a suicide note tends to use shorter, simpler words, his vocabulary is less diversified, he is more repetitious, he uses more simple action expressions (nouns and verbs) and fewer discriminative qualifiers (adjectives and adverbs), and his messages are more easily filled in (*cloze* procedure) by others. He also uses more polarized "allness" terms. The effects of the suicidal *directive state* are also clearly evident—in higher distress-relief quotients, in the greater frequency of evaluative terms, and in the smaller proportion of evaluative assertions that are positive in direction. Suicide notes also display the demanding, commanding, pleading nature of this state by higher frequency of *mands.* Suicide notes yield evidence of greater *conflict* of motives—by greater qualification of verb phrases, more ambivalence constructions, and a larger percentage of evaluative assertions about Ego and significant others that are ambivalent in sign. Most of these differences were significant at the .01 level, and they substantiate our general hypotheses about the effects of heightened drive level upon language encoding.

One major prediction was not borne out: there was no evidence for greater *disorganization* of encoding behavior in suicide notes as compared with ordinary letters to friends and relatives. We conclude that the suicide state, at least at the time a note is penned, does not represent a sufficiently high degree of motivation to cause disruption of language skills, but the negative result could also indicate that our measures of disorganization were inadequate or that the hypothesis was wrong. The failure of the time orientation measure to yield any differences may also mean that our notions were wrong. It is also possible that this measure was confounded with that for *mands*; mands usually have future reference and are significantly more frequent for suicide notes.

The comparison of genuine suicide notes with simulated suicide notes, matched for age, education, and general social status, can be considered, on the one hand, a more stringent test of the hypotheses or, on the other hand, an indication of the degree to which a nonsuicidal person can intuit and adopt the encoding content and style of the suicidal person. From the former point of view, we would have to conclude that most of our measures fail to distinguish significantly between the genuine and pseudo notes (excepting the *noun-verb/adjective-adverb ratio*, *mands*, *length of independent segments*, and perhaps the *proportion of ambivalent assertions*). Nevertheless, the quantitative indices that differentiated suicide from ordinary letters, and which might be expected to differentiate genuine from faked notes, did so for 10 out of the 13 matched pairs to which they could be applied.

How well can nonsuicidal writers adopt the encoding content and style of the suicide state? First, nonsuicidal people can obviously intuit the superficial *content* of suicide notes—the distress-expression, the use of evaluative terms, and the decrease in positive evaluative assertions. Less superficially, however, we note interesting differences in the words used (more positively toned terms, expressing the ambivalence of the true suicidal state, and more concrete terms generally) and in the contingencies among content categories (less stereotyped, "story-book" associations in the true suicide cases). Second, although the over-all reduction in significance of differences, as compared with the suicide versus control analysis, shows that the *style* of the suicidal person can be adopted to some degree by a person merely instructed to write such a note, there are certain exceptions. The person faking a suicide note fails to reflect the demanding, commanding, pleading style (*mands*), the reduced qualification (*noun-verb/adjective-adverb ratio*), and the evaluative ambivalence toward self and others of the genuine suicide notes.

One criticism that could be leveled at this study is that other determinants than motivation might be responsible for the results. It is known that many of the indices used here as tests of motivational effects can be affected by other source characteristics as well. For example, stereotypy measures like length of words and TTR are influenced by the education and IQ level of the source. Our control sample of ordinary letters to friends and relatives could be matched with the suicide notes in terms of sex and age, but that was all. Could the differences we found be accounted for simply on the basis that our suicide note writers were less intelligent and/or less well educated? If we explain the differences in stereotypy in this way, we are unable to explain why the same notes showed no differences in structural disturbances (ordinary English composition, for the most part) and, in fact, for males showed *longer* integrated sentence segments. Furthermore, this would not explain the directive-state differences (e.g., in *mands*). Also, in the genuine-pseudo comparison, where these factors were controlled by matching, differences for the most part were in the same direction, although not as large.

SUMMARY

Theoretical analysis of the effects of motivation level upon language encoding led to several hypotheses. Messages produced under heightened drive level should (*a*) be more stereotyped, (*b*) be more disorganized, if the motivation level is extremely high, (*c*) reflect the specific nature of the motives operating, and (*d*) reflect conflict of responses if two or more competing motives are operating. These hypotheses were tested by (*a*) a comparison of suicide notes with ordinary letters to friends and relatives and (*b*) a comparison of genuine suicide notes with simulated suicide notes, written by nonsuicidal people. In the first comparison, all of the hypotheses were clearly borne out except that concerning disorganization of encoding skills. In the second comparison, differences were smaller, only certain measures, the *noun-verb/adjective-adverb ratio*, Skinner's *mands, length of sentence segments*, and *proportion of ambivalent evaluative assertions* still discriminating significantly. Implications of these result for psycholinguistic theory and for stylistics are considered in the discussion, along with certain criticisms that could be made of the study.

NOTE

[1]This method is described in some detail in Pool, 1959.

REFERENCES

Boder, D. P. The adjective-verb quotient. A contribution to the psychology of language. *Psychol. Rev.*, 1940, 3: 309–343.

Dollard, J., & Mowrer, O. H. A method of measuring tension in written documents. *J. abnorm. soc. Psychol.*, 1947, 42: 3–32.

Hebb, D. O. Drives and the C. N. S. (conceptual nervous system). *Psychol. Rev.*, 1955, 62: 243–254.

Johnson, W., Fairbanks, Helen, Mann, Mary Bachman, & Chotlos, J. W. Studies in language behavior. *Psychol. Monogr.*, 1944, 56: No. 2 (Whole No. 255).

Mainland, D., & Murray, I. M. Tables for use in fourfold contingency tests. *Science*, 1952, 116: 591–594.

Osgood, C. E. *Motivational dynamics of language behavior.* In M. R. Jones (ed.), *Nebraska symposium on motivation.* Lincoln: University of Nebraska Press, 1957.

Osgood, C. E., Saporta, S., & Nunnally, J. C. Evaluative assertion analysis. *Litera*, 1956, 3: 47–102.

Pool, I. (ed.) *Trends in content analysis.* Urbana: University of Illinois Press, 1959.

Skinner, B. F. *Verbal behavior.* New York: Appleton-Century-Crofts, 1957.

Spence, K. W., Farber, I. E., & McFann, H. H. The relation of anxiety (drive) level to performance in competitional and noncompetitional paired-associates learning. *J. exp. Psychol.*, 1956, 52: 296–305.

Taylor, W. L. Recent developments in the use of "Cloze Procedure." *Journalism Quart.*, 1956, 33, No. 1.

Zipf, G. K. *Human behavior and the principle of least effort.* Cambridge, Mass.: Addison-Wesley, 1949.

Part Eight

LINGUISTIC DIMENSIONS OF PERSUASION

32

THE EFFECT OF VARIATIONS IN NONFLUENCY ON AUDIENCE RATINGS OF SOURCE CREDIBILITY

Gerald R. Miller
Murray A. Hewgill

INTRODUCTION

In the literature of speech, communication, and psychology, considerable attention has been directed to the problem of source credibility. Interest in the variables affecting credibility has stemmed from the long-accepted dictum that the audience's perception of the source will influence the response to his message. Generally, the research supports the soundness of this dictum.

For the most part, credibility has been investigated by manipulating factors apart from the source's actual presentation of the message. Thus, a number of studies have demonstrated that, with presentation and content held constant, variations in such source characteristics as competence and trustworthiness will lead to differential amounts of attitude change on the part of audience members.[1] Kelman, in research conducted to test certain propositions of his theoretic model of the processes of social influence,

Reprinted from *Quarterly Journal of Speech* 50, No. 1 (February 1964): 34–44.

has demonstrated that the duration of attitude change induced by a persuasive message is partially dependent on the source of the speaker's power.[2]

Although studies such as these are of considerable theoretical and practical interest to students of speech, it would appear that one potentially significant area has been overlooked in the previous research on source credibility. While considerable emphasis has been placed on the "who the source is" dimension, little consideration has been given to "how the source says it." Or, expressed in a more scientific idiom, investigators have largely ignored those classes of physical and vocal variables likely to influence the audience's perception of the source's credibility.

At the common-sense level, all of us are aware that such physical and vocal variables play a part in shaping our reactions to a speaker, if for no other reason than that various personality stereotypes are associated with certain physical and vocal characteristics. Thus, the speaker who consistently fails to look directly at his audience may be perceived as untrustworthy, while the speaker who does maintain audience contact will probably be regarded as direct and straightforward. Similarly, a speaker's delivery may be one of the determinants of his credibility, in that it may influence the listeners' perception of him.

In the present study, interest is directed toward one class of vocal variables that may influence an audience's perception of a source's credibility. Specifically, the study had as its purpose the investigation of possible relationships between the quantity and type of nonfluency presented by a speaker and audience ratings of source credibility.

HYPOTHESES OF THE STUDY

The following hypotheses were investigated in the study:

(1) As the number of nonfluencies presented by a speaker increases, audience ratings of the speaker's credibility will decrease.

This hypothesis suggests that quantitiy of nonfluency and audience perception of source credibility are negatively related. It is clear, however, that the label, "nonfluency," encompasses a wide variety of verbal behaviors. A number of factors should function to produce differences in the magnitude of audience response to various types of nonfluencies. For example, if a particular type of nonfluency occurs with great frequency among the general population of speakers, it can be suggested that a listener will be extensively exposed to discourse containing this type of nonfluency, and that this extensive exposure will lead to a reduction in the cue properties associated with the nonfluency. On the other hand, if the type of nonfluency involved occurs less frequently among the general population of speakers, the nonfluency should possess definite cue properties for the listener. This consideration leads to the second hypothesis:

(2) The effect hypothesized in (1) above will be greater for some types of nonfluency than for others; specifically, the effect will be greater for a nonfluency typed "repetition" than for a nonfluency typed "vocalized pause."[3]

METHOD

The stimulus employed in this study was a taped message in which the speaker argued that the practice of granting scholarships to college or university students on the basis of athletic ability should be abolished. The entire message was based on the contention that athletic scholarships are antithetical to the basic purpose of a college or university: enrichment of the mind.

Nine versions of this message were taped for presentation. These nine versions were intended to differ only in the number of nonfluencies and type of nonfluency occurring within each. The message containing no nonfluencies was 1054 words in length and was of approximately seven minutes and fifteen seconds duration. In the other eight versions the amount and type of nonfluency were systematically varied. Four of these messages contained vocalized pauses and four contained repetitions. The frequencies of vocalized pauses in the four speeches were 25, 50, 75, and 100, or one vocalized pause every 42, 21, 14, and 10.5 words respectively. The frequency of repetitions in the other four speeches was varied in a pattern identical to that for the vocalized pauses.

All messages were recorded by a faculty member in the department of speech at Michigan State University, who is a trained speaker and actor. Considerable care was taken to keep all other elements of the message as constant as possible. As in all studies of this kind, some minor variation in presentation is to be expected. Even so, the skill of the speaker and the care exercised in the preparation of the messages combined to produce speeches that were quite similar save for differences in amount and type of nonfluency.

Operationally, the two types of nonfluency were defined as follows: a vocalized pause was defined as the utterance of the "uh" (phonetically, [ə] to [ʌ]) sound between two words of the message. Thus, subjects in the vocalized pause treatments would hear such statements as, "For 'uh' Newman, it was the unique environment of the university. . . ." A repetition was operationally defined as the utterance of the first syllable of a word, followed by the utterance of the short "uh" (phonetically [ə]) sound, followed by the utterance of the complete word.[4] Thus, subjects in the repetition treatments would hear such statements as, "For New- 'uh' Newman, it was the unique environment of the university. . . ." As indicated earlier, the nonfluencies were systematically inserted into each of the messages, so that an approximately equal number of words separated each nonfluency. The points of insertion were determined by dividing the total number of words in the message by the number of nonfluencies to be inserted.

PROCEDURE

Subjects were members of ten undergraduate speech classes at Michigan State University. The classes ranged in size from seventeen to twenty-two members; however, subjects were randomly discarded from the larger classes to obtain an n of sixteen for each of the treatment groups.

Each class was randomly assigned to one of the treatment groups. Although the design of the study permitted the utilization of a single treatment group for both the o Vocalized Pause and o Repetition conditions, the availability of subjects made it possible to employ a separate treatment group for each of the two conditions. This method had the double advantage of simplifying the analysis and providing information concerning the degree of response consistency to be expected among treatment groups exposed to the same stimulus.

Subjects in each treatment group heard the message during a

regular class meeting. The message was introduced to each group with a non-directive statement concerning communication research which was intended to mask the true purpose of the study. Subjects were given no information about the source they heard on the tape.

Immediately after hearing the speech, each subject completed a rating instrument dealing with the perceived credibility of the anonymous source who had presented the message. The factors employed and the scales utilized in this instrument were based on previous factor analytic research conducted by Berlo and Lemert on the dimensions of source credibility.[5] These investigators arrived at a three-factor solution, encompassing the dimensions of *competence, trustworthiness,* and *dynamism.* A listing of the individual scales utilized and the factor loadings for each may be found in Figure 1.

Each scale was scored by assigning a value of seven to the response indicating the highest degree of perceived source credibility and a value of one to the response indicating the lowest degree of perceived source credibility. Each factor score was obtained by summing across the four scales; thus, a score of twenty-eight on a factor would represent maximum perceived source credibility for a subject on that factor, while a score of four would represent minimum credibility.

Completion of this instrument terminated the experiment, and at that time the study was explained to the subjects and its true purpose divulged to them.

Figure 1. Credibility Factors and Scales Utilized in the Study

Factor	*Scale*	*Factor loading*
Competence	Experienced-inexper'n'd	90
	Expert-ignorant	90
	Trained-untrained	90
	Competent-incompetent	88
Trustworthiness	Just-unjust	82
	Kind-cruel	78
	Admirable-contemptible	77
	Honest-dishonest	75
Dynamism	Aggressive-meek	73
	Bold-timid	72
	Energetic-tired	65
	Extroverted-introverted	64

RESULTS

For all statistical tests, the .05 level of significance was required. Analysis of the data yielded the following results.

The means for subjects' ratings of perceived source credibility on the *competence* factor are found in Table 1. Two-factor analysis of variance resulted in a nonsignificant F for the test of the Quantity of Nonfluency by Type of Nonfluency interaction ($F = < 1$). The F's obtained for both of the main effects were significant (F, Quantity of Nonfluency = 12.34; F, Type of Nonfluency = 9.51).

Use of the critical-difference technique[6] revealed a total of twenty-one significant differences among the forty-five possible comparisons of Competence means. These differences, which are summarized in Table 2, provide support for both hypotheses. In terms of number of nonfluencies, subjects in the o Vocalized Pause and o Repetition conditions rated the source significantly higher on Competence than did subjects in any of the other conditions except the 25 Vocalized Pause condition.

It should be pointed out, however, that this reduction in mean ratings of source Competence is not consistent across all treatments, but is most marked between subjects hearing speeches containing no nonfluencies and subjects hearing speeches containing 50, 75, or 100 nonfluencies. The mean ratings of source Competence by subjects in the 50, 75, and 100 Vocalized Pause conditions are almost identical; the mean ratings of source Competence by subjects in the 50, 75, and 100 Repetition conditions, although demonstrating a steady decline, do not differ significantly from one another.

In terms of type of nonfluency, mean Competence ratings of the source were lower for Repetition conditions than for Vocalized Pause conditions at each level of quantity of nonfluency except o Vocalized Pause and o Repetition. This effect is most marked at the 100 nonfluency level; at this level subjects in the Vocalized Pause condition rated the source as significantly more Competent than did subjects in the Repetition condition. Although none of the other comparisons shows a significant difference, the consistently lower mean ratings of the source's Competence at each level of nonfluency by subjects in the Repetition conditions suggests that Repetition leads to a greater decrease in the perceived Competence of the source than does Vocalized Pause.

The means for subjects' ratings of perceived source credibility on the *trustworthiness factor* are found in Table 3. Two-factor

Table 1.   Mean Ratings of Source Credibility on the Competence Factor

Type of nonfluency	Frequency of nonfluency				
	0	25	50	75	100
Vocalized pause	22.81	18.94	15.94	16.31	15.56
Repetition	21.94	15.31	14.13	13.44	10.75

Table 2.   Critical Difference Matrix for Mean Ratings of Competence

	0 R	25 VP	25 R	50 VP	50 R	75 VP	75 R	100 VP	100 R
0 VP	+.87	+3.87	+7.50*	+6.87*	+8.68*	+6.50*	+9.37*	+7.25*	+12.06*
0 R		+3.00	+6.63*	+6.00*	+7.81*	+5.63*	+8.50*	+6.38*	+11.19*
25 VP			+3.63	+3.00	+4.81*	+2.63	+5.50*	+3.38	+ 8.19*
25 R				− .63	+1.18	−1.00	+1.87	− .25	+ 4.56*
50 VP					+1.81	− .37	+2.50	+ .38	+ 5.19*
50 R						−2.18	+ .69	−1.43	+ 3.38
75 VP							+2.87	+ .75	+ 5.56*
75R								−2.12	+ 2.69
100 VP									+ 4.81*

*$p = <.05$; c.d. $= 3.98$.

Table 3.   Mean Ratings of Source Credibility on the Trustworthiness Factor

Type of nonfluency	Frequency of nonfluency				
	0	25	50	75	100
Vocalized pause	18.38	20.00	15.75	18.00	16.44
Repetition	18.31	17.69	19.94	17.50	15.25

Table 4. Critical Difference Matrix for Mean Ratings of Trustworthiness

	0 R	25 VP	25 R	50 VP	50 R	75 VP	75 R	100 VP	100 R
0 VP	+.07	−1.62	+ .69	+2.63	+2.44	+ .38	+ .88	+1.94	+3.13*
0 R		−1.69	+ .62	+2.56	+2.37	+ .31	+ .81	+1.87	+3.06*
25 VP			+2.31	+4.25*	+4.06*	+2.00	+2.50	+3.56*	+4.75*
25 R				+1.94	+1.75	− .31	+ .19	+1.25	+2.44
50 VP					− .19	−2.25	−1.75	− .69	+ .50
50 R						−2.06	−1.56	− .50	+ .69
75 VP							+ .50	+1.56	+2.75
75 R								+1.06	+2.25
100 VP									+1.19

*$p = <.05$; c.d. $= 3.02$.

analysis of variance resulted in a nonsignificant F for the test of the Quantity of Nonfluency by Type of Nonfluency interaction ($F = <1$). Likewise, the F obtained for the Type of Nonfluency was not significant ($F = 2.01$). However, the test of the Quantity of Nonfluency yielded a significant F of 2.79.

Use of the critical-difference technique revealed only six significant differences among the forty-five possible comparisons of Trustworthiness means. Table 4 contains a summary of these comparisons. It can be seen that subjects in the 25 Vocalized Pause condition rated the source significantly higher on Trustworthiness than did subjects in the 50 Vocalized Pause, 50 Repetition, 100 Vocalized Pause, and 100 Repetition conditions. In addition, subjects in the 0 Vocalized Pause and 0 Repetition conditions rated the source significantly higher on Trustworthiness than did subjects in the 100 Repetition condition. Taken as a whole, the findings on Trustworthiness provide only minimal support for the first hypothesis of the study and fail to provide support for the second hypothesis.

The means for subjects' ratings of perceived source credibility on the *dynamism* factor are found in Table 5. Two-factor analysis of variance yielded a significant F of 2.86 for the test of the Quantity

Table 5. Mean Ratings of Source Credibility on the Dynamism Factor

Type of nonfluency	*Frequency of nonfluency*				
	0	25	50	75	100
Vocalized pause	22.44	21.81	20.06	18.56	21.19
Repetition	22.38	17.44	15.00	17.31	13.81

of Nonfluency by Type of Nonfluency interaction. Examination of the plotted means revealed that the interaction resulted from differential rating behavior by subjects in the Vocalized Pause and Repetition conditions at the 75 and 100 nonfluency levels. Whereas the mean rating of source Dynamism decreases from the 50 nonfluency to the 75 nonfluency level and then increases from the 75 nonfluency to the 100 nonfluency level in the Vocalized Pause conditions, the opposite occurs in the Repetition conditions; that is, the mean rating of source Dynamism increases from the 50 nonfluency to the 75 nonfluency level and then decreases from the 75 nonfluency to the 100 nonfluency level. Reasons for these differences in rating behavior are difficult to specify.

Because of the significant interaction effect, the data were analyzed by analysis of variance technique for simple, rather than main, effects. The analysis showed no significant differences among the five Vocalized Pause groups. Differences among the five Repetition groups, however, were significant ($F = 6.5$). The four analyses for type of nonfluency showed that the two 25 frequency groups were significantly different ($F = 9.5$), as were the 50 and 100 frequency groups ($F = 8.3$ and 12.7 respectively). The two 75 frequency groups were not significantly different.

Further analysis of the Dynamism means by use of the critical-difference technique revealed a total of twenty-four significant differences among the forty-five possible comparisons of Dynamism means. These differences, which are summarized in Table 6, provide support for both hypotheses of the study. In terms of number of nonfluencies, the predicted effect is more pronounced in the Repetition conditions. Subjects in the o Repetition con-

Table 6. Critical Difference Matrix for Mean Ratings of Dynamism

	0 R	25 VP	25 R	50 VP	50 R	75 VP	75 R	100 VP	100 R
0 VP	+.06	+.63	+5.00*	+2.38	+7.44*	+3.88*	+5.13*	+1.25	+8.63*
0 R		+.57	+4.94*	+2.32	+7.38*	+3.82*	+5.07*	+1.19	+8.57*
25 VP			+4.37*	+1.75	+6.81*	+3.25	+4.50*	+ .62	+8.00*
25 R				−2.62	+2.44	−1.12	+ .13	−3.75*	+3.63*
50 VP					+5.06*	+1.50	+2.75	−1.13	+6.25*
50 R						−3.56*	−2.31	−6.19*	+1.19
75 VP							+1.25	−2.63	+4.75*
75 R								−3.88*	+3.50*
100 VP									+7.38*

*$p = <.05$; c.d. = 3.43.

dition rated the speaker significantly higher on Dynamism than did subjects in the 25, 50, 75, and 100 Repetition conditions, and subjects in the 25 and 75 Repetition conditions rated the speaker significantly higher on Dynamism than did subjects in the 100 Repetition condition. By contrast, only one comparison is significant in the Vocalized Pause conditions; subjects in the o Vocalized Pause condition rated the speaker significantly higher on Dynamism than did subjects in the 75 Vocalized Pause condition.

In terms of type of nonfluency, it can be seen that subjects in the o Vocalized Pause and o Repetition conditions assigned almost identical mean ratings to the source on the Dynamism factor. At each of the other four levels of quantity of nonfluency the mean ratings of source Dynamism are higher in the Vocalized Pause condition than in the Repetition condition; three of the four differences are statistically significant. Thus, the findings indicate that Repetition leads to a greater decrease in the perceived Dynamism of the source than does Vocalized Pause.

DISCUSSION

The findings of this study provide support for the two hypotheses that were investigated. Generally, it appears that as the quantity of nonfluency presented by a speaker increases, audience ratings of perceived source credibility decrease. Also, this effect is somewhat more pronounced when the nonfluent behavior involves repetitions rather than vocalized pauses.

This result, however, does not emerge clearly for all three credibility factors employed in the study. The most consistent reductions in source credibility ratings occurred on the Competence and Dynamism factors, with few significant differences resulting from audience ratings of Trustworthiness.

Several factors may account for these differential results. First, it is possible that the Trustworthiness factor and nonfluency, as defined in this study, are relatively independent of each other. For example, it is probable that an audience would consider a stutterer to be as trustworthy as a nonstutterer but might consider him less competent.

Second, it is possible that the classroom context in which the speech was presented cued the audience to attend more closely to some aspects of the presentation than to others. Whereas general considerations of competence and dynamism are usually relevant criteria in evaluating a classroom presentation, the trust-worthiness of the speaker is seldom challenged. It could be, there-fore, that questions concerning the speaker's honesty were not particularly salient to the audiences involved.

A third consideration which may provide a partial explanation for the relative lack of emphasis placed on the Trustworthiness dimension was the source's anonymity. Prior research indicates that in a situation involving inadequate performance by an un-familiar individual, others will reduce their ratings of the individ-ual's competence more than their ratings of his likeability.[7] Since the scales used to measure Trustworthiness touch directly upon desirable and undesirable personal traits (Kind-Cruel, etc.), it is conceivable that this phenomenon was operating in the present experimental situation. Subjects may have tended to avoid judg-ments of Trustworthiness by reasoning that the speaker was prob-ably a nice fellow, but incompetent in terms of presentational skills. Such reasoning would thus enable them to place emphasis on a dimension of credibility somewhat removed from the source's personal control.

Probably the most significant finding of the study is the indica-tion that different types of nonfluent behavior elicit differences in audience ratings of perceived source credibility. It would appear that the level of analysis must be reduced from the broad category "Nonfluency," if one wishes to gain a reasonably comprehensive understanding of the effects of various verbal behaviors on audience reactions to a speaker. In the present study, vocalized pauses and repetitions were employed as categories of verbal disturbance likely to affect audience judgments of the speaker. Future research, however, might well focus on operationalizing and manipulating other types of nonfluency in order to determine their effects on audience response.

Future research might also employ attitude change measures along with source credibility ratings to determine what effect differ-ences in quantity and type of nonfluency have on amount of audi-ence attitude shift. In the present study, interest was directed entirely at source credibility differences. It is probable, however, that the audience's perception of the source's credibility is di-rectly related to the amount of attitude shift that the source may be expected to induce. The inclusion of attitude change measures would enable one to investigate this possibility.

Perhaps the most intriguing direction for future research lies in combining extra-presentational and intra-presentational variables that are potentially related to source credibility in order to study their possible interactive effects in shaping audience response to the speaker.[8] For example, one could use the standard introductory technique utilized in prior credibility research to create a positive or negative audience set toward the speaker prior to his presentation. Then, by systematically varying the amount and type of nonfluency occurring within the message itself, it would be possible to obtain an indication of the effects of both prior set and presentational differences on audience ratings of source credibility.

Since the present study is only a beginning step, it is felt that further attention to the physical and vocal cues affecting audience reaction to a speaker is warranted. Further investigation of these variables should provide a more complete understanding of the factors that are relevant to the construct of source credibility.

SUMMARY

The purpose of this study was to investigate possible relationships between the quantity and type of nonfluency presented by a speaker and audience ratings of source credibility. Specifically, it was hypothesized: (1) that as the number of nonfluencies presented by a speaker increases, audience ratings of the speaker's credibility will decrease; and (2) that this effect will be greater for a nonfluency typed *repetition* than for a nonfluency typed *vocalized pause*.

Ten treatment groups, each containing sixteen subjects, were utilized in the study. Each of these groups heard a message that differed only in the amount and type of nonfluency it contained. The treatment conditions were as follows: 0 Vocalized Pause, 25 Vocalized Pause, 50 Vocalized Pause, 75 Vocalized Pause, 100 Vocalized Pause, 0 Repetition, 25 Repetition, 50 Repetition, 75 Repetition, and 100 Repetition. The messages were recorded by a trained speaker in order to minimize other presentational differences.

Immediately after hearing the speech, each subject completed a rating instrument designed to measure his perception of the source's credibility. Three dimensions of credibility were included in the instrument: Competence, Trustworthiness, and Dynamism.

Analysis of the data obtained from subjects' ratings produced the following results:

(1) On the Competence factor, subjects who heard the speech that contained no nonfluencies rated the speaker significantly

higher than did subjects who heard the speeches containing 50, 75, or 100 nonfluencies. Also, the decrease in ratings was more marked in the Repetition conditions than in the Vocalized Pause conditions. Thus, the findings on Competence tend to support both hypotheses of the study.

(2) On the Trustworthiness factor, there were only six significant differences among all possible comparisons of treatment means. The data on Trustworthiness were interpreted as providing only minimal support for the first hypothesis of the study and no support for the second hypothesis.

(3) On the Dynamism factor, subjects who heard the speech that contained no repetitions rated the speaker significantly higher than did subjects who heard the speeches containing 25, 50, 75, and 100 repetitions. The decrease in Dynamism ratings was not as pronounced in the Vocalized Pause conditions, with only the comparison between the 0 Vocalized Pause and 75 Vocalized Pause conditions reaching significance. Thus, the findings on Dynamism tend to support both hypotheses of the study.

The findings were discussed in terms of their relationship to the hypotheses of the study, and implications for further research were considered.

NOTES

[1]See, for example, Carl I. Hovland and Walter Weiss, "The Influence of Source Credibility on Communication Effectiveness," *Public Opinion Quarterly*, XV (Winter 1952), 635–650; Carl I. Hovland and Wallace Mandell, "An Experimental Comparison of Conclusion-Drawing by the Communicator and by the Audience," *Journal of Abnormal and Social Psychology*, XLVII (July 1952), 581–588.

[2]Herbert C. Kelman, "Processes of Opinion Change," *Public Opinion Quarterly*, XXV (Spring 1961), 57–79; Herbert C. Kelman, "Compliance, Identification, and Internalization: Three Processes of Attitude Change," *Journal of Conflict Resolution*, II (March 1958), 51–60.

[3]Content analysis by Mahl indicates that vocalized pauses occur almost as frequently in uninterrupted speech as all other types of speech disturbances combined. See George F. Mahl, "Measuring the Patient's Anxiety During Interviews from 'Expressive' Aspects of His Speech," *Transactions of the New York Academy of Sciences*, XXI (January 1959), 256.

[4]The "uh" was utilized in operationalizing repetition because vocalizations such as "New-Newman" appear artificial when no vocal transition links the two sounds.

[5]David K. Berlo and James B. Lemert, "A Factor Analytic Study of the Dimensions of Source Credibility." Paper presented at the 1961 convention of the SAA, New York.

[6]E. F. Lindquist, *Design and Analysis of Experiments in Psychology and Education* (Boston, 1956), pp. 93–94.

[7]Edward E. Jones and Richard deCharms, "Changes in Social Perception as a Function of the Personal Relevance of Behavior," in Eleanor E. Maccoby, Theodore M. Newcomb, and Eugene L. Hartley, *Readings in Social Psychology* (New York, 1958), pp. 102–110.

[8]Since this study was originally submitted, a similar suggestion has been made by two other writers; see Kenneth Andersen and Theodore Clevenger, Jr., "A Summary of Experimental Research in Ethos," *Speech Monographs*, XXX (June 1963), 78.

33

LANGUAGE VARIABLES AFFECTING THE PERSUASIVENESS OF SIMPLE COMMUNICATIONS

David E. Kanouse
Robert P. Abelson

In the typical persuasive-communication situation, a communicator wishes to establish or strengthen for his audience the credibility of a particular set of assertions. Experimental research on the factors presumably critical to the effectiveness of persuasion has focused on such variables as the credibility of the communicator, the emotion-arousing qualities of the communication, the discrepancy between the positions of communicator and recipient, and motivational tension arising from imbalance, incongruity, or dissonance. Little attention, however, has been directed toward the problem area of subjective logic; namely, the nature of the cognitive-processing rules an individual applies to determine whether or not a communicator's arguments establish the validity of the communicator's position.

A series of recent studies reported elsewhere by Gilson and

Reprinted from *Journal of Personality and Social Psychology* 7, No. 2 (1967): 158–63. Copyright 1967 by The American Psychological Association, and reproduced by permission.

Abelson (1965) and by Abelson and Kanouse (1966) has furnished some suggestive leads in this area. Simple assertions containing a subject, verb, and object were presented to subjects, together with mixed evidence bearing on the truth of the assertion; that is, some of the evidence supported and some contradicted the truth of the assertion. Subjects were required to state whether they felt the assertions were true or false in the light of the given evidence. Of the various forms of evidence used in these studies, two types in particular will concern us here. In one type, evidence about the object of the assertion was specified in *concrete* terms as in the following example:

> Altogether there are three kinds of bees: bumble bees, honey bees, and carpenter bees.
> Committees need bumble bees.
> Committees do not need honey bees.
> Committees do not need carpenter bees.
> Do committees need bees?

In the second type, evidence about the object of the assertion was specified in abstract terms, as in this example:

> All bees are flying, stinging, furry insects.
> Committees need flying insects.
> Committees need stinging insects.
> Committees do not need furry insects.
> Do committees need bees?

Evidence of the first type requires the subject to induce the credibility of the assertion from the lower-level, concrete evidence, whereas the second type requires a deduction down to the assertion from higher-level abstract evidence.

In the Abelson and Kanouse studies, subjects were given a systematic collection of items such as those in the examples. They were instructed not to regard the items as a test of logic, but to respond on the basis of intuitive reaction using the given information. The major findings which emerged are that the particular sentence subjects and objects contained in an assertion make very little difference in the credibility of the assertion, at least for the relatively neutral content material employed. However, the nature of the particular verb contained in the assertion seems to be of critical importance. Moreover, the Abelson and Kanouse studies found the effect of the verb to be markedly different for concrete versus abstract evidence. The strongest effect in the data pitted verbs which might be called "positive manifest" verbs against others which might be classified "negative subjective" verbs, as follows:

Assertions containing verbs which express positive, manifest relationships appear to be established very readily by concrete evidence, but only with great difficulty by abstract evidence. Verbs of this type include have, buy, approach, recommend, and produce.

Assertions containing verbs which express negative, subjective relationships are readily established by means of abstract, deductive evidence, but are extremely difficult to establish with concrete, inductive evidence. Verbs belonging to this class include hate, fear, avoid, and ignore.

To put the matter another way there is a preferred evidence form appropriate to particular verbs: concrete evidence for positive manifest verbs, and abstract evidence for negative subjective verbs.[1]

The reasons for this somewhat surprising finding are by no means clear as yet, and the foregoing categorization of verbs furnishes a convenient description of the results rather than an explanatory schema. Nevertheless, it seems apparent that the processes of subjective inference are quite sensitive to verb differences.

Inasmuch as these studies represent somthing of an innovation both in subject matter and in method, the question of their relevance to other problem areas in psychology, and to communications research in particular, is of some importance. The method in previous studies utilized assertions which are relatively lacking in meaningful content. Moreover, subjects were instructed to base their answers solely on the information provided in a single item. Thus it seems likely that subjects adopted a detached, problem-solving orientation toward the task of evaluating the assertions. This raises the question of whether similar results would obtain for the situation in which a subject is asked to indicate his agreement or disagreement with a concrete position on a meaningful issue. The present study is designed to provide some evidence on this question.

Directly applying the previous results concerning the preferred evidence form for different verb classes, the hypothesis is suggested that, other things being equal, the most persuasive communications are those in which assertions containing positive, manifest verbs are supported by concrete evidence, and sentences containing negative, subjective verbs are supported by abstract evidence. Conversely, the weakest (least persuasive) communications should be those in which all assertions are supported by the *nonpreferred* evidence form for the verb of the assertion; that is, concrete evidence for negative, subjective verbs and abstract evidence for positive, manifest verbs.

Communications

Four brief communications were constructed on the following topics: the desirability of buying complicated dolls for children; the effects of hunting regulations on the numbers of predatory birds; the effect of United States agricultural assistance on Central American good will; and the need for industrial facilities in a town in northern Alaska. The topics were selected as representing issues with which the subject was likely to be relatively unfamiliar (since the issues were largely created for the purposes of the study), but which he was likely to perceive as relatively meaningful albeit not personally ego-involving. Any one of the topics might have been the subject of an article appearing in a popular magazine such as *Reader's Digest*. Each communication contained a core which was syllogistic in style; that is, it was made up of two one-sentence premises and a conclusion. The two premises were designed in such a way that when considered in conjunction they posed a problem or dilemma; the conclusion then presented a value judgment on a particular course of action relevant to the problem. Acceptance of the two premises lent credence to the conclusion, although the conclusion was never completely dictated by the premises. Perhaps an example may clarify matters:

> Figures released by U. S. Wildlife officials show that Nebraskan hunting regulations are producing a large increase in the number of Nebraskan crested hawks. This indicates that the regulations are producing a large increase in the number of legally protected birds.
> A recent issue of the Farm Journal reports that Nebraskan farmers fear a large increase in the number of government-preserved wildlife, because of the danger of destruction of crops and livestock. From this it is apparent that Nebraskan farmers fear a large increase in the number of legally protected birds.
> Therefore, the laws against hunting legally protected birds are too strict.

The core of this sample consists of the two premises stating, respectively that the hunting regulations produce, and farmers fear, an increase in the number of legally protected birds, together with the conclusion recommending one particular corrective remedy. The verb of one premise was subjective and negative (fear), while the verb of the other premise was manifest and positive (produce). Other particular positive and negative verb pairs appeared with the other three communication topics.[2] In the example just presented, concrete evidence was used with the positive verb and abstract evidence with the negative verb. The regulations were said to produce an increase in hawks, the farmers to fear an increase in wildlife. Denoting positive verbs by the letter "p" and negative verbs by the letter "n," using upper case for abstract evidence and lower case for concrete evidence, the foregoing communication may be denoted the pN version.

Leaving the remainder of the communication exactly the same, the connections between verbs and evidence forms can be interchanged, using abstract evidence with the positive verb and concrete evidence with the negative verb. The regulations can be said to produce an increase in wildlife and the farmers to fear an increase in hawks. This is how the interchanged communication (the Pn version) reads:

> Figures released by U. S. Wildlife officials show that Nebraskan hunting regulations are producing a large increase in the number of government-preserved wildlife. This indicates that the regulations are producing a large increase in the number of legally-protected birds.
>
> A recent issue of the Farm Journal reports that Nebraskan farmers fear a large increase in the number of Nebraskan crested hawks, because of the danger of destruction of crops and livestock. From this it is apparent that Nebraskan farmers fear a large increase in the number of legally protected birds.
>
> Therefore, the laws against hunting legally protected birds are too strict.

According to our hypothesis, the first (pN) version of this communication should be more persuasive than the second (Pn) version, even though the two are almost identical. The only difference is a simple interchange of "government-preserved wildlife" with "Nebraskan crested hawks."

For control purposes, two more versions of each communication were introduced by simple reversal of the order of presentation of the two premises, putting the assertion with the negative verb first. (These two versions may be denoted Np and nP.) In the Nebraskan communication, for example, the paragraph with the United States Wildlife figures can come after rather than before the paragraph with the Farm Journal's report. Four communication versions are thus defined by the Two Orders of Presentation × Two Verb-Evidence Form Combinations.

METHOD

Subjects and Design

The subjects were 48 Yale undergraduates who received course credit for their participation. They were assigned randomly to four groups of 12 each. Each group received all four communication topics, each communication in a different version. The order in which the versions occurred was balanced over the four groups according to the 4 × 4 Latin square shown in Table 1. The order of presentation of communication *topics* was the same for all four groups.

Procedure

Each subject received a test booklet containing instructions and four communications. The instructions indicated that the subject was to read four brief essays on a variety of topics, and that each essay would present evidence in support of a conclusion. The subject was to read each essay carefully and critically, and to indicate his agreement or disagreement with the conclusion on a scale located beneath the essay. On a separate scale (located on the page

Table 1.   Summary of Experimental Design

Communi-cation version	Topic			
	Toys	*Hunting*	*Central America*	*Alaska*
pN	I	II	III	IV
Np	IV	III	II	I
Pn	III	I	IV	II
nP	II	IV	I	III

*Roman numerals refer to the group which received a particular combination of condition and topic.

following the essay) he was then to indicate how convincing he found the evidence. Beneath this scale the subject was encouraged to make additional comments on the reasons for his answers. Additional oral instructions illustrated the use of the scales (which are 31-point scales with verbally labeled end points), emphasizing that the subject should use the extremes of the scale only when he felt truly extreme in his opinion.

RESULTS

Table 2 displays the agreement data, by topics and versions. The means represent responses on a 31-point scale, with the maximum value defined as "I agree completely" and the minimum defined as "I disagree completely."

A number of things are noteworthy about these data. First, the overall level of agreement with the conclusions is quite low. In only 3 of the 16 cells does agreement rise about the midpoint (16.00) of the agreement scale. In the other cells agreement ranges from slightly to considerably below this theoretical point of neutrality. The general low level of agreement can perhaps best be attributed to the fact that the communications were extremely cryptic and sketchy in presenting arguments, consequently appearing excessively doctrinaire. Such an explanation finds some informal support in the written comments of subjects. One of the most frequently recurring themes was that the evidence was insufficient in quantity and strength. Many subjects may, therefore, have reacted negatively to the gratuitously authoritative style of the arguments.

Table 2. Mean Agreement with Conclusions by Topic and Version

| Communica-tion version | Topic | | | | |
	Toys	Hunting	Central America	Alaska	M
pN	18.92	9.25	12.83	13.75	13.69
Np	12.50	10.25	16.75	17.25	14.19
Pn	12.67	6.58	8.33	9.75	9.33
nP	15.25	8.42	9.17	13.00	11.46
Strong (pN + Np)	15.71	9.75	14.79	15.50	13.94
Weak (Pn + nP)	13.96	7.50	8.75	11.38	10.40

Turning now to the relative effects of the conditions on agreement, we find in Table 2 that the array of means at the bottom of the table (strong versus weak conditions) appears to support the hypothesis; that is, conditions Pn and nP produce greater mean agreement with the conclusions than conditions Pn and nP. The effect was in the predicted direction for all four topics. The size of the effect was approximately 2 rating-scale points for the toys and hunting topics, 6 points for the Central America topic, and 4 points for the Alaska topic.

An analysis of variance was performed to test the significance of this and other effects. This analysis is summarized in Table 3. The design of the study permitted a systematic test of the main effects of order of presentation of verbs (i.e., whether the positive or negative verb occurred first), order of presentation of evidence (whether the abstract or concrete evidence was given first), and the interaction between these two effects, the latter representing a test of the hypothsized strength effect. The appropriate error term for these tests is the error (within).

As indicated in the table, the anticipated interaction between order of presentation of verbs and of evidence was highly significant. The main effects themselves did not approach significance, and the only other significant effect in the study was that of topic. Since the communications on the several topics were quite disparate, and were not in any way designed to be equally persuasive, the finding of a significant topic main effect is of relatively little interest, particularly inasmuch as this effect does not interact significantly with the communication versions variable.

Table 3.   Analysis of Variance of Agreement Scores

Source	*df*	*MS*	*F*
Between Ss			
Groups	3	48.13	<1.00
Ss within groups	44	61.03	
Within Ss			
Topic	3	342.82	7.51*
Version:			
Verb order	1	82.69	1.81
Evidence order	1	31.69	<1.00
Verb Order × Evidence Order (Strength)	1	602.08	13.19*
Topic × Version Residual	6	70.87	1.55
Error (within)	132	45.64	

*$p < .001$.

Table 4. **Mean Ratings of Convincingness of the Evidence by Topic and Version**

Communica-tion version	Toys	Hunting	Central America	Alaska	M
pN	17.00	7.75	12.50	11.58	12.21
Np	13.42	8.42	18.33	15.00	13.79
Pn	10.00	6.42	9.00	7.75	8.29
nP	9.67	6.83	9.33	9.42	8.81
Strong (pN + Np)	15.21	8.08	15.42	13.29	13.00
Weak (Pn + nP)	9.83	6.62	9.17	8.59	8.55

Thus the analysis confirms the general impression given by the means in Table 2: namely, that agreement with the conclusions is dependent to a large extent on the nature of the pairing of verb type and evidence form. This generalization seems to hold with consistency over four communications differing in content.

What now of the effect of the experimental conditions on the perceived "convincingness" of the evidence in the communications? Table 4 displays the mean perceived "convincingness" of the arguments in the communication, as a function of communication topic and version. It is readily apparent from inspection of the table that the same general pattern of results obtains as for the agreement data, except that the effect is still more striking. Again, the strong communications appear much more convincing to sub-

Table 5. **Analysis of Variance of Convincingness Ratings**

Source	df	MS	F
Between Ss			
Groups	3	34.58	<1.00
Ss within groups	44	66.48	
Within Ss			
Topic	3	273.23	5.88*
Version:			
Verb order	1	53.13	1.14
Evidence order	1	13.55	<1.00
Verb Order × Evidence Order (strength)	1	949.63	20.47*
Topic × Conditions Residual	6	59.98	1.29
Error (within)	132	46.39	

*$p < .001$.

jects than the weak communications; this effect appears strongly and consistently over all four communications.

The analysis of variance for these data is summarized in Table 5. It can be seen that, again, the highly significant interaction due to verb and evidence pairing appears, together with the significant but unexciting main effect of topic.

DISCUSSION

The results of the study lend strong support to the hypothesis that the persuasiveness of a communication is affected by the relationship between the type of verb in an assertion and the form of evidence used to bolster that assertion. The results show with great consistency that the more persuasive communications are those which employ concrete evidence to establish assertions containing a positive, manifest verb, and abstract evidence when the verb in the assertion is negative and subjective. This confirms the results of previous studies by Gilson and Abelson (1965) and by Abelson and Kanouse (1966), extending the findings to situations involving content material which is more meaningful than that employed in previous studies, and to evidential arguments which, although still extremely simple, are more complex than those previously studied.

The results therefore lend some credence to the suggestion advanced elsewhere by Abelson and Kanouse (1966) that the study of fine details of language-processing behavior is an approach having general relevance to communications research. The present study, of course, did not involve a full-blown communications situation; the issues used, although meaningful, were relatively non-involving for the subjects in a personal sense, and the persuasive arguments lacked the complexity and sophistication of typical real-life communications. It is anticipated that further research can profitably be pursued at two different levels. At one level, further clarification is needed of the underlying processes involved in subjective inference. At the other level, it will be necessary to determine what role these processes play in a wide variety of more complex situations, and how they interact with other variables in these situations.

NOTES

[1]"Positive subjective" verbs (love, like, trust) and "negative manifest" verbs (destroy, fight, harm) fall in between these two extreme categories, exhibiting no strong tendency for either concrete or abstract evidence to be preferred. The reader may note that the distinction between *manifest* and *subjective* verbs is less obvious than that between *positive* and *negative* verbs. In general, *manifest* verbs express a relationship which is directly observable and relatively delimited in time; *subjective* verbs express an orientation of the subject toward the object which is relatively enduring and not directly observable. Not all of our verb examples fit this categorization in all respects, having been selected on empirical rather than theoretical grounds. Research currently under way is aimed at pinpointing which differences between these categories are most crucial.

[2]The verb pairs for the other topics were as indicated in the following "cores." Toys topic: Many families *buy* complicated dolls for their children; most children *ignore* complicated dolls; therefore, a lot of money is being wasted on complicated dolls. Alaska topic: The town of Atanik, Alaska, *needs* industrial facilities; the people of Atanik *hate* industrial facilities; therefore, it would be desirable if the Alaskan government would launch an information campaign designed to dispel Atanik's hatred of industrial facilities. Central America topic: Johnson's advisers are *recommending* more agricultural aid to Central America; Central America would *resent* more U. S. agricultural assistance; therefore, the potential United States policy . . . would not be helpful in winning Central American good will.

REFERENCES

Abelson, R. P., & Kanouse, D. E. The subjective acceptance of verbal generalizations. In S. Feldman (Ed.), *Cognitive consistency: Motivational antecedents and behavioral consequents.* New York: Academic Press, 1966. Pp. 171-197.
Gilson, C., & Abelson, R. P. The subjective use of inductive evidence. *Journal of Personality and Social Psychology,* 1965, 2: 301-310.

34

ATTITUDINAL EFFECTS OF SELECTED TYPES OF CONCLUDING METAPHORS IN PERSUASIVE SPEECHES

John Waite Bowers
Michael M. Osborn

For the several thousand years since written records of public speeches have been accumulating, the verbal behavior of speakers has indicated a continuing faith in the power of metaphor. According to the assumptions implicit in numerous addresses, metaphor helps the speaker to move his audience, to make his argument memorable, and to enhance his prestige in the eyes of his listeners. This belief in the strength of metaphor is especially evident in the conclusions of speeches. There the speaker frequently develops a bold metaphor as a culmination of the attitude and argument contained in the body of the address. Notable examples are Demosthenes' "On the Crown" and Cicero's "First Oration against Catiline," both of which develop in their conclusions the metaphors of sickness and pestilence; William Pitt's "On the Abolition of the Slave Trade," which concludes with an elaborate light-dark metaphor; Lincoln's "First Inaugural Ad-

Reprinted from *Speech Monographs* 33 (1966): 147–55. Footnotes have been renumbered.

dress," which ends in an interesting musical image; Bryan's "The Cross of Gold," for which the closing imagery has come to provide a title; and Franklin Roosevelt's "First Inaugural Address," in which war imagery develops throughout the speech and culminates in the conclusion.

Supporting the implicit assumptions of speakers are the analyses and precepts of rhetoricians. The idea that metaphor aids a speaker in moving his audience rests upon firm traditional foundations. Principally, rhetoricians respect metaphor because it pleases the audience by enlivening the discourse in which it occurs, by appealing directly to the senses, by stimulating mental processes in a manner which is intrinsically pleasurable. Thus, Quintilian concluded shrewdly, metaphor "contributes to the case," since, in the process of pleasing, metaphor makes it easier to attend, disposes us to be grateful to the speaker who has provided this pleasure, and makes us receptive to his point of view.

This gratitude to the speaker is one of the principal supports in traditional rhetorics for a second evident assumption, that metaphor enhances the credibility or *ethos* of a speaker. The traditional theorists never draw an explicit relationship between metaphor and ethical proof, but their analyses give ample basis for the supposition that such relationships do exist. In addition to Quintilian's notion of gratitude felt toward the speaker, both Cicero and Aristotle argue that apt and appropriate metaphor is taken by an audience as a sign of high mental ability. For this reason, we might expect the use of metaphor to increase audience respect for the speaker.

Scanty evidence from contemporary research indicates a possibility that the ancients and the practitioners who follow their percepts may be wrong. Bowers found that highly intense or emotional language boomerangs for audiences whose initial attitudes are incongruent with those expressed in the speech.[1] That is, a highly intense speech against a concept initially favored by the audience is less effective in changing attitudes than is a less intense speech. Furthermore, in another study, Bowers found that certain types of metaphors are judged as extremely intense.[2] Hence, unless metaphors behave differently from other kinds of intense language, one would expect them to have a boomerang effect, to be less effective in changing attitude negatively toward an initially-favored concept than more literal, less intense expressions.

At least two avenues are open for conciliation of the seemingly contradictory evidence of tradition and experiment. (1) The effects of metaphor may, indeed, be different from the effects of other kinds of intense language. Bowers did not discriminate in his experiment between metaphorical intensity and other kinds. If metaphorical conclusions were found to be more effective than literal conclusions, the difference could be attributed to the fact that the conclusions were *metaphorically* intense. (2) Intense expressions abounded throughout the speeches in the Bowers experiment. Possibly, the boomerang effect would not have occurred if the audiences had been prepared for highly intense conclusions by less intense value statements early in the speeches. Intense metaphorical expressions of value may be more effective that literal expressions when they occur *late* in persuasive speeches.

METHOD AND RATIONALE

The experiment we are reporting was designed to begin to answer the most important basic question about the use of intense metaphor in conclusions of persuasive speeches: Are they more effective in changing attitudes than literal conclusions? We tested the following hypotheses:

> (1) Intense metaphorical conclusions differ from literal conclusions in their effects on attitude change toward the main concepts of persuasive speeches.
> (2) Intense metaphorical conclusions differ from literal conclusions in their effects on judgments of credibility of the sources of persuasive speeches.
>> (a) They differ in their effects on judgments of the competence of the source.
>> (b) They differ in their effects on judgments of the trustworthiness of the source.
>> (c) They differ in their effects on judgments of the ingenuity of the source.

Criterion measures for testing the hypotheses were change in attitude and judgments of credibility (post- minus pre-test score) as indicated by appropriate semantic-differential type scales.

As stimulus materials we used two tape-recorded, 750–1000-word persuasive speeches, each of which had an intense and sustained metaphorical conclusion and a literal conclusion. One speech was against the concept "Protective Tariffs" and was allegedly delivered by a political science professor. The other was against the concept "Government Aid to Needy Students" and was allegedly delivered by an economics professor. The metaphorical conclusions embodied extended versions of those metaphors Bowers found to correlate highly with intensity. The metaphorical conclusion to the protective-tariff speech was an extended sex metaphor, while the speech on government aid to needy students incorporated an extended death metaphor in its figurative version. Transcripts of the four conclusions follow:

> *Protective tariff, literal.* From what we've learned here today it is obvious that we have listened too long to the voices of those who represent special interest groups. Too long, we ourselves have stood by and permitted the ruination of our western economies by those who have proclaimed the doctrine of protective tariff. We have neglected our larger interests for the sake of the smaller interests of these special groups, and the result has been—not a vigorous, protected economy—but rather economic stagnation.
>
> I say the time has come to listen no longer in our legislatures to these short-sighted lobbyists. For only when we shut our ears to them, and remove the tariff barriers which stand as so many harmful restrictions on our general welfare, can we achieve the goal of free trade, giving to the entire world new economic hope and a new sense of economic well-being.
>
> *Protective tariff, metaphorical.* From what we've learned here today it is obvious that we have listened too long to the seductive whispers of special interest groups. Too long, we ourselves have stood by and permitted the rape of western economies by those who have proclaimed the doctrine of protective tariff. We have prostituted our own interests to satisfy the lust of these special interest groups, and the result of this impotent union has been—not a vigorous and healthy economy—but economic abortion.
>
> I say the time has come to banish from our legislative chambers these economic seducers. For only when we shut our ears to them, and remove the barriers which stand like so many ill-advised parental restrictions, can liberty and economy lie side by side, stimulating each other, giving through free trade a new birth of hope to the world and a new manhood of economic well-being.
>
> *Government aid to needy students, literal.* So today we must learn, I believe, that governmental aid is no

substitute for individual initiative. Must we allow, then, our government to replace our own individuality? Can we afford to lose the basis of our national strength under the so-called protective influence of Washington? How soon will we learn that "freedom" and "individual" are interchangeable words? Will it be when, filled with the words of would-be idealists, we turn to find that freedom is no longer with us? I pray that we will not permit these things to happen, that we will come to realize that in education governmental help is not compatible with our national goals.

Government aid to needy students, metaphorical. So today we must learn, I believe, that governmental aid is no substitute for individual initiative. Must we allow, then, our government to slowly strangle our own individuality? Can we permit the basis of our national strength to rot away under the so-called protective influence of Washington? How soon will we learn that the death of the individual is the death of freedom? Will it be when, behind the sweet words of would-be idealists, we hear the sickening death-rattle of liberty in the throat of America? I pray that we will not permit this gentle murder of our values, that we will come to realize that in education the kiss of governmental help is the kiss of death.

In the context of this study, a metaphor is defined as a term requiring "some effort, however slight, . . . to transfer its denotation from that with which it [is] conventionally associated to that with which it [is] associated in the context of the communications. Michael M. Osborn and Douglas Ehninger call this effort 'puzzlement-recoil.'"

We made every effort to keep delivery constant across the two versions of each speech, dubbing the sustained metaphors on the tape of the introduction and body of the speeches used for the literal conclusions. In order to make the figurative/non-figurative contrasts as clear as possible, we avoided any important use of metaphor within the bodies of the speeches. All tapes were introduced by a recorded announcer as "the first in a series of exercises in critical listening."

Each subject in the study heard both the speech on government aid to needy students and the protective-tariff speech, one with a literal and the other with a metaphorical conclusion. The following figure shows the combination of variables to which each group of subjects was exposed:

Group	Speech	Conclusion
I (33ss)	Protective Tariff	Sex metaphor
	Government Aid to Needy Students	Literal
II (33ss)	Protective Tariff	Literal
	Government Aid to Needy Students	Death metaphor
III (33ss)	Protective Tariff	Death metaphor
	Government Aid to Needy Students	Literal
IV (33ss)	Protective Tariff	Literal
	Protective Tariff	Sex metaphor

This combination of variables permitted a Lindquist Type II design, in which the effects of A (topic and other speech and source variables) and B (metaphor-literal conclusions) are both within subjects effects.[3] Only the AB interaction is a between-subjects effect. We tried to keep the men/women ratio about constant across the groups. Differences due to variable A, of course, are to be expected. The real source of interest was the metaphor effect, variable B. The design does not permit meaningful conclusions about the relative effectiveness of the two types of metaphors employed, since that variable is confounded with the topic/speech variable. All differences were tested for significances at the .05 level.

RESULTS

Pre-tests

Subjects were generally favorable initially toward both concepts and sources. Where the most negative score would be 5 and the most positive 35, the pre-test mean toward "Government Aid to Needy Students" was 28.075, toward "Protective Tariff," 24.424.

Three separate scores were collected for each source, each reflecting a dimension of credibility.[4] On the competence dimension the lowest possible score was 4, the highest, 28. On this dimension the mean pre-test score toward the economics professor was 24.242, toward the political science professor, 24.59. On the trustworthiness dimension with the same upper and lower limits, initial evaluation of the economics professor was 21.745, of the political science professor, 21.393. The ingenuity dimension consisted of only one scale with limits of 1 and 7. On this scale the economics professor scored 4.287, the political science professor, 4.848. Hence, on all three credibility dimensions the two professors were assigned positive ratings.

Attitude Change Toward Concepts

Hypothesis 1, which predicted that the effects of intense metaphorical conclusions would differ from the effects of literal conclusions toward the main concepts, was confirmed. For both speeches, the metaphorical conclusions brought about more change in the direction advocated than did the literal conclusions. Table 1 shows the mean attitude change toward concepts for each cell in the design.

Surprisingly, neither source/speech combination was more successful than the other in bringing about attitude change toward the respective concepts. The only significant effect in the Type II design was for metaphor.

Judgments of Source Credibility

Hypothesis 2, which predicted that the effects of intense metaphorical conclusions would differ from the effects of literal conclusions for judgments of source credibility, was confirmed. However, the relationships were considerably more complex than those revealed for attitude change toward concepts. Type II analyses of variance for all three dimensions of credibility revealed significant interactions between metaphorical conclusions and other elements in the speaker/speech complex of variables.

Table 2 shows the mean change in evaluation of competence of the sources, Table 3 the mean change in evaluation of trustworthiness of the sources, and Table 4 the mean change in the evaluation of ingenuity of the sources. In order to detect the source of the interactions, simple randomized analyses of variances were executed for each speaker separately.

On the competence dimension, the analysis revealed that negative reaction toward the economics professor was significantly greater when he concluded with the metaphor (death metaphor) than when he concluded literally. The effect of metaphor on the assessment of the political science professor (sex metaphor) was in the opposite direction but not significant.

Change toward the two sources on the trustworthiness dimension followed exactly the same pattern as on the competence dimension. Subjects changed significantly more negatively toward the economics professor when he employed the death metaphor than when he concluded literally. For the political science professor using a sex metaphor the difference was in the opposite direction but not significant.

Table 1. Mean Attitude Change Toward Concepts in the Direction Advocated

Concept	Literal	Metaphorical*
Government Aid to Needy Students	3.606	4.515**
Protective Tariff	3.939	5.303**

*The speech on government aid, delivered by the economics professor, ended in the death metaphor; the protective-tariff speech, delivered by the political science professor, ended in the sex metaphor.

**The difference between the literal and metaphorical treatments was significant at the .05 level ($F = 4.43$; necessary for significance, 3.92).

Table 2. Mean Change on Competence Dimension*

Speaker, concept, and type of metaphor	Literal	Metaphorical
Economics Professor, Government Aid to Needy Students, Death	.545	−1.393
Political Science Professor, Protective Tariff, Sex	−1.030	− .090

*A (topic, speech, source)/B (metaphor) interaction significant ($F = 10.614$; necessary for significance, 3.92).

Table 3. Mean Change on Trustworthiness Dimension*

Speaker, concept, and type of metaphor	Literal	Metaphorical
Economics Professor, Government Aid to Needy Students, Death	− .030	−2.515
Political Science Professor, Protective Tariff, Sex	−1.909	− .606

*A (topic, speech, source)/B (metaphor) interaction significant ($F = 10.614$; necessary for significance, 3.92).

Table 4. Mean Change on Ingenuity Dimension*

Speaker, concept, and type of metaphor	Literal	Metaphorical
Economics Professor, Government Aid to Needy Students, Death	1.121	.030
Political Science Professor, Protective Tariff, Sex	− .303	.666

*A (topic, speech, source)/B (metaphor) interaction significant ($F = 12.902$; necessary for significance, 3.92).

On the ingenuity dimension the interaction was of the same type as on the competence and trustworthiness dimensions. Subjects changed less positively toward the economics professor speaking metaphorically than speaking literally. For the political science professor, however, the metaphorical conclusion had the opposite effect. On this dimension both differences were significant.

On all three dimensions, then, the evaluation of the economics professor was more negative when he employed a metaphorical conclusion (death metaphor) than when he employed a literal one. The sex metaphor employed by the political science professor, on the other hand, enhanced subjects' evaluation of him on all three credibility dimensions, though the difference between metaphorical and literal conditions was significant only on the ingenuity dimension.

DISCUSSION

In the context of this study certain kinds of extended, intense concluding metaphors have significant effects on attitude change toward concepts. Several avenues are available for the explanation of this effect, which conflicts at a superficial level with an earlier experimental test of the effects of language intensity. We have already mentioned the two leading explanations. (1) Metaphors have effects different from other kinds of intense language. Thus, the strictly metaphorical variable in this study did not have the boomerang effect reported in the earlier study where various kinds of language intensity were used. (2) High language intensity, whether methaphorical or not, is more effective than less intense language when it occurs in the conclusions of speeches after audiences have been appropriately prepared for strong value terms by the introduction and body. A third possibility is that the two variables interact: that the effect of metaphor is different from the effect of other kinds of intense language, and this difference is enhanced by a late position in persuasive speeches.

Because of the interaction between metaphor and other aspects of the speech situation, the change in attitude toward sources is more difficult to discuss. The two speeches differed in several significant ways other than the type of concluding metaphor employed. Within the limits of the design, it is impossible to assess confidently the source or sources of the interaction in the speeches and speakers themselves. Among the possible sources are the following. (1) Initial attitude toward the concept "Government Aid to Needy Students" was more favorable than that toward "Protective Tariff." Thus, the economics professor encountered *stronger incongruity* in opposing government aid than did the political science professor in opposing protective tariffs. (2) The government-aid speech ended in a *death metaphor,* the protective tariff speech in a *sex metaphor.* (3) Obviously, the two speeches differed in the *arguments employed.* (4) Although care was taken to avoid strong differences, the two speakers varied in their *delivery.* Because of the multitude of causes which might have contributed to the interaction, then, what follows must be considered a tentative, *post hoc* explanation of the results.

The fact that neither speech/speaker combination brought about more attitude change toward concepts than the other makes us suspect that explanations (3) and (4) can reasonably be discarded. Our guess is that explanations (1) and (2) account for the interaction between metaphor and the speech/speaker complex of variables.

Although both professors increased incongruity with their more intense, metaphorical conclusions, audiences reacted to the political science professor more favorably when he used a metaphorical conclusion than when he used a literal conclusion. As far as the congruity possibilities are concerned, then, the only difference between the economics professor and the political science professor was that the former faced stronger incongruity than the latter. If the metaphorical speeches had brought about more negative reactions to both speakers than the literal speeches, the congruity principles would have supplied an adequate explanation even though the differences for the economics professor were greater than the differences for the political science professor. But the fact is that the difference for the two sources was not only in degree but also in kind. The most reasonable explanation for this discrepancy is the nature of the metaphors employed. On this basis it would be argued that the economics professor's death metaphor negatively affected audience assessment of his competence, trustworthiness, and ingenuity and that the political science professor's sex metaphor positively affected audience assessment of his competence, trustworthiness, and ingenuity.

Several explanations could account for the different effects of the metaphors used, the one we most favor being the relative conventionality of the two metaphors. References to murder, strangling, death rattle, etc. are fairly common, especially among speakers and writers who oppose change in a political or economic system. Indeed, these expressions are trite to the extent that we would almost predict that a contemporary, conservative speaker would employ them when discussing the effects of a given proposal on existing political ideology. The sex metaphor, on the other hand, has not been so widely used that it has become predictable in an intense statement of attitude. It retains originality, which may, as Cicero says, appeal directly to the senses and stimulate mental processes. Thus, although the political science professor may have been no more intense in his statement of attitude toward the concept, he was more original than the economics professor. This originality apparently enhanced audience assessment of his competence and trustworthiness. The economics professor's trite statement of attitude boomeranged. The metaphor detracted from audience assessment of his competence, trustworthiness, and ingenuity.

Apart from conventionality, audiences could have reacted to the intrinsic content of the two metaphors as provided by their generic items for association and especially as specified by their extensions. That is to say, the sex metaphor could have been intrinsically attractive, the death metaphor intrinsically repulsive for these audiences; such reactions could have been generalized to the speakers. Knapp offers some indirect support for this conclusion.[5] When a speaker develops at some length a disturbingly strong death metaphor, audiences may feel that they are in the presence of a mentally unhealthy individual. One might expect their impressions of such a person to be lowered, especially on the trustworthiness dimension. The strongest reaction against the economics professor was on that dimension.

The two metaphors differ radically in one other respect, formal development. The sex metaphor develops with extensions which at first suggest negative or unattractive aspects of sexuality, but then turns abruptly in the concluding section of the image to stress positive or healthy aspects. The death metaphor, on the other hand, is negative throughout. If anything, the secondary sex metaphor hinted in the latter part of the death image tends to make its meaning all the more repugnant. Thus, although it raises anxiety in the manner of the sex metaphor, it does not reduce that emotion through a reassuring recommendation, but instead augments anxiety through an additional metaphoric strategy.

This experiment resulted in confirmation of the hypotheses that certain types of metaphorical conclusions to persuasive speeches bring about effects different from those resulting from literal conclusions to the same speeches. Specifically, the metaphors employed here brought about more attitude change in the direction advocated than did their literal counterparts. A complex relationship emerged between the two types of metaphor and their effects on assessments of source credibility.

NOTES

[1]"Language Intensity, Social Introversion, and Attitude Change," *Speech Monographs*, XXX (November 1963), 345–352.

[2]"Some Correlates of Language Intensity," *Quarterly Journal of Speech*, L (December 1964), 415–420.

[3]E. F. Lindquist, *Design and Analysis of Experiments in Psychology and Education* (Boston, 1953), pp. 273–281.

[4]For competence and trustworthiness scales see Murray A. Hewgill and Gerald R. Miller, "Source Credibility and Response to Fear-Arousing Communications," *Speech Monographs*, XXXII (June 1965), 97. The ingenuity scale was: "clever-dull."

[5]Robert H. Knapp, "A Study of Metaphor," *Journal of Projective Techniques* 24 (December 1960), 394–295.

35

FRUSTRATION AND LANGUAGE INTENSITY

Carl W. Carmichael
Gary Lynn Cronkhite

The effect of "frustration"[1] on attitude change was the focus of an often quoted experiment in social psychology. Briefly Weiss and Fine found that subjects who had been deliberately "frustrated" but prevented from aggression toward the "frustrating" agent changed attitudes significantly more in response to a punitively oriented communication than did "nonfrustrated" subjects.[2]

Bowers referred to this experiment in attempting to explain unexpected results of his study of the effect of language intensity upon attitude change.[3] The finding that "negative" speeches were much more effective than "affirmative" speeches, he suggested, might be a result of "scapegoating" by students who were frustrated by the requirement that they perform an unpleasant task.[4] Further, Bowers found that the versions of the speeches using intense language produced less attitude change than their moderate counterparts—exactly the opposite of what he predicted.[5] Although Bowers does not suggest that this, too, was an effect limited to "frustrated" subjects, the experiment was so designed that this could have happened. As will be explained later, such an effect can be inferred from evidence that organisms already highly

Reprinted from *Speech Monographs* 32 (1965): 107–11.

aroused tend to reject stimulation that would further increase their level of arousal.

The present experiment was designed to test one major hypothesis: *"Frustrated" listeners will show a greater tendency toward agreement with speeches using language of low intensity, whereas this pattern will not occur among "nonfrustrated" listeners.*

The test of this major hypothesis was replicated using two of Bowers' speeches that were maximally different: the concepts differed in that one speech pertained to the Peace Corps and the other dealt with women's fashion changes; the speeches differed in that one called for a favorable change in attitude and the other called for an unfavorable change; one of the communicators was male and the other female; and the communicators differed in prestige in that one was introduced as a prominent U. S. Senator and the other as a home economist.

Beyond the value of replication, the addition of this dimension to the design made it possible to test Bowers' suggestion that the cause of differences in attitude change observed between his speeches was the inadvertent "frustration" of his subjects. Hence, the use of two speeches made it possible to test incidentally a second hypothesis: *that "frustrated" listeners will agree more with the speech in which the home economist opposes women's fashion changes than will "nonfrustrated" listeners, whereas this pattern will not occur for the speech in which the U. S. Senator favors the Peace Corps.* The specific hypothesis is not of so much interest as the more general methodological implication. If it is true that Bowers' results were caused by the unintentional "frustration" arising from the very nature of the experimental tasks, the argument is strong that "frustration" is a variable that may limit the validity of generalizing the results of experiments using captive subjects.

PROCEDURE

The subjects were thirty-six students enrolled in two sections of the freshman communication course at the University of Iowa. In the section chosen for the frustration treatment, the experimenter appeared at the beginning of a regular class period and represented himself as an assistant to the director of the program and as the official in charge of special education. Most students in freshman communication at Iowa are required to undergo a series of practical examinations at the end of the course, and failure in any one of those requires the students to enroll in a remedial class in speaking, writing, or reading. The experimenter informed the "frustrated" section of students that the department intended to conduct an evaluation of its testing procedures the next year and needed a control group of inferior students who had never taken the practical examinations. He then told them that their instructor had recommended them as an inferior group and that he had assured himself that they were indeed inferior by reading some of their themes, which he felt were among the worst he had ever read. Consequently, he said, the members of the section would not be permitted to attempt the examinations, but would be automatically enrolled in all three remedial classes. Finally, the experimenter announced a heavy and unexpected series of assignments for the remaining days of the semester.

In the section chosen for the "nonfrustration" treatment, the experimenter, introducing himself in the same way as described above, attempted to provide ego-satisfaction for the subjects in order to overcome any possible "frustration" resulting from the interruption of the normal class procedure. He told them that they had been designated a superior section and that he had read some of their themes and was convinced that they were superior. He promised to recommend that their instructor exempt them entirely from the practical examinations.

Independent Variables

"Frustrated" and "nonfrustrated" as terms describing one pair of variables, it should be emphasized, are not used here in the popular sense and do not refer to some hypothesized internal emotional state of the individual. The use is the technical one describing an external set of circumstances imposed upon subjects. The circumstances, as designated by Dollard *et al.* in *Frustration and Aggression*, are two: (1) the existence of a desired goal response, and (2) the blocking of this response.[6] In the present instance, exemption from three remedial skills courses is clearly a desired goal of freshman students, and the experimental manipulations in one instance blocked the goal-response and in the other case facilitated it. The terms *goal-blocked* and *goal-facilitated* could be substituted for *"frustrated"* and *"nonfrustrated,"* but to do so would be to invent unnecessary jargon.

As for the language intensity variable, the method of constructing the speeches of relatively high and low intensity was that described by Bowers:

> (1) Argumentative speeches were written. . . . (2) All words and phrases which, in the writer's judgment, expressed the speaker's attitude toward the concept were replaced with numbered blanks. (3) In a separate booklet, sets of at least three alternative words were supplied for each numbered blank. (4) Fifteen or more judges drawn from students in the freshman speech and composition course at the State University of Iowa rated each word or phrase according to its intensity. These ratings were made in context with the judges instructed to imagine that the expressions were to be inserted in the appropriate blanks in the manuscripts of the speeches. (5) The words and phrases with the highest mean intensity ratings were inserted in all of the blanks, thus creating high intensity speeches on each of the . . . topics; similarly the words and phrases with the lowest mean intensity ratings were inserted to produce . . . low intensity speeches. The two versions of each of the speeches were essentially identical in evidence, in organization, in denotative content, and in all other respects with the exception of intensity.[7]

Experimental Design and Measurement of the Dependent Variable

The subjects in both the "frustrated" and the "nonfrustrated" classes were assigned randomly to two subgroups. Both subgroups from both sections then heard recordings of two speeches: one alleged to be that of a prominent home economist was against women's fashion changes; the other which was alleged to be that of a prominent U. S. Senator was in favor of the Peace Corps. Forms of these two addresses using high levels of language intensity were given to one subgroup of each class, and forms using low levels of language intensity were given to the other two subgroups. The speeches and the two versions of each were identical to the two used by Bowers, except that they had been retaped by graduate students in speech.

The dependent variable in this experiment, which was of an after-only design, was the extent to which the subjects agreed with the speeches. The measuring instrument was a set of sixteen seven-point evaluative scales of the semantic differential type.

Immediately after the subject heard the two speeches they rated the relevant concepts on each of the scales. Since the experimenters had placed the higher numbers at the appropriate ends of the scales, the higher numbers in all instances indicated agreement with the position advocated in the speech.

Statistical Analysis

A Lindquist Type III analysis of variance was used to test the hypotheses.[8] "Frustration" level and language intensity constituted the between-subjects variables, and the replications were the within-subjects variable. Stated in terms of this design, the first hypothesis was a prediction of significant interaction between "frustration" level and language intensity, and the second hypothesis was a prediction of significant interaction between "frustration" level and replications. The five percent level was preset as the minimum level at which the null forms of these hypotheses would be rejected.

RESULTS

Hypothesis 1: Interaction between "frustration" level and language intensity was significant ($F = 8.93$; significant at the one percent level). The first hypothesis thus clearly was supported. As Table 1 shows, "frustrated" subjects who heard versions of the speeches using language of low intensity were more favorable toward the viewpoints of those speeches than were the "frustrated" subjects who heard the high-intensity versions. This pattern did not occur

Table 1. Means of the Scores Showing the Extent to Which "Frustrated" and "Nonfrustrated" Subjects Agreed with the Concepts in High and Low Intensity Speeches on Two Topics

	High intensity speeches	*Low intensity speeches*
Frustrated subjects	67.11 ($n = 9$)	74.35 ($n = 19$)
Nonfrustrated subjects	69.50 ($n = 8$)	68.39 ($n = 9$)

**Table 2.   Means of the Scores Showing the Extent to
Which "Frustrated" and "Nonfrustrated"
Subjects Agreed with the Concepts
in Speeches on Two Topics**

	"Peace Corps" speech	*"Fashion change" speech*
Frustrated subjects	81.79 ($n = 19$)	60.05 ($n = 19$)
Nonfrustrated subjects	85.35 ($n = 17$)	52.47 ($n = 17$)

for "nonfrustrated" subjects; although those who heard the highly intense versions showed somewhat greater agreement with the speeches than did those who heard the low-intensity forms, the t-test for the difference between these means was nonsignificant.

Hypothesis 2: Interaction between "frustration" level and replications was significant ($F = 9.00$; significant at the one per cent level), and thus the second hypothesis also was supported. Further analysis through an application of the t-test to differences between the pairs of means (see Table 2) showed that the "fashion change" speech was significantly·more effective with "frustrated" than with "nonfrustrated" subjects, whereas the difference between the two sets of subjects for the speech on the Peace Corps was nonsignificant.

DISCUSSION

Of the two findings, the first, that "frustrated" subjects tend to agree more closely with speeches using language of relatively low intensity, deserves the greater amount of attention. Since the only difference between the two versions of each speech was in the choices of words on the basis of a pretest of levels of intensity among groups of near synonyms, the chance for confounding was slight. Secondly, this part of the study warrants careful attention because the result is founded upon a replication involving two different speeches advocating two directions of change with regard to widely different concepts and attributed to speakers with unlike characteristics.

This effect of language intensity clearly was to be inferred from the results of Bowers' experiment if one assumes that his subjects were "frustrated." Frustration-aggression theory alone, however, does not account for the finding. Instead, two steps are necessary. First, there is evidence that subjects who are aroused "emotionally" or physiologically are more persuasible.[9] This theory, if applicable here, would mean that both subgroups of "frustrated" subjects would be more in agreement with the messages than were those who were "nonfrustrated." Since this was not true, the writers turned to the "activation theory" of Fiske and Maddi, who have argued that whether an organism increases or decreases its activation level depends upon what level is appropriate to the time of day and the task at hand.[10] Thus a subject at a high drive or activation level tends to reject stimuli that would further increase his activation. Observations during the course of the experiment and later interviews with the subjects make this explanation credible. The subjects in the "frustrated" section obviously were highly aroused, and the theory that they tended to reject the further arousing of such verbal stimuli as the words *deranged, licentious*, and *squandered* is tenable. This effect, moreover, is somewhat similar to the finding of Janis and Feshbach that subjects exposed to a minimum fear appeal conformed less to the advocated behavior than did subjects exposed to a maximum fear appeal, and it is still more highly similar to their later finding that this result was especially true among those chronically the most anxious.[11]

A careful distinction, however, should be made between intense language on topics *irrelevant* to the reason an audience is aroused and that designed to excite listeners or to direct highly emotional persons into relevant action. Nothing in the present results negates the observations of Quintilian, Longinus, and many others that passionate language is appropriate only when an audience "shares the inspiration of the speaker."[12] In other words, intense language that is relevant and appropriate to the task at hand is something quite different from the emotional stimulation attempted in the present study. An interesting follow-up experiment would be one using speeches of low and high language intensity urging the abolition of the freshman communication course after subjects had been "frustrated" as described earlier. Under such circumstances the highly intense language might be acceptable to the "frustrated" subjects, for they might perceive the higher arousal level as appropriate to the task of abolishing the "frustrating" course.

Less significant than the first result but still one of considerable interest is the significant interaction found between the replications and the "frustration" level. This finding supports Bowers' suggestion that inadvertent "frustration" may have been responsible in part for the difference in effectiveness between his speeches. Bowers believes that the effect confirms Weiss and Fine's conclusion that "punitively-oriented communications" are more acceptable to "frustrated" than to "nonfrustrated" subjects. This possibility certainly may be true, but differences in concepts, messages, and speakers seriously confounded this replication dimension.

No matter which of the confounded variables was responsible for the significant results, the findings in Bowers' and the present experiments suggest that the unintentional "frustration" of a captive audience is a condition that future experimenters should either avoid or control. In recruiting subjects the choice is between allowing them to volunteer, in which case self-selection may bias the sample, and requiring participation, in which case the subjects may be "frustrated." Either procedure, without some method of control, restricts the population about which the research worker can generalize.

NOTES

[1]The term "frustration" is here applied to the act of preventing an individual from reaching a desired goal—that is, to the blocking of a goal-response. Because this use of the term is not wholly consonant with popular use, which sometimes implies the arousal of a specific "emotion," in this paper the term is enclosed in quotation marks. The theory, well substantiated by research, is that goal-blocking "frustration" increases the probability of aggression not only toward the frustrating agent but also, if such aggression is inappropriate, toward other environmental stimuli in proportion to their resemblance to the frustrating agent. For a theoretical discussion of the relationship between "frustration" and aggression, see John Dollard, Leonard W. Doob, Neal E. Miller, O. Hobart Mowrer, and Robert R. Sears, *Frustration and Aggression* (New Haven: Yale University Press, 1939).

[2]Walter Weiss and Bernard J. Fine, "The Effect of Induced Aggressiveness on Opinion Change," *Journal of Abnormal and Social Psychology*, LII (Jan., 1956), 109–114.

[3]John Waite Bowers, "Language Intensity, Social Introversion, and Attitude Change," *SM*, XXX (Nov., 1963), 345–352.

[4]*Ibid.*, p. 352.

[5]*Ibid.*, p. 349.

[6]Dollard et al., p. 11.

[7]Bowers, pp. 346–347.

[8]E. F. Lindquist, *Design and Analysis of Experiments in Psychology and Education* (Boston: Houghton Mifflin Co., 1953), pp. 281–284.

[9]John A. McNulty and Richard H. Walters, "Emotional Arousal, Conflict, and Susceptibility to Social Influence," *Canadian Journal of Psychology*, XVI (Sept., 1962), 211–220.

[10]Donald W. Fiske and Salvatore R. Maddi, "A Conceptual Framework," in *Functions of Varied Experience*, ed. Donald W. Fiske and Salvatore R. Maddi (Homewood, Ill.: Dorsey Press, 1961), pp. 11–56.

[11]Irving L. Janis and Seymour Feshback, "Personality Differences Associated with Responsiveness to Fear-Arousing Communications," *Journal of Personality*, XXIII (Dec., 1954), 154–166.

[12]Longinus, *On the Sublime*, tr. G. M. A. Grube (New York: Liberal Arts Press, 1957), sec. 32.